Tribal Health and Nutrition

Tribal Health and Nutrition

Edited by
S.N. CHAUDHARY

RAWAT PUBLICATIONS
Jaipur • New Delhi • Bangalore • Hyderabad • Guwahati

ISBN 978-81-316-0512-7

Published with financial assistance from Tribal Research and Development Institute, Bhopal.

Published by
Prem Rawat for **Rawat Publications**
Satyam Apts, Sector 3, Jawahar Nagar, Jaipur 302 004 (India)
Phone: 0141 265 1748 / 7006 Fax: 0141 265 1748
E-mail: info@rawatbooks.com
Website: www.rawatbooks.com

New Delhi Office
4858/24, Ansari Road, Daryaganj, New Delhi 110 002
Phone: 011 2326 3290

Also at *Bangalore, Hyderabad* and *Guwahati*

Typeset by Rawat Computers, Jaipur
Printed at Chaman Enterprises, New Delhi

Contents

Foreword

Health and nutrition are the two fundamental dimensions of the social development process. Without having intake of nutritious food on a continuous basis sound health status is a distant dream. But nutritious food is a necessity and not a condition for good health. There are other factors – both hereditary and environmental – which also influence one's health status. Status of health has both positive and negative impacts on the process of development at the levels of individual, community and society. If the health status of population, irrespective of their social background, is good as per the observation of health experts, it has positive socio-economic impact at all levels. Such population is considered physically fit to participate in the development process. But if the population is sick and suffering from various diseases and is also deprived of nutritious food, they have to suffer at all levels, including economically and educationally. Hence, it is very appropriate to say that "health is wealth".

The situation is not rosy if we see the health and nutrition status of tribal population, who roughly constitute about 8.2 per cent of the total population of the country. Number of factors may be held responsible for this state of affair. This does not mean that historically there has been absence of societal interventions to improve their health status and address food security related issues. Number of institutional interventions have been made to improve health status of tribal masses. Also, number of efforts are in progress to ensure availability of rich food. Public Distribution System (PDS) has special package for them. Role of civil society and tribal culture is also praiseworthy in this context. Traditional knowledge may also be appreciated to address their health and nutrition related challenges since long.

As a result of all these interventions, there is significant improvement in both health and nutritional conditions of tribes. They are now friendly to modern initiatives. The increasing life longevity, decreasing mortality, decreasing number of underweight infants and children etc., are few among several examples of success. Today, hundreds and thousands of tribal men, women and children can be seen visiting at the PHCs and CHCs working in the tribal areas. But, this is one side of the picture. The other side is relatively alarming. Even today a large number of tribals are the victim of so many diseases. Many children and mothers are the victim of malnutrition. Many of them are failed to avail modern health facility, even if available at the village level. Hence, issues of health and nutrition need urgent consideration and intervention with fresh mood. Without improvement in the health sector, their association with the new development process cannot be ensured. Keeping these objectives in mind, a two-day National Seminar on Tribal Health and Nutrition was organized in March 2011 by Tribal Research and Development Institute, Bhopal in collaboration with Rajiv Gandhi Chair in Contemporary Studies, Barkatullah University, Bhopal. This book is the outcome of that seminar.

I am extremely thankful to the Minister for Scheduled Tribes and Scheduled Castes Welfare, Government of Madhya Pradesh, Kunwar Vijay Shah, who finalized the theme and permitted to hold seminar. The seminar reflected the variety of visions that dominated all discussions on its theme. The main objective behind publication of this volume is to disseminate the deliberations of the seminar at different levels. I am confident that this volume will be useful for planners, policy makers, NGOs and students of tribal studies.

I congratulate S.N. Chaudhary, Rajiv Gandhi Professor, Barkatullah University, Bhopal for editing this volume in a short span of time.

Devendra Singhai
Director
Tribal Research and Development Institute
Bhopal

Preface

Health and nutrition are the two interrelated issues which have drawn attention of scholars from across the various social science disciplines from research and teaching points of view. In course of investigation scholars have adopted both subjective and objective approaches to understand the concepts of health and nutrition. Neither health nor nutrition can be understood in isolation from the socio-economic background of people and macro-micro level socio-political undercurrents. In this context scholars have also underlined the importance of culture, including indigenous knowledge, in the management of issues relating to health and nutrition. And, the roles of culture and tradition have been intensively examined while discussing health and nutrition of Scheduled Tribes (STs). Such studies carry both academic and social importance from understanding and policy formulation points of view. The book is an extension of previous academic effort as mentioned above. For this purpose, a two-day national seminar on Tribal Health and Nutrition was organized by Tribal Research and Development Institute, Government of Madhya Pradesh in collaboration with Rajiv Gandhi Chair in Contemporary Studies, Barkatullah University, Bhopal. Many officials, scholars and volunteers have helped in the successful organization of the seminar. And it is our moral responsibility to acknowledge their contribution.

Initially it was the decision of the Minister, Scheduled Tribes and Scheduled Castes Welfare, Government of Madhya Pradesh, Shri Kunwar Vijay Shah to organize seminar. We are extremely thankful to him. He also encouraged us at all levels to ensure success of the seminar. Shri

Harishankar Khatik, MOS, Scheduled Tribes and Scheduled Castes Welfare, was kind enough to grace the inaugural function of the seminar. We are thankful to him. Credit also goes to Shri Devendra Singhai, Director, Tribal Research and Development Institute for inviting the Rajiv Gandhi Chair to hold the seminar in joint collaboration. He also extended logistic support to organize the seminar. We extend heartfelt gratitude to him. Also, officials of Tribal Research and Development Institute, especially Shri G.C. Bhalavi, and Dr G.P. Patel, both Joint Director, Shri S.P. Bhatt, Research Assistant and Smt Sangeeta Chaudhary extended support every now and then to ensure success of the seminar. We extend sincere thanks to all of them.

The Vice-Chancellor of Barkatullah University, Professor Nisha Dube deserves special thanks for permitting the Rajiv Gandhi Chair to hold the seminar in joint collaboration as well as to preside over the inaugural function of the seminar.

I am extremely thankful to Professor Buddhadeb Chaudhuri and Dr Almas Ali for delivering keynote address and valedictory address respectively. We are thankful to all those scholars, policy makers and NGO representatives, who participated in the seminar as a chairperson, co-chairperson, chief guest and paper presenters.

There are 21 papers in this volume. I am thankful to all those, who on my request, submitted revised version of their articles for publication.

Last but not the least, I extend my thanks to scholars of Rajiv Gandhi Chair in Contemporary Studies, viz., Dr Manish Mishra, Post-Doctoral Research Associate, Shri Narayan Mohanty and Ms Bhawana Shakyawar, Junior Research Fellow, Shri Pitamber Mohanta, Project Fellow, Dr Manoj Sharma and Shri Sarvan Uikey, Field Assistant, for their help in the success of the seminar. Here I would like to mention the name of Dr Manish Mishra, who also helped me in editing the papers for their publication in this volume.

Towards the end, I am thankful to Shri Pranit Rawat of Rawat Publications, Jaipur for publishing the book within the stipulated time frame.

S.N. Chaudhary

Contributors

A. Kavishwar, Faculty, Regional Medical Research Centre for Tribals (ICMR), Jabalpur (Madhya Pradesh)

Aalok Ranjan Chaurasia, Professor, Shyam Institute, Bhopal (Madhya Pradesh)

Anjali Dash, ICSSR Doctoral Fellow, Madhya Pradesh Institute of Social Science Research, Ujjain (Madhya Pradesh)

Buddhadeb Chaudhuri, Former Dr Ambedkar Chair Professor, Calcutta University, Kolkata (West Bengal)

Chaturbhuj Sahu, Professor, Department of Anthropology, Vinoba Bhave University, Hazaribagh (Jharkhand)

Chura Giri, Faculty, Department of Sociology, Margherita College, Dibrugarh (Assam)

D. Debnath, Associate Professor, Sociology and Community Development, Indian Institute of Forest Management, Bhopal (Madhya Pradesh)

D.C. Jain, Faculty, Regional Medical Research Centre for Tribals (ICMR), Jabalpur (Madhya Pradesh)

J.J. Roy Burman, Professor, Tata Institute of Social Sciences, Mumbai (Maharashtra)

Jay Palak, Ranchi Institute of Medical Sciences (RIMS), Ranchi (Jharkhand)

Kali Nath Jha, Faculty, Department of Sociology, Ranchi University, Ranchi (Jharkhand)

Parul Joshi, State Quality Monitor, Mid-Day Meal Programme, Rural Development Department, Bhopal (Madhya Pradesh)

Pradeepta Ranjan Pattanayak, Faculty, Department of Sociology, P.N. College, Khurda, Bhubaneswar (Odisha)

R. Shankar, Professor and Head, Department of Sociology, Bharthidasan University, Tiruchirappalli (Tamil Nadu)

Ram Narayan Sahu, Faculty, Department of Anthropology, Sarv Narayan Singh – Ram Kumar Singh College, Saharsa (Bihar)

S.N. Chaudhary, Professor, Rajiv Gandhi Chair in Contemporary Studies, Barkatullah University, Bhopal (Madhya Pradesh)

S.N. Tripathy, Professor, Gokhale Institute of Politics and Economics, Pune (Maharashtra)

Soubhagya Ranjan Padhi, Faculty, Department of Sociology, Aeronautics College, Sunabeda, Koraput (Odisha)

Suneel Qamra, Faculty, Regional Medical Research Centre for Tribals (ICMR), Jabalpur (Madhya Pradesh)

Swapan Kumar Kolay, Associate Professor, Bastar University, Bastar (Chhattisgarh)

Tapas Dalapati, Assistant Professor, Madhya Pradesh Institute of Social Science Research, Ujjain (Madhya Pradesh)

V. Jaisee Geetha, Faculty, Department of Sociology, Queen Mary's College, Chennai (Tamil Nadu)

V.K. Shrivastava, Ex-Director, National SC&ST Commission, Bhopal (Madhya Pradesh)

Vinita Singh, Faculty, Department of Sociology, Ranchi Women's College, Ranchi (Jharkhand)

Y.G. Joshi, Professor Emeritus, Madhya Pradesh Institute of Social Science Research, Ujjain (Madhya Pradesh)

Yatindra Singh Sisodia, Professor, Madhya Pradesh Institute of Social Science Research, Ujjain (Madhya Pradesh)

Introduction

S.N. CHAUDHARY

Health and nutrition are two sides of the same coin. They are complementary to each other. Without having intake of proper food as determined and prescribed by nutrition experts appropriate health status can neither be attained nor can it be retained. And, between the interplay of health and nutrition, the role of pollution-free environment as well as easy and affordable access to medical facility, especially in need, is immense. If there is freedom of opportunity to avail prescribed food, clean environment and proper treatment facility, definitely, the health status will improve. Here, by health, we mean its understanding based on both subjective and objective interpretations. The definition of health provided by WHO is largely based on objective interpretation. Health refers to a state of complete physical, mental and social well-being and not merely the absence of disease and infirmity. But, the definition provided by Lewis (1954) is based on both subjective and objective considerations. To him, if various organs work well enough not to draw attention to themselves and their owner is free from pain or discomfort, he usually supposes to be in good health. This criterion is then a subjective one. But if he avails himself of the mass X-ray service and in consequence learns that his lungs show strong evidence of tuberculosis disease he ceases to be considered in good health. The criterion now he adapts is an extraneous one, viz., the assertion of a physician who relies on objective or pathological data.

So far as the concept of nutrition is concerned, it refers to a key element in any strategy to reduce the burden of disease. Hunger, malnutrition, obesity and unsafe food all cause disease, and better nutrition will translate into large improvement in health among all of us, irrespective of our wealth and home country (Brundtland, 2000). Hence, nutrition is a pre-condition of health. Neither health nor nutrition can move in the opposite direction. But none of these two can operate in isolation from social reality. It is necessarily determined by number of births and other attributes such as caste and community background, geographical area of habitation, class and gender, political will, social processes, level of assertiveness on the part of change agents dealing with health-related issues, carrying capacity of the expected beneficiaries, inclination of change agent in favour of change and overall assertiveness on the part of beneficiaries.

If we examine tribes of India from the point of view of these attributes in order to understand their health and nutrition status, the picture is largely frustrating. Besides historical factors, institutional attention towards tribal health has remained inadequate in the past. Three reasons are held responsible. These are: (a) there was a general thinking that living close to nature, they enjoyed an environment which is conducive to good health, (b) they have been regarded as not very amenable to western system of medicine as they still depend very much on supernatural cure, and (c) the difficult terrain which they occupy where it is difficult to reach health care services adequately (Sachchidananda, 2010).

How can tribes, most of whom live in remote villages having degraded state of affairs and where not only their livelihood is based on primary sources which are both meagre as well as uncertain, their income is also low and infrequent, ensure themselves quality food in a sufficient manner? Needless to mention that most of the poor and manual labourers come from this category. Most of their time is consumed in meeting basic requirements. Actually they are the victim of marginality in the sense that due to interplay of variety of factors the quantity as well as the quality of locally available natural resources, especially forests, which worked as a source of their material and non-material culture since long, has massively deteriorated. Today, the existing forests largely failed to meet their ever-increasing demands of fuel and fodder. As a result, in contrary to the past when tribes were constructively dependent on forests, many of them are today destructively dependent on forests. Of course, during the last 60 years, a number of general as well as area-specific and tribe-specific development schemes have been introduced. During the Fifth Five-Year Plan, for example, the strategy of Tribal Sub-Plan was introduced, but the success level is not as per expectation. Factors like local culture, seasonal outmigration, availability of tribal elites, social and ecological movements etc., are largely incapable to improve the quality of life of tribal masses in a meaningful manner. Tribals at large have also been unable to associate themselves with secondary and tertiary sector occupations to earn their livelihood. Thousands of seats are lying vacant in government departments for want of suitable and appropriate candidates from tribal community. The process of development radiating from the modernization forces has made them like a straw man. If some of them have availed institutional benefit they have been forced to become dependent prone. Many of them have been forced to pay cultural cost of their development. Loss of identity may be taken as an example.

Also, the level of environmental degradation in the tribal belt has significantly increased especially since the introduction of globalization process in July 1991. How can a pollution-free environment is possible when the rate of deforestation is very high due to mega-development projects such as power plants, industries, roads, mines etc., in the tribal areas in 'national interest' without respecting local ecology, local environment and local concerns? Needless to mention that in the name of development (which is very controversial issue these days) hundreds of thousands of tribals are constantly displaced from their traditional habitats which results in their movement from both material and non-material culture and lifestyle. Under this situation, how they can ensure their regular income, proper food, clean environment and medical facility suiting to their need, psychology and carrying capacity?

Table 1

Status of Tribes on the Basis of Health Indicators

Indicators	*Scheduled Tribes*	*Others*
Prevalence of fever	31.4	30.4
Prevalence of diarrhoea	21.41	19.20
Children with anaemia	79.3	72.7
Women with anaemia	64.9	47.6
Children underweight	55.9	41.1
Infant mortality	84.00	61.8
Child mortality	46.3	22.2
Under-5 mortality	126.0	82.0
Life expectancy at birth	62 years	65 years

Source: NFHS, 1998–99.

There is no doubt that tribals' dependence on forests has significantly decreased in many parts of the country which has affected them adversely in the following ways: (a) continuous deforestation has reduced availability of desired forest produce; (b) whatever forest produce is available, there is continuous tug of war between the locals and outsiders, who have now link with the market forces, and the role of the state is directly or indirectly in favour of the latter; and (c) psychological, cultural and spatial mobility of tribals in favour of non-tribal lifestyle, food habit, dress pattern, means of entertainment and so on which force them to withdraw from forest-based century old culture and lifestyle.

As stated at the outset, the status of health and nutrition amongst tribals is not satisfactory. Their condition is not even at par with the non-tribal population living in the neighbourhood, although the latter group is also lagging far behind the required level of health and nutrition. And amongst tribes disparity exists between men and women and between primitive and non-primitive tribes. In many cases traditional institutions exist to address health and disease. Also, amongst many tribes, even today, fatalistic interpretation of disease is made. Chaudhuri (1986) reported that among the tribals the diseases are commonly related to the belief in different deities and spirits. According to Mahapatra (1994) diseases are usually perceived to occur among many tribes due to (a) belief in supernatural forces, any negative act against such forces may cause harm to the self and the community, and (b) physical factors like living in unsanitary conditions. According to Swami (1994), the metaphysical causes of sickness as perceived by tribes may be classified as under: (a) soul loss, (b) breach of taboo, (c) sorcery, (d) ghosts of ancestors, (e) ancestral spirits and supernatural power, (f) evil eye, evil mouth, (g) manna, and (h) fetish. According to Kumar and Verma (2010), some of the tribal groups in Madhya Pradesh prefer to go to the local witch doctors initially on the grounds that the process is inexpensive and can save money if it works. The Saharias undertake superstitious practices to ward off illness because they feel that it has significance and involves less expenditure. When it fails they visit the local quack and only in the last resort do they visit the hospital.

Partly because of availability of institutional facilities and partly due to change in the mindset of a section of tribes, the traditional institutions are not seriously taken. This does not mean that the role of traditional medicine men has completely disappeared from the scene. The traditional healers are still found in large numbers and tribals do not hesitate to visit them. In case of some of the diseases tribals visit both the traditional and modern medicine men. In some of the cases, viz., snakebite, the traditional healers are approached on priority basis (Chaudhary, 2010).

Many more studies on fatalistic interpretation of health and disease may be cited. Documentation of such interpretation is essential from policy point of view.

So far as the modern institutions are concerned they have still to establish their credibility and legitimacy in the tribal world. Success of such institutions depend on the degree of its response to health challenges faced by tribal masses. Responsiveness also includes constant presence and availability of trained doctors, nurses and other health workers, sufficient number of required medicine, friendly attitude of health personnel to the tribals and so on. However, if we examine the grassroots situation, the picture is not necessarily encouraging. In many cases structure such as Aanganwadi centre or Primary Health Centre (PHC) or Sub-Centre is there but there is no sufficient staff, medicine and so on. Kumar and Verma (2010) reported that PHCs hardly provide proper care. Most do not even have proper medicine kits and the medicines have to be obtained from the open market. The Saharias of Madhya Pradesh, for example, complain that the behaviour of the doctors and nurses leaves much to be desired. They do not listen to their problems. This is why they do not go to the hospitals until the situation becomes really serious. Similarly, according to the Saur tribals, in some areas, the PHCs hardly function and their main task is vaccination. In several areas inhabited by Bhils, the PHC is run by the paramedical staff since the doctor is either absent or has not been appointed. More or less similar is the situation with Aanganwadi centre.

Also, there is no effort, at the village level, on the part of health institutions to address health and nutrition issues in a holistic perspective. They are not even serious on preventive measures. Issues such as the proper functioning of PDS, awareness programme for environment upgradation, inclusion of preventive measures in the syllabus of primary classes are perceived by the health institutions beyond their domain. In spite of having tall claims most of the modern health institutions working in the tribal areas are unable to become part of their culture. And without becoming part of their culture how they can win the heart of tribes, especially those who have historically perceived indigenous practices with high regard and prestige?

Joshi (2010) opined that continuity, social sanction and cultural legitimacy are the three attributes of traditional healing systems. Such practices, therefore, are traditional, sustainable, experimental and holistic. There are different types of healers such as ethno-orthopaedics, ethno-pediatrics, ethno-psychiatrist, ethno-dentists, ethno-physicians, etc.

There may be disagreement on the issue of relationship between traditional and modern health, nutrition and disease management mechanism, but effort, especially in the light of local ecology, to integrate the two is largely missing. Is it not possible to enlist the traditional healers in the tribal villages, most of whom are tribals themselves, and also men, and delink them from blind faith and superstition and train them to work as village level health workers? They have century-old acceptance, there is no linguistic barrier and they will seldom run from pillar to post for transfer and lucrative posting. But the effort to integrate the two methods are missing mainly because the ethnomedicine and its practitioners are largely underestimated by modern policy formulators and change agents. They consciously or unconsciously perceive these two methods as opposite to each other. And, by perceiving situation in such a manner, they overlook local level situation and carrying capacity of poor tribals. Hopefully, they also undermine globally accepted importance of traditional healing practices. The policy makers must recall that according to WHO estimation 80 per cent of population in Africa, 60 per cent in India and 40 per cent in China uses indigenous medicine. Indigenous medicine is known as CAM in Australia, Canada, the USA, Belgium and France wherein 48 per cent, 70 per cent, 42 per cent, 38 per cent and 75 per cent cases respectively it is used. The report also disclosed that in Malaysia, the annual expenditure on indigenous medicine is US$ 500 million as against US$ 300 million for allopathic medicines. In countries like the USA and the UK expenditure on indigenous medicine per annum is US$ 2,700 million and 2,300 million respectively (quoted in Joshi, 2010). On this basis it may safely be said that indigenous medicine is used globally. And, there is no point of disagreement if indigenous and modern medicines are perceived with equal respect.

These are some of the broader issues which carry social and academic importance. From policy perspective also these issues need to be examined especially in the era of globalization when we have huge opportunities but these are confined to a handful of population. From national integration and sustainable development points of view opportunity created by globalization must also reach to the poor people, especially tribals. In order to debate on all these issues, a two-day national seminar was organized with the following specific objectives:

1. Tribal Health and Nutrition: Conceptual, Theoretical and Philosophical Issues
2. Health and Nutrition Management Policies/Schemes with Reference to Tribes: Historical Overview
3. Status of Tribal Health and Nutrition: Role of Local Institutions, Indigenous Knowledge and Socio-cultural Practices
4. Functioning and Implications of Modern Health and Nutrition Management Schemes on Tribes with Reference to Aanganwadi centre, Primary Health Centre and Community Health Centre

5. Integration of Traditional and Modern Health and Nutrition Management Practices with Reference to Tribes: Status and Possibilities
6. Ensuring Sustainable Health and Nutrition Status of Tribes: Agenda for Action

II

The volume starts with an introduction to the theme as well as papers included in it. In the first paper, Buddhadeb Chaudhuri writes that many tribals living in remote areas have a better health status and eat more balanced food than those living in less remote areas. Again, in many cases, it has been noted that certain diseases may be common in specific areas but are under control because of certain food habits based on vegetation available locally or practices which have been generated through tradition. There is no doubt that any disturbance in the eco-system is likely to adversely affect the ecological balance as well as the concerned population. By citing other studies he says that tribes engaged in shifting cultivation like the Padam, Riang etc., were having better nutritional status than the settled agricultural tribes like the Santal and Ho. Again, in the context of deforestation, the hunting and gathering tribes were having lower nutritional status. Physical well-being of the tribals is inextricably linked up with the forest ecology. In fact, rapid disappearance of forests, commercialization of minor forest produce, replacement of food crops by cash crops and tendency towards monoculture forestry and lastly privatization of communal lands may affect the health, nutrition and physical well-being of the tribal population in a negative manner. The implication of such a trend, in countries where health insurance is unaffordable to the majority, is unimaginable. In this changing situation, the condition of the poor, particularly the tribals, has become more critical and difficult. There is thus a need to develop indigenous science and technology instead of replacing it in the name of scientific development and modernization.

R. Shankar and V. Jaisee Geetha, in their paper, underlined that problems of tribes, especially related to health, are complex and challenging. Meagre financial and trained technical manpower resources play severe constraints on development plans in general and health care programmes in particular which cannot be considered in isolation. The intrinsic value of an effective health plan under such circumstances would depend upon laying down correct priorities and judicious use of resources. Hence, the paper emphasizes on corrective measures which need to be taken by all the change agents dealing with the problem of health and nutrition of tribal masses. There is also need to maintain transparency and objectivity at the level of programme implementation.

Using the data from the latest District Level Household and Facility Survey (DLHS) 2007–08 Aalok Ranjan Chaurasia analysed the living conditions and health status of Scheduled Tribes (STs) in India and its constituent states. The analysis indicates that among different states and union territories, STs in Himachal Pradesh enjoy the best living conditions and health status while in Madhya Pradesh, Meghalaya, Odisha, Bihar and Uttar Pradesh, are relatively poor. Finally, the author suggests that improvement in the income levels of STs remain the most daunting challenge for the development of this most marginalized population group.

The paper of S.N. Tripathy deals with existing disparity between tribal and non-tribal populations in health services in the state of Madhya Pradesh. Based on secondary data, the paper covers the issues of infant and child mortality, malnutrition, death of girl child, maternal care and health and expenditure to deal with all these issues. It also examines recent initiatives taken by the Government of Madhya Pradesh from gram panchayat level onwards to improve the health status of marginalized groups, especially STs and SCs. It suggests that by formulating efficient health delivery mechanisms curbing loopholes in the delivery system, curbing the magnitude of corruption found at all the levels, sensitizing health service providers at the block and panchayat levels etc., not only disparity on health sector can be mitigated but also overall health status of tribals can be improved.

The paper of V.K. Shrivastava is cross-cultural in nature. It deals with the nutrition status of tribes with particular reference to the tribes of Madhya Pradesh. It also examines the problems of genetic disorder, infant mortality rate, mortality and morbidity and reproductive wastage. To him, the state of affairs is alarming at all the levels. As a conclusion, some steps have been suggested to improve their health and nutritional status.

J.J. Roy Burman, in his paper, highlights interface between ethno-medicine among the Bhutias and Lepchas of Sikkim. To him medicinal practices of these tribes are linked intimately with religion. In between and after the declaration of merger with India and state formation an inclination towards modern western medicine had been noticed. With the creation of the Health Department and establishment of hospitals, PHCs and sub-centres lots of people started visiting them frequently. But ethnic politics culminating into competition with the large-scale migrant Nepalese population, the Bhutias and Lepchas have withdrawn back to activism and a distinct shift towards the traditional herbal and medico-psychiatric practices can be noticed. The Tibetan medical practices based on Buddhist aetiology too have emerged. The paper makes a modest attempt in unfurling these dynamics based on ethno-medicine.

Suneel Qamra and colleagues attempted to assess the prevalence of different grades of nutritional status (thinness) of Gond children with reference to Gond-dominated Mandla district of Madhya Pradesh. They observed that nearly 80 per cent of Gond children were having nutritional deficiency of grade I, II and III variety. Needless to say that nutritional status of Gond children, irrespective of sex, is dismal and needs attention. The poor weight alone aggravates morbidities and infections. The paper asserts that Grade I thinness was higher among boys compared to girls. The mean values of light, weight and BMI, when compared with national and international standards, was matching to 10th percentile. However, the weight was more deficient to height.

The paper of Swapan Kumar Kolay reflects the nutritional status of pre-school children, identifies the influencing factors and estimates the degree of nutritional status index. Conducted in nine villages of Gujarat, the study used data from selected rural households, haemoglobin estimation and anthropometric measurements of pre-school children. Kolay observed that about 59 per cent boys and 60 per cent girls suffer from mild to moderate forms of malnutrition according to weight for height whereas 58 per cent of boys and the same number of girls suffer from mild to moderate forms of undernutrition with respect to height for age. Similarly, 77 per cent of girls and 84 per cent of boys suffer from mild to moderate forms of malnutrition with respect to weight for age. The study found boys to be more vulnerable as compared to girls in weight for age. Dietary consumption, mother's education, mother's position among housewives and child's height were positively related to the child's nutritional status. Also, mother's age, child's age and dependency ratio had negative influence on nutritional status. The paper suggests that by providing education to women and also by decreasing dependence of women on external forces, their health and nutritional status may be improved.

The paper of Pradeepta Ranjan Pattanayak has made a fairly comparative analysis of the health situation (especially of maternal and child health) among the tribals of Odisha, along with the other social groups and communities, to bring to the fore the magnitude of the chasm that exists between these groups and the other non-tribal social groups and communities of the state, so that remedial steps may be taken to bridge the gap in the greater interests of the society. The data for the purpose was selectively taken from NHFS-II and III, Census Reports, HDR 2004 and 2005, Government of Odisha. The paper remarks that tribes of Odisha suffer from the terrible syndrome of relative deprivation as compared to other groups so far as their health status is concerned.

Yatindra Singh Sisodia and Tapas Dalapati examined health status of Saharia primitive tribe in relation with different institutional measures. To them, the major diseases among the Saharias are malaria, diarrhoea and cholera, which are caused by poor sanitation habits and poor food intake. The sense of sanitation among Saharias is very poor. The authors warn that in order to improve the health of children and mothers, health facilities should be exclusively targeted for Saharias and not to be clubbed with any general programme meant for the mainstream communities. Despite all such efforts, there is also an urgent need to create awareness, sensitization and capacity building among tribes. Schemes need to be reformulated on the basis of needs assessment of the people. There is a culture of silence in the Saharia society and therefore the need of the hour is to make it aware and responsive so that they can become active participators in the whole process.

The paper by S.N. Chaudhary is an empirical study of a tribal village of Madhya Pradesh which is inhabited by Gond tribe. He underlined that historically villagers have followed traditional healing practices in the past and their perception about health and disease was fatalistic. Indigenous treatment facility was available at the local level. In many cases they were also indifferent towards the disease and treatment. But today amount of objective interpretation of health and disease has significantly increased. The attributes of a physically fit person as narrated by villagers are similar to those expressed by doctors. Also, the number of those who were not attending to any healing method in the past has decreased significantly. Their dependence on modern health practices has increased. This does not mean that today traditional medicine men are totally out of the scene. Actually, villagers simultaneously follow both the techniques. Institutional interventions operating in the form of PHC, Aanganwadi centre, CHC working at the block level, Janani Suraksha Yojna, Deendayal Mobile Hospital and private doctors working at Sahpur are more popular among tribal people these days. However, some of the pertinent doubts which originate out of this conclusion relate to sincerity and commitment on the part of PHC and CHC, resourcefulness as well as availability of such facility in need without facing problems. Looking to the carrying capacity of tribals, the paper suggests an integration of indigenous and modern health and disease management mechanism.

D. Debnath, in his paper, writes that due to large-scale degradation of natural resources and unhygienic habitation tribal population suffers from a number of communicable and parasitic diseases. Hence, the utility of the herbal medicinal species in curing the diseases and maintaining their sound health conditions is emphasized. Today, the forest management initiatives have been taken to promote the in-situ conservation and ex-situ cultivation of herbal medicines. This has been followed by the creation of National Medicinal Plants Board under the Ministry of Health and Family Planning, Government of India. For the large-scale production of herbal medicine species public-private partnership has been adopted. But, the outcome is not so praiseworthy. Finally, the paper suggests some measures to deal with the health problems of primitive tribes.

The paper of Y.G. Joshi is based on the survey conducted in 40 Baiga-dominated villages of Shahdol, Sidhi, Mandla, Balaghat, Surguja, Bilaspur and Rajnandgaon districts of undivided Madhya Pradesh. The total Baiga households covered in the study are 983. Besides, 600 households from other communities also were included in order to have a comparative view. The paper underlines that in spite of significant investment under the special assistance programme for the development of this primitive tribal group, the ground realities are far from being satisfactory. The high death rate among females during child birth, high child mortality rate and a majority of deaths occurring due to preventable diseases, like malaria, jaundice and diarrhea, speaks itself of the sorry state of affairs with respect to the availability and effectiveness of health care facilities. To the author, besides poor geographical accessibility, access, affordability and lower education and lower awareness levels, the corruption and non-helping attitude of the functionaries, together with mismanagement and poor coordination between different components of health care delivery system, are largely responsible for the poor state of health of this primitive tribal group. To the researcher, in isolation, the health programmes cannot achieve the target. This calls for formulation and implementation of health schemes in relation with other development measures.

Chaturbhuj Sahu, in his paper, underlines the health and nutritional status of Santhal and Birhor tribes of Hazaribagh district of Jharkhand. They are known as expert herbal doctor. They are not only specialized in sterilization of women temporally as well as permanently, but are also aware of the herbs to induce abortion. The data have been collected from Churchu block for Santhal tribe and three Birhor Tandas, viz., Demotanr (Sadar block), Kandsar (Katkamsandi block) and Sijhuwa (Ichak block) of the district. Regarding maintenance of good health, the Santhals have become more conscious of taking advantage of allopathic treatment in comparison to Birhors, who still follow the traditional pattern of treatment. The Santhals' condition is better than the Birhors. Finally, the paper warned that until the holistic efforts are not made, health status of both these tribes cannot be improved.

The paper of Anjali Dash is based on a field study in Odisha state. It highlights that in spite of the meaningful advancement in the field of preventive and curative medicine, the health care delivery system in tribal areas, especially Odisha, is still poor and needs amelioration and strengthening with sustenance on the guidelines suggested to achieve the targeted goals of health for all in India. Unless locality-specific, tribe-specific and need-based health care delivery system is evolved, which is appropriate, acceptable, accessible and affordable, the goal of health for all would remain a utopia and affect both health and nutritional status of the tribal people. The paper also suggests that many of the infections and parasitic diseases can be prevented from timely intervention, health awareness and education made available to tribes.

Vinita Singh and Jay Palak, in their paper, makes an attempt to explore the linkages between the larger issues of socio-economic, political and ecological factors with the accessibility, affordability and availability of health services to understand the health of tribal women, especially maternal and child health. To them, given the complex intertwining among so many issues involved in tribal health, the entire gamut of tribal health poses challenges for the social scientists as well as health workers especially in the context of mainstream development process. The paper concludes with a retrospective note that tribal health has to be analysed within the context of an interdisciplinary perspective so as to make it more viable from theoretical as well as practical points of view.

The paper by Ram Narayan Sahu and Chaturbhuj Sahu deals with the consumption pattern and nutritional profile of Birhor tribe of Jharkhand state. According to the authors, an average Birhor individual of study area is able to consume 700 gm/day of various food stuffs consisting of 65 per cent cereals and negligible amount of fat and other minerals which are essential for healthy growth. All the food consumed by them except roots/tubers is inadequate. The dietary intake of nutrients is observed as 1,700 kcal energy, 35 gm protein, 400 mg calcium, 28 mg iron, 8 mg Niacin in an average Birhor individual. All the nutrients are found to be inadequate as compared to recommended daily intake and their consumption pattern.

The paper of Kali Nath Jha is based on macro-level situation in health sector, specially with reference to Jharkhand state. It covers gender dimension of health and nutrition, decreasing sex ratio and gender violence, trafficking of tribal women and their encounters with HIV/AIDS and availability of both traditional and modern health providers. The paper concludes that looking to the poor health status of tribal women one may easily understand their pitiable social status.

In her paper, Chura Giri highlights the role of culture, tradition and indigenous knowledge in the management of health and nutrition among Hajong and Lisu tribes of the north-east region. The author is of the view that in the absence of comprehensive and well-structured modern health management institutions, these two tribes not only have their own definitions of health and disease but in order to take care of conception and pregnancy, birth, name giving ceremony, child caring and rearing, taking care of old age people, issue of death and overall health of women at all these levels indigenous practices are extensively followed. The author noticed gender disparity in all aspects contributing to poor health. Ultimately, the paper underlines some suggestions to translate goals of National Health Mission into action for qualitative improvement in health and nutritional status of these two tribes.

The paper of Parul Joshi is based on an intensive study carried out on three tribes, namely, Bhils, Bhilala and Pataliya, in Dhar district of Madhya Pradesh. She has analysed the issue of breastfeeding as a necessary condition for improvement in the health status of infants in relation to some of the independent variables relating to parents such as caste/community, age at marriage, age of delivery, type of family, occupation and annual income. She observed that because of blind faith and tradition, which is sustained by high level of illiteracy among parents, in many families mothers do not allow breastfeeding for three days after birth because they perceive that initially breast milk is not fit for infant. The paper also examines the adoption of supplementary food to babies. The paper concludes that due to ignorance both breastfeeding and supplementary food are not provided to both infants and minor children as per the nutritional requirement. As a result, the level of malnutrition among infants and children is very high among all the three tribes.

The last paper by S.R. Padhi deals with the problem of health and disease with reference to tribes from Korapat district of Odisha from human rights perspective. It highlights infrastructural profile and social and cultural practices to deal with poor health status. It underlines how poor infrastructural arrangements attribute to poor health status of tribes of Odisha in general and tribes of the studied area in particular. Also, an attempt has been made to map impact of poor health conditions on the empowerment process. The paper ends with a positive note that the question of health and disease may be meaningfully addressed provided there is an integration of traditional and modern health institutions and practices.

III

On the basis of an overview of 21 papers included in this volume, most of which are field-based and exploratory, it may be safely said that in spite of the presence of modern health management institutions, functioning of traditional healing system, tribal development initiatives launched by the state and some of the efforts made by tribal themselves, their status of health and nutrition is not as per the norms prescribed by Indian Medical Association. Their condition is unsatisfactory. And, because of poor health and nutrition, they are the victims of various types of diseases. As a result, they lead a poor quality of life and living standard. Number of historical and contemporary factors have been held responsible for this state of affairs. Most of the authors have underlined the increasing role of state in dealing with health and nutrition-related issues. But they have also expressed fear about sustainability, sincerity and commitment on the part of the change agents. However, rays of hope have also been traced. Delinking the local medicine practitioners from blind faith and superstition and integrating them with modern health institutions and empowering and restructuring the latter in the light of the local requirement and carrying capacity of tribal masses may be a viable exercise. Also, efforts need to be made to ensure effective and value-free functioning of development schemes operating at the village level. Scholars are also of the view that effort from below is the need of the hour. And, this calls for social capital formation amongst the tribal masses.

References

Brundtland, G.H. (2000): World Economic Forum, Director, WHO.

Chaudhary, S.N. (2010): In Search of Sustainable Development: Scenario in a Tribal Village of Madhya Pradesh (Unpublished Report), Bhopal: Rajiv Gandhi Chair in Contemporary Studies, Barkatullah University.

Chaudhuri, B. (1986): "Medical Anthropology in India with Special Reference to Tribal Population", in B. Chaudhuri (ed.), *Tribal Health: Socio-Cultural Dimensions*, New Delhi: Inter-India Publications.

Joshi, P.C. (2010): "Traditional Healing Practices of Scheduled Tribes: Status, Challenges and Future", *Special Bulletin* (Workshop Proceedings), Bhopal: Tribal Research and Development Institute.

Kumar, Y. and H. Verma (2010): "Status of Health and Development in Tribal Groups: District and Tribewise Situation Analysis in Madhya Pradesh", *Special Bulletin* (Workshop Proceedings), Bhopal: Tribal Research and Development Institute.

Lewis, A. (1954): "Health as a Social Concept", *British Journal of Sociology*, Vol. IV, pp. 109–124.

Mahapatra, L.K. (1994): "Concept of Health among the Tribal Population Groups of India and its Socio-Economic Correlates", in S. Basu (ed.), *Tribal Health in India*, Delhi: Manak Publications.

Sachchidananda (2010): "Tribal Health Management and Strategies for Future Action", *Special Bulletin* (Workshop Proceedings), Bhopal: Tribal Research and Development Institute.

Swami, S. (1994): As quoted in "Practice of Ethno-Medicine among the Tribals", in S.R. Padhi and B. Padhi (eds.), *Trends and Issues in Tribal Studies*, Delhi: Abhijeet Publications.

1

Tribal Health, Traditional Wisdom and Knowledge

Challenges and Opportunities

BUDDHADEB CHAUDHURI

The World Health Organisation (WHO) defines health as "a state of complete physical, mental and social well-being and not merely the absence of disease and infirmity". It is well recognised that health is not the exclusive domain of medical science because every culture, irrespective of its simplicity and complexity, has its own beliefs and practices concerning diseases. No culture works in a meaningless fashion in its treatment of diseases. Every culture evolves its own system of medicine in order to treat diseases in its own way. Thus, treatment of disease may vary from group to group. To understand health and health-related problems in a proper perspective, it is very important to consider the socio-cultural issues, economic dimensions and environmental aspects. This is more relevant in the context of tribal people particularly living in the rural areas.

The National Health Policy formulated in 1983 and 2002 have yielded results but in several areas, the outcome has not been as expected. Government initiatives in the pubic health sector have recorded some noteworthy successes over time. Diseases like smallpox and guinea worm have been eradicated from the country; polio is on the verge of being eradicated; leprosy and kala azar can be expected to be eliminated in the near future. There has been a substantial drop in the Total Fertility Rate (TFR) and Infant Mortality Rate (IMR). The success of the initiatives taken in the public health field is reflected in the progressive improvement of many demographic indicators over time.

Table 1

Demographic Changes/Achievements Through the Years: 1951–2000

Indicator	*1951*	*1981*	*2000*
Life Expectancy	36.7	54	64.6
IMR	146	110	70

While noting that the public health initiatives over the years have contributed significantly to the improvement of these health indicators, it is to be acknowledged that public health indicators/disease-burden statistics are the outcome of several complementary initiatives under the wider umbrella of the developmental sector, covering rural development, agriculture, food production, sanitation, drinking water supply, education, etc. Despite the impressive public health gains as revealed in the Table 1, one cannot deny the fact that the morbidity and mortality levels in the country are still unacceptably high. These unsatisfactory health indices are, in turn, an indication of the limited success of the public health system in meeting the preventive and curative requirements of the general population.

Out of the communicable diseases which have persisted over time, the incidence of malaria staged resurgence in the1980s before stabilizing at a fairly high prevalence level during the 1990s. Over the years, an increasing level of insecticide-resistance has developed in the malarial vectors in many parts of the country. In respect of TB, the public health scenario has not shown any significant decline in the pool of infection amongst the community, and there has been a distressing trend in the increase of drug resistance to the type of infection prevailing in the country. A new and extremely virulent communicable disease – HIV/AIDS – has emerged on the health scene since the declaration of the NHP 1983. As there is no existing therapeutic cure or vaccine for this infection, the disease constitutes a serious threat, not merely to public health but to economic development in the country. The common water-borne infections – gastroenteritis, cholera, and some forms of hepatitis – continue to contribute to a high level of morbidity in the population, even though the mortality rate may have been somewhat moderated.

Life expectancy at birth has increased for male and female in India. It is 64.1 years for males and 65.8 years for females (2005). This has revealed the decrease in death rate and the better improvement of quantity and quality health services in India. However, there are inter-state, inter-district and rural-urban differences in life expectancy at birth due to low literacy, differential income levels and socio-economic conditions and beliefs. In Kerala, a person at birth is expected to live for 73 years while in states like Bihar, Assam, Madhya Pradesh, Uttar Pradesh, etc., the expectancy is in the range of 55–60 years.

The infant mortality rate (IMR) has declined in India from 70 infants per 1,000 live births in 1999 to 57 in 2005–06 per 1,000 live births. Under-5 mortality rate per 1,000 live births was 85 in 2002. Maternal mortality ratio (MMR) per 100,000 live births was 301 in 2003.

A diverse set of factors are thought to be associated with maternal mortality: factors that influence delays in deciding to seek medical care, in reaching a place where care is available, and in receiving appropriate care. The Tenth Plan document of India has targeted to reduce the IMR to 45 per 1,000 live births by 2007 and 28 per 1,000 live births by 2012. The main causes of high MMR being socio-economic status of women, inadequate antenatal care, the low proportion of institutional deliveries, and the non-availability of skilled birth attendants in two-thirds of cases.

A World Health Report (1999) gives the main causes of mortality in India as non-communicable diseases (48%), communicable diseases (42%) and injuries (10%).

Table 2

Variations in Health Status Amongst States

Sector	*Population BPL (%)*	*IMR/Per 1000 Live Births (1999–SRS)*	*<5Mortality per 1000 (NFHS-2)*	*Weight For Age – % of Children Under 3 years (<-2SD)*	*MMR/Lakh (Annual Report 2000)*
India	26.1	70	94.9	47	408
Rural	27.09	75	103.7	49.6	—
Urban	23.62	44	63.1	38.4	—
Better Performing States					
Kerala	12.72	14	18.8	27	87
Maharashtra	25.02	48	58.1	50	135
Tamil Nadu	21.12	52	63.3	37	79
Low Performing States					
Odisha	47.15	97	104.4	54	498
Bihar	42.60	63	105.1	54	707
Rajasthan	15.28	81	114.9	51	607
Uttar Pradesh	31.15	84	122.5	52	707
Madhya Pradesh	37.43	90	137.6	55	498

In the period when centralized planning was accepted as a key instrument of development in the country, the attainment of an equitable regional distribution was considered one of its major objectives. Despite this conscious focus in the development process, the facts given in Table 2 clearly indicate that the attainment of health indices has been very uneven across the rural-urban divide.

The statistics bring out the wide differences between the attainments of health goals in the better-performing states as compared to the low-performing states. It is clear that national averages of health indices hide wide disparities in public health facilities and health standards in different parts of the country. Given a situation in which national averages in respect of most indices are themselves at unacceptably low levels, the wide inter-state disparity implies that, for vulnerable sections of society in several states, access to public health services is nominal and health standards are grossly inadequate. Despite a thrust in the NHP-1983 and 2002 for making good the unmet needs of public health services by establishing more public health institutions at a decentralized level, a large gap in facilities still persists.

The National Rural Health Mission (NRHM) under the Ministry of Health and Family Welfare (MOHFW), Government of India has brought out a document (2008) entitled "India Guaranteeing Quality Primary Health Care for All: An Agenda for Action". The public health problems have been identified statewise and the key challenges are as follows:

Table 3

Health Problems in Different States

Indicator	*States with high incidence/low performance*
Infant mortality	MP, UP, Odisha, Rajasthan, Chhattisgarh, Bihar, Assam
Maternal mortality	Assam, Bihar, MP, Odisha, Rajasthan, UP
High expenditure in government hospitals	Bihar, Haryana, Punjab, Rajasthan, UP, Assam, Karnataka, Odisha
High TB cases/suspect cases	Jharkhand, Bihar, Gujarat, UP, West Bengal, Assam, Andhra Pradesh, Tamil Nadu
High TFR	MP, UP, Bihar, Jharkhand, Chhattisgarh, Rajasthan
Full immunization	Rajasthan, UP, MP, Bihar, Jharkhand
Diabetes	Kerala, Tamil Nadu, Tripura, Goa, West Bengal, Delhi
Asthma	West Bengal, Kerala, Mizoram, Sikkim, Tripura
Malaria	Assam, Maharashtra, Karnataka, West Bengal, Odisha, Rajasthan, UP, Gujarat, Chhattisgarh, Jharkhand, MP, Arunachal Pradesh, Meghalaya

Cont'd...

...Cont'd

Tobacco and alcohol	Rajasthan, Chhattisgarh, MP, Bihar, Jharkhand, Odisha, West Bengal, Mizoram, Meghalaya, Tripura, Nagaland, Assam, Arunachal Pradesh, Sikkim, Andhra Pradesh, Goa, Kerala, Tamil Nadu, Punjab, Chhattisgarh
Diarrhoea and availability of ORS	UP, Assam, Rajasthan, Nagaland, Jharkhand
HIV prevalence	Manipur, Andhra Pradesh, Karnataka, Maharashtra, Tamil Nadu

The above demographic features show a number of disturbing trends. But the most disturbing feature is the child sex ratio which shows a gradual decline at the national level. It speaks of a demographic imbalance in future. Even though there is some improvement in the context of infant mortality rate in many states, still it is quite high. Again, the prevalence of anaemia is quite conspicuous.

Indicating a continuing preference for boys in society, the child sex ratio in India has dropped to 914 females against 1,000 males – the lowest since independence – in the provisional 2011 Census report released on 31st March, 2011.

Table 4

Situation of Sex Ratio, Child Sex Ratio, IMR and Aneamia among Children and Women at the National Level

Sex Ratio (1991, 2001)				
	1991	2001	Absolute Change	
India	927	933	+ 6	
Child Sex Ratio (1991, 2001) (Girls per 1,000 boys)				
	1991	2001	Absolute Change	
India	945	927	–18	
Infant Mortality Rate (IMR)				
	1971	1981	1991	2001
India	129	110	73	66
Anaemia among children (6–59 months) and women (15–59 years)				
	Any Anaemia (children)	Any Anaemia (women)		
India	69.5	55.3		

Despite a slew of laws to prevent female foeticide and schemes to encourage families to have girl child, the ratio has declined from 927 females against 1,000 males in 2001 to 914 in 2011, which was described as a "matter of grave concern" by Census Commissioner of India. The highest child sex ratio has been reported in Mizoram (971 females against 1,000 males) and Meghalaya (970). Incidentally, these are the two states having majority tribal population.

Access to, and benefits from, the public health system have been very uneven between the better-endowed and the more vulnerable sections of society. This is particularly true for women, children and the socially disadvantaged sections of society. The facts given in Table 5 highlight the handicap suffered in the health sector on account of socio-economic inequality.

Table 5

Variations in Health Status among Socio-Economic Groups

Indicator	*Infant Mortality/1000*	*Under-5 Mortality/1000*	*Children Underweight (%)*
India	70	94.9	47
Social Inequity			
Scheduled Castes	83	119.3	53.5
Scheduled Tribes	84.2	126.6	55.9
Other Disadvantaged	76	103.1	47.3
Others	61.8	82.6	41.1

So it is seen that child mortality including under-5 child mortality and underweight children are more found among the Scheduled Tribes (STs), than Scheduled Castes (SCs) and other disadvantaged groups. Considering these negative health indicators, it is obvious that these communities, particularly the tribals need special attention.

The different tribal communities in India do not represent a homogenous group. There is considerable variation in the context of economy, life style, behaviour and practices. Similarly, variations are also there in the context of demographic features. Thus, population of communities varies from around 20 to over 40 lakh. Thus in one context, the survival of the community may be the most crucial factor while in another context economic development may be more important. In case of some communities, there is a definite decline, threatening the survival of the community. In this context, the study of socio-cultural habits and health practices becomes imperative. The decline might not be only because of a lower rate of fertility but also owing to high mortality and problems in the existing health practices. The decline may be related to their food habits or certain types of food that the tribals consume which may adversely affect the fertility of the concerned population. Again, it may be worthwhile to examine what is the minimum viable population of a group. In other words, it may be examined, whether the size of the population is, in any way, related to decline, if so, what is the size. Unfortunately, till today, we do not have many studies to answer some of these crucial questions.

There is one factor common among all tribal communities except the north-east, it is the educational backwardness. The tribals form the bulk of the illiterate population in India and the close link between education and health is all well-known. It has also been noted that child mortality, under-5 child mortality are the highest among the tribals. It has also been noted that among the tribals there is high incidence of communicable diseases including (a) vector-borne malaria, dengue, (b) water-borne diarrhoea and hepatitis, and (c) air-borne pneumonia, measles, TB Incidentally, all these diseases are due to poverty, malnutrition and certain environmental factors like poor sanitation and unsafe drinking water. Now, there is a growing trend to give more emphasis on non-communicable diseases than on communicable diseases which affects a much larger segment of the population, primarily the disadvantaged people and this can be reduced, if not eliminated, if certain efforts are made and without much financial commitment.

Health and Culture

The belief in the interference of supernatural agency is particularly strong in the case of their main economic pursuits and in the context of health and disease. The different economic activities are associated with rituals. Similarly, different deities and spirits are connected with various types of diseases. Most of their socio-cultural activities revolve around gods and spirits. Thus, they have specific gods for their health and disease, for calamities, for the cattle and so on.

It is important to understand and identify the cause of illness as the nature of treatment is intimately connected with it. The present author has noted this link in his study of the Mundas; Valunjkar and Chaturvedi (1967) too have noted this relationship. Religious performances occupy a prominent place in the treatment of disease, like smallpox and plague which are associated with supernatural causes. Lewis (1958) too had noted that the advantage in learning about the indigenous beliefs and practices of the community is the insight that give into the world view of the people as concepts of disease causation are part of a society's total world view, which is also reflected in other spheres such as agriculture, politics and interpersonal relations.

Health, Medicine and Community

Health and treatment reflect the social solidarity of a community. In a tribal community, for example, illness and the consequent treatment is not always an individual or familial affair, but the decision about the nature of treatment is taken at the community level. In the rural areas, in case of some specific diseases, not only the diseased person or his/her family, but the total village community is affected. All the other families in the village are expected to observe certain taboos or norms and food habits. The non-observance of such practices often calls for action by the village council. One cannot deny the impact of this psychological support in the context of treatment and cure.

In most of the tribal communities, there are number of folklores related to health. Certain practices are suggested to avoid illness or diseases, while some are prescribed to have better health. These should not be ignored as mere folk-beliefs, but need careful attention. There are different folklores to avoid illness, during illness, regarding food and so on. Documentation of such folklores available in different socio-cultural system may be very rewarding and may provide the model for appropriate health practices in a given ecosystem.

Food, Nutrition and Tribal Health

Health and nutrition, particularly in the tribal societies, is intimately connected with forest. It has been reported in various studies that the tribals who are living in remote areas have a better health status and more balanced food than those living in less remote and depleted forest areas. (Chaudhuri, 1986a, 1989, 1991) In the Report of the Roy Burman Committee (1982) on Forest and Tribals, it has been noted that, "it has been possible for the tribal community to subsist for generations with a reasonable standard of health because forest provided their food such as fruits, tubers, leafy vegetables, shoots, honey, flowers, juices, grass, game, fish, etc". Medicinal herbs and plants which they have been using for treatment of diseases and maintaining health are today the source of modern medicine. In two studies related to tribal health (Chaudhuri, 1990a), it has been noted the various roots and tubers available in the forest or small animals they can hunt supply a more balanced nutritional status of the tribals, but due to deforestation as most of the roots and tubers are not available in many areas, the health and nutrition have been affected. Again, in many cases, it has been noted that certain diseases may be common in certain areas but remained controlled due to certain food habits based on vegetation available locally. Forest helps to maintain a balanced ecosystem in nature and supplies sufficient food to the people who depend on it. So any type of degradation in the forest environment is likely to affect the balance and thereby adversely affecting the concerned population.

Table 6

Items Collected from Forest/Nature (Midnapur)

Items	*No. of Varieties*			*Type and Number of Families Involved*		
	Beliaguri	Chonsoro	Jamunasole	Beliaguri	Chonsoro	Jamunasole
Fruits	3	3	10	Kul (14), Kurchi (2), Bahara (4)	Tamarind (44) Kul (18) Khejur (3)	Guava (62), Jam (65), Jackfruit (59), Kend (35), Khejur (62), Kul (67), Mango (58), Kurchi (29) Tamarind (64), Bahara (26) Bel (47)
Drinks	2	2	2	Rana Rani (14) Mahua (8)	Rana Rani tree(15), Mahua (11)	Rana Rani tree (67), Mahua (68)
Vegetable	1	1	5	Mushroom (22)	Mushroom (19)	Mushroom (71), Sajne (65), roots and tubers (62), green vegetables (63)
Other types of food	1	1		Honey (1)	Honey (4)	Honey (18), small bird (22), small animals (20), eggs of ant (26), rarely wild pigs and deer during animal hunting festivals (36)
Medicine	4	0	6	Kurchi (2), Neem + Neem twigs (8), Kalmegh (1), Amloki (1)	—	Dudhi lata (62), Kurchi (37), Neem + Neem twigs (66), Kalmegh (24), Amloki (39) Bel (47) Anantamul (26) Satamul (27)
Fuel	Many varieties			All families collect dry leaves, dry twigs and wood of mainly eucalyptus and other plants available nearer to Beliaguri and Chonsoro villages.		All families collect dry leaves, dry twigs and wood of different plants available in the forest
Wood and Bamboo	1	1	5	Eucalyptus	Eucalyptus	Sal (70), Gamar (20), Mango (40), Jackfruit (27), Bamboo (70)

Cont'd...

...Cont'd

Fodder		Many		Mainly straw supplemented by leaves of Jackfruit, Jam and Mango		Grazing in the forest fodder generally not problem
Oil	0	0	2	—	—	Kusum (32), Sal (29), Kachra (37)
Other items	2	2	3	Sal (12), Khejur (4)	Sal (15), Khejur (2)	Kendu leaves for biddi (42), Sal leaf (73), Khejur leaf (65)
				N: 44	N: 44	N: 73

Beliaguri and Chonsoro – degraded forest situation; Jamunasole –better preserved forest area

Table 7

*Items Collected from Forest (Rangamati, Jharkhand)**

Items	*No. of Varieties*	*Type and Number of Families Involved*
Fruits	11	Amra (26), Bhurru (22), guava (46), Jackfruit (42), Jam (47), Kul (52), mango (46), papaya (23), Kend (26), tamarind (49), lemon (32)
Drinks	1	Mahua (55)
Vegetable	6	Sajne (45), green Jackfruit (25), green mango (28), mushroom (46), roots and tubers (37), green vegetables (28),
Other types of food	5	Honey (18), small birds (25), small animal (28), eggs of ant (33), rarely wild pigs and deer
Medicine	9	Amla/Amlaki (38), Hartaki (24), Boyra (16), Satamuli (18), Arjun (12), Kalmegh (12), Neem (42), Brahmi (14), Puduna/Pudina (33)
Fuel	Many	All families collect dry leaves, dry twigs and wood of different plants available in the forest
Wood and Bamboo	4	Sal (55), mango (32), Jackfruit (27) and bamboo (28)
Fodder	Many	Grazing in the forest fodder generally not problem
Oil	2	Kusum (48), Sal (22)
Other items	7	Kendu (32), Sal(55), Palash (20), Peepul (15), Tara tree (34), Sali tree (22), Edel tree (16)

N: 55 * Rangamati – a forest village

Table 8

Different Plants Supplying Food in the Degraded Forest Situation of West Midnapore District, West Bengal

Village Name	*Name of Trees*	*Past Situation (about 25 years back)*	*Present Situation*
Beliaguri and Chonsoro	Sal (Shorea robusta)	Available in plenty; fruits – consumed as vegetables.	Very less available; fruits – as vegetable – occasional.
	Bhungru (also Bhurru)	Fruits available in plenty	Fruits available much less
	Mohul *(Modhuca longofolia)*	Flower-plenty as vegetables, liquor preparation widely used; fruits – plenty; Seeds-extracted oil (Kochra) – extensively used.	Flower – rare as vegetables; used for preparing liquor fruits – limited; seed – Kachra oil, if necessary purchase from selected markets.
	Kend (not known)	Fruits – plenty (green) as vegetables; ripe – delicious, tasty; widely available in seasons.	Fruits – not available locally; available in markets.
	Bon Khejur (Phoenix species)	Fruits available in June-July-plenty.	Fruits available in June-July – very less.
	Neem *(Azadirachta indica)*	leaves – consumed as vegetables; trees available in plenty.	Leaves – consumed as vegetables; number of trees less.
	Aam (Mango, *Magifera indica)*	Fruits – available in plenty.	Fruits – available but very limited.
	Kanthal (Jackfruit)	Fruits – green as vegetable; ripe one as fruit; available in plenty.	Fruits – green as vegetables; ripe as fruit; available mostly in market.
	Kul/Charkul *(Zizyphus jujuba)*	Available in plenty.	Fruits – not available in plenty.
	Kham/Bon Alu *(Dioscaria)*	Roots – regularly available as vegetables.	Roots – very rare.
	Kundri (wild)	Fruits as vegetable; readily available.	Fruits – very rare.
	Mushroom	Consume as vegetable; readily available	Consume as vegetable; readily available.
	Tamarind *(Tamarindus Indica)*	Fruits – ripe one as fruit; trees available in plenty	Fruits – ripe one as fruit; trees available in plenty.

Table 9

Community, Medicine and Use

Tribe	*Local Name*	*Scientific Name*	*Diseases*
Ho	Orkho	Calotropis giganzia	Tuberculosis
Ho	Begnamadant	Dendrophthoe falcata	Snake bites, abortion, birth control
Ho	Makorkenda	Diospyros embryopteris	Dog bite, diarrhoea, dysentery, blood dysentery, jaundice, abdomen pain
Ho	Sajna	Moringa cleifera	Snake bites, migraine, headache
Ho	Hantipajar	Ooxylum indicum	Fever, leprosy, paralysis, rangbad, rheumatoid
Ho	Sarpagandha	Rauwolfia serpentine	Arthritis, Snake bite
Ho	Chirata	Swartia Puchella	Headache
Ho	Arjun	Terminalia arjuna	Skin boils
Ho/Santal/ Lodha	Anantmul	Hemidesmus indicus	—
Ho/Santal/ Lodha	Satamul	—	—
Ho/Santal/ Lodha	Bel	—	Digestion, stomach elements
Ho/Santal	Lebu/Nimbu	—	T.B
Ho/Santal	Kalmegh	Anographis paniculata	Fever
Lodha	Kuchila	Strychnos nuxvom ica	Cancer, malaria, leprosy, rheutamoid
Lodha	Nirbish	Typhonium trilobatum	Dog bite, cancer, filarial, snake bites, whitlow
Lodha	Mirhilata	Urena lobata	Filarial
Lodha	Kurchi	—	Dysentery
Santal	Apang	Achyranthes aspra	Abortion, Dysentery, Dhatu, Epilepsy, Menstrual disorder, Post-burn etc
Santal	Manthal	Antidesma diandrum	Dhatu, eclampsia, filarial, rheumatoid, otitis
Santal	Sialkanta	Argemone maxiana	Whitlow
Santal	Khapra	Boerhavia diffusa	Vomiting, diarrhoea, dhatua, labour pain, dog bite, menstrual disorder
Santal	Changer	Clerodendrum viscosum	Snake bites, asthma
Santal	Chinnibuta	Scoparia dulcis	Jaundice
Santal	Sal	Shorea robusta	Dysentery, blood dysentery, rangbat, menstrual disorder, dhatu
Santal	Narichirchira	Sida cordifolia	Malaria, mumps
Santal	Atkir	Smilax Macrophylla	Cancer, jaundice, headache, anaemia, typhoid, oedema, pneumonia etc
Santal	Ruhini	Soy mida febrifuga	Fever, diarrhoea, tuberculosis, dhatu
Santal	Katkutjaung	Viscum articulatum	Menstrual disorder, malaria

Medicine Men in Tribal Communities

Amongst the tribals, there are a group of specialists – the priests and/or magicians or medicine men whose services are sought after, depending on the cause of the illness. The dependence on and confidence in traditional medicine men or magicians and *shamans* are again often responsible for the non-acceptance of modern medicine. The traditional approach establishes faith and assurance in the patients, while modern medicine lacks this. As the *shamans* or what are called traditional medicine men and magicians share the common cultural beliefs and practices of the patients, naturally they have more faith in them. Carstairs (1955), a medical psychiatrist and anthropologist, pointed out that the difference between the points of view of the physician and the village folk with regard to theories of etiology, techniques of curing and conceptions of roles of the physician, resulted in misunderstandings between himself, a physician, and his clients. Marriott (1955) has shown how the contrasts and conflicts between the roles assumed by the indigenous and the western medical practitioners resulted in obstacles to the acceptability of western medicine.

Again, in many cases, it has been noted that certain diseases may be common in certain areas but they remain controlled because of certain food habits based on vegetation available locally or certain practices which have been generated through tradition. There is no doubt that any disturbance in the ecosystem is likely to affect the balance and adversely affect the concerned population. Another survey has shown that contrary to the general expectation, the shifting cultivating tribes like the Padam, Riang were having better nutritional status than those of the settled agricultural tribes like the Santal and the Ho. Again, in the context of deforestation, the hunting and gathering tribes were having lower nutritional status. Physical well-being of the tribals is inextricably linked up with the forest ecology. In fact rapid disappearance of forest, commercialization of minor forest produce, replacement of food crops by cash crops and tendency towards monoculture forestry and lastly privatization of communal lands may affect the health and nutrition and physical well-being of the tribal population.

Health, Forest and Nutrition

It has been noted by many that tribals living in remote areas have a better health status and more balanced food than those living in less remote areas (Chaudhuri, 1986b, 1989). In two projects related to tribal health, it has been noted that the various roots and tubers available in the forest or small animals can supply a more balanced nutritional status of the tribals as most of the roots and tubers are not available (Chaudhuri, 2003). Again, in many cases, it has been noted that certain diseases may be common in certain areas but they remain controlled because of certain food habits based on vegetation available locally or certain practices which have been generated through tradition. There is no doubt that any disturbance in the ecosystem is likely to affect the balance and adversely affect the concerned population.

It is quite significant that death rates are consistently lower than the national average in some of the tribal predominant states. Roy Burman (1990) has noted that physical well-being of the tribals is inextricably linked up with the forest ecology. In fact, rapid disappearance of forest, commercialization of minor forest produce, replacement of food crops by cash crops and tendency towards monoculture forestry and lastly privatization of communal lands may affect the health and nutrition and physical well-being of the tribal population.

Health and Forest

The relation of forest with nutrition may be mentioned. It has been noted by many that the tribals living in remote areas have a better health status and more balanced food than those living in less remote areas. The various roots and tubers available in the forest or small animals they can hunt supply a balanced nutrition to them. There is no doubt that deforestation is likely to affect the nutritional status of the tribals as most of the roots and tubers are not available. Again, in many cases, it has been noted that certain diseases may be common in certain areas but they are controlled because of certain food habits based on vegetation available locally, or certain practices which have been generated through tradition. There is no doubt that any disturbance in the ecosystem is likely to affect the balance and same diseases may spread very quickly. The mode of utilization of available natural resources often determines the long-term impact on health. A number of scholars have pointed out the nature of health hazards in the context of unplanned/uncontrolled use of insecticides and pesticides for agricultural development. It has also been observed how this may affect the nutritional status of people, particularly the tribals. The use of insecticides and pesticides has killed the small fishes in the paddy field and thus the poorer families, who generally consumed this protein, were deprived of it. This is also true in case of many tribal areas. Thus the whole development strategy needs critical analysis as it may adversely affect the environment and consequently the health status of the people, particularly the tribals.

Forest happens to be the main source of getting medicinal plants and animals. Naturally, the different forest acts restricting the use and exploitation of forest resources are adversely affecting the health and treatment in tribal societies. Thus, though apparently there does not exist any relation between the forest and health of an individual, in reality, the forest acts; deforestation and certain types of afforestation programmes may adversely affect the health of the tribals. In some of our studies on the health care system in the tribal areas, we observed how the tribal medicine men were facing difficulties in getting medical plants. Most of the traditional medicine men, who came from the three states of Jharkhand, Odisha and West Bengal, while discussing the problems they faced in practising their profession, all clearly pointed out the difficulties they were facing in gathering medicinal plants mainly from the forest. The success of their approach has to be analysed in this context, even if their treatment is not successful in one context.

The relation of treatment and nutrition with forest among the rural population, particularly among the tribal communities is quite obvious. The traditional herbal treatment is rather a people's knowledge and an oral tradition. In many cases, many persons in the concerned community have the knowledge and in some cases, a few selected persons, the traditional medicine men are more knowledgeable. But in any case, people depend on nature, particularly on forest for these medicinal plants. Thus deforestation and commercial afforestation of mono-plant forest may seriously affect the availability of these medicinal plants. Even the nutrition may be similarly affected. Access to forest resources can affect treatment and nutrition. Some of the major problems the tribal communities are facing in general and the traditional medicine men in particular in this context are as follows:

1. Deforestation and non-availability of medicinal plants and animals.
2. Commercial afforestation and more emphasis on commercially important plants – consequently non-availability of herbs.
3. Forest laws and acts restricting the use and exploitation of forest resources.
4. Non-availability of medicinal plants because of commercial interest in many areas.

In the past, this knowledge base was oral and almost always transmitted verbally from one generation to another. Such knowledge is in fact still used today in many areas all over the world in the day to day living of many indigenous people. In several parts of Asia, apart from the folk traditions there is also a parallel classical tradition of knowledge. These classical knowledge systems have very sophisticated theoretical foundations and are codified and documented in thousand of manuscripts. They represent non-western knowledge systems of the world and very different in their world view, concepts and principles from the western knowledge systems. Traditional knowledge in medicine and health has been time tested over generations. It is a holistic concept covering a broad base from disease prevention, health promotion and healing. It has and can deal with health problems ranging from the common cold, air and water-borne diseases to orthopaedics and other complicated cases.

This system is also based on a wide range of biological resources using thousands of plant species, hundred of animal species and animal parts and various minerals and metal sources. Unfortunately, over the years, traditional knowledge and skills have been neglected and a prejudice has been engineered and encouraged by powerful nations and multinationals in order to subjugate non-western cultures.

Science in Society: Indigenous Wisdom and Knowledge

Despite our entire technological breakthrough, we still live in a world where a fifth of the developing world's population goes hungry every night, a quarter lacks access to even basic necessity like safe drinking water and a third lives in a state of abject poverty – at such a margin of human existence that words simply fail to describe it. In both developing and industrial countries, the threats to health security are usually greater for the poorest, people in the rural areas particularly the indigenous people. Spending on health programmes is also very different and it is quite low in the developing countries; for example it is only US$ 7 per individual per year in Bangladesh. Considering this alarming situation, out of the seven important targets put forward for human development in the Agenda for Social Summit, four were related to health. They are as follows:

1. Primary health cares for all with special stress on the immunization of children.
2. Severe malnutrition to be eliminated and moderate malnutrition rates to be halved.
3. Family planning services for all willing couples.
4. Safe drinking and sanitation for all.

The prevailing health and medical system – the western system – has unfortunately failed to meet the need of the world's majority. The failure of the Alma Ata Declaration in fulfilling its objectives of achieving Health for All by the year 2000 gives more urgency for looking for an alternative. In most countries a very frightening policy change is being manoeuvred by agencies like the World Bank and IMF (International Monetary Fund) to give less and less emphasis to the social and welfare sectors and higher emphasis to the economic and infrastructure sectors. As such, the financial allocation for health is going down in most Asian countries. The implication of such a trend in countries where health insurance is unaffordable to the majority is unimaginable. Based on current trends in health care financing and the failure of the Alma Ata Declaration to take a grip of the situation there is an imperative need for evolving an alternative. In this whole changing situation, the condition of the poor, particularly the indigenous people has become more critical and difficult.

Generally, when we talk or think about science, we refer to the western or industrial society. In the context of scientific development, we prefer to discuss more about the so-called modern scientific innovations assuming that science is only there in those societies and quite often implying that scientific rigour or interest is absent in other societies. The role of science is to help mankind to meet the various demands exploiting the natural resources in the best possible way without adversely affecting the environment. People have developed their own science and technologies based on the demands of the concerned societies, but quite often these are ignored. What I want to impress here is that we need to look at indigenous science and technology particularly when an exiting body of knowledge is available: perhaps it is better to develop it instead of replacing it in the name of scientific development and modernization.

Opportunities and Challenges

A number of myths have been systematically created against the non-western system in general and indigenous system in particular.

Often it is said that health is the exclusive domain of medical science. By restricting it in this way, the socio-economic, cultural and environmental issues are often ignored.

Following the above logic, more and more expenditure on sophisticated research is promoted. It is not my intention to discourage research but when the resources are limited, it is to be seen how best possible way the resources can be utilized and whether it should provide more expensive sophisticated facilities to a few or minimum less expensive facilities to a larger population. Perhaps there is a need to make a balance between the two.

Quite often, it is said that the rural people, particularly most of the tribals, are all superstitious. Thus, if a tribal worship a deity for cure, automatically it is assumed that they are superstitious and would not accept the so-called modern health practices, but when the same thing is done in the cities of India, it becomes tradition and when it is done in the churches of Europe, it is levelled as convention. The question of rationality cannot be judged or examined in isolation, without examining the ecosystem, health facilities available and economic condition. Again, the mere presence of a health centre does not necessarily mean that people would depend on it, if proper and adequate facilities are not available or if the people are not convinced about its efficiency. In fact, bulk of the social scientists, who have studied health culture on the rural population in India have been overenthusiastic in discussing superstitious health beliefs and practices and have not paid adequate attention to the forces which have been instrumental in causing decay and degeneration of their health culture.

The advocacy of traditional method of treatment does not mean that something counter to development is suggested. The point is that there may be many positive aspects in a traditional system, which should be encouraged and propagated. In fact, the need is to provide all the alternatives and not to depend on only one system.

The argument often put forward in favour of the introduction of the modern system (and of the replacement of the traditional) is that tribal and similar traditional approaches do not have an answer to many diseases. This is an undeniable fact but does not necessarily reflect a limitation of the traditional system. Apart from the fact of the non-availability of many herbs, one should add that many of these diseases were formerly unknown. Naturally, the question of any traditional system having a remedy for them does not arise. In fact, for the same reason, modern medicine also does not have remedies for many diseases.

Documentation of traditional knowledge in health and medicine is urgently necessary. Most of the research and publications available in this field is purely academic in nature. Society in general is schooled into thinking that adopting traditional health skill and culture is inferior as compared to modern medicine. This attitude has contributed to the further degeneration of this knowledge. Documentation is also urgently needed because the traditional knowledge is mostly an oral tradition and hence documentation is necessary before they are forgotten. Loss of this rich and diverse ecosystem based knowledge systems and skills will be no ordinary loss.

Documentation should be made and at the same time one has to be aware of the risks involved and the use the commercial interest can put to it. Hence, it should be done with certain reservations. Cases are not lacking, when after the publication of research reports on traditional medicinal plants used by the tribals, many such plants were collected in bulk by outside big industries for commercial use for profit. As a result, they are no more available to the traditional medicine men which are so essential for treatment. As a result, the tribals are deprived of their traditional system without the modern system becoming accessible to them.

A knowledge and documentation of traditional tribal medicine are also urgently necessary. It is important for the modern system to begin with the base existing in the tribal society and build on it, rather than replace it. In order to achieve this, information about tribal medicinal practices should be documented before they are forgotten. A study of indigenous method of treatment may help to identify new methods of treatment of various diseases with certain modifications. In fact, a number of ethno-botanical studies have helped to identify a number of medicinal plants used by the tribals to treat different types of diseases. Many of them may be very useful to treat diseases and it is urgently necessary to document them and try them after proper scientific experiment. This has been observed in the few studies that have been made on tribal medicine, especially in terms of efficiency, which is very encouraging. This, however, needs to be further substantiated by sustained research. It may be said that the achievement of tribal medicine is quite revealing. However, to utilize the research findings for further development and application for benefiting the vast majority of the rural poor, particularly the tribals who are living in areas which have very little or no modern medical facilities, needs an integrated and multi-disciplinary research and follow-up dissemination efforts.

Legal and policy issues involving protection of traditional knowledge also needs to be examined. A legislative framework is required whereby the knowledge is kept with the people and recognition, financial or otherwise, is accorded to the individual or community by commercial firms who have to use their knowledge.

The changing forest policies and the changing development scenario in Asian countries has adversely affected the strength of the biological resources used in traditional medicine as much of these resources are being depleted through deforestation. The mono-plant afforestation programmes where emphasis is given on commercial plants has not helped the people much. There is a need to promote conservation measures for saving medicinal plants in various ecosystems and habitat.

A number of studies have pointed out the nature of health hazards in the context of unplanned/uncontrolled use of insecticides and pesticides. It has been noted how they have killed the small fishes in the paddy field and thus the poorer families, who generally consumed this protein were deprived of it. This is also true in case of many tribal areas. Thus the whole development strategy needs critical analysis as it may adversely affect the environment and consequently the health status of the people, particularly the tribals.

Multinational drug companies, medical lobby and the western media have played a major role in disrupting and negating the indigenous knowledge system while on the other hand exploited this traditional knowledge and resource base to develop new drugs. Current efforts at research in ethnic pharmacology have often proved to be counter-productive to the development or advancement of local cultures as the objective is not to strengthen the traditional knowledge and resource base but to get information for multinational drug companies. It is well known that drug multinationals have been robbing traditional knowledge for their own interests.

There is a need to perpetuate and revive the traditional/indigenous system, which is close to the people, non-commercial in nature and curative in approach. It this context, it may be necessary, for

(a) identification of factors responsible for erosion of indigenous health care system and formulation of action programmes to countermand it,
(b) formulation of appropriate methodology to institute traditional health care system in rural/tribal areas and
(c) identification of methodology for more intensive and integrated documentation, research and development.

References

Banerjee, D. (1986): *Social Science and Health Service Development in India*, New Delhi: Lok Prakash.

Carstairs, G.M. (1955): "Medicine and Faith in Rural Rajasthan", in B.D. Paul (ed.), *Health, Culture and Community*, New York: Russell Sage Foundation.

Chaudhuri, Buddhadeb (1979): Cultural Dimensions of Health: A Study on West Bengal Villages, 1st International Congress on Traditional Asian Medicine, Canberra, Australia.

——. (1986a): *Tribal Health: Socio-Cultural Dimensions*, New Delhi: Inter-India Publications.

——. (1986b): "Social and Cultural Aspects of Health", *Journal of Social and Economic Studies* (n.s.): 379–388.

——. (1989): "Social Science, Health and Culture: The Tribal Situation", *Social Action*, 39(3): 243–253.

——. (1990a): "The Case of Tribal Medicine", in J.V. Narlikar and others (eds.), *The Philosophy of Science*, Shimla: Indian Institute of Advanced Study.

——. (1990): *Cultural and Environmental Dimensions on Health*, New Delhi: Inter-India Publications.

——. (1993): "Health, Culture and Environment: The Tribal Situation in India", in Mrinal Miri (ed.), *Continuity and Change in Tribal Society*, Shimla: Indian Institute of Advanced Study.

——. (2003): *Forest, Health and Development: The Tribal Situation*, New Delhi: Inter-India Publications.

Chaudhuri, Buddhadeb, D. Dasgupta and K.K. Chatterjee (eds.) (1989): *Tribal Medicine*, Midnapore: Regional Research and Study Centre.

Jain, S.K. (1968): *Medicinal Plants*, New Delhi: National Book Trust.

Joseph, A.N.T. (1992): "Ethnozoology of Reptiles in Relation to Health Care among Tribals in Madhya Pradesh", in Walter Fernandes (ed.), *National Development and Tribal Deprivation*, New Delhi: Indian Social Institute.

Lewis, Oscar (1958): *Village Life in Northern India*, New York: Random House.

Marriott, McKim (1955): "Western Medicine in a Village of Northern India", in B.D. Paul (ed.), *Health, Culture and Community*, New York: Russell Sage Foundation.

Population Foundation in India (2010): *Population, Health and Social Development*, New Delhi: PFI.

Roy Burman, B.K. (1982): *Report of the Committee on Forest and Tribals*, New Delhi: Government of India.

——. (1990): "Development Hazards to Health in Tribal India", in Buddhadeb Chaudhuri (ed.), *Cultural and Environmental Dimensions on Health*, New Delhi: Inter-India Publications.

Roy, Chandreyee (2009): Forest and Tribals: Right to Access Over Natural Resources, Ph.D. Thesis, Human Rights, Kolkata: Calcutta University.

Valunjkar, T.N. and H.R. Chaturvedi (1967): "Religion and Illness in Hindu Society", *Journal of the M.S. University of Baroda*, 15 and 16(2): 45–52.

WHO (1999): "Regional Health Situation, India: Trends in Health Status", 7.2. Regional Office of South East Asia, www.searo.who.int/en/Section313/Section1519_10855.htm

2

Health and Nutritional Status of Tribes in India

R. SHANKAR AND V. JAISEE GEETHA

India is a homeland of different tribal groups inhabiting widely varying ecological and geo-climatic conditions in different concentration throughout the country. These aboriginals face several problems such as widespread poverty, illiteracy, malnutrition, absence of safe drinking water and sanitary living conditions, poor maternal and child health services and ineffective coverage of national health and nutritional services. Various problems faced by tribals have been traced out in several studies as contributing factors to dismal health conditions prevailing among the tribal population in India. The health and nutrition problems of the vast tribal population of India are as varied as the tribal groups themselves who present a bewildering diversity and variety in their socio-economic, socio-cultural and ecological settings.

Tribal Map of India

The tribal population groups of India are known to be the autochthonous people of the land. Tribals are often referred to as *Adivasi*, *Vanyajati*, *Vanvasi*, *Pahari*, *Adimjati* and *Anusuchit Jan Jati*, the latter being the constitutional name. The concept of tribe emerged in India with the coming of the British. Gradually, the concept of reservation emerged and through that emerged the idea of Scheduled Tribe in independent India.

According to Article 342 of the Constitution, the Scheduled Tribes (STs) are the tribes or tribal communities or part of or groups within these tribes and tribal communities which have been declared as such by the President through a public notification. STs are spread across the country mainly in forest and hilly regions (2001 Census). The essential characteristics of these communities are (this criterion is not spelt out in the Constitution but has become well established):

- Primitive traits
- Geographical isolation
- Distinct culture
- Shy of contact with community at large
- Employed mostly in primary sector
- High levels of poverty and illiteracy, low nutritional levels

The Constitution incorporates several provisions for the promotion of educational and economic interest of STs and their protection from social injustice and all forms of exploitation.

In India, 427 groups have been recognized as STs. These tribal groups inhabit widely varying ecological and geoclimatic conditions (hilly, forest, desert, etc.) in different concentration throughout the country with different cultural and socio-economic backgrounds.

Due to their remote and isolated living, tribal groups are difficult to reach. According to 2001 Census of India, the tribal population in India is more than 83 millions. It is 8.08 percentage of the total population. The STs differ considerably from one another in race, language, culture and beliefs. Notwithstanding so much diversity, there are certain broad similarities between the mutually divergent tribal groups. Striking similarities are noticed in their modes of living, each tribe lives in a definite area, has common dialect, cultural homogeneity and unifying social organization. The tribal population of India has been found to speak 105 different languages and 225 subsidiary languages indicating a great deal of variety (IGNOU, 1990). Languages spoken by Indian tribes can be classified into four major families of languages, namely, Austro-Asiatic family, Tibeto-Chinese family, Dravidian family and Indo-European family. On the basis of racial features, B.S. Guha (1935) considers that the tribal population of India belongs to three races, namely, the Proto-Australoids, the Mongoloids and the Negritos. Literacy among the tribals is very low (25.9%) and especially so among the tribal females (14.5%) (NSSO, 1991). The level of education among most of the STs is up to primary level. The lowest level of literacy among females was found in Rajasthan (4.1%). Sex ratio (females per thousand males) reflects the status of socio-cultural, maternal and child health care programmes existing in the population. In the 1991 Census, the sex ratio of the tribal population was 972 females per thousand males against 927 for the total population. The highest sex ratio for STs among various states has been reported from Odisha (1,002) and the lowest from Goa (889).

STs are at different stages of social, cultural and economic development. The cultural pattern varies from tribe to tribe and region to region. The economic life of the tribals is specific in nature. Based on the manner in which the tribals primarily and distinctly make their living, the Indian tribals can be classified into seven groups:

(i) *Food Gatherers and Hunters:* For example Cholanaicken, Malapandaram and the Arahdan tribal groups of Kerala, Rajis of Uttar Pradesh, Birhor of Bihar, Hill Maria of Madhya Pradesh, Juangs of Odisha, Chenchus of Hyderabad, Kadars of Cochin, Jenu-Kuruba of Karnataka, the Onge, the Jarwa and the Andamanese of Andaman islands.

(ii) *Shifting (Jhum) Cultivators:* For example Khasis of Meghalaya, Nagas of Assam, Korwa of Bihar, Saora of Odisha, Muria and Maria of Madhya Pradesh.

(iii) *Settled Agriculturists:* For example major tribes like Santhal, Munda, Ho, Oraon, Gond, Bhil, Mina, etc.

(iv) *Artisans:* The number of tribes subsisting on crafts like basket making, tool making, spinning and weaving is small, e.g., Kota of Nilgiri Hills, Birhor of Bihar.

(v) *The Pastoralists and Cattle Herders:* For example Todas of Nilgiris, Gujar, the Bakerwal and Gaddi in Himachal Pradesh.

(vi) *The Folk Artists:* For example Pradhans of Madhya Pradesh.

(vii) *Wage Labourers:* Large chunks of tribal territories have come under plantations, mining and industrial development. Tribals of Chhotanagpur have gone to north-east India to work on tea plantations. The Santhals have been employed in coal mines of Bihar.

Tribal scene does not present a uniform canvas. The Dhebar Commission (1961) observed four different layers among the tribal population. On top is the acculturated layer whose Scheduled Tribe members have adopted more or less the way of life of non-tribal sections forming the upper crust of the society, e.g., Minas. They have travelled the farthest from original tribal habitat. The second are the settled Scheduled Tribes agriculturists, e.g., Santal, Munda, Oraon, Gond, etc., in the fringe plains who have come quite some way from the tribal highlander, being no longer isolated and they are in the process of transformation. The third category is that of the highlanders who having hardly shifted from their habitat, have undergone little transformation and may still practice shifting cultivation, e.g., Khasis, Muria and Maria. The last category, (at the base) a class of tribals, which is in an extremely underdeveloped stage, isolated backward groups, including the so-called 'primitive groups', who, encysted in their original habitat, have been little exposed and, consequently, preserve original socio-economic-cultural traits, e.g., Cholanaicken, Kadars, Onge, etc.

Tribal groups constitute about 8.2 per cent of the total population in India (Indian Government Census, 2001). According to government statistics, tribes can be found in approximately 461 communities (Singh, 1994) with almost 92 per cent of them residing in rural areas, mostly in remote underserved forest regions with little or no basic civic amenities like transport, roads, markets, health care, safe drinking water or sanitation (Indian Government Census, 2001). Tribal communities therefore lag behind other communities with respect to attainment of income, education, health and other requisites for good community nutrition (Srinivasan and Mohanty, 2004). A study by Mishra (2005) using the National Family Health Survey (NFHS-2) found that in almost all the states of India, tribal households had a higher incidence of childhood stunting (52.3%) than non-tribal households (42.8%). Tribal population still largely depend on agriculture and forest products for their livelihood and they follow a relatively homogenous lifestyle with their food habits, dietary practices and general pattern of living (Patwardhan, 2000). Most tribes still rely on their indigenous foods, which usually consist of wild unconventional forest products although some cultivate grains and other farm products for subsistence (Singh and Arora, 1978). The most frequently used cereals are maize, millet or rice and these form part of a major meal at least once daily (Kapil et al., 2003). Since the tribal diet is usually plant based with significant amounts of anti-nutritional factors, which limit the absorption, and/or bioavailability of zinc and because very limited amount of animal source foods are consumed, these population are at high risk for zinc deficiency.

The Concept of Health

Health is a prerequisite for human development and is an essential component for the well-being of the mankind. The health problems of any community are influenced by interplay of various factors including social, economic and political ones. The common beliefs, customs, practices related to health and disease in turn influence the health seeking behaviour of the community. There is a consensus agreement that the health status of the tribal population is very poor and worst among the primitive tribes because of their isolation, remoteness and being largely unaffected by the developmental processes going on in the country.

The term 'health' is understood differently by different people developing upon the specific social, economic, cultural and political situations in which they happen to be expressed

Politically powerless would consider himself to be in a state of health so long his body permits him to perform his duties and tasks and earn minimum subsistence. Even rich men will think that in the same way though he may seek immediate medical care. Several definitions focused the individuals as responsible for their ill-health and thus failed to bring out the nexus between diseases and the external factors which are social and political. Talcott Parsons gave a definition of health in a restricted form. According to Parsons, health may be defined as the state of optimum capacity of an individual for the effective performance of the roles and tasks for which he has been socialized. It is thus defined with reference to the individual's participation in the social system. This view is further correlated by the following definition: "Health may be thought of as the extent of an individual's continuing physical, emotional, mental and social ability to cope with his environment". This views shows that the individual is responsible for what he is suffering from. They go to say that if a person is suffering from diarrhea caused by unsafe drinking water the individual is blamed for not boiling the water instead of blaming the social system which failed to provide safe drinking water owing to lack of political will.

The above concept of health is not based on any system analysis. A few of the contemporary views on health, though they reflect an attempt to consider the extraneous factors also. Ronald Ftakberg and Joyce Lesson added sociological dimension to the concept of health. They attempt towards a clear 'conceptualization' of health by different committees and organizations on various occasions finally culminated in the formation of a widely accepted definition given by the World Health Organization. According to WHO, "health is a state of complete physical, mental, social well-being, and not merely an absence of disease (or) infirmity". Though this definition underlines the social dimension of health, it has not taken into account the existing gap which prevails between the people and the 'health providers' in the contemporary situation. Besides, WHO's definition is also too general and it has not specified the level which can indicate 'complete' physical, mental, and social well-being of individuals. It varies among different social categories depending upon their social status and the political power they enjoy. According to them, health in non-industrialized countries (and perhaps elsewhere) is not, we shall argue, to be seen in medical and economic terms alone, all the traditional concerns such as role, class, age, sex, stage in life cycle, conflict and reference group also involved. A shift from 'individual' to 'social' responsibility is expressed in the above explanation, and it is also true that every social phenomenon has a direct bearing on the health of the people. Those aspect is further validated by the definition given by the Survey and Development Committee. According to this committee, the term 'health' implies more than an absence of sickness in the individual and indicates a state of human functioning of the body and mind in relation to his physical and social environment so as to enable him to enjoy life to the fullest possible extent and to reach his maximum level of productivity.

The health status of any community is influenced by the interplay of health consciousness of the people, socio-cultural, demographic, economic, educational and political factors. The common beliefs, traditional customs, myths, practices related to health and disease in turn influence the health seeking behaviour of autochthonous people (Balgir, 2004a). If general health of an average non-tribal Indian is inferior to the Western and even many Asian counterparts, the health of an average Indian tribal is found to be much poorer compared to the non-tribal counterparts. The health status of tribal population is very poor and worst of primitive tribes because of the isolation, remoteness and being largely unaffected by the developmental process going on in India. The United Nations (UN) members met in 2000 and set themselves eight goals to be achieved by 2015. In these goals, reducing child mortality, improving maternal health, and combatting HIV/AIDS, malaria and other diseases related to the health segment were included. The first goal of 'eradicating extreme poverty and hunger' also contains a nutritional element which is health related. In the developing world, death rates in children under-5 are dropping, but not fast enough. Eleven million children are still dying every year, from preventable or treatable causes. More than half a million women die each year during pregnancy or childbirth. AIDS has become the fourth largest killer worldwide, and in parts of Asia, HIV is spreading at an alarming rate. The blight of malaria and tuberculosis continues.

Tribal communities in general and primitive tribal groups in particular are highly disease-prone. Also, they do not have required access to basic health facilities. They are most exploited, neglected, and highly vulnerable to diseases with high degree of malnutrition, morbidity and mortality (Balgir, 2004). Their misery is compounded by poverty, illiteracy, ignorance of causes of diseases, hostile environment, poor sanitation, lack of safe drinking water and blind beliefs, etc. The chief causes of high maternal mortality rate are found to be poor nutritional status, low haemoglobin (anaemia), unhygienic and primitive practices for parturition. Average calorie as well as protein consumption is found below the recommended level for the pregnant as well as lactating women. Some of the preventable diseases such as tuberculosis, malaria, gastroenteritis, filariasis, measles, tetanus, whooping cough, skin diseases (scabies), etc., are also high among the tribals. Some of the diseases of genetic origin reported to be occurring in the Indian tribal population are sickle cell anaemia, alpha- and beta-thalassemia, glucose-6–phosphate dehydrogenase (G-6-PD) deficiency, etc. (Balgir, 2004b). Night blindness, sexually transmitted diseases are well-known public health problems of tribals in India.

Health and Its Correlates

The UNDP Human Development Index (HDI) comprises three components, i.e., health, education and income generating capacity. Health is a function, not only of medical care, but also of the overall integrated development of society – cultural, economic, educational, social and political. The health status of a society is intimately related to its value system, philosophical and cultural traditions, and social, economic and political organization. Each of these aspects has a deep influence on health, which in turn influences all these aspects. Hence, it is not possible to raise the health status and quality of life of people unless such efforts are integrated with the wider effort to bring about overall transformation of a society. Health development can be integrated with the larger programme of overall development in such a manner that the two become mutually self-supporting. Good health and good society go together. This is possible only when supportive services such as nutrition and improvements in the environment and in education reach a higher level.

Every social group, from a primary group such as a family to a complex nation group, and extending beyond it, the human society as a whole, strives for the betterment of health of its members. Nothing on the earth is more international than diseases said Paul Russel. Health and disease have no political or geographical boundaries. Disease in any part of the world is a constant threat to other parts.

Around 68 per cent (Census 2011) of the Indian population lives in rural areas. Their food consumption is far below standard, their housing condition is inadequate, their methods of performing productive activities is primitive, their educational horizons is limited, and their accessibility to technological innovations is far-reaching. What are the causes and what are the effects? Widespread preventable diseases unquestionably serve as a barrier to progress in any direction be it economic, social or political. A population that is chronically ill understandably has decreased productivity. Uncontrolled diseases in the environment and the continuance of conditions that breed unproductivity and illiteracy also discourage investment as well as the industrial development. Finally, a low economy and standard of living attributable directly or indirectly to widespread ill-health is a constant encouragement to social unrest. Under such circumstances people have many reasons for discontentment and very little to lose in resorting to violence. There is a vicious circle. Disease breeds poverty and poverty in turn breeds more disease. A similar relationship exists between disease with illiteracy, social problems and many other factors. It is difficult or impossible to state which factor is primary, which is cause and which is effect. Once the cycle is established however, it is clear that each factor contributes to the continuance of all other undesirable factors. This has been referred to as 'multiple causation' and 'cumulative causation'.

Health Culture

The culture of community determines the health behaviour of the community in general and individual members in particular. The health behaviour of the individual is closely linked to the way he or she perceives various health problems; what they actually mean to him or her, on the one hand, and on the other his or her access to various relevant institutions. The holistic concept of health culture provides a valuable framework for analysing the work of anthropologists in health fields. However, a very few studies are available in this direction, specially among the tribal population.

Tribal Health Culture

Tribal communities are mostly forest dwellers. Their health system and medical knowledge over ages known as 'traditional health care system' depend both on the herbal and the psychosomatic lines of treatment. While plants, flowers, seeds, animals and other naturally available substances formed the major basis of treatment, this practice always had a touch of mysticism, supernatural and magic, often resulting in specific magico-religious rites (Balgir, 1997). Faith healing has always been a part of the traditional treatment in the tribal health care system, which can be equated with rapport or confidence building in the modern treatment procedure. For example, the doctor priests of the Saora tribe utilize several herbs and roots in conjunction with their magico-religious rites in Odisha. Health problems and health practices of tribal communities have been profoundly influenced by the interplay of complex social, cultural, educational, economic and political practices. The study of health culture of tribal communities belonging to the poorest strata of society is highly desirable and essential to determine their access to different health services available in a social set-up.

The common beliefs, customs, traditions, values and practices connected with health and disease have been closely associated with the treatment of diseases. In most of tribal communities, there is a wealth of folklore associated with health beliefs. Knowledge of folklore of different socio-cultural systems of tribals may have positive impact, which could provide the model for appropriate health and sanitary practices in a given ecosystem. The health culture of a community does not change so easily with changes in the access to various health services (Balgir, 2004a). Hence, it is required to change the health services to conform to health culture of tribal communities for optimal utilization of health services.

Tribal Health and Nutrition Problem

The health problems need special attention in the context of tribal communities of India. Available research studies point out that the tribal population has distinctive health problems which are mainly governed by their habitat, difficult terrains and ecologically variable niches. The health, nutrition and medico-genetic problems of diverse tribal groups have been found to be unique and present a formidable challenge for which appropriate solutions have to be found out by planning and evolving relevant research studies. Primitive tribal groups of India have special health problems and genetic abnormalities like sickle cell anaemia, G-6-PD red cell enzyme deficiency and sexually transmitted diseases (Commissioner Report for Scheduled Tribes and Scheduled Castes, 1986–87). Insanitary conditions, ignorance, lack of personal hygiene and health education are the main factors responsible for their ill-health. The primary health care infrastructure provides the first level of contact between the population and health care providers and forms the common pathway for implementation of all the health and family welfare programmes. It provides integrated, preventive, curative and rehabilitative services to the population close to their hearth and home. A majority of the health care needs of the tribal population are taken care of either by the trained health personnel at the primary health care level or by their own traditional indigenous health practitioners at village level. Those requiring specialized care are referred to secondary and tertiary sector. The tribal population is not a homogeneous one. There are wide variations with regard to education and health status, access and utilization of health services among the tribal population (Balgir, 2000a).

Keeping in view that most of the tribal habitation is concentrated in far-flung areas, forest land, hills and remote villages, and in order to remove the imbalances and provide better health care and family welfare services to STs, the population coverage norms of establishment of rural infrastructure have been relaxed. The primitive tribes in India have distinct health problems, mainly governed by multi-dimensional factors such as habitat, difficult terrains, varied ecological niches, illiteracy, poverty, isolation, superstitions and deforestation. The tribal people in India have their own lifestyles, food habits, beliefs, traditions and socio-cultural activities.

The health and nutritional problems of the vast tribal population are varied because of bewildering diversity in their socio-economic, cultural and ecological settings (Balgir, 2000a). However, data analysis in view of their ecological, ethnological, cultural and biological diversity is lacking in India. The health care services and challenges in rural and tribal areas are a complicated phenomenon such as:

- Concept of health and disease is rather traditional which results in their not seeking treatment at an early stage of physical maladjustment and frequent refusal of preventive measures in rural areas and their idea of medical care is some treatment not easily accessible and available. There is a lack of motivation of people for availing medical care at the initial stage of the disease.
- Limited paying capacity or habit of getting treatment always free of cost.
- Comparative inaccessibility of medical care services due to underdeveloped communication and transport facilities.
- Non-availability of qualified medical practitioner in the village.
- Qualified health workers and professional medical and paramedical staff do not want to work in rural and tribal areas because of professional, personal and social reasons.
- Non-availability of private or governmental doctor as and when need arises.

A look into the pattern of rural health services shows that the scarcity of trained manpower for health is a major problem and obstacle to the extension of health services to rural and tribal areas. Moreover, the qualified health workers do not want to work in rural and tribal areas because of professional, personal and social reasons. The health problems of rural and tribal population cannot automatically be overcome by establishing more primary health centres and subcentres and also imparting training to more health personnel or providing integrated health services by a single authority or by a number of agencies. An integrated health services would be operated on a teamwork basis by division of labour so that the greatest possible use of professional skills could be made. While the physician is the central figure in the health centre complex, the efficiency and output of health services would depend upon the supporting personnel consisting of nurses, various categories of paramedical (laboratory technician, pharmacist, multipurpose health worker, genetic/marriage counsellor, Aanganwadi worker, etc.) and auxiliary staff. Managerial skills and controlling power of the doctor to coordinate various activities and maintenance of infrastructures including vehicles and procurement of equipment, medicines, vaccines, etc., on regular basis are highly desirable. There is a complete lack of managerial training, financial empowerment and facilities available to the doctor to efficiently and effectively monitor and carry out public health duties in the rural setting and tribal areas. This drastically affects the well-being and tribal health. Frequent transfers and absenteeism of the staff, favouritism and corrupt practices hinder the smooth functioning of the Primary Health Centre (PHC), which have adverse health effects on the tribal population. Due to a combination of geographic isolation, economic status, societal attitudes, traditional beliefs, and provider inadequacy, tribal population throughout India have often been denied access to allopathic health services. Comprising of around 10 per cent (100 million) of India's population, they demonstrate some of the poorest health outcomes in India. With a large population and consanguineous marriage practices, there is a dangerously high prevalence of genetic disorders among tribal population in India. The presence of sickle cell anaemia among tribal population has surged to the forefront as a critical public health problem among tribal groups. A congenital haemolytic anaemia that results from a defective haemoglobin molecule, sickle cell disease causes red blood cells to roughen, become sickled, and rupture (haemolyze) leading to sickle cell crisis. This results in an impaired circulation and chronic ill-health. Half of the patients with sickle cell disease die before 20 years of age due to organ failure from repeated crises. Epidemiological studies confirm that sickle cell anaemia is prevalent in the tribal populace; the prevalence of heterozygotes (carriers) for the sickle gene is calculated to be over 20 per cent in some areas. The sickle gene was first described in tribal groups in South India, and studies illustrate its presence in various parts of India including Tamil Nadu, Madhya Pradesh, Odisha, and Kerala. Genetic diseases have traditionally received little attention from urban health services in India, and even less so in tribal areas. As a result, virtually all studies carried out regarding tribal population and sickle cell anaemia have strongly recommended that genetic health services be integrated into existing primary health care and medical services to combat the disease. Few health care delivery systems, however, have implemented these recommendations.

Improper Nutrition

Food is that which nourishes the body. Nutrients are those 50 (or) more chemical substances in food that are needed by the body and are divided in to six classes: normally proteins, fats, carbohydrates, mineral elements, vitamins and water. Nutrition refers to the processes in the body for making use of food. It includes eating the right kind and amount of food for the body's needs; digestion of foods so that the body can use nutrients; absorption of the nutrients in to the blood stream; use of individual nutrients by the cells in the body for the production of energy, maintenance and growth of cells, tissues and organs; and elimination of wastes.

Nutritional care is the application of the art and science of nutrition to the feeding of the people. It deals with the assessment of the nutritional status; the planning of meals according to physiology and psychologic needs. Certain changes associated with poor nutrition include overweight, underweight, growth failure, sudden loss of weight, poor posture, protruding abdomen, lack of padding of fat (or) excessive fat, dry, scaly, pale skin, poorly fonned jaw with teeth poorly aligned, dull dry, hair, dull eyes, sensitivity to light, burning, itching, circles and puffiness under eyes, poor appetite, complaints of indigestion, diarrhea, constipation, fatigue and worried, depressed sake of mind. The principal target of nutritional improvement in the community is the family and the instrument for combatting malnutrition is nutrition education.

The tribal population is recognized as socially and economically vulnerable. Their lifestyles and food habits are different from that of their rural neighbours. They depend on minor forest produce and manual labour for livelihood. They may not have adequate income. Their food consumption pattern is dependent on the vagaries of nature and varies from extreme deprivation (in the lean seasons) to high intakes (in the post-harvest period).

Somnath Ray's study from the nutritional point of view, opines that the Indian society is a dual society, consisting of a small group of welfare and very large group of undernourished. The high income groups are showing disease of affluence which is found in the developed countries.

On the other hand, malnutrition is often found among the low income groups. Malnutrition is particularly found among certain vulnerable groups like rural agriculture labours, tribal population, urban slums and children. The specific nutrition problems in the country are:

(a) *Protein and energy malnutrition:* In sufficiency of calories – so-called "food gap" – appears to be the chief cause of PRM among children. Its incidence among rural children between 1 and 5 years in different parts of the country is estimated around 1.2 per cent. Nutrition experts consider this to be an underestimate because it does not include the mild and moderate forms of PRM.

(b) *Anaemia:* The second important nutritional problem in India is anaemia, which is very common especially among women of the reproductive age group and pre-school children. A modest estimate shows that 50 per cent of all pregnant and lactating women have nutritional anaemia.

(c) *Vitamin deficiencies:* Vitamin 'A' deficiency is an important public problem especially in the age group 3–5 years. It is an important cause of preventable blindness in children in many parts of Asia including India. Deficiency of other vitamins is also quite frequent.

(d) *Goiter:* Surveys reveal that nearly 40 million people are suffering from varying degrees of goiter and 140 million are estimated to be living in the known goiter endemic regions of the country which exist in the states.

Malnutrition is high among the tribal population. Nutritional deficiency leads to diseases like endemic goiter, anaemia, pellagra and beriberi deficiency disease occurring when the human body has insufficient amount of thiamine (Vitamin B_1). The deficiency may result from improper diet, e.g., nutritional anaemia is a major problem for women in India and more so in the rural and tribal belt. This is particularly serious in view of the fact that both rural and tribal women have heavy workload and anaemia has profound effect on psychological and physical health. Anaemia lowers resistance to fatigue, affects working capacity under conditions of stress and increases susceptibility to other diseases. Maternal malnutrition is quite common among the tribal women especially those who have many pregnancies too closely spaced. Tribal diets are generally grossly deficient in calcium, Vitamin A, Vitamin C, riboflavin and animal protein.

A study by Mishra (2005) using the National Family Health Survey (NFHS-2) found that in almost all the states of India, tribal households had a higher incidence of childhood stunting (52.3%) than non-tribal households (42.8%). Using the same dataset, Nagda (2004) reported an anaemia prevalence of more than 80 per cent among tribal children. Several studies have also reported deficient intake of calories and protein among tribal populations relative to the Indian RDA, which may be an explanation for the high rates of stunting among this group (Rao et al., 1994; Yadav and Singh, 1999; Agte et al., 2005; Mittal and Srivastava, 2006). Iron deficiency is recognized as the major cause of anaemia in tribal communities (Reddy et al., 1995; Vyas and Choudhry, 2005) and several studies have reported that deficiencies of micronutrients such as iron and zinc often occur together.

Hence, the high rates of anaemia among tribal populations provide additional evidence of the possibility of marginal zinc deficiency in tribal areas. This is further supported by the high prevalence of stunting and the highly deficient dietary energy intakes in the tribal population since intake of both zinc and iron are known to be highly correlated with dietary energy intake (Willett, 1998). At least one study has shown that zinc intake of population in tribal regions was significantly lower than that of any of the other regions studied (Agte et al., 2005). Tribal population still largely depend on agriculture and forest products for their livelihood and they follow a relatively homogenous lifestyle with their food habits, dietary practices and general pattern of living (Patwardhan, 2000). Most tribes still rely on their indigenous foods, which usually consist of wild unconventional forest products although some cultivate grains and other farm products for subsistence (Singh and Arora, 1978). The most frequently used cereals are maize, millet or rice and these form part of a major meal at least once daily (Kapil et al., 2003). Earlier studies indicated that, comparatively, the overall health of the tribal population is inferior to that of people elsewhere in India and that poor environmental sanitation and unhygienic personal practices predispose tribal population to high risk of infection (Nagda, 2004; Mishra, 2005). Findings from a recent national survey showed that 82.4 per cent of tribal households did not have latrines and 78.1 per cent did not have drainage facilities in their homes (NFHS-2, 1998), a situation that predisposes children to diarrheal disease. The survey also found that the prevalence of diarrhea and Acute Respiratory Infection (ARI) was higher among tribal children than children of non-tribal mothers. Similarly, the study by Nagda (2004) suggested that childhood diarrhea, ARI, anaemia and fever were major causes of infant mortality in tribal areas.

India's abysmal track record at ensuring basic levels of nutrition is the greatest contributor to its poverty as measured by the new international Multidimensional Poverty Index (MPI). About 645 million people or 55 per cent of India's population is poor as measured by this composite indicator made up of ten markers of education, health and standard of living achievement levels.

Developed by the Oxford Poverty and Human Development Initiative (OPHI), the MPI attempts to capture more than just income poverty at the household level. It is composed of ten indicators: years of schooling and child enrolment (education); child mortality and nutrition (health); and electricity, flooring, drinking water, sanitation, cooking fuel and assets (standard of living). Each education and health indicator has a 1/6 weight, each standard of living indicator a 1/18 weight.

The recent data also shows that even in states generally perceived as prosperous such as Haryana, Gujarat and Karnataka, more than 40 per cent of the population is poor by the new composite measure, while Kerala is the only state in which the poor constitute less than 20 per cent. The MPI measures both the incidence of poverty and its intensity. A person is defined as poor if he or she is deprived on at least 3 of the 10 indicators. By this definition, 55 per cent of India was poor, close to double India's much-criticized official poverty figure of 29 per cent. Almost 20 per cent of Indians are deprived on 6 of the 10 indicators.

Nutritional deprivation is overwhelmingly the largest factor in overall poverty, unsurprising given that half of all children in India are undernourished according to the National Family Health Survey III (2005–06). Close to 40 per cent of those who are defined as poor are also nutritionally deprived. In fact, the contribution of nutrition to the overall MPI is even greater in urban than rural India.

Multi-dimensional poverty is highest (81.4% poor) among Scheduled Tribes within India's Hindu population, followed by Scheduled Castes (65.8%), Other Backward Class (58.3%) and finally the general population (33.3%).

Among tribal households, there were serious deficiencies in the intake of pulses and legumes, milk and milk products, fats and oils, and sugar and jaggery. Anthropometric indices also show high levels of malnutrition. Generally, a balanced diet provides all the food substances needed by the body for healthy growth and development. Good nutrition also includes eating the proper amount of food each day. It helps keep the body healthy and fit. When they are not able to get two meals a day, how is the concept of nutritious food applicable to them. The nutritional problems of different tribal communities located at various stages of development were full of obscurities and very little scientific information on dietary habits and nutrition status was available due to lack of systematic and comprehensive research investigations. Malnutrition was common and greatly affected the ability to resist infection, led to chronic illness and in the post-weaning period led to permanent brain impairment. Good nutrition was a requirement throughout life and was vital to women in terms of their health and work. Nutritional anaemia was a major problem for women in India and more so in the rural and tribal belt. In developing countries, it was estimated that at least half of the non-pregnant and two-thirds of the pregnant women were anaemic (U.N.,1984). The situation was particularly serious in view of the fact that both rural and tribal women had a heavy workload and anaemia had a profound effect on their psychological and physical health. Aneamia lowered resistance to fatigue, affected working capacity under conditions of stress and increased susceptibility to other diseases. Maternal malnutrition, which was quite common among the tribal women, was also a serious health problem, especially for those having many pregnancies too closely spaces, and reflected the complex socio-economic factors that affected their overall situation. The nutritional status of pregnant women directly influenced their reproductive performance and the birth is crucial to an infant's chances of survival and to its subsequent growth and development. Nutrition also affected location and breast feeding which were key elements in the health of infants and young children and a contributory factor in birth spacing. Scanning through available data, it was observed that among most of the tribal groups the staple diet was rice or minor millets except the Mompas of Assam who consumed wheat also (Basu et al., 1985). Birds, fish and other meat products were also consumed by the tribals occasionally. Diet of not a single tribal in the different states of India can be said to be satisfactory. Tribal diets were generally grossly deficient in calcium, Vitamin A, Vitamin C, riboflavin and animal protein. Diets of South Indian tribes in general, and of Kerala in particular, were grossly deficient even in respect of calories and total protein. Studies carried out at the National Institute of Nutrition (1971) and Planning Commission of India (Sixth Five-Year Plan, Government of India) reported a high protein calorie malnutrition along the rice-eating belts. Studies available on the dietary status and health of the Bihar and Maharashtra found deficiency calorie as well as protein and essential amino acids in their diets though major signs of nutritional deficiencies were not observed (Chitre, 1976).

Surveys on the nutritional deficiencies (Gopalan, 1971) among the tribals reported a high incidence of goitre, angular stomatitis among the Mompas of Assam and Vitamin A deficiency among the Onges. A high incidence of malnutrition was observed (Ali, 1980; Basu et al., 1990; Mahapatra and Das, 1990) in some primitive tribal groups in Phulbani, Koraput and Sundergarh districts of Odisha and also among Bhils and Garasia of Rajasthan, Padars, Rabris and Charans of Gujarat and Bondas of Odisha (Haque, 1990). Studies of tribal communities in Odisha conducted by Ali (1992) found that an ecological imbalance caused by rapid deforestation had resulted not only in depleting food resources, but in prolonged droughts, adding to hunger and starvation.

Higher prevalence of undernutrition in tribal population is due to

- poverty and consequent undernutrition;
- lack of awareness about, access to and utilization of the available nutrition supplementation programmes; and
- social barriers preventing the utilization of available nutrition supplementation programme and services.

- poor environmental sanitation and lack of safe drinking water, leading to increased morbidity from water-borne infections;
- environmental conditions that favour vector-borne diseases;
- lack of access to health care facilities resulting in increased severity and/or duration of illnesses.

Social and Cultural Issues

There are so many political, cultural, social, economic and educational problems of this community, but the important problems are related to health, nutrition and educational development. The main problem is their exploitation. As they are coming in contact with outsiders, they are being treated like a commodity and use them as slaves. Their social and cultural structure is being disturbed and disorganized. After independence, first time it was considered that their security is as important as security of others. To develop their identification, separate development programmes have been introduced. Although, much work has been done in fields of economic, social and political spheres, yet there is a great need to make new and practical programmes.

High Disease Burden

Any tribe must be encouraged to organize itself in order to take advantages of the programmes designed for the development and health in the light of human genetics, prophylactic immunization, socio-cultural traditions and eco-friendly environment. It has been observed that the tribal communities are vulnerable as well as have major threat of the following major health problems:

Communicable Diseases

The people in their daily life consciously or subconsciously modify the environment and ecological aspects of their habitat, which in turn increase the risk for communicable diseases. The communication of diseases is dependent either on the direct contact or on the indirect agents like breathing, sputum, stool, saliva, urine, etc. The venereal diseases are communicated through direct contact and tuberculosis is communicated through indirect contact such as breathing. Thus, the communicable diseases are those diseases, which pass from infected person to a healthy person by direct or indirect contacts through infectious agents. Sometimes, viral or bacterial infections cause death in large numbers (in epidemic form) and threaten the survival of mankind.

There are several communicable diseases prevalent among the tribals of India. These are: tuberculosis, hepatitis, sexually transmitted diseases

(STDs), malaria, filariasis, diarrhoea and dysentery, jaundice, parasitic infestation, viral and fungal infections, conjunctivitis, yaws, scabies, measles, leprosy, cough and cold, HIV/AIDS, which is spreading like wild fire, etc., due to lack of sanitation and unhygienic living (Balgir, 2005a). They frequently become victims of repeated epidemics of the above mentioned contagious diseases.

Leprosy is communicated through intimate and prolonged contact with the patient. The unhygienic conditions play a major role and disease is manifested in skin, mucous membrane and nerves and caused by mycobacterium leprae. Poor diet and nutrition enhances susceptibility of communication to infectious diseases. Besides, lack of personal and domestic hygiene, overcrowded living are also the causative factors responsible for this kind of disease. Beside the other communicable diseases like diarrhea, measles, typhoid, and influenza are also reported among the tribals. Lymphatic filariasis (LF) is one of the major tropical diseases associated with disfigurement of grossly swollen limbs and genitals. Globally around 40 million people almost in 80 countries where the disease is endemic have clinical LF, and another 80 million are infected with the parasite. More than 1,000 million people live in the endemic areas and are at risk of becoming infected. Human infection with the parasite leads to damage in the lymphatic vessels that lead to a wide range of temporary or permanent disabilities. The LF can be eliminable. The Global Programme to Eliminate Lymphatic Filariasis (GPELF) recommends that all those who live in endemic communities be treated once in a year with a single dose of appropriate antifilarial drug like diethylcarbamazine (DEC). Though this drug has limited effect on adult filarial worm, it clears microfilariae from infected humans and deprives mosquitoes for opportunity to pick up infection from affected host to healthy individual. Elimination of LF by 2015 is the goal prescribed in National Health Policy of India.

Local outbreaks due to malaria are of frequent occurrence, and the morbidity and mortality associated with the disease is alarming. The environment is conducive to mosquito proliferation, survival and longevity; all these prerequisites lend to active transmission of the malaria pathogen. Owing to the heavy rainfall and high humidity, mosquito fauna is rich and breeding habitats are diverse. The transmission of malaria is perennial and persistent. This type of malaria is often termed as tribal malaria. In the tribal pockets, most people live under poor socio-economic conditions and are vulnerable to malaria transmitted by efficient vectors. Resistance to chloroquine (the commonly used anti-malarial) in Plasmodium falciparum (Pf) infection is widespread. Plasmodium vivax (Pv) is highly susceptible to chloroquine and, thus, should always be the first line of treatment, but recently it has been reported that malaria has also become chloroquine resistance in some tribal pockets. The problem is further compounded by the poor administrative control for organized malaria control operations. Malaria is the foremost public health problem in India.

Though the tribal communities constitute nearly 8 per cent of the total population of India, they contribute 25 per cent of the total malaria cases and 15 per cent of the total Pf cases, leading to 30–50 per cent malaria deaths in India. A high transmission of Pf is in the forest regions because malaria control in such settlements is unattainable due to technical and operational problems. Insecticide impregnated mosquito nets popularly known, as medicated nets is one such approach to ward off the dreaded vectors to reduce the man mosquito contact. This strategy is simple, cost-effective, environment friendly, sustainable and involves the much needed community participation which is vital to the success of any health programme. This method of vector control when integrated with health education, inter-sectorial cooperation and biological control, coupled with early detection and prompt treatment will provide a long-lasting solution in keeping with the global strategy for malaria control.

Diarrhoeal disorders are communicable water-borne diseases like gastro-intestinal disorders including acute diarrhea and are responsible for high morbidity and mortality. In tribal areas, the diarrheal/dysentry diseases including cholera occur throughout the year attaining peak during the rainy season (from June to October). The acute diarrheal problems were basically due to poor environmental hygiene, lack of safe drinking water, improper disposal of human excreta, aggravated by low literacy, socio-economic status coupled with blind cultural belief, lack of access to medical facilities leading to serious public health problems.

Non-communicable Diseases

Education, especially the female education, is generally considered a key factor to development. Female education is believed to have a great influence on the maternal and child health as it enhances the knowledge and skills of the mother concerning age at marriage, contraception, nutrition, prevention and treatment of diseases. This also means that the higher infant and child mortality rates among the poorly educated mothers are due to their poor hygienic practices. Moreover, maternal education is related to child health because it reduces the cost of public health related to information on health technology. It is expected that the increase in literacy rate of a community would reduce the fertility, morbidity and child mortality or in other words, improve the health status of the community as a whole. Mortality decline can be achieved by widely distributed public health services such as information technology, immunization, sanitation, nutrition, adding preventive and curative services to improve the maternal and child health. Lack of proper health education, poverty, faulty feeding habits and irrational beliefs aggravate the health and nutritional status of these underprivileged people in India (Balgir, 2000a).

As malnutrition is known to lead susceptibility to infectious diseases to death, the mortality rate in primitive tribes may be attributed to malnutrition. Aneamia was more common in females than males. The majority of these tribals showed microcytic and hypochromic blood picture suggestive of iron deficiency anaemia. There was a positive correlation between hookworm infestation and anaemia due to indiscriminate defecation, bare foot and lack of health awareness.

Deficiency of essential dietary components leads to malnutrition, protein calorie deficiency and micronutrient deficiencies like Vitamin A, iron and iodine deficiency.

Public health policies are not adopted and implemented in vacuum; they are the outcome of social and political change. The forces of change need to be understood in the interest of public health. Conditions of environmental sanitation are deficient, combined with limited access to preventive and curative health care, result in high incidence of infectious diseases and high state of morbid conditions in the tribal population. It is well established that undernutrition impairs body's defence mechanism and undernourished children are more susceptible to various infections. It is observed that higher fertility and higher infant and child mortality and also maternal mortality are interlinked phenomenon based on health and nutritional status of a community. Consumption of hooch is a habit with most tribals and considered to be the main reason for the community's backwardness. More people die of hooch-related causes in tribal areas. With the literacy rate being low, most tribals spend their hard-earned money on liquor instead of finding a way out of poverty. But the bulk of the earning is spent on buying hooch. Hooch gets the boot in tribal population. Liver cirrhosis due to excessive drinking of country made alcohol, hypertension due to excessive salt intake, chronic respiratory diseases due to excessive smoking, oral cancer (due to regular betel nut chewing), malnutrition, nutritional deficiency disorders like iron deficiency anaemia, iodine deficiency (goitre), avitaminosis, etc., form a major chunk. Cardio-vascular diseases are very uncommon among the tribals. There are several other environmentally caused health hazards due to poor sanitation, poor disposable facilities for human excreta, animal waste, sewerage and sullage, etc., associated with illiteracy, extreme exploitation by the local elites, etc.

However, in some tribes the indigenous way of treatment for some common ailments using herbs and other forest flora or fauna products is much more advanced than the modern allopathy in some cases.

Silent Killer Genetic Diseases

Genetic disorders are gaining prominence and have profound health implications in morbidity status of tribals. Sickle cell anaemia and glucose-6–phosphate dehdrogenase (G-6–PD) enzyme deficiency are the two important genetically determined disorders, which play an important role in human health and disease. Recently, the G-6–PD enzyme deficiency among the tribes (Bathudi, Bhuyan, Munda and Santal tribes) of India has been identified as a new variant, which had only 10–20 per cent of the normal enzyme activity and normal electrophoretic mobility, but had five-fold higher Michael's constant for the substrates which actually translates roughly into five-fold lower activity at limiting substrate concentrations and showed the increased thermostability than normal enzyme (Kaeda et al., 1995). This means that the anti-malarial drugs like primaquine and many other compounds such as phenacetin, furadantin, certain sulphonamides and acetyl salicylic acid (aspirin), etc., should be administered with caution among the tribal population of India, which may cause hemolytic crisis and, sometimes may even be fatal. Hereditary hematological disorders such as hemoglobinopathy and thalassemia syndrome (Balgir and Sharma, 1988; Balgir, 1996a, 1996b), glucose-6–phosphate dehydrogenase enzyme deficiency (Balgir, 1989) and hemophilia, and colour blindness (Balgir, 1999a), chromosomal aberrations, congenital malformations, inborn errors of metabolism, etc., are encountered among the tribal population.

Reproductive Health

After India's independence, government institutions were gradually opened in rural areas inhabited by indigenous people. Male officers from the developed coastal plains were posted in these government offices temporarily, usually for a period of two to three years. Since the tribal areas were underdeveloped and lacked necessities of modern lifestyle, the officers who were posted in tribal areas did not bring their families with them. During their stay, some of them entered into bigamy by marrying innocent young tribal women. This did not cost them much and provided a solution to their loneliness and physical or sexual needs. Two or three years later, they could leave the area leaving the tribal wife and children without any support. This illegal and inhuman practice by the government officials remained unknown to the public in the coastal plains. Further, the dark side of these activities was the grabbing of land by outside people in the tribal areas, sexual exploitation of innocent tribal women, and extortion of forest produces by non-tribal traders, stood as a challenge before the indigenous women living in the forests. This has led to the spread of certain diseases common among the tribals. In tribal areas there is a lack of infrastructure particularly related to the supply of drinking water, electricity and educational and health services. The tribal territory is rich in mineral, forest and water resources, but the poorest of the poor live there. The area has also an abundance of rare flora-fauna and is rich in biodiversity. Despite this, tribes have to migrate in search of their livelihood, have low access to health care and education and have higher morbidity and mortality. Thus, it is required that the development processes are speeded up in the tribal areas ensuring that the fruits of development must reach the tribal communities. The development process has displaced sizable number of tribal people from their natural habitat and from the sources of their livelihood in recent times. This has further kept them below poverty line. The infant mortality rates were very high in primitive tribes, the life expectancy was low with the high death rate. The unhygienic and primitive parturition practices were mainly responsible for high maternal mortality. Among some tribe, the delivery was conducted by the mother herself in a half squatting position holding a rope tied to roof of the house. This helps her in applying pressure to deliver the child. In complicated labour, obviously, it might lead to maternal as well as child mortality. The respiratory diseases including upper respiratory tract infections were more commonly prevalent which accounted for a high infant mortality due to inadequate vaccination, lack of early diagnosis and treatment and prevention.

Factors Contributing to High Disease Burden

Generally, a balanced diet provides all the food substances needed by the body for healthy growth and development. Good nutrition also includes eating the proper amount of food each day. It helps keep the body healthy and fit. When they are not able to get two meals a day, how is the concept of nutritious food applicable to them.

Lack of medical facility is another problem for them. The poor tribals do not get food regularly so they fall sick. Doctors recommend that people should have medical care at the first sign of any illness. Early care can result in quicker cure. But the tribals are deprived of all these basic needs. Due to mosquitoes bites, skin diseases, jaundice, natural calamities, they suffer and do not get any treatment on time.

Hygiene problem is very common in rural as well as in tribal areas. Due to unhygienic conditions their children suffer with many diseases like measles, mumps, polio, tetanus, and whooping cough. Prevention of disease is an important part of medical care. Parents should make sure that their children receive immunization against diphtheria, German measles, measles, mumps, polio, tetanus, and whooping cough. But tribal parents are ignorant of these things.

As already mentioned, food is one of our most basic needs. We cannot live without it. Food gives us the energy for everything we do—walking, talking, working, playing, reading, and even thinking and breathing. Food also provides the energy our nerves, muscles, heart, and glands need to work. In addition, food supplies the nourishing substances our bodies require to build and repair tissues and to regulate body organs and systems.

Government Initiatives

In tribal health, several health policies were implemented by the government, of which, the National Health Policy of 1983 dealt with the primary health care services to all and access to basic services. Basic services usually consist of diagnostic, preventive, and routine restorative services. such as water supply and sanitation. The quality of available health services depends on individual responsibility and the quality of environment.

Yet another landmark health policy, implemented in 2002, aims at achieving good health among the general population of the country through universal provision of comprehensive primary health care services. The approach would be to increase access to the decentralized public health system by establishing new infrastructure in deficient areas and by upgrading the infrastructure in the existing institutions. The strength of India's health care system is its elaborate network of health care infrastructure. The goal of strengthening primary health care requires effective, affordable and comprehensive primary level health care services.

Both the Government of India and the Government of Tamil Nadu have been implementing several programmes for the health care development of the tribal communities. In such attempts, the National Health Policies dealt with primary health care consisting of nutrition for all, immunization, maternal and child health care, prevention of food adulteration, water supply and sanitation, environmental protection, school health programmes, occupational health services, prevention and control of epidemic diseases. The tribal communities have their own systems of medicines, dispensed through the medium of *shamans*, herbalists and witchdoctors, which also act as a barrier in the implementation of health care programmes. With all these, tribals suffer from chronic diseases and health problems. It is due to low income and other socio-economic factors. As a result, the health status of the tribals remains in a precarious condition.

Strategies to Improve Health Care in Tribal Areas

- Ensuring availability of adequate infrastructure and personnel.
- Area specific RCH programmes.
- 100 per cent central plan funds for NMEP.
- Effective implementation of the health and family welfare programmes.
- Close monitoring, early detection of problems in implementation and midcourse correction.

Suggestions

Health care is one of the most important of all human endeavours to improve the quality of life especially of the tribal people (Balgir, 1997, 2000a, 2005a). It implies the provision of conditions for normal, physical and mental development and functioning of human being individually as well as in a group. A great realization has come from the medical scientists that human being can no longer be treated as an anatomical and physiological entity, and that man's individuality should be understood in terms of perceptions, culture and belief system (Balgir, 2000a). Studies by anthropologists indicate that traditional medicines do exist and persist even though the health consumer has now access to western medicine. There is a need to study scientifically the traditional tribal medicines and healing systems and combine them with modern allopathic system so as to make it available and affordable for the poor tribal population.

As we know that the health comes by evolution, not by revolution, health must meet the needs of the people, as they perceive them. Health cannot be imposed from outside against people's will. It cannot be dispensed to the tribal people. They must want and be prepared to do their share and to cooperate fully in whatever the health programmes a community develops (Balgir, 2000a). The problems of shortage of food, poverty, population expansion, malnutrition, health, hygiene and disease burden still persist in 60 per cent rural population in India. Proper health and balanced nutrition are, therefore, considered as some of the prime requirements for application of biotechnology in improving the quality of life of rural poor. It implies sufficient knowledge about the culture, environment, natural and human resources, skill endowments and the belief systems of a set of people (Balgir et al., 2002, 2005a). This approach is best suited to study the behaviour of the people in health and disease, encompassing the biocultural and eco-environmental aspects of the concerned tribal population. It is envisaged to upgrade the health and nutritional status of tribal poor using emerging applied tools such as

- Improvement of health care infrastructure.
- Developing a flawless referral system.
- Provide diagnostic facilities for genetic defects.
- Follow up of aneamic and other severe patients.
- Carry out population genetic survey programmes.
- Health education.
- Genetic counselling.
- Marriage counselling.
- Provide prenatal diagnosis.

Conclusion

It is necessary to continue with primary health care educational activities, national health and tribal health programmes and other measures of providing proper nutrition and counselling and with the help from experts from multi-disciplinary fields, the health status of the tribal population can be improved. The health status of a society is intimately related to its value system, philosophical and cultural traditions, and social, economic and political organization. Each of these aspects has a deep influence on health, which in turn influences all these aspects. Hence, it is not possible to raise the health status and quality of life of people unless such efforts are integrated with the wider effort to bring about overall transformation of a society. Health development can be integrated with the larger programme of overall development in such a manner that the two become mutually self-supporting. Good health and good society go together. This is possible only when supportive services such as nutrition and improvements in the environment and in education reach a higher level.

References

Balgir, R.S. (1989): "Ethnic and regional variations in the red cell glucose-6–phosphate dehydrogenase deficiency in India", *Indian J Hemat*, Vol. 7: pp. 101–109.

——. (1996a): "The prevalence of sickle cell hemoglobinopathy in India", in T. Madhava Menon, C. Sivathanu, K.P. Prasanth, M. Sasikumar and P.R.G. Mathur (eds.), *Encyclopedia of Dravidian Tribes*, Trivandrum: The International School of Dravidian Linguistics, pp. 21–29.

——. (2000a): "Human genetics, health and tribal development in Orissa", in P. Dash Sharma (ed.), *Environment, Health and Development: An Anthropological Perspective*, Ranchi: S.C. Roy Institute of Anthropological Studies, pp. 87–104.

——. (2004a): "Dimensions of rural tribal health, nutritional status of Kondh tribe and tribal welfare in Orissa: A biotechnological approach", Proceedings of the UGC Sponsored National Conference on 'Human Health and Nutrition: A Biotechnological Approach' (Lead Lecture), 12–13th December, Thane, pp. 47–57.

——. (2004c): "Medical genetics in Orissa: An urgency in health and disease", Proceedings of the 8th Orissa Bigyan Congress on 'Science for Sustenance' held during 11–12th December, Bhubaneswar, pp. 20–23.

——. (2005a): "Biomedical anthropology in contemporary tribal society of India", in Deepak Kumar Behera and Georg Pfeffer (eds.), *Contemporary Society: Tribal Studies,* Vol. 6, *Tribal Situation in India*, New Delhi: Concept Publishing Company, pp. 292– 301.

Banerji, D. (1982–86): *Poverty, Class and Health Culture in India*, Vol. I, New Delhi: Prachi Prakashan.

Basu, Salil (1994): "The state of the art: Tribal health in India", in Salil Basu (ed.), *Tribal Health in India*, Delhi: Manak Publishers.

——. (1994): *Genetic Disorders and Health Care*, Delhi: Shri Kala Prakashan.

——. (1996): "Health and socio-cultural correlates in tribal communities", in R.S. Mann (ed.), *Tribes of India: Ongoing Challenges*, Delhi: M.D. Publications Pvt. Ltd.

Basu, Salil et al. (1993): Study for Socio-cultural, Demographic Characteristics, Maternal and Child Health and Sexually Transmitted Diseases among the Polyandrous' Jaunsaris of Jaunsar-Bawer, Dehradun: NIHFW, Mimeo.

Bhasin, M.K. and H. Walter (2001): *Genetics of Castes and Tribes of India*, Delhi: Kamla-Raj Enterprises, pp. 26–78.

Bimla (1995): "How healthy are village women", *Social Welfare*, 42(3): 16–17.

Census of India (1991): 1 of 1992. Final Population Tools, Registrar General and Census Commissioner of India, New Delhi.

Dasgupta, Supriya (1988): "Tribal women", in Supriya Dasgupta (ed.), *Understanding the Tribal Dilemma: Tribal Women and Forest Dweller Economy*, New Delhi: Indian Social Institute.

David, Grembowski (2001): *The Practice of Health Program Evaluation*, New Delhi: Sage Publications.

ICMR Report (1984): Growth and Physical Development of the Indian Infants and Children, Tech. Rep. Ser. No. 18, New Delhi: Indian Council of Medical Research.

Keith, Tones S. and Jackie Green (2004): *Health Promotion: Planning and Strategies*, New Delhi: Sage Publications.

Menon, Geeta (1987): "Tribal Women: Victims of the Development Process", *Social Action*, Vol. 37.

Park, J.E. and K. Park (1976): *Text Book of Preventive and Social Medicine*, New Delhi: Banarasidas, p. 12.

Singh, K.S. (1994): *The Scheduled Tribes,* Delhi: Oxford University Press.

Srinivasan, S. (1987): "Health care in rural India: Problems and challenges", in A.K. Kalla and K.S. Singh (eds.), *Anthropology, Development and Nation Building*, New Delhi: Concept Publishing Company, pp. 211–220.

Sujatha, V. (2003): *Health by the People: Sociology and Medical Care*, Jaipur: Rawat Publications.

Vidyarthi, L.P. (1983): "Tribes in India", in *Peoples of India: Some Genetical Aspects*, XV International Congress of Genetics, December 12–21, New Delhi: ICMR.

3

Living Conditions and Health Status of Scheduled Tribes in India

Evidence from DLHS 2007–08

AALOK RANJAN CHAURASIA

The Scheduled Tribes (STs) are tribes notified under the Article 342 of the Constitution of India, which makes special provision for tribes, or tribal communities which are notified by the President of India. The word 'tribe' has however not been defined or described in the Indian Constitution and, in fact, there is no satisfactory definition anywhere. Generally, tribal people are distinguished through characteristics specific to them including self-identification, language, distinctive social and cultural organization, geographic location, etc. The Hindi word used for the term 'tribe' is *Adivasi* which comprises of two words *Adi* meaning aboriginal and *Vasi* meaning inhabitants (Ranjan, 2006). According to this interpretation, tribal people are aboriginal inhabitants of the country India.

India has the largest tribal population in the world (Ali, 2003). At the 2001 population census, the ST population in the country was enumerated to be 84.33 million accounting for almost 8.2 per cent of the total population (Ranjan, 2006). There is however no estimate of the tribal population in India as many population groups regarded as *Adivasi* are not included in the list of STs described in the Schedule V of the Indian Constitution. The list of STs described in the Indian Constitution was prepared in 1950 on the basis of two criteria – primitiveness and backwardness (Sachchidananda and Prasad, 1998). The proportion of STs varies widely across states and union territories.

Classification of the population by caste – Scheduled Castes, Scheduled Tribes and non-Scheduled Castes/Tribes – is a regular feature of the Indian population census, although, ST population is not a socially, culturally and ecologically homogenous entity. Similarly, large scale surveys like National Family Health Survey, District Level Household and Facility Survey and Coverage Evaluation Survey also classify the households and individuals surveyed by caste. This classification provides an opportunity to analyse the living conditions and health status of STs across the states and union territories of the country.

Information about living conditions and health status of STs as a whole is available through the National Family Health Survey and the District Level Household and Facility Survey. In this paper, we use the information available through the latest District Level Household and Facility Survey (DLHS) 2007–08 to analyse how living conditions and health status of STs vary across the states and union territories of the country.

The paper is organised as follows. The next section of the paper provides a brief account of the DLHS 2007–08 and outlines the methodology, while the third section presents the country level scenario of the living conditions and health status of STs on the basis of the information available through DLHS 2007–08. The fourth section of the paper analyses inter-state variations in different dimensions of living conditions and health status of STs while the last section discusses the policy and programme implications of the analysis.

II

Data and Methodology

The present analysis is based on the information available through the District Level Household and Facility Survey (DLHS) 2007–08 (IIPS, 2010). DLHS 2007–08 was one of the largest ever demographic and health surveys carried out in India, with a sample size of about seven lakh households covering all states and union territories and all districts of the country. DLHS were initiated in the year 1997 with a view to assess the utilization of public health care facilities and people's perceptions about the quality of health services. DLHS 2007–08 was the third in the series of district surveys. Like the two earlier rounds, DLHS 2007–08 was designed to provide estimates of important indicators of maternal and child health, family planning and other reproductive health services. The survey was carried out during the period 2007–08 with a reference period from 1st January, 2004 through the survey date which varied from place to place. A multi-stage stratified sampling design was used to select the households for the survey. For every district of the country an independent sample of households was drawn for the survey. At household level, direct interview approach was adopted to collect the information during the survey. Bilingual questionnaires – in English and in the local language – were developed and pre-tested for the purpose of the interview.

DLHS 2007–08 covered more than 700 thousand households in the country out of which 112 thousand were ST households. We use the information available from 101 thousand households in the rural areas to analyse and discuss the living conditions and health status of STs in the country and in its constituent states and union territories. We also compare the situation of STs with that of non-STs (Scheduled Castes, other backward classes and other classes) in the rural areas. Information about non-STs is also available through the DLHS 2007–08.

The analysis has been carried out at the national level as well as at the state level but not at the district level as the sample size at the district level was too small to carry out such an analysis. Moreover, the proportion of STs may be too small to a meaningful analysis. During the analysis, it was observed that a number of indicators used for analysing the living conditions and health status of STs were found to be strongly correlated to each other. As such, for the state level analysis, we have applied the factor analysis procedure to group the living conditions and health status variables into dimensions or factors of living conditions and health status. Factor analysis attempts to simplify the complex and diverse relationship that exists among a set of observed variables by uncovering common dimensions or factors that link together seemingly unrelated variables, and consequently provides insight into the underlying structure of the data (Dillon and Goldstein, 1984). Factors extracted through the factor analysis technique are actually linear combinations of the original variables used in the analysis. The factors have the additional property that they are not correlated to each other. This property of factor analysis solution helps in identifying different dimensions of the phenomenon under study – living standards and health status in the present case. The factor analysis solution help in analysing how different states and union territories of the country faired on different factors or dimensions of living conditions and health status of STs.

The application of the factor analysis procedure in the present case revealed that the 12 indicators used in the present analysis can be grouped into three factors of living standards and health status as discussed later in this paper. Results of the application of factor analysis procedure greatly helped in analysing the inter-state variations in the living conditions and health status of STs in the country.

III

National Scenario

The low level of income of ST households is well reflected in terms of the house in which they were living at the time of the survey. According to DLHS 2007–08, almost 70 per cent of the ST households in the country were living in kuchcha houses, whereas this proportion was less than 40 per cent in non-ST households. On the other hand, the proportion of ST households living in pucca houses was less than 7 per cent but almost 24 per cent in the non-ST households. The proportion of non-ST households living in semi-pucca houses was also substantially higher than the ST households. This observation supports the earlier observation that income levels of most of the ST households in the country remain low and there is very limited wealth accumulation or assets creation which has implications for the health of the people. It is obvious that STs constitute the most disadvantaged population group in the country.

The third standard of living indicator that we have considered in the present analysis is the source of drinking water. This indicator is important as the quality of drinking water has direct relevance to the health status and a firsthand idea about the quality of the drinking water can be made from the source of water. DLHS 2007–08 suggests that more than 35 per cent of the ST households covered during the survey had an unprotected drinking water source such as unprotected well or pond or lake or river, even rainwater, etc., whereas this proportion was only 14 per cent in case of non-ST households. In case of piped drinking water supply, however, there was not much difference between the ST and non-ST households. However, in case of handpump, the difference between ST and non-ST households is again very substantial. Under the safe drinking water initiative, handpumps have been installed in rural and remote areas where the piped drinking water supply is not operationally and financially feasible. However, information available through the DLHS 2007–08 suggests that the ST population has only a limited access to handpumps. Most of the ST population in the country continues to fetch water from an unprotected source.

Another standard of living indicator which has a direct relevance to the health of the people is the toilet facility. Interestingly, the information available through the DLHS 2007–08 suggests that the proportion of ST households having no toilet facility very much the same as the non-ST households in the rural areas of the country. However, the proportion of households having flush latrines is substantially higher in non-ST households as compared to ST households (Figure 4). In any case, DLHS 2007–08 suggests that open field defecation continues to be widely prevalent in rural India despite a lot of emphasis on sanitation under the Total Sanitation Campaign (TSC) of the Government of India.

The foregoing discussion depicts the poor living conditions of the ST households in rural India as compared to non-ST households. The information available through DLHS 2007–08 clearly indicates that at least two-third of the ST households in the rural areas of the country continue to live in conditions that may, at best, be termed as precarious. The prevailing living conditions of STs in the rural areas also suggest that economic growth and associated development that the country is currently witnessing appears to have contributed only marginally in improving the living conditions of the STs in the country. The STs in the country continue to remain largely devoid of the benefits of the social and economic progress of the country. They continue to be the most marginalized population group in the country. Despite all efforts, they continue to live at the margin.

Health Status

The impact of the poor living conditions of the ST households is well reflected on the health status of the ST women. During DLHS 2007–08, information about the care received by women who had their last delivery in the three years preceding the survey was collected. The proportion of ST women receiving full antenatal care – at least three antenatal check-up, at least one tetanus toxoid injection and at least 100 iron folic acid tablets or equivalent syrup – was found to be only around 12 per cent, compared to very close to 15 per cent in the non-ST women (Figure 5). Similarly, the proportion of ST women reporting that their last delivery during the reference period of DLHS 2007–08 was a safe delivery – either institutional delivery or home delivery attended by professionally trained persons – was only about 32 per cent compared to more than 45 per cent in non-ST women. The very fact that a very small proportion of ST women received full antenatal care and more than two-third of the deliveries reported by ST women at DLHS 2007–08 were unsafe deliveries indicates that most of the ST women are exposed to the hazards of pregnancy and child birth which has implications to their health as well as health of their children. The institution base delivery of reproductive health services does not appear to fit in the cultural and traditional ethos of STs and, therefore, utilization of these services by ST women remains low.

In case of postnatal care also, the situation is no different. The proportion of ST women who reported a delivery during the reference period of DLHS 2007–08 and their new born receiving postnatal care was found to be substantially lower than the proportion of non-ST women (Figure 6). Only around 30 per cent of the ST women reported that they received postnatal care within 48 hours of the delivery while their new born was examined within 24 hours of birth. Although, these proportions are not very high in non-ST population also, yet the gap between ST and non-ST women indicates towards exclusion of ST women in the delivery of basic reproductive health services in the rural areas. Some of this exclusion, no doubt, is because of cultural and traditional factors. However, this exclusion also indicates the inefficiency of maternal health services, either public or private, in meeting the reproductive health needs of ST women.

In case of complete immunization – proportion of children 12–13 months of age receiving BCG, 3 doses of OPV, 3 doses of DPT and measles – the coverage rate is abysmally low in both STs and non-STs which indicates that in the rural areas of the country very few children are completely immunized – a reflection again to the poor efficiency of health services. However, even at this abysmal level, the proportion of fully immunized children is lower in STs.

Similarly, use of family planning methods is lower in STs than in non-STs, although the difference is not very large according to DLHS 2007–08. The relatively lower use of family planning methods in STs as compared to non-STs is reflected in the proportion of 1st and 2nd order births in the total births reported during the reference period by ST women as compared to non-ST women (Figure 7). Like the maternal health services, the relatively lower use of family planning methods in STs may be due to both cultural and traditional factors as well as due to the poor efficiency of health and family welfare services.

In case of common childhood diseases, however, the prevalence is found to be lower in ST children as compared to non-ST children (Figure 8). For all children below five years of age identified during DLHS 2007–08, it was enquired from the household whether the child suffered from diarrhoea, cough or fever during the two weeks prior to the survey and reported prevalence of the three common childhood diseases was found to be higher in the non-ST population. It may however be pointed out that the prevalence rate presented in Figure 8 are based on the response of household members and the difference between STs and non-STs may be because of the difference in the perceptions about common childhood diseases. In any case, the proportion of ST households reporting disease symptoms is quite high.

The foregoing analysis suggests that STs in the country continue to have, in general, poorer living conditions and health status as compared to non-ST population. In order to explore further the living conditions and health status of STs, we have analysed the variability across ST households in the country in terms of key variables of living conditions and health status using the factor analysis procedure. As discussed above, factor analysis combines the variables under study into factors or dimensions which are the linear combinations of original variables. These factors are not correlated to each other.

For the purpose of factor analysis, every ST household was given a score of 1 or 0 in each of the 14 variables in the following manner:

- A score of 1 if the wealth index score of the household falls in the richest wealth quintile group and 0 otherwise.
- A score of 1 if the household lives in a *pucca* house and 0 otherwise.
- A score of 1 if the source of drinking water is piped water supply and 0 otherwise.
- A score of 1, if the house in which the household lives has a flush latrine and 0 otherwise.
- A score of 1 if the women who delivered during the reference period of DLHS 2007–08 received full antenatal care during her pregnancy and 0 otherwise.
- A score of 1 if any delivery in the household during the period of reference was the safe delivery and 0 otherwise.
- A score of 1 if the woman of the household who delivered during the reference period of DLHS 2007–08 was examined during the first 48 hours of the delivery and 0 otherwise.
- A score of 1 if a child born in the household during the reference period of DLHS 2007–08 was examined within 24 hours of the birth and 0 otherwise.
- A score of 1 if the birth order of the birth reported during the survey was either 1st or 2nd order birth.
- A score of 1 if a child aged 12–23 months at the time of the survey received full immunisation and 0 otherwise.
- A score of 1 if couples in the reproductive age group were using any family planning method and 0 otherwise.

- A score of 1 if a child less than five years of age reported diarrhoea during two weeks prior to the survey and 0 otherwise.
- A score of 1 if a child less than five years of age reported fever during two weeks prior to the survey and 0 otherwise.
- A score of 1 if a child less than five years of age reported cough during two weeks prior to the survey and 0 otherwise.

Using these scores, the correlation matrix of the 14 variables of living conditions and health status was prepared and this correlation matrix was used for the application of the factor analysis procedure. The initial factors so generated were rotated using the Varimax criterion with Kaiser normalization. The analysis was carried out using the SPSS software package.

Using factor analysis procedure, four factors were extracted from 14 indicators described above. The principal component method was used to extract the factor. This method extracts that factor first which accounts for highest proportion of the variance. The four factors, so extracted account together, for more than 50 per cent variance in all 14 variables and at 40 per cent of the variation in individual variables except in case of full antenatal care, full immunization and piped water supply. As discussed above, factors are estimated as a linear combination of original variables and are interpreted by examining the combination of variables that are most highly correlated with them (highest factor loading in factor analysis terms). In order to facilitate interpretation, factors are rotated after identification for which several methods are available. In the present analysis, we have used Varimax method which minimizes the number of variables that have high loadings on a factor. Note than rotation does not change the total variance explained by the factors or the goodness of fit of a factor analysis solution. However, rotation changes the proportion of variance explained by individual factors. In Table 1 the extracted factors are labelled. These labels try to best describe dimensions of living conditions and health status of ST households that each factor seems to represent based on what the variables with the highest loadings (loading after rotation 0.25 or more) on that factor appear to have in common.

The factor analysis solution suggests that the living conditions and health status of STs in the country can be described in terms of four dimensions – the dimension of maternity services, the dimension of living status, the dimension of childhood diseases and the dimension of family welfare. An important observation of Table 1 is that no variable is loaded on more than one factor which suggests that some of the variables are highly correlated whereas there is little correlation between other variables. For example, all variables related to maternity services are highly correlated but these variables are not related with variables such as use of family planning methods and childhood immunization. Interestingly, living status variables – wealth index score, amenities in the house and source of dinking water – have not been found to be correlated with the use of maternity services and practice of family planning, etc. On the other hand, indicators of childhood diseases have not been found to be correlated with service variables as well as living status variables.

In order to utilize the factor patterns described in Table 1 to evaluate living conditions and health status of ST households, factor score coefficients were calculated using the regression method. These factor score coefficients were than used to calculate factor score for each Scheduled Tribe household. On the basis of these scores, a household was classified as poorest, poor, average, good and best on each of the four dimensions and the proportion of households falling in different categories were calculated. The distribution of ST households in the five categories on the four dimensions of living conditions and health status are shown in Figure 9.

Figure 9 provides interesting insight into the living conditions and health status of STs in the country. For example, as far as the use of maternity services are concerned, the ST households are almost evenly divided. However, in the context of the living status, a whopping 55 per cent of the households are classified in the poorest category compared to only about 30 per cent in the best category. Similarly, in case of use of family planning methods, fertility and immunisation of children also, the status, more than 60 per cent of ST households are classified in poorest category, whereas this proportion was almost 30 per cent in case of the dimension of childhood diseases. The divergence of ST households on the four dimensions of living conditions and health status identified in the present analysis is very much evident from Figure 9. The situation gets more complicated because of the mutual exclusiveness of the dimensions.

IV

State Scenario

Among different states and union territories of the country, the distribution of ST households across the five categories described above varies widely. Moreover, there is a lot of divergence in a state/union territory across the four dimensions of living conditions and health status of STs. This is expected as the social and economic status and living conditions vary widely across states and union territories. These inter-state and intra-state variations in different dimensions suggest that the living conditions and health status of STs vary widely across states and union territories of the country.

In order to rank different states and union territories in terms of the living conditions and health status of STs, we have first ranked the states and union territories on different dimensions of living conditions and health status identified in the present analysis on the basis of the proportion of ST households in the best category. and then calculated the average rank for each states/union territory. The ranks so obtained were then averaged to estimate the rank in the four dimensions combined (Table 2).

The above exercise suggests that the living conditions and health status of STs in the rural areas are the best in Kerala and poorest in Bihar amongst the states and union territories of the country. The living conditions and health status of STs in the rural areas are also relatively better in Lakshadweep, Daman and Diu and Tamil Nadu. On the other hand, in Uttar Pradesh, Odisha, Jharkhand, Tripura and Chhattisgarh, the living conditions and health status of STs in the rural areas appear to be the poorest in the country on the basis of the information available through DLHS 2007–08. It is also clear from Table 2 that there is no state/union territory in the country which is ranked best in all the four dimensions of living conditions and health status of STs in the rural areas. Similarly, there is no state/union territory which appears to be the worst in all the four dimensions vis-à-vis other states/union territories of the country. The regional diversity in different dimensions of living conditions and health status of STs in the rural areas is very much evident from Table 2.

The average rank measures the variation in living conditions and health status across states/union territories. It gives little idea about the variation in the rank across the four dimensions in a state/union territory. This variation can be captured through calculating the range of the rank in the four dimensions – the wider is the range the larger is the variation of a state/union territory across different dimensions. When the range of the rank is narrow, the rank of the state/union territory in all the four dimensions are close to each other irrespective of the absolute rank. Obviously, when the rank is the same in all dimensions, the range of rank is zero.

According to this exercise, the range of the rank on the four dimensions was the narrowest in Gujarat followed by Jammu & Kashmir, Arunachal Pradesh and West Bengal. All these state rank in the middle in the four dimensions of living conditions and health status across states and union territories of the country (Table 1). On the other hand, the range of the rank has been found to be the widest in Lakshadweep and Bihar followed by Kerala and Jharkhand. Lakshadweep has the best rank in the dimension II (living status) but the worst rank in the dimension III (childhood diseases) whereas Bihar has the best rank in dimension III but the worst rank in the remaining three dimensions. A similar situation appears to prevail in Kerala and Jharkhand also. The worst rank in dimension III in Lakshadweep and Kerala implies that the reported prevalence of childhood diseases in Lakshadweep and Kerala is the highest in the country. On the other hand, the best rank in this dimension in Bihar and Jharkhand means that the reported prevalence of childhood diseases in these states is the lowest in the country. It may however be pointed out here that the reported prevalence of childhood diseases may be seriously biased because of the knowledge and awareness of the respondent. One reason that the reported prevalence of childhood diseases is very high in Kerala and Lakshadweep may be due to high to very high awareness of the people in Lakshadweep and Kerala about childhood as well as other diseases conditions. On the other hand, one of the reasons for very low reported prevalence of childhood diseases in Bihar and Jharkhand may be due to poor knowledge and awareness about childhood diseases in these states. If we exclude the factor III in the estimation of overall rankings, the scenario changes radically.

V

Conclusions

STs in India continue to lag behind the non-STs in some key elements of living conditions and health status. However, living conditions and health status of STs are relatively better in Lakshadweep, Kerala, Tamil Nadu and Maharashtra but poorer in Bihar, Odisha, Uttar Pradesh, Jharkhand, Tripura and Chhattisgarh.

Another important conclusion that emerges from the present analysis is that there appears a disconnect between different dimensions of living conditions and health status of STs. This means that improvements in one dimension do not mean improvements in other dimensions also. This feature of the lop-sided development is a common anomaly of India's development discourse. Development management in India has been and continues to be the responsibility of an outdated development administration system while the development philosophy that India pursues has essentially been borrowed from the west and is based on six killer applications – competition, modern science, private property rights, modern medicine, consumer society and work ethics. These killer applications, unfortunately, are contrary to the traditional ethics and lifestyle of STs which is driven largely by compromise and companionship, tradition and culture, common property, traditional medicine, subsistence society, and family ethics.

References

Ali, A. (2003): "Health status of tribals in India: An overview", in D.K. Adak, B.N. Bhattacharya, R. Ghosh, M. Pal, P. Bharti and T.S. Vasulu (eds.), *Demography and Health Profile of the Tribals*, New Delhi: Anmol Publications.

Dillon, W.R. and M. Goldstein (1984): *Multivariate Analysis: Methods and Applications*, New York: John Wiley & Sons.

International Institute for Population Sciences (2010): District Level Household and Facility Survey 2007–08, India, Mumbai: International Institute for Population Sciences.

Ranjan, Alok (2006): "The age and sex structure of tribal population in Central India", *Tribal Health Bulletin*, 12(1 and 2): 1–17.

Sachchidananda and R.R. Prasad (1998): *Encyclopedic Profile of Indian Tribes*, New Delhi: Discovery Publishing House.

Table 1

Factors for Different Dimensions of Living Conditions and Health Status of Scheduled Tribes in India

Factor No.	*Assigned factor label*	*Variables most correlated with the factor (loading 0.25 and more after rotation) and factor loading after rotation*
I	Maternity services	Full antenatal care (0.34) Safe delivery (0.81) Postnatal examination of woman within 48 hours of delivery (0.91) Examination of the newborn within 24 hours of birth (0.91)
II	Living status	Flush toilet (0.72) Piped water supply (0.49) Pucca house (0.65) Richest wealth quintile group (0.75)
III	Childhood diseases	Diarrhoea (0.62) Fever (0.81) Cough (0.78)
IV	Family welfare	Birth order 1 and 2 (0.59) Use of family planning method (0.73) Full immunization of children (-0.51)

Table 2

Ranking of States/Union Territories in Terms of Different Dimensions of Living Conditions and Health Status of Scheduled Tribes

State/Union Territory	*Rank in dimension*					*Rank of the mean rank*	*Range of the rank*
	I	*II*	*III*	*IV*	*Mean rank*		
Andhra Pradesh	10	9	18	9	11.5	9	9
Arunachal Pradesh	14	16	12	14	14.0	14	4
Assam	16	19	9	17	15.3	17	10
Bihar	28	28	1	28	21.3	28	27
Chhattisgarh	23	20	10	23	19.0	23	13
Dadra & Nagar Haveli	13	10	17	12	13.0	11	7
Daman & Diu	2	2	27	3	8.5	2	25
Gujarat	15	14	15	16	15.0	15	2
Himachal Pradesh	6	8	22	6	10.5	6	16
Jammu & Kashmir	12	13	14	15	13.5	12	3
Jharkhand	26	27	2	26	20.3	25	25
Karnataka	7	7	23	7	11.0	8	16

Cont'd...

...Cont'd

Kerala	1	3	26	1	7.8	1	25
Lakshadweep	3	1	28	2	8.5	2	27
Madhya Pradesh	19	21	6	21	16.8	19	15
Maharashtra	8	6	20	8	10.5	6	14
Manipur	20	22	7	20	17.3	20	15
Meghalaya	21	23	5	22	17.8	22	18
Mizoram	11	12	21	11	13.8	13	10
Odisha	25	25	8	25	20.8	26	17
Rajasthan	9	15	16	10	12.5	10	7
Sikkim	17	11	19	13	15.0	15	8
Tamil Nadu	4	4	25	4	9.3	4	21
Tripura	24	24	4	24	19.0	23	20
Uttar Pradesh	27	26	3	27	20.8	26	24
Uttarakhand	22	18	11	19	17.5	21	11
West Bengal	18	17	13	18	16.5	18	5

Source: Author's calculations

Table 3

Living Conditions and Health Status of Scheduled Tribes and non-Scheduled Tribes in India, 2007–08

	Wealth quintiles				
	Poorest	Second	Middle	Fourth	Richest
ST	37.69	24.44	19.96	13.08	4.83
Others	21.21	23.94	23.14	20.30	11.42
	Type of house				
	Kachcha	Semi-Pucca	Pucca		
ST	69.87	23.74	6.37		
Others	39.41	36.47	23.85		
	Source of drinking water				
	Pipe	Handpump	Protected well/spring	Unprotected source	
ST	25.26	24.15	16.65	33.93	
Others	27.39	42.65	13.04	14.02	
	Toilet in the house				
	Flush	Pit	Dry	Others	No
ST	15.58	7.87	5.67	10.12	60.76
Others	21.78	4.85	1.25	3.10	69.02

Cont'd...

...Cont'd

	Reproductive health			
	Full antenatal care	Safe delivery	Postnatal care to woman within 48 hours	Postnatal care to new born within 24 hours
ST	12.05	32.35	29.01	29.89
Others	14.79	45.71	41.47	41.90
	Childhood diseases			
	Cough	Diarrhoea	Fever	Full-immunization
ST	16.65	10.31	17.42	11.58
Others	22.73	13.69	22.50	12.92
	Family planning			
	Proportion of 1st and 2nd order births	Current use of family planning		
ST	55.24	32.87		
Others	56.80	38.11		

Table 4

Distribution of Households by Factor Scores in the Dimension of Maternity Services

Union Territory/State	*Poorest*	*Poor*	*Average*	*Good*	*Best*
Andhra Pradesh	13.90	11.55	24.37	21.84	28.34
Arunachal Pradesh	26.62	21.18	9.15	19.35	23.69
Assam	20.36	13.09	26.68	17.84	22.04
Bihar	35.51	17.08	25.17	17.08	5.17
Chhattisgarh	17.80	12.50	33.86	22.23	13.62
Dadra & Nagar Haveli	16.60	11.06	23.40	24.26	24.68
Daman & Diu	7.69	1.28	3.85	19.23	67.95
Gujarat	16.05	14.24	21.44	26.09	22.17
Himachal Pradesh	16.55	9.15	19.01	15.85	39.44
Jammu & Kashmir	17.60	15.01	19.25	22.77	25.36
Jharkhand	30.04	12.29	35.08	14.59	7.99
Karnataka	10.35	9.44	16.13	30.59	33.49
Kerala	7.46	1.49	5.97	4.48	80.60
Lakshadweep	3.45	1.53	1.92	34.10	59.00
Madhya Pradesh	18.02	19.88	28.10	15.05	18.95
Maharashtra	9.58	9.22	13.96	36.88	30.36
Manipur	27.45	16.99	21.64	15.07	18.85

Cont'd...

...Cont'd

Meghalaya	36.65	14.52	18.42	14.48	15.93
Mizoram	19.27	11.90	17.47	23.69	27.67
Odisha	24.76	14.86	29.68	21.98	8.72
Rajasthan	15.56	11.40	27.98	15.46	29.60
Sikkim	30.58	9.30	12.59	26.09	21.44
Tamil Nadu	4.81	7.69	12.50	17.31	57.69
Tripura	19.50	20.68	28.51	18.76	12.56
Uttar Pradesh	28.02	25.14	19.19	20.54	7.10
Uttarakhand	26.83	17.07	15.85	24.39	15.85
West Bengal	15.10	16.27	27.25	21.57	19.80
Rest	12.90	8.60	6.45	24.73	47.31
India	21.75	14.45	23.83	19.98	19.99

Source: Author's calculations

Table 5

Distribution of Households by Factor Scores in the Dimension of Living Status

Union Territory/State	*Poorest*	*Poor*	*Average*	*Good*	*Best*
Andhra Pradesh	42.96	3.79	1.99	7.94	43.32
Arunachal Pradesh	53.78	1.30	0.91	10.16	33.85
Assam	56.52	1.73	0.89	11.61	29.25
Bihar	74.83	1.35	0.90	10.79	12.13
Chhattisgarh	54.43	7.49	1.49	8.94	27.65
Dadra & Nagar Haveli	46.38	2.55	1.28	8.09	41.70
Daman & Diu	10.26	1.28	1.28	1.28	85.90
Gujarat	47.33	3.03	0.83	12.24	36.56
Himachal Pradesh	33.80	4.93	4.23	7.39	49.65
Jammu & Kashmir	47.52	1.55	2.07	10.25	38.61
Jharkhand	71.59	4.48	0.83	7.06	16.04
Karnataka	27.25	3.50	4.11	14.76	50.38
Kerala	11.94	0.00	2.99	0.00	85.07
Lakshadweep	5.75	1.15	0.00	0.38	92.72
Madhya Pradesh	62.56	2.53	0.51	9.88	24.52
Maharashtra	26.29	2.85	2.34	12.53	55.99
Manipur	61.42	3.23	0.77	10.63	23.95
Meghalaya	64.52	2.07	2.07	8.20	23.15
Mizoram	41.92	2.18	2.89	12.88	40.12
Odisha	60.92	4.34	3.31	14.28	17.15
Rajasthan	46.83	6.18	0.96	11.66	34.36

Cont'd...

...Cont'd

Sikkim	44.68	2.85	1.65	10.34	40.48
Tamil Nadu	20.19	0.96	3.85	0.96	74.04
Tripura	66.17	0.44	1.33	13.59	18.46
Uttar Pradesh	70.63	0.77	0.77	10.94	16.89
Uttarakhand	52.44	3.66	2.44	10.98	30.49
West Bengal	50.98	3.14	2.75	11.37	31.76
Rest	23.66	0.00	2.15	6.45	67.74
India	54.42	3.25	1.50	10.37	30.47

Source: Author's calculations

Table 6

Distribution of Households by Factor Scores in the Dimension of Childhood Diseases

Union Territory/State	*Best*	*Good*	*Average*	*Poor*	*Poorest*
Andhra Pradesh	41.70	15.16	0.54	0.54	42.06
Arunachal Pradesh	51.76	14.54	0.05	0.19	33.46
Assam	56.37	14.38	0.20	0.40	28.66
Bihar	74.16	13.71	0.22	0.00	11.91
Chhattisgarh	54.06	18.34	0.37	0.25	26.99
Dadra & Nagar Haveli	44.68	13.62	0.00	0.85	40.85
Daman & Diu	10.26	3.85	0.00	2.56	83.33
Gujarat	46.60	16.94	0.24	0.29	35.93
Himachal Pradesh	28.52	22.18	0.35	0.35	48.59
Jammu & Kashmir	46.69	14.80	0.72	0.52	37.27
Jharkhand	71.20	12.78	0.31	0.16	15.55
Karnataka	25.42	24.35	1.22	1.22	47.79
Kerala	11.94	2.99	0.00	0.00	85.07
Lakshadweep	4.98	2.68	0.38	0.38	91.57
Madhya Pradesh	62.10	13.41	0.07	0.07	24.34
Maharashtra	25.47	18.80	0.76	0.56	54.41
Manipur	61.32	14.74	0.11	0.05	23.78
Meghalaya	63.51	13.51	0.23	0.27	22.48
Mizoram	39.25	20.91	0.71	0.60	38.54
Odisha	60.82	22.03	0.44	1.27	15.45
Rajasthan	46.07	19.61	0.05	0.20	34.06
Sikkim	41.67	18.14	0.45	0.45	39.28
Tamil Nadu	18.27	7.69	1.92	0.00	72.12
Tripura	66.03	15.51	0.30	1.03	17.13

Cont'd...

...Cont'd

Uttar Pradesh	70.44	12.67	0.19	0.00	16.70
Uttarakhand	52.44	17.07	1.22	1.22	28.05
West Bengal	50.39	17.84	0.20	0.00	31.57
Rest	23.66	8.60	1.08	0.00	66.67
India	53.59	16.03	0.32	0.36	29.70

Source: Author's calculations

Table 7

Distribution of Households by Factor Scores in the Dimension of Family Welfare.

Union Territory/State	*Poorest*	*Poor*	*Average*	*Good*	*Best*
Andhra Pradesh	0.00	51.08	2.35	15.88	30.69
Arunachal Pradesh	1.93	56.96	4.57	9.44	27.11
Assam	0.30	62.70	4.59	9.49	22.92
Bihar	0.45	80.90	4.49	8.54	5.62
Chhattisgarh	0.12	66.27	2.94	14.07	16.60
Dadra & Nagar Haveli	0.43	51.91	2.13	17.45	28.09
Daman & Diu	1.28	11.54	1.28	11.54	74.36
Gujarat	0.15	54.33	4.41	16.40	24.72
Himachal Pradesh	2.46	43.66	2.46	8.80	42.61
Jammu & Kashmir	0.72	52.69	4.24	15.42	26.92
Jharkhand	0.03	78.58	3.13	9.06	9.21
Karnataka	0.00	39.57	5.78	17.96	36.68
Kerala	0.00	14.93	0.00	1.49	83.58
Lakshadweep	1.53	5.36	0.38	15.71	77.01
Madhya Pradesh	0.02	68.74	4.46	7.48	19.29
Maharashtra	0.05	34.54	4.28	24.81	36.32
Manipur	0.11	70.36	3.62	6.14	19.78
Meghalaya	0.82	71.00	2.65	8.35	17.17
Mizoram	0.38	51.26	4.26	14.08	30.02
Odisha	0.05	72.56	6.68	11.01	9.70
Rajasthan	0.15	58.54	4.66	6.59	30.06
Sikkim	3.15	50.67	2.55	16.04	27.59
Tamil Nadu	0.00	25.00	0.00	11.54	63.46
Tripura	0.15	70.75	5.91	10.49	12.70
Uttar Pradesh	0.77	74.66	5.18	11.32	8.06
Uttarakhand	1.22	59.76	7.32	10.98	20.73
West Bengal	0.39	59.41	5.49	12.55	22.16
Rest	2.15	25.81	2.15	16.13	53.76
India	0.41	62.06	4.08	11.43	22.02

Source: Author's calculations

Figure 1

Distribution of households by wealth quintiles

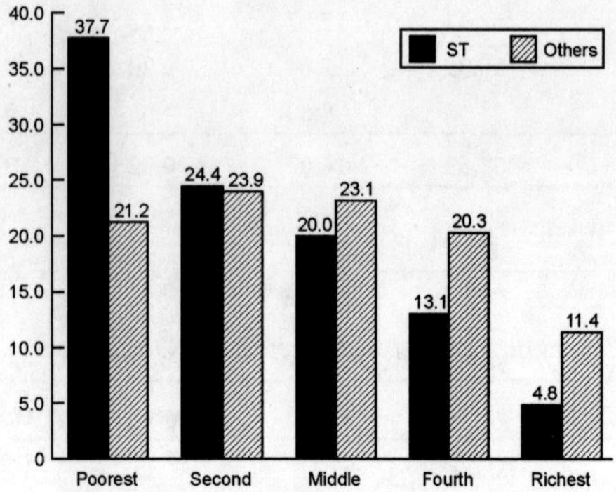

Figure 2

Type of house of Scheduled Tribes and non-Scheduled Tribes

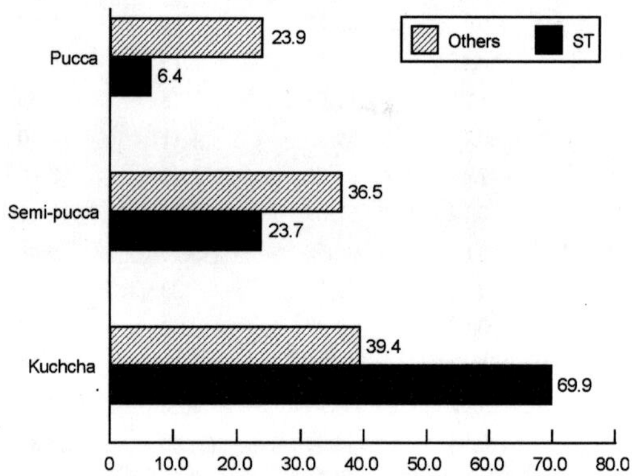

Figure 3

Source of drinking water

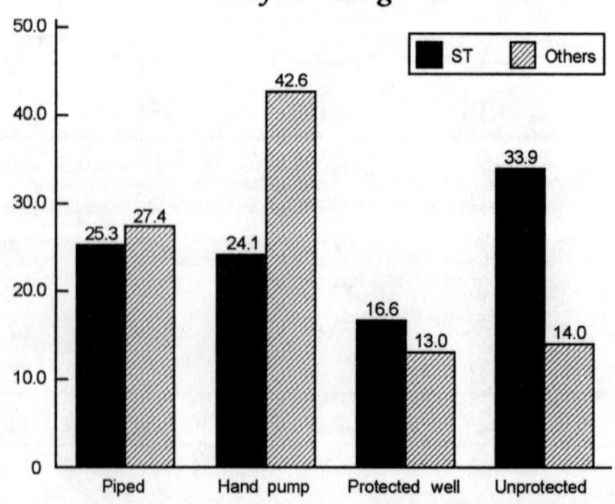

Figure 4

Availability of toilet in the house

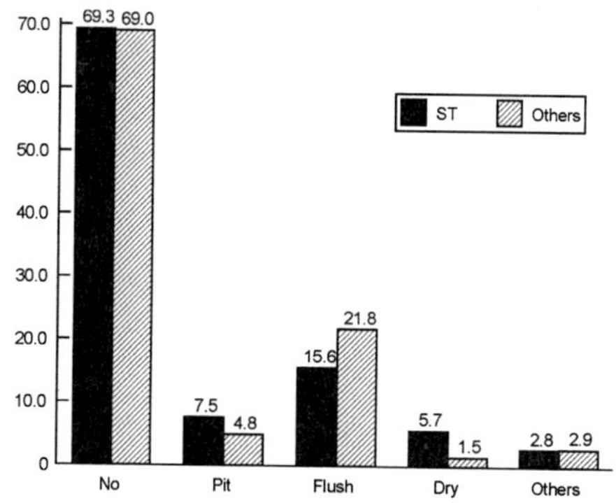

Figure 5

Maternity services

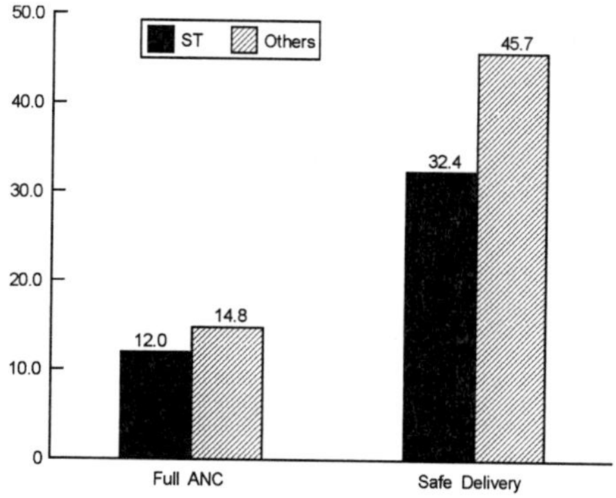

Figure 6

Postnatal care

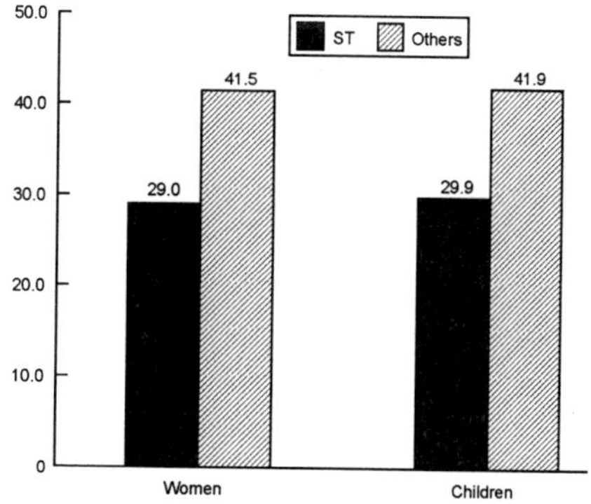

Figure 7
Immunization and family planning

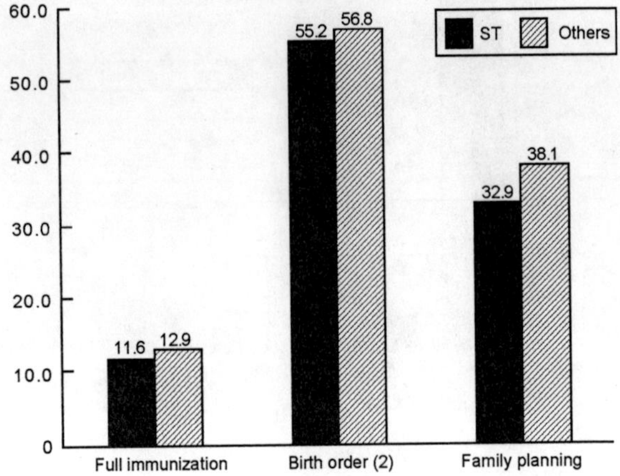

Figure 8
Childhood diseases

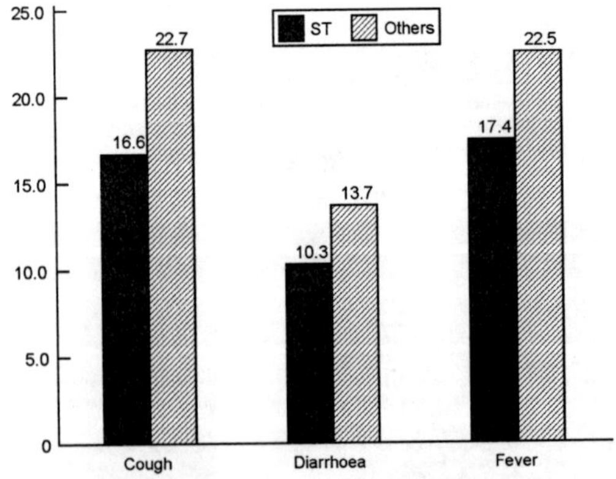

Figure 9

Distribution of Scheduled Tribes households on different dimensions of living conditions and health status

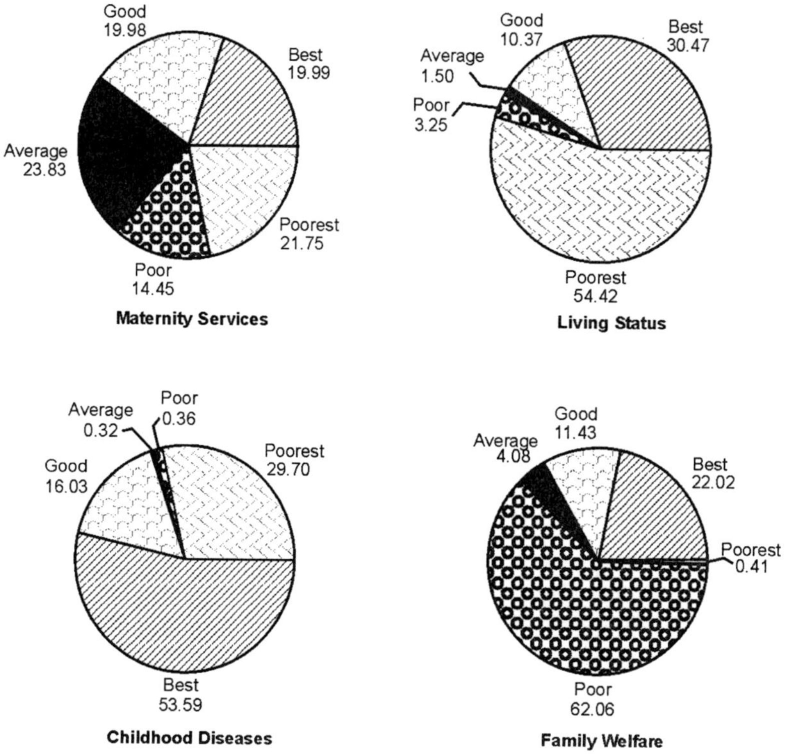

Figure 10

Distribution of Scheduled Tribes households on different dimensions of living conditions and health status in states and Union Territories in India

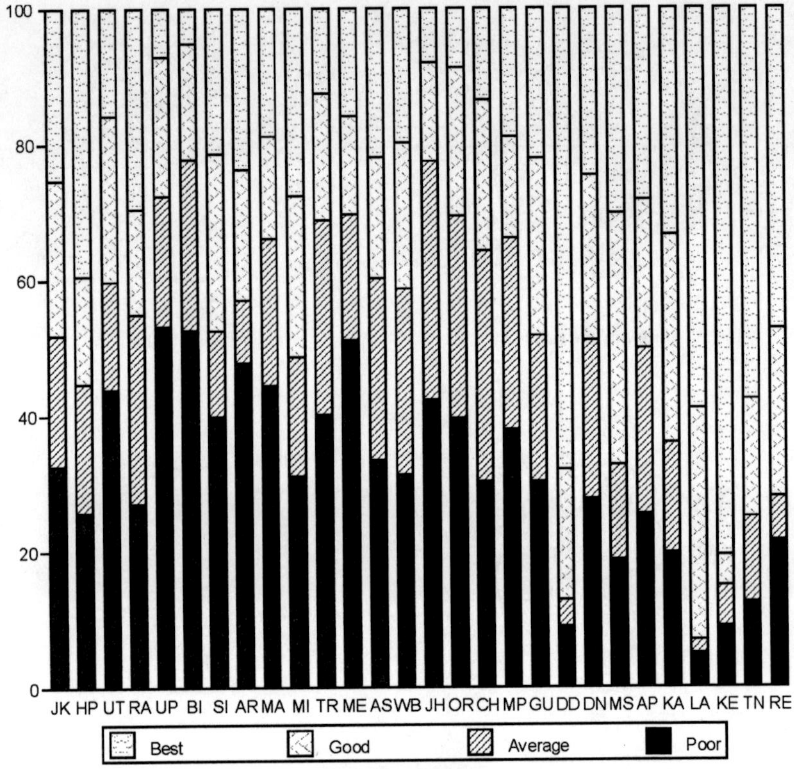

Maternity Services

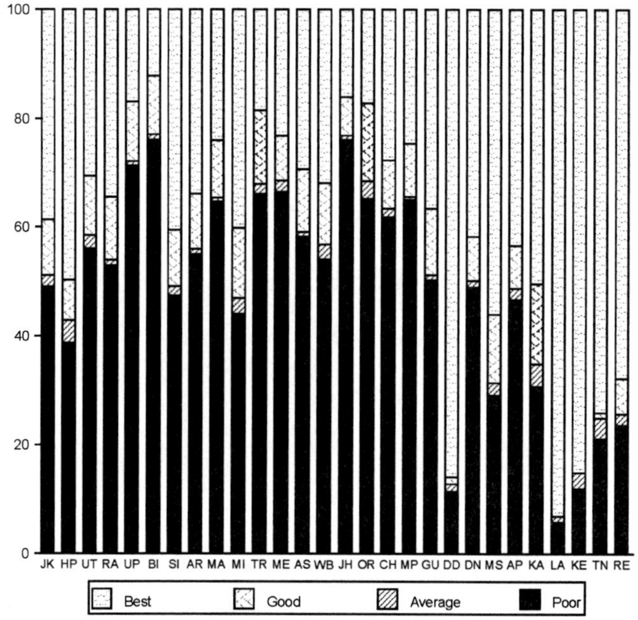

Living Status

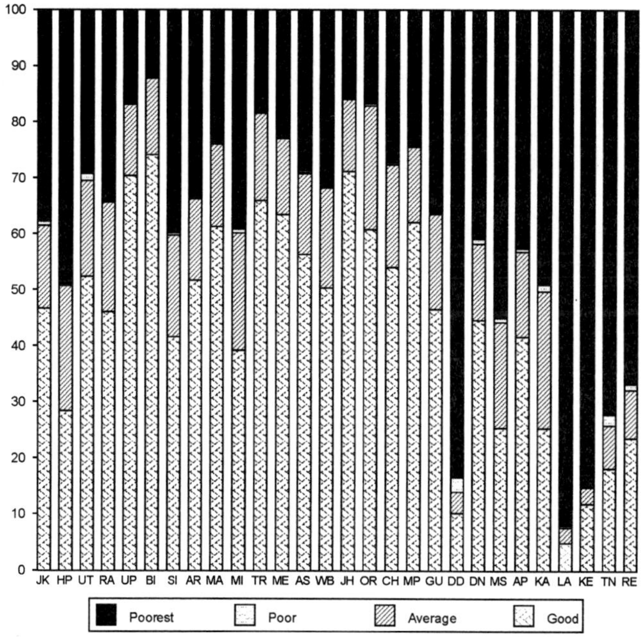

Childhood Diseases

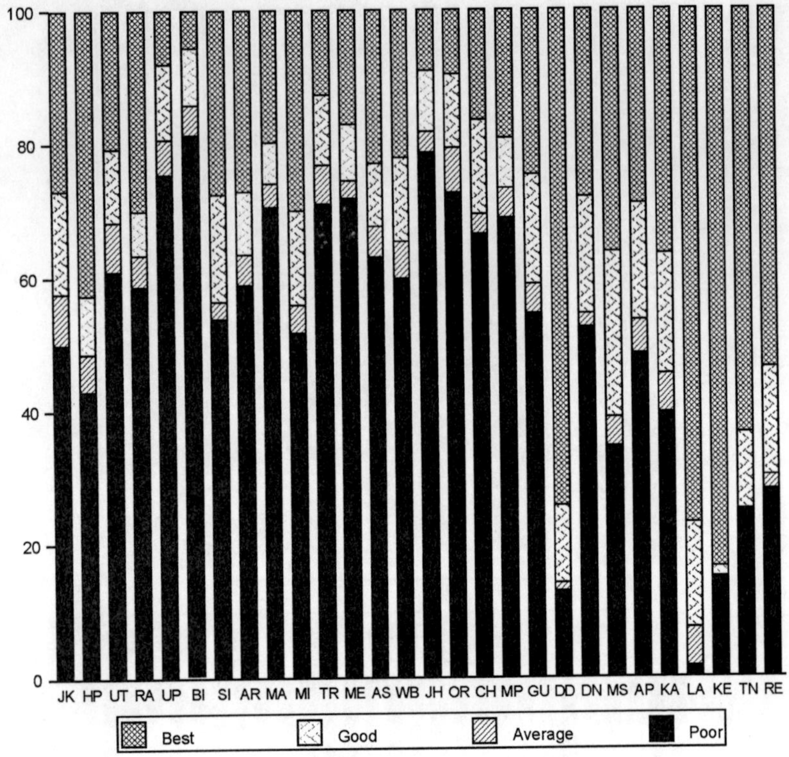

Family Welfare

4

Disparity in Health Services with Reference to Tribes of Madhya Pradesh

S.N. TRIPATHY

According to the Census 2001, Scheduled Tribes (STs) constitute approximately 8.2 per cent of India's total population and the Indian Constitution has recognized about 573 communities as STs, which confers entitlements to affirmative action programmes. However, the majority of tribal communities languishing in poverty and persistently remained vulnerable as compared to the general population which has been apparently evident from their socio-economic problems. About 45.86 per cent STs in rural areas having been classified as living below the poverty line (BPL) and 34.75 per cent in urban areas in 1999–2000. The Fifth Schedule of the Indian Constitution designates 'Scheduled Areas' where more than 50 per cent of the population is tribal. The Fifth Schedule (see Annexure 1) covers tribal areas in nine states of India, namely, Andhra Pradesh, Jharkhand, Gujarat, Himachal Pradesh, Maharashtra, Madhya Pradesh, Chhattisgarh, Odisha and Rajasthan. The north-eastern states such as Assam, Meghalaya, Tripura and Mizoram are covered by the Sixth Schedule and are not included in the Fifth Schedule. The notified tribal districts of the country under Fifth Schedule are indicated in the Annexure 1. It is distinguished that Bihar, Karnataka and West Bengal are not covered under this schedule.

In addition, tribes confront other economic and social challenges when attempting to avail of health services: poverty, low levels of education, poor access to medical care, and isolation from the mainstream economy are the norms. Tribal communities have distinct languages, cultural behaviours and mistrust of outsiders; and their knowledge of disease prevention and treatment is limited. Due to a combination of societal attitudes, unstable belief systems, and the apathy of the government, tribal population throughout India have long been deprived of basic health care. As a result, gaping disparities in health status of tribes, when compared to metropolitan areas, are apparent. Genetic abnormalities and infectious diseases such as sickle-cell anaemia, malaria, tuberculosis, leprosy, typhoid, and cholera are rampant in areas of Madhya Pradesh, Maharashtra, Tamil Nadu, Odisha and Assam states. In addition, malnutrition, birth disorders, and gastrointestinal diseases are pervasive among the tribal population, and stark deficiencies have been detected in gross amount of calcium, Vitamin A, Vitamin C, riboflavin, and animal protein. Certain tribal groups are even facing extinction due to endemic diseases and an unusually low sex ratio.

The health problems of any community are influenced by interplay of multitude of factors including social, economic and political ones. The common beliefs, customs, practices related to health and disease in turn influence the health seeking behaviour of the community. There is a consensus agreement that the health status of the tribal population is very poor and worst among the primitive tribes because of their isolation from the main stream of civilization, remoteness and being largely unaffected by the developmental processes going on in the country.

Health Problems of Tribes

With regard to Madhya Pradesh, one of the poorest states in India, has more than 37 per cent of its total population constituting 60 million are in the midst of abject poverty. Scheduled Castes (SCs) and Scheduled Tribes (STs), two most marginalized groups, constitute 35 per cent of the population and account for 60 per cent of the poor. Gender-based discrimination is reflected in the unequal sex ratio (916/1,000) against an already worrying national average of 933/1,000 (in 2001 Census) and lower human development indicators for women.

Health being a prerequisite for human development and an essential component for the well-being of the mankind, in Madhya Pradesh, despite progress in recent years, it has still been among the highest rates of maternal and infant mortality of all states in India. Total fertility rate and incidence of vector-borne and communicable diseases are also much higher than average. In order to examine disparities among different social groups with regard to 'access to' and 'utilization' of health care services in some of the tribal concentrated states, data have been collected from third round of

National Family Health Survey (NFHS-3), 2005–06. This survey has been considered as the storehouse of data for a number of health indicators on national and states level separately. At the all-India level the sample of the survey includes 19 per cent SCs, 8 per cent STs, 40 per cent OBCs and 33 per cent general category households. This survey is quite consistent with their respective proportion in total population of the country. The survey is modelled after the 'Demographic and Health Survey' conducted in many countries in the world and has been based on pre-tested scientific sampling designs. The NFHS-3 data indicated that Madhya Pradesh had the highest rates of undernourishment in children less than three years (60%) in the country. The performance of the public health delivery system in Madhya Pradesh faces several constraints: vacancies of staff and infrastructure gaps, particularly in the poorest ten districts and tribal areas; lack of drugs and other essential supplies at local level; weak implementation and monitoring system; poor accountability of staff and low staff motivation and management capacity. The poor quality and low funding of the public health system has resulted in the growth of an uncontrolled and poor quality private sector. For poor households, use of the private sector has led to high out-of-pocket expenditures (often pushing people further into poverty).

It is revealed from the Human Development Report, 2007 that states like Assam, Bihar, Gujarat, Haryana, Karnataka and Kerala have better life expectancy at birth as compared to Madhya Pradesh. Even the state of Bihar which is counted among one of the most backward states in the country, life expectancy at birth for males and females (2001–06) stood at 65.66 years and 64.79 years respectively, much higher than that of Madhya Pradesh.

National Family Heath Survey-3 (2005–06)

Various studies undertaken in our country illustrate that the primitive tribes have distinct health problems, mainly governed by multidimensional factors like their habitat, difficult terrain, ecologically variable niches, illiteracy, poverty, isolation, superstition and deforestation. Hence, an integrated multidisciplinary approach has been adopted by different researchers to study the tribal health problem. Madhya Pradesh has the largest population of tribes among all the states of India. They constitute nearly one-fourth of India's total tribal population. There are as many as 46 different tribal groups in the state among which Gonds, Bhils, Kols, Kanwars are predominant. National Family Health Survey-3 (2005–06) data indicates that health outcomes for tribes are poor compared to the general population, and even when compared to SCs. Not only do tribes have poorer health outcomes, their access to health services is also considerably worse: less than 20 per cent of tribal women give birth in an institution as compared to 40 per cent of women in the general population and 35 per cent of SC women; and only about 31 per cent of tribal children are fully immunized as compared to about 44 per cent in the general population and 40 per cent among SCs. It is fair to conclude that their access to other health services would be equally poor, including the services aiming to prevent and treat vector-borne diseases. Further, NFHS-3 data shows that girls, tribal and dalits have worse infant and child mortality indicators than other groups. Analysing trends in NSS data, the Human Development Institute predicts that in 2015 the incidence of poverty amongst tribes will be 37.9 per cent which is the same as the all India figure was in 1993–94 (DFID, UK, May 2007).

Genesis of Child Mortality among Excluded Sections in Madhya Pradesh

The state specific report of NFHS-3 demonstrates out a very grim picture of health indicators among tribal communities. It points out that 140 tribal children perish on every 1,000 live births which means 14 per cent children are not surviving to celebrate their 5th birthday and die before it. It is much higher than the Madhya Pradesh average under-5 mortality of 94.2 per one thousand live births.

Table 1 depicts that the state of Madhya Pradesh has the highest percentage of SC/ST mortality among the states under review. Chhattisgarh with 90.6 per cent of infant mortality occupies the second highest infant mortality among the states. The position of Maharashtra is comparatively better among the tribal states under study.

Table 1

Health Outcomes: Madhya Pradesh in Comparative Perspective (Infant Mortality Rate)

States	*SC*	*ST*	*General*
Madhya Pradesh	81.9	95.6	68.8
Maharashtra	45.2	51.4	40.5
Odisha	73.7	78.7	53.1
Chhattisgarh	63.1	90.6	83.1
Gujarat	65.4	86.0	47.3
All India	66.4	62.1	57

Note: Based on 250–499 unweighted cases.

Source: NFHS 2005–06.

Table 2

Infant Mortality Rate among STs and Total Average of the Major States of India

States	*Infant Mortality Rate (per 1,000 Live Births)*			
	STs	*N*	*Total*	*N*
Odisha	70	527	64	1905
Madhya Pradesh	87	870	71	3597
Uttar Pradesh	43	138	69	11758
Assam	62	161	61	993
Bihar	86	35	60	5868
Maharashtra	48	546	42	4235
Gujarat	87	289	52	2603
Chhattisgarh	65	386	65	1222
Karnataka	51	177	45	2357
Rajasthan	55	559	70	3454
West Bengal	58	242	50	3443
Jharkhand	84	514	70	1756
Andhra Pradesh	89	259	48	3143

Note: STs: Scheduled Tribes, N: total number of cases (live births).

Source: The rates are calculated from unit level data of NHFS-3.

It is revealed from Table 2 that the infant mortality in those states having high concentration of SC and ST population is higher compared to other poor states in India. The table also shows that across the states the IMR among the STs varies; infant mortality among the tribes is higher among the states like Andhra Pradesh, Gujarat, Madhya Pradesh and Bihar.

Table 3

Under-5 Mortality

States	*SC*	*ST*	*General*
Madhya Pradesh	110.1	140.7	79.9
Maharashtra	50.2	69.8	47.4
Odisha	91.8	136.3	64.2
Chhattisgarh	78.1	128.5	(109.3)
Gujarat	86.6	115.8	55.7
All India	88.1	95.7	57

Note: Based on 250–499 unweighted cases.

Source: NFHS 2005–06.

IMR is very high and alarming in states of Odisha, Uttar Pradesh, Madhya Pradesh, Assam and Rajasthan compared to the national average. The NFHS-3 unfolds that under-5 death rates are 88 and 96 per 1000 live births for SCs and ST population. With regard to SC and ST population, under-5 death rate is the highest in Madhya Pradesh, which is 110.1 and 140.7 respectively (Table 3).

Table 4

Statewise Present Rate of Malnutrition in India (NFHS-3, 2005–2006 and 2007–2012) (percentage)

States/UTs	*Children under 3 Years*		*Women (15–49) Years with BMI Below Normal (18.5)*		*Eleventh Plan Goal – Reduction by 50%*
	Underweight	*Anaemia*	*Body Mass Index*	*Anaemia*	
Gujarat	47.4	80.1	32.3	55.5	23.7
Madhya Pradesh	60.3	82.6	40.1	57.6	30.2
Chhattisgarh	52.1	81.0	41.0	57.6	26.1
Maharashtra	39.7	71.9	32.6	49.0	19.9
Odisha	44.0	74.2	40.5	62.0	22.0
All India	45.9	79.2	33.0	56.2	23.0

Notes: 1. Figures for current level are that of NFHS 2005–06.
2. For state-level figures, pro-rata reduction has been applied on the basis of targetedreduction at all-India level.
3. Figures for other states are not available. Compiled from the statistics released by: Lok Sabha Unstarred Question No. 4589, dated 8.05.2007, and Planning Commission, Government of India.

The overall rate of malnutrition among children (less than three years) has been depicted in Table 4, which indicates that the state of Madhya Pradesh has the highest percentage of underweight children (60.3%) and also (82.6%) anaemic.

Table 5

Vulnerability of Madhya Pradesh in IMR and Child Mortality among Scheduled Tribes

State	*IMR*	*Under-5 Mortality*
Madhya Pradesh	95.6	140.4
Chhattisgarh	90.6	128.5
Rajasthan	73.2	113.8
Gujarat	86.0	115.8
Jharkhand	93.0	138.5
Odisha	78.7	136.3

Table 6

Vulnerability of Madhya Pradesh in IMR and Child Mortality among Scheduled Tribes

State	*IMR*	*Under-5 Mortality*
Madhya Pradesh	95.6	140.4
Chhattisgarh	90.6	128.5
Rajasthan	73.2	113.8
Gujarat	86.0	115.8
Jharkhand	93.0	138.5
Odisha	78.7	136.3

More than 56 children die within just 28 days of birth, whereas it is 44.9 for the state and 95 die without celebrating their first birthday, in comparison to the state average of 69.5 for the state. The status of child survival among tribal communities is a serious matter of concern for Madhya Pradesh.

The state of Madhya Pradesh is the one of the biggest contributors of total neonatal and child mortality in the country. The report of National Family Health Survey (NFHS-3) India presents the terrible situation of child care in the state but the data on caste-based classification of child fatality in Madhya Pradesh by the latest state report of NFHS-3 Madhya Pradesh paints an offensive state of affairs of efforts made to protect the right of survival of every child. Providing safe childhood to their young children is just a day-dreaming for parents belonging to downtrodden castes/tribes in the state. In Madhya Pradesh 56.5/1,000 new-born in STs had to pay the cost of taking birth in STs by giving away their life. As many as 56.5 neonates born in STs died in the first 28 days of birth per thousand live births. Similarly, 50.2 neonates per thousand live births from SCs died off in neo-natal period. The SCs (15.17%) and STs (20.27%) together form 34.44 per cent of total population in Madhya Pradesh but it is unfortunate that these section of the society are not assured whether their child will survive or not by tomorrow.

In comparison to the 94.2/1,000 less than 5 mortality, the chance of survival is much lower among SC/ST child population under five years of age with 110 and 140 mortality per thousand live births.

No Sincere Efforts to Save the Girl Child

The girl child is the most vulnerable and neglected category in Madhya Pradesh. The life chart of a disadvantaged girl child reflects the strong element of discrimination at every step of her life. It is clearly visible in the latest state specific report of NFHS-3 Madhya Pradesh.

Table 7

Infant and Child Mortality Rate – Castewise

Caste/Tribe	*Neonatal Mortality*	*Infant Mortality*	*Under-5 Mortality*
India	39	57	74.3
Madhya Pradesh	44.9	69.5	94.2
SC	50.2	81.9	110.1
ST	56.5	95.6	140.7
OBC	53.3	79	97.6
Other	39.6	66.8	79.9

It is found from the Table 7 that in terms of neonatal mortality, infant mortality and under-5 mortality in Madhya Pradesh is much higher than the national average. It is much higher among the tribes compared to other social groups, i.e., SC, OBC and 'Other'.

Discrimination in the provision of adequate and timely nutrition and health inputs to the girl child is a persisting problem and as a result of which these groups suffer from various problems like underweight, malnutrition, anaemia, micronutrient deficiencies, stunted growth etc. But it is appalling that she even do not diverse the right to care when falls ill. While during fever 72.2 per cent male child under five years of age for whom treatment was sought from health facility/provider but more than 30 per cent girl child are not taken to any health provider. About 50.4 per cent young girls with diarrhoea are not given any medical aid although 63.9 per cent were taken to health facility.

Table 8

Statewise Expenditure on Health Sectors in India in IX Plan (1997–98 to 2001–02)

(*₹ in lakh*)

State	*1997–98*	*%*	*1998–99*	*%*	*1999–00*	*%*	*2000–01*	*%*	*2001–02*
Gujarat	17180.00	9.07	17179.00	7.62	20650.00	8.03	21805.00	7.79	14319.00
MP	7031.00	3.71	14524.00	6.44	12269.00	4.77	11702.00	4.18	11210.00
Maha-rashtra	13811.00	7.29	16224.00	7.20	17082.00	6.65	21023.00	7.51	20174.00
Odisha	5198.00	2.74	7042.00	3.12	7546.00	2.94	8808.00	3.15	11018.00
Total	189497.22	100	225480.16	100	257014.42	100	279795.14	100	301815.96

Source: Lok Sabha Starred Question No. 415, dated on 21.12.2005.

Table 9

Statewise Expenditure on Health Sectors in India in X Plan (2002–03 to 2006–07)

(₹ in Lakh)

State	*2002–03*	*%*	*2003–04*	*%*	*2004–05*	*%*	*2005–06*	*%*	*2006–07 Approved Outlay*	*%*
Chhattisgarh	5550.00	2.19	11736.00	3.82	12462.52	3.09	12122.33	2.22	33249.90	4.72
Odisha	7283.09	2.87	9256.11	3.02	10281.41	2.55	14448.19	2.65	4052.20	0.58
MP	14520.93	5.72	15444.43	5.03	17763.95	4.40	17604.29	3.23	16961.91	2.41
Maharashtra	21637.15	8.53	33244.78	10.83	31192.05	7.73	77874.10	14.28	88228.54	12.53
Gujarat	15192.32	5.99	21472.13	7.00	25294.00	6.27	43494.00	7.98	45994.00	6.53
All India	253695	100	306867	100	403572	100	545337	100	704000	100

Note: Above data depend on MEDICAL AND PUBLIC HEALTH head. Table 9 illustrates the latest position of percentage of health expenditure in Madhya Pradesh during the year 2006–07. It exhibits 2.41 per cent which is much lower than that of Maharashtra (12.53) and Gujarat (6.53).

Source: Complied by state financial performance of state's Tenth Plan.

Table 10

Statewise Maternal Care Indicators for Births Five Years Preceding the Survey in India (2005–06)

States	*%age Who Received All Recommended Types of Antenatal Care*[1]	*%age of Births Delivered in a Health Facility*	*%age of Deliveries Assisted by Health Personnel*[2]	*%age of Deliveries With a Postnatal Check-up*[3]	*%age of Deliveries With a Postnatal Check-up Within Two Days of Birth*[3]
Chhattisgarh	11.3	14.3	41.6	36.5	28.4
MP	7.2	26.2	32.7	33.8	28.5
Odisha	18.4	35.6	44.0	40.9	33.3
Gujarat	25.6	52.7	63.0	61.4	56.5
Maharashtra	21.6	64.6	68.7	64.0	58.7
All India	15.0	38.7	46.6	41.2	37.3

Notes:
1. For the last live birth in the five years preceding the survey, mother received three or more antenatal check-ups (with the first check-up within the first trimester of pregnancy), received two or more tetanus toxoid injections, and took iron and folic acid tablets or syrup for three or more months.
2. Doctor, auxiliary nurse midwife, nurse, midwife, lady health visitor, or other health personnel.
3. Based on the last live birth in the five years preceding the survey. Postnatal check-ups are checks on the woman's health within 42 days of the birth. Compiled from the statistics released by the Ministry of Health and Family Welfare, Government of India.

Table 8 illustrates that among the states under review, we find that the percentage of health expenditure was 3.71 during the year 1997–98 in Madhya Pradesh which was higher than Odisha (2.74), but much lower than Gujarat (9.07) and Maharashtra (7.29). The percentage of health expenditure in Madhya Pradesh hiked to 6.44 in the year 1998–99 and finally, culminated to 7.51 in the year 2000–01.

Table 10 shows that with regard to the percentage who received all recommended types of antenatal care, Madhya Pradesh has the lowest (7.2%), followed by Chhattisgarh (11.3). Similarly, with regard to percentage of births delivered in a health facility, Madhya Pradesh is the second lowest state (26.2) next to Chhattisgarh (14.3). Likewise, regarding the percentage of deliveries with a postnatal check-up, Madhya Pradesh is at the lowest (33.8), much below the national average (41.2).

Maternal Health

There has been a perceptible change in recent years regarding the focus of development policies and priorities. In India, and globally, development goals are no longer defined in terms of economic growth exclusively. The vital link between health and development is increasingly recognized and attempts have been made to reformulate health policies and programmes. Since women constitute nearly half of the total population, the emphasis on women health in developmental policies and programmes has become pertinent. The slogan, "Healthy Women, Healthy World" embodies the fact that as the custodian of family health, women play a unique role in maintaining the health and well-being of communities. Hence, the issue of women's health in general and reproductive health in particular came into prominence with the deliberations of the International Conference on Population and Development at Cairo in 1994 and Fourth World Conference of Women at Beijing in 1995. At these conferences, it was accepted that women's health and reproductive rights are important means of women's empowerment and quality of life.

The concept of women's health today has become a major concern in India because of high prevalence of infant, child, and maternal mortality and deteriorating quality of life. Available evidences in India show that women have been suffering from many health problems and deprived of health facilities. Though India has made considerable progress in social, economic, cultural, demographic and political arenas in recent decades, while, it lagged behind in the improvement of women's health. India is one of the few countries where males significantly outnumber females (933 females for 1,000 males) and its maternal mortality rate in rural areas is highest among the world. Women experience malnutrition, anaemia, infectious diseases and illness more than men, and they are less likely to receive timely medical treatment.

Women, especially the poor, rural women and tribal women, are often trapped in cycle of ill-health exacerbated by childbearing, hard physical labour and deprivation of medicare services. Rural women in India are among the most disadvantaged people in terms of their health status. Access to appropriate health care information, a comprehensive, adequate and affordable health services are still to be achieved for the rural women. Rural women are especially vulnerable to pregnancy and childbirth related deaths. Poor health of women and nutritional status in India are inextricably interwoven with social, cultural and economic factors. These factors severely constrain the ability of women and adolescent girls to acquire good health services. Longstanding and entrenched gender inequities affect women's health, their allocation of assets, power, rights, status and opportunities. Women have less access to basic resources such as social, health, educational as well as in other service systems. Though the Indian government is committed to improve women's health through various policies and programmes, problems and the inequities in women's health continue to exist in our society. Hence, it is necessary to recognize and to evolve mechanisms to overcome barriers, such as poverty and illiteracy and several socio-economic constraints. There is a need to adopt a justifiable gender sensitive and women-friendly approach to the women's health.

According to the Sample Registration Survey, 2001–03, around 78,050 pregnant women die in India every year. For every hundred thousand live births, there are 301 maternal deaths, the survey depicts. According to the White Ribbon Alliance of India (WRAI), nationwide initiative that promotes safe motherhood, there has been no significant decline in India's maternal mortality rate (MMR) since the 1990s. Surveys of the causes of the high MMR show how inaccessible timely medical attention still is to many pregnant women. An inadequate health care system, lack of awareness, bad roads and poverty are some of the major factors that come in the way of safe deliveries for pregnant women. Internal bleeding, eclampsia and obstructed labour are just some of the factors that are responsible for the high number of maternal mortality deaths in Madhya Pradesh. Every five minutes, India suffers from one maternal death.

1. Surveys have also found that the maximum number of maternal deaths is recorded among the SCs, STs and other backward classes.
2. With a maternal mortality rate of 379, Madhya Pradesh is among the six worst affected states in the country.

3. Only 17 per cent of births to women who belong to STs were assisted by a doctor, compared with 47 per cent births to women who do not belong to an SC, ST or OBC.
4. The majority of women in all religious groups receive antenatal care; nonetheless, there is a substantial variation by religion in the likelihood of women receiving antenatal care. Antenatal care was received by 73 per cent Muslim women and 78 per cent Hindu women, compared with almost all Jain women and 90 per cent Sikh women. By caste/tribe, the likelihood of receiving any antenatal care and care from a doctor is lowest for ST mothers and highest for mothers who do not belong to an SC, ST or OBC.
5. The likelihood of having received antenatal care at all, as well as antenatal care from a doctor, increases sharply with the household's wealth index. Among mothers in household with the lowest wealth quintile, 59 per cent received antenatal care and only 23 per cent received antenatal care from a doctor. By contrast, among mothers in households in the highest wealth quintile, 97 per cent received antenatal care and 86 per cent received antenatal care from doctors.
6. One out of five women in India did not receive any antenatal care for their last birth in the five years preceding the survey. Women not receiving any antenatal care tend disproportionately to be older women, women having children of high birth orders, ST women, women with no education and women in the household with lowest wealth quintile. These differentials suggest that improving the coverage of antenatal programmes requires special efforts to reach older and higher parity women and women who are socio-economically disadvantaged.
7. Madhya Pradesh (32.6%) comes at the third lowest position, following Bihar (29.1%) and Uttar Pradesh (22.5%) when it comes to antenatal care of women by doctor. Almost 93 per cent urban women and 77 per cent rural women have not received any antenatal care. During their contact with health workers pregnant women are expected to be told about pregnancy related complications and where they should go if they have any complications. NFHS-3 depicts that most women did not receive information on specific pregnancy related complications and where to go if they experience any of these signs. Only 20 per cent were told about prolonged labour as a sign of a pregnancy complication, and even fewer (15–17%) were told about convulsions and

vaginal bleeding as signs of pregnancy complication. Urban women, more educated women and women in the households in the highest wealth quintile were better informed about the each pregnancy complication. In Madhya Pradesh, only 16.9 per cent women have had any contact with the health worker.

8. Births assisted by a doctor/nurse/LHV/ANM/other health personnel (%) – 37.1 per cent (urban – 66.4%, rural – 28%). The report reveals that less than 40 per cent of births in India take place with the help of health facilities. More than half take place in the woman's own home and 9 per cent take place in the parental home. Two-third deliveries (67.3%) in urban areas and 29 per cent of deliveries in rural areas take place with health facilities. Though the state government has taken innumerable steps and initiated several programmes for promoting institutional deliveries but there are just 29.7 per cent institutional deliveries in the state. The data shows that only 20.2 per cent institutional deliveries takes place in rural areas. This depicts the quagmire of health care facilities and personnel in the rural areas.
9. Maternal care indicator highlights that percentagewise data who received all recommended types of antenatal care – Madhya Pradesh (7.2%) comes at fifth position from the lower when it comes to percentage women who received all recommended types of antenatal care, following by Nagaland (1.9%), Uttar Pradesh (4.1%), Bihar (5.8%) and Arunachal Pradesh (6.5%).
10. Anaemia is a major cause of maternal mortality. The survey data show that nearly 82.6 per cent of the children in the age group of six to 35 months are anaemic; 40.1 per cent of women have a body mass index (BMI) below normal; 57.9 per cent of pregnant women and 57.6 per cent of women who were ever married are anaemic.

Policy Paradigms

At the macro level, the Government of India has undertaken number of steps under the National Rural Health Mission (NRHM) launched in April 2005 to (i) augment and ensure appropriate public health focus, peoples, orientation and ownership of public health programmes; (ii) encourage community-based approaches to disease control; (iii) promote public-private partnership in service provision; (iv) involve local bodies and Panchayati Raj Institutions (PRIs); and (v) promote gender equity. These initiatives are intended to improve access to primary health care, thereby impacting the prevention and control of communicable diseases, reduction of infant mortality rate and maternal mortality ratio by 50 per cent by year 2012 and promotion of healthy lifestyles.

The Government of Madhya Pradesh has undertaken a series of steps in the recent decades ameliorating the functioning of the health system and facilities, which have been documented by the Government of India's central line ministry, the Ministry of Health and Family Welfare (MoHFW). Madhya Pradesh has set the instance for other Indian states in promoting decentralized planning under MoHFW's flagship programme – the National Rural Health Mission (NRHM). Madhya Pradesh has already signed a memorandum of understanding (MoU) with the Government of India, committing itself to: increase public expenditure on health, increased decentralization and community participation, providing funding for community level health workers and granting functional autonomy to local health facilities.

A perusal of the aforesaid analysis concludes that the formidable challenges for the development of health programme are how to reallocate scarce resources to districts and blocks that are at present deprived and underserved and secondly to increase access for the poorest women, girls, dalits and tribes to health services. This necessitates representation of underserved communities mainly the tribes on decision making committees at the district, block and Gram Panchayat level. There is an imperative need to provide proper training to cater to the need of the vulnerable groups. The PRIs or locally elected governments need to be involved in preparations of district health plans which would help in making these more responsive to local needs. Community monitoring of services and client satisfaction surveys need to be picked up with proper accountability of the system.

In short, evolving an efficient delivery mechanism, plugging the loopholes in the service delivery system to the much neglected tribes, curbing the magnitude of corruption, and the need to generating demand for the service providers, etc., will go a long way in mitigating the health disparity among the tribes in Madhya Pradesh.

References

Health of Tribal Population in India: Results of Some ICMR Studies (1998): Indian Council of Medical Research, New Delhi, p. 1.

Madhya Pradesh Health Sector Reform Programme (2007): Programme Memorandum, Government of Madhya Pradesh, Government of India, DFID, UK.

Annexure 1: Fifth Schedule Areas

Andhra Pradesh	:	Visakhapatnam, East Godavari, West Godavari, Adilabad, Srikakulam, Vizianagaram, Mahboobnagar, Prakasam (only some mandals are scheduled mandals)
Jharkhand	:	Dumka, Godda, Devgarh, Sahabgunj, Pakur, Ranchi, Singhbhum (East and West), Gumla, Simdega, Lohardaga, Palamu, Garwa, (some districts are only partly tribal blocks)
Chhattisgarh	:	Sarbhuja, Bastar, Raigad, Raipur, Rajnandgaon, Durg, Bilaspur, Sehdol, Chindwada, Kanker
Himachal Pradesh	:	Lahaul and Spiti districts, Kinnaur, Pangi tehsil and Bharmour sub-tehsil in Chamba district
Madhya Pradesh	:	Jhabua, Mandla, Dhar, Khargone, East Nimar (Khandwa), Sailana tehsil in Ratlam district, Betul, Seoni, Balaghat, Morena
Gujarat	:	Surat, Bharauch, Dangs, Valsad, Panchmahl, Vadodara, Sabarkanta (parts of these districts only)
Maharashtra	:	Thane, Nasik, Dhule, Ahmednagar, Pune, Nanded, Amravati, Yavatmal, Gadchiroli, Chandrapur (parts of these districts only)
Odisha	:	Mayurbhanj, Sundargarh, Koraput (fully scheduled area in these three districts), Raigada, Keonjhar, Sambalpur, Baudakondmals, Ganjam, Kalahandi, Bolangir, Balasor (parts of these districts only)
Rajasthan	:	Banswara, Dungarpur (fully tribal districts), Udaipur, Chittorgarh, Sirohi (partly tribal areas)

5

Status of Tribal Health and Nutrition

Agenda for Action

V.K. SHRIVASTAVA

There is a general agreement among scholars and researchers that in spite of constant effort made by the state and civil society organizations during last sixty years the health status of the tribal population is very poor. However, it has been brought out by a number of studies that the health problems commonly found among the tribals are nutrition deficiency among the children and anaemia among mothers, hematological disorders, sickle cell, seasonal diseases like diarrhoea among children below five years of age, malaria, tuberculosis, skin diseases, leprosy, goiter etc. Yaws is also prevalent in certain tribal pockets. The health problems among primitive tribes are a cause for greater concern. For example, the health and nutritional survey of the Saharia tribe in Madhya Pradesh suggests that 19 per cent were found to have cervical lymaphadenopahty and 42 per cent were found to be suffering from respiratory infection. Genu valgum was found in 83 per cent of children of Abujmaria tribe of Chhattisgarh state and in Madhya Pradesh about half of the adult population and 10 per cent of children of Bharia were found suffering from goiter. Sickle cell haemoglobin was found in 13 per cent of Bharias, and 20 per cent of Gonds. Out of 1.89 million cases of malaria in the country as per the report of the Ministry of Health and Family Welfare (1994–95), 0.67 million were P. Flciparum and 60 per cent of these cases were contributed by the tribal population.

Primitive tribal groups of India have special health problems and genetic abnormalities like sickle cell anaemia, G-6-PD red cell enzyme deficiency and sexually transmitted diseases were prevalent among some of them (Commissioner for STs & SCs, 1986–87). Insanitary conditions, lack of personal hygiene, health education and ignorance are the main factors responsible for their ill-health.

Many primitive tribal communities are facing extinction like the Onges, Jarawas and Shompens in Andaman and Nicobar Islands. Possible reasons need to be explored although these may differ from population to population and are probably multiple (Verma, 1976). Some of the factors as indicated by investigations include: (a) endemic diseases like malaria; disease introduced from outside like tuberculosis, influenza, dysentery, high infant mortality and malnutrition; (b) venereal diseases, induced abortion, inbreeding, addiction to opium, custom of eating tubers of 'DIOSCERA' (may cause sterility as they contain substances used in oral contraception); and (c) high sex ratio leading to shortage of women.

Urgent studies are, therefore, required on different primitive tribal groups of India which are small in size and are inhabiting in inhospitable environment, to elicit their fertility, mortality, morbidity patterns, consanguinity status, food habits, physical growth trends, genetico-environment disorders and factors affecting them in order to delineate the high risk groups. The paper is divided into five parts. The opening part deals with status of nutrition among different tribes of the country with emphasis on certain tribes of Madhya Pradesh. The second part examines types and causes of genetic disorders among different tribes. Part three examines the state of morbidity and mortality. It underlines both communicable and non-communicable diseases. In the fourth part of the paper, an attempt has been made to discuss infant mortality rate among different tribes. In the last part some suggestions have been provided to bring improvement in health and nutritional conditions of tribes.

I
Nutrition

The nutritional status of various tribes varies from tribe to tribe depending on the socio-economic, socio-cultural and ecological background. Though no systematic and comprehensive research investigation have been carried out, but it appears that malnutrition among the tribals, especially tribal children and women, is fairly common, debilitating their physical condition, lowering resistance to disease, and in the post-weaning period, leading at times even to permanent brain impairment. Experts have opined that not a single tribe in the different states of India can be said to have a satisfactory dietary pattern. Tribal diets are frequently deficient in calcium, Vitamin A, Vitamin C, riboflavin and animal protein. Diets of some South

Indian tribes are deficient even in respect of calories and total protein. A high incidence of malnutrition is observed among some primitive tribal groups in Phulbani, Koraput and Sundergarh districts of Odisha and also among the Bhils and Garasias of Rajasthan and the Padana, Rabris and Charans of Gujarat.

North Eastern Frontier Agency (NEFA) have got diets which can be said to be superior to the average non-tribal diet of any state of India. Studies carried out at National Institute of Nutrition (NIN) (1971) and Planning Commission of India (Sixth Five-Year Plan, Government of India) reported a high protein caloric malnutrition along the rice-eating belts. Studies available on the dietary status and health of the tribals of Bihar and Maharashtra observed deficiency of their diet in calories as well as protein and essential amino acids content though, major signs of nutritional deficiencies were not observed (Chitre et al., 1976). Similar results were obtained from the studies among the pre-school tribal children of Andhra Pradesh and tribals of Kalahandi, Koraput, Madhya Pradesh and Maharashtra (Pingle, 1975). Surveys on the nutritional deficiencies (Gopalan, 1971) among the tribals reported a high incidence of goiter, angular stomatitis among the Mompas of Assam and Vitamin A deficiency among the Onges. A high incidence of malnutrition was observed (Ali, 1980; Basu et al., 1990; Mahapatra and Das, 1990) in some primitive tribal groups in Phulbani, Koraput and Sundergarh districts of Odisha and also among Bhils and Garasias of Rajasthan, Padar, Rabri and Charans of Gujarat and Bonda of Odisha (Haque, 1990). Nutritional investigations carried out by NIN among the tribal groups of Jhabua, Bastar and Sarguja districts of Madhya Pradesh showed following trends:

(a) Severe anaemia was very high in Bastar, followed by Jhabua and was minimal in Sarguja.
(b) The intake of foods and nutrients was more in Sarguja as compared to Bastar and Jhabua.
(c) Overt cases of protein-energy malnutrition (PEM), namely, Kwashiorkor, Marasmus and vitamin deficiency sings like Bitot's spot and Angular stomatitis were conspicuous by their very low prevalence compared to general rural population.

Studies carried out by National Institute of Health and Family Welfare (NIHFW) among the Gond (Muria and Madia), Bhatra, Halba tribal groups of Bastar district of Chhattisgarh showed following trends (Basu et al., 1989):

(a) The average protein calorie intake was found to be much less in the Gond children as compared to Bhatra and Halba children.
(b) Higher frequencies of Biot's spot, Angular stomatitis and motling of teeth were found among Gond children as compared to Bhatra and Halba children.

(c) Muscular wasting was noticed to be higher in Gond children as compared to Bhatra children.

Data on the nutritional deficiency disorders among other tribal groups are scarce. Multidisciplinary and comprehensive studies providing information on habitant, local food products, determinants of malnutrition, dietary practices, economic and social system and its relationship with nutritional status are urgently required. To evolve a suitable strategy to overcome the nutritional deficiencies among the tribals and promulgate preventive and promotive health care, the various socio-economic concomitants and cultural variants have to be taken into consideration. So the nutritional status of any population is a complex and complete entity being a reflection of overall socio-economic status and disinfection, livelihood and food dietary life household food disposition patterns, food related practice including dietary habits. To understand the actual requirement of the creeds and to assess the nutritional status, it is advisable to evaluate the disposable income available to a household and the related expenditure is one of the most important determinants of quantity and quality of the household's food intake in the rural areas. From this an estimate of the households of the tribal areas could be ascertained. In this context, the mean per capita expenditure for month for rural India is ₹ 287 (NCAER, India Human Development Report, 1999).

The tribal population of Madhya Pradesh including Chhattisgarh is specially vulnerable regarding food security and food intake. One major factor is the process of alienation from traditional natural resources which many such tribal communities have undergone in the last few decades due to various reasons such as, deforestation, land degradation, influx of non-tribal population and incoming of major irrigation projects and industries. Poor agriculture and additional stress due to drought contribute to lapping the balance critically towards serve food insecurity. Due to this inadequacy of protein/caloric intake is quite striking among the tribal children below 10 years of age. It is found that only about one-third of these tribal children receive diet adequate in caloric and protein. Similarly, among elder children (10–12 years) and pregnant and lactating women, only around half of the population in these groups has adequate protein and caloric intake.

It could be noted that an intake of less than 20 per cent of the recommended daily allowance (RDA) constitute a serious dietary deficiency. However, about one-fourth of tribal children not receive even this bare minimum cereal intake exposing them to serve malnutrition. It is evident from the Table 1 given below:

Table 1

Adequacy of Intake of Major Food Categories in Tribal Children in Madhya Pradesh

Major Food Categories	*Age 1–3 Years >=70% RDA*	*Age 4–6 Years > = 70% RDA*
Cereal and billets	77.4	77.2
Pulses	35.4	45.8
Leafy vegetable	11.1	11.4
Other vegetable	32.4	31.4
Roots and tubers	39.7	36.8
Milk and milk products	0.3	0.9
Tats and oils	3.9	0.9
Sugar and jaggery	0.5	0.2

Source: National Nutrition Monitoring Bureau, NIN: Diet and Nutritional Status of Tribal Population, Report on First Report Survey-2000.

Table 2

Nutritional Status of Women in Madhya Pradesh including Chhattisgarh

Background Characteristics	*Percentage of Women with BMI 18.5*
Residence	
Urban	28.2
Rural	41.8
Region	
Vindhya	50.0
Central Madhya Pradesh	30.5
Malwa Plateau	36.3
South-Central Madhya Pradesh	47.1
South-Western Madhya Pradesh	33.8
Caste/Tribe	
Scheduled Caste	39.3
Scheduled Tribe	49.2
Other Backward Class	37.4
Others	27.2
Total	38.2

BMI: Body Mass Index-A. BMI less than 18.5 denotes undernourished.

Source: NFHS-2 Madhya Pradesh including Chhattisgarh (National Family Health Survey, 1998–99).

As regards the nutritional status of tribal women in the state of Madhya Pradesh including Chhattisgarh (representing large tribals of belt of central India), it is found that they (tribal women) have extremely poor nutritional status in comparison to the other sections of women population. It is because of their poor socio-economic condition. It is a revealing fact that the prevalence of undernutrition among the tribal women is almost twice of those in the other category. Overall, about 38.2 per cent of women in Madhya Pradesh and Chhattisgarh are undernourished. It is also found that the disparities among various social strata are responsible for even higher levels of undernutrition. Rural women are one and half times more likely to be undernourished than urban women. There are significant regional disparities too, with women from South-Central area faring much worse than those from Vindhya and Central Madhya Pradesh. It would be clear from the Table 2.

As regards the nutritional status of tribal children in Madhya Pradesh including Chhattisgarh, it is found that tribal children are worse off compared to those from other social groups of children. The National Nutrition Monitoring Bureau Report (2000) shows that almost three-fourths of the tribal children in Madhya Pradesh including Chhattisgarh are underweight (74.1%) and stunted (73.4%) (This is higher than the NFHS proportion, perhaps because of sampling variation). What is more worrisome is very high proportion of severely underweight tribal children, at about 42 per cent, this being a group which is most vulnerable in situation of fluctuation of food supply or infection illness. Table 3 given below shows the nutritional status of tribal boys and girls falling under different height and weight.

Table 3

Nutritional Status of Children in Tribal Areas of Madhya Pradesh including Chhattisgarh

Sex	*Below 3SD*		*Below 35 D-2SD*		*Total Below 2–SD*	
	Wt. for age	*Ht. for age*	*Wt. for age*	*Ht. for age*	*Underwt.*	*Stunting*
Boys	42.5	53.0	31.6	21.7	74.1	74.7
Girls	41.3	54.1	32.9	18.2	74.2	72.3
Both	41.3	53.6	32.2	19.9	74.1	73.5

Source: National Nutrition Monitoring Bureau, NIN, Diet and Nutritional Status of Tribal Population, Report on First Report Survey, 2000.

In order to assess the dietary intake and nutritional status of tribal population especially the girls falling in the age groups of 11–13 years, a study has been done by Rajni Talia and Priti Taneja in 13 blocks of Dhar tribal district of western Madhya Pradesh in the year 1999. The tribal girls under the study belong to Bhil, Bhilala and Patalia tribal communities. About half of the tribal families (49.01%) under study were engaged in their own agriculture and agricultural labour. About 23.13 per cent families were earning their livelihood as wage earners. The findings of the study are as under:

(a) Consumption of cereal was 70 per cent of RDA and pulse was 25 per cent of RDA.
(b) The intake of green leafy vegetable was low.
(c) 77 per cent subjects were non-vegetarian, but consumption of non-vegetarian food was negligible.
(d) Data regarding nutrition intake indicated deficient intake of all most nutrition.
(e) A two-meal pattern per day was found in 73 per cent cases and three meal pattern was in 27 per cent cases. Generally, rice was not consumed by these families.

Due to poor nutrition condition, the tribal women and children are the victim of anaemia. Significant micronutrient deficiency is responsible for anaemia. The prevalence of anaemia among the tribal women and children is an index, which reflects the combine impact of availability of nutrition foods to the households, gender equity of food distribution within the household, and effectiveness of iron folic acid supplementation through the health services.

Data from NFHS-2 (1998–99) of west Madhya Pradesh shows that tribal women seem to be suffering most, with almost three-fourths (70.3%) being anaemic and almost one-fourth (23.8%) having moderate or serve anaemia in comparison to the other sections of women in the state of Madhya Pradesh, including Chhattisgarh.

A survey in the drought hit tribal district Barwani in west Madhya Pradesh was conducted by CEHAT (Centre for Enquiry into Health and Allied Themes) during the years 1998–2000 in collaboration with local organization to have an idea of impact that drought has had on nutrition in the region. A sample of 712 under-5 tribal children from two blocks were taken and studied for their nutritional status based on 'weight-for-age'. Of these 84 per cent children were found to have some degree of malnourishment and 21.9 per cent children had severe malnourishment. This figures correlate with the findings of the special study report of NNBM on nutritional status of tribal children. This study found 20.4 per cent of the sample of tribal children in Madhya Pradesh to be severely malnourished.

A similar study was conducted by NNMB[1] among the adult tribal population having BMI of below 18.5, i.e., some grade undernutrition. According to NNMB data collected from the tribal areas in Madhya Pradesh, 49 per cent of the tribal adults were undernourished (BMI<18.5) and 8 per cent were severely undernourished (BBI<16).

The nutritional status of tribal women directly influences their reproductive performances and the birth weight of their children, which is crucial to the infant's chances of survival, growth and development. Thus, the STs in India are thus caught in a vicious cycle of malnutrition and ill-health.

Reproductive Wastage

The nutritional status of tribal women directly influences their reproductive performances and the birth weight of their children, which is crucial to the infants' chances of survival, growth and development. The Scheduled Tribes of India are thus caught in a vicious cycle of malnutrition and ill-health. Data on reproductive wastage among tribal population are meagre. Collection of these sensitive information was found to be difficult in tribal situation, mostly these information were underreported. The incidence of abortion was reported to be 2.5 per cent among Muria and 0.2 per cent among Bhatra mothers, 7.50 per cent in Zemi women of Nagaland (Choudhury et al., 1971, cited from Malhotra, 1986). The incidence of still-births was found to vary from 0.09 per cent in Kota of Tamil Nadu to 7.4 per cent in Mishings of Assam (Malhotra, 1986).

The Report of Planning Commission prepared on the eve of Tenth Five-Year Plan (Chapter 4.2, pp. 460–61) also found that condition of tribal health and nutrition is inadequate. The Report says,

> Although the National Health Policy, 1983 accords high priority to extending organized services to those residing in the tribal, hilly and backward areas as well as to the detection and treatment of endemic diseases affecting tribals, yet the tribals continues to be one of the fragile population, mainly due to their poor health and nutritional status. Tribal health is one of the important areas for action in the health sector. The major contributors to the increased disease risk amongst tribal communities includes: (i) poverty and consequent undernutrition; (ii) poor environmental sanitation, poor hygiene and lack of safe drinking water leading to increased morbidity from water and vector-borne infections; (iii) lack of access to health care facilities resulting in the increased severity and duration of illnesses; (iv) social barriers and taboos preventing utilization of available health care services; (v) vulnerability to specific diseases like G-6-PD deficiency, Yaws and other endemic diseases like malaria, etc.,

also, the tribal population, being heterogeneous, there are wide variations in their health status, access to and utilization of health services.

Malnutrition is fairly common amongst the tribals, especially their children and women, debilitating their physical condition and lowering their resistance to disease, leading at times even to permanent brain impairment. As most tribal women suffer from anaemia which lowers resistance to fatigue, this affects their working capacity and increase susceptibility to disease particularly for those having closely-spaced frequent pregnancies. The nutritional status of tribal women directly influences their reproductive performances and the birth weight of their children, which is crucial to the infant's chances of survival, growth and development. Almost all the tribals in the country do not have a satisfactory dietary pattern as their diets are frequently deficient in calcium, Vitamin A, Vitamin C, Riboflavin and animal protein. The tribals are thus caught in a vicious cycle of malnutrition and ill-health.

II
Genetic Disorders Causing Health Problem, Haemoglobinopathies and Allied Disorders

These are hereditary haemotologic disorders and encompass thalassaemias, abnormal haemoglobin syndromes and glucose-6–phosphate dehydrogenase (G-6–PD) deficiencies. They produce haemolytic anaemia of varying severity and are problems of considerable public health importance (Basu, 1978). In the haemoglobinopathies, the actual chemical structure of haemoglobin is abnormal and the alternation in structure may affect the rate at which haemoglobin is synthesized in the body, or the fate of the red cells that contain abnormal pigment. Since thalassaemias, abnormal haemoglobin syndromes and G-6–PD deficiency produce varying grades of heamolytic anaemia, there is an urgent need to study their present state of distribution, causes of variation, probable susceptibility or resistance with diseases (like malaria, etc.) in particular ecological and social settings. This would be useful with a view to evaluate the nature and extent of selective forces operating in a population so that necessary effective steps could be taken from public health point of view.

Haemoglobin S (HbS) (Sickle-Cell Haemoglobin)

The presence of HbS among Indian tribes was first reported by Lehmann and Cutbush (1952). Since then several studies have reported presence of sickle cell trait from a large number of tribes from different parts of India (Kate et al., 1975, 1978; Brittenham et al., 1978; Negi, 1970, etc.). It may be noted that HbS is widely spread in central, western and southern India with indications of increase in frequency from central to western and then to southern India (Das, 1986). Some South Indian tribes like Mullukurumba, Paniyan, Pradhan, Irula, Adiyans, Konda Kamara show high percentage of HbS (more than 30%). It has also been observed that sickle cell trait (HbAs) in heterozygous condition, confers protection against falciparum malaria. It has been estimated by Malhotra (1986) that about 50 lakh tribal persons are carrying sickle cell trait (HbAs) and they are more prone to certain diseases like pulmonary disorders, haemolytic crisis, mild jaundice, infections, kidney disorders, etc. About 1.6 lakh tribal individuals will be homozygous HbSS. These homozygous individuals with a few exceptions do not survive upto adulthood.

III
Morbidity and Mortality

The principal causes of morbidity are: (a) infective and parasitic diseases (communicable diseases), (b) malnutrition, (c) non-communicable diseases, and (d) diseases associated with genetic disorder, morbid conditions due to malnutrition and genetic disorders. All these causes of morbidity and mortality are largely found among tribes.

Communicable Diseases

From the available studies (Roy Burman, 1986; Mukherjee and Nandy, 1986; Reports of Commissioner for SCs & STs, 1986–87) communicable diseases like Yaws, tuberculosis, leprosy, malaria and veneral diseases are found with high frequency among tribes.

Non-communicable Diseases

Very little information is available about the prevalence of non-communicable diseases in tribal population. Studies carried out by NIN (1971) among the tribals of Sarguja, Jhabua and Bastar districts of erstwhile Madhya Pradesh showed high incidence (53.9%) of goitre (enlarged thyroid gland) in tribals of Sarguja district. Eye condition like cataract, corneal opacity, etc., were found to be in high frequencies (20.3%) in Bastar district. Cases of dental caries (5.1%) were noted in Jhabua. A few instances of cardiovascular diseases like hypertension, valvular heart diseases were clinically found in Jhabua, Sarguja and Bastar.

IV
Infant Mortality Rate (IMR)

State of infant and child mortality would be perhaps to the best assessment of the state of basic health care, quality and reach of health delivery, general environment for health, crucial health, determinants such as nutrition, sanitation, safe drinking water, etc. It would also be a very good determinant of the performance of the development initiatives that focus on poverty, backwardness, green equity and even empowerment. Infants and children (upto the age of five) die prematurely of causes such as low birth weight phenomena and certain vaccine prevent diseases, etc.

IMR is considered as one of the most sensitive indicators of health status. Some valuable information of infant morality rates of tribal population of different states of India (Registrar General, Ministry of Home Affairs, 1973, cited from Malhotra, 1986), shows that infant mortality rates have been found to vary from a minimum of 36/1,000 in Kerala to a very high rate of 168/1,000 in Uttar Pradesh. Very high infant mortality rates (more than 140/1,000) have been observed in the tribal population belonging to the states of Andhra Pradesh, Gujarat, Madhya Pradesh and Uttar Pradesh. But very little information is available on individual tribes about IMR and its etiological factors. Investigations carried out among the tribal groups of Bastar district (Basu, 1986) showed a very high rate of infant mortality among Bhatras (148.56) followed by Murias (123.35) whereas Marias (85.44) and Halbas (92.78) from the same area displayed relatively lesser frequencies. Similar inter-tribe variation of IMR was observed in several tribes inhabiting the same area of Andhra Pradesh (range 68 to 213.33/1,000) (Malhotra, 1986). These inter-tribal differences of IMR from the same geographical area need further in-depth investigation.

The male and female rates in IMR is even more alarming. While the girl child would normally survive better than the boy child being biologically healthier. In case of tribal population the IMR rate is not separately available, neither for girl child nor for boy child. It is available for whole state. As per the available information IMR is lowest for Kerela state and highest in Madhya Pradesh state.

V
Strategies

The following strategies may be followed for the health development of the tribal population:

Socio-cultural and Environment Awareness

- Formulation of realistic development plans based on needs of specific tribal group.

- Adequate understanding of socio-cultural background of different tribal groups, perception of diseases, their beliefs and taboos, study of health culture at micro-level. Positive tribal culture/values, traditional skills should be encouraged and to be inducted to the mainstream of life.
- In most of the tribal communities, there are number of folklores related to health. Documentation of folklores available in different socio-cultural systems may provide the model for appropriate health and sanitary practices in a given ecosystem.
- Identification of indigenous herbs for medicinal use and their preservation and documentation.
- Development of ethno-botanical and ethno-zoological museum at the divisional headquarters, collection, preservation and display.
- Efforts on sanitation, personal hygiene, provision of safe drinking water, dispelling the misbeliefs and taboos, magico-religious practices, etc., awareness of hazards of consanguineous marriages.

Nutrition

- Development of horticulture with emphasis on local fruits.
- Development of poultry and fisheries.

Maternal and Child Health

- Hundred per cent immunization of mothers and children with special emphasis on measles vaccination.
- Distribution of Vitamin A free of cost
- Oral rehydration therapy and education.

Genetic Disorders

- To hold training camps of medical and para-medical staff for awareness of genetic disorders and marriage counselling.
- Training of laboratory technicians in the technique of simple genetic tests like sickling, G-6–PD enzyme deficiency, etc.
- Screening of villages for sicklers and G-6–PD deficient individuals, identified persons can be tattooed with dot marks.
- Sensitization of medical and para-medical staff with the management of genetico-environmental disorders prevalent among the tribal population.

Health Education

- Distribution of leaflets and playing of audio and where possible video cassettes, preferably in local dialects and weekly markets, ghotuls, schools, etc.

- Development of effective communication strategies on health education and health care among tribal groups.

Training

- Organization of short term orientation courses on tribal culture for health workers at district and sub-divisional headquarters.
- Identification of traditional health practioners and their training in pubic health.
- Training of tribal girls/women as nurses, midwives to generate better response.
- Strengthening of tribal research institutes which may serve as base laboratories.

Other Measures

- In difficult tribal/hilly areas, mobile health teams should be formed to provide professional services for medical care and research and collect health information.
- In tribal areas, 'Haats' (weekly market centres) are the focal point of activity. Each 'Haat should be brought under a Primary Health Centre (PHC).
- As some primitive tribal groups are reported to be stagnant/ declining efforts should be made to delineate the causative factors.

Note

1. Source: National Disaster Management Committee Weekly Drought Report No. 10, copy of Madhya Pradesh Memorandum of Scarcity, Diet and Nutritional Status of Tribal Population, report on First Report Survey by National Nutrition Monitoring Bureau (NNMB), 2000, Article on pp. 38–39, Store Science and Technology Features, October 2001.

References

Ali, Almas (1980): "Health and genetic problems of Kutia Kondhas of Burlubaru village, Phulbani district, Orissa", *The Newsletter*, Vol. 1, No. 2, Government of India, Ministry of Home Affair, Tribal Development Division, New Delhi.

Basu, S.K., A. Jindal, G. Kshatriua, P. Singh, P. Roy and K.K.N. Sharma (1989): "Epidemiological investigation of haemoglobinrtopathies and allied disorders, nutrition and physical growth trends, health profile, health seeking behaviour and their environment correlates for promotion of health care among scheduled tribes and scheduled castes of Bastar district, Madhya Pradesh", PAC Report, NIHFW, New Delhi, Mimeo.

Basu, S.K., A. Jindal, G. Kshatriya, S.K. Chetapalli and A.S. Khan (1990): "Genetic and socio-cultural determinations of tribal health, Kutia of Pulbani district", Orissa Annual Report, NIHFW, New Delhi, Mimeo.

Brittenham, G., B. Lozoff, D.B. Sastry and S. Narsimhan (1978): "Haemoglobinopathes in the Nilgiri Hills of Southern India", in I.C. Verma (ed.), *Medical Genetics in India*, Aroma Enterprises, New Delhi, pp. 75–80.

Chitre, R.G., M. Dixit, V. Agate and V. Vailekar (1976): "The concept of essential amino acid in human nutrition: A need for reassessment", *Ind. J. Nutr. Dietet.*, 13: 101.

Choudhury and others (1971): cited in K.C. Malhotra (1986): "Genetico-environmental disorders and their impact on mortality and morbidity profiles among tribal population", presented at Genetic and Socio-cultural Determinants of Tribal Health, NIHFW, New Delhi.

Das, B.M. (1986): "Frontiers of genetic research among tribals of India", presented at Genetic and Socio-cultural Determinants of Tribal Health, NIHFW, New Delhi.

Gopalan, C. (1971): *Nutritional Atlas of India*, ICMR, New Delhi.

Haque, M. (1990): "Height, weight and nutrition among the six tribes of India", in B. Chaudhuri (ed.), *Cultural and Environment Dimension on Health*, Inter-India Publications, New Delhi, pp. 192–206.

Kate, S.L, B.N. Mukherjee, K.C. Malhotra, M.A. Phadke, C.S. Sainani and G.S. Mutalik (1975): "Red cell glucose 6 phosphate dehydrogenase deficiency and haemoglobin variants among some castes and tribes of Maharastra and West Bengal", *Second. Ann. Conf. Ind. Soc. Hum. Genet.*, Calcutta.

Kate, S.L., M.C. Mutalik, M.A. Phadke and G.S. Sainani (1978): "Sickle cell haemoglobin and G-6–PD deficiency in tribal groups of Maharastra", in I.C. Verma (ed.), *Medical Genetics in India*, Aroma Enterprises, New Delhi, pp. 89–92.

Lehmann, H. and M. Cutbush (1952): "Sickle cell trait in Southern India", *Brit Med. Jt.*

Mahapatra, L.K. and Jagannath Das (1990): "Nutritional ecosystem of Orissa tribes", in B. Chaudhuri (ed.), *Cultural and Environmental Dimensions on Health Care*, Inter-India Publications, New Delhi, pp. 293–326.

Malhotra, K.C. (1986): "Genetico-environmental disorders and their impact on mortality and morbidity profiles among tribal population", presented at Genetic and Socio-cultural Determinants of Tribal Health, NIHFW, New Delhi.

Mukherjee, D.P. and S.K. Nandy (1986): "Anthropology of tribal health: The case of the Asur in Netarhat Plateau", in B. Chaudhuri (ed.), *Tribal Health: Socio-cultural Dimensions*, Inter-India Publications, New Delhi, pp. 247–258.

National Institute of Nutrition (1971): Indian Council of Medical Research, Hyderabad, Annual Report.

Negi, N.S. (1970): "Ethnic component in the distraction of sickle cell trait in India", Bio-anthropological Research in India.

Pingle, U. (1975): "Some studies in two tribal groups of Central India", *Plant Foods for Man*, 1: 195–208.

Planning Commission of India, Sixth Five-Year Plan.

Verma, O.P. (1976): "The working composition of the Ranchi tribal labourers in Andaman and Nicobar Islands", *Journal of Social Research*, 19(2): 114–123.

6

Ethno-medicine among the Bhutias and Lepchas of Sikkim

Some Dynamics

J.J. ROY BURMAN

The laity in India generally believes that traditional medicinal practices are on the wane and are being replaced by biomedicine. The state too, by and large, has reposed greater faith on allopathy and is promoting it in a big way. However, of late, the efficacy of ethno-traditions is being reasserted and has gained significant popularity. In the state of Sikkim too the traditional aetiology of Bhutias and Lepchas has continued to thrive in spite of deep inroads having made by allopathy. In fact, the Bhutia, Lepcha and the Nepalis who predominate the state numerically are witnessing an ethnic strife and due to it along with atavism the older practices have resurfaced very prominently and the state government has been compelled to accommodate the role of *shamans* and blend the traditional system with modern allopathic health care practices. This paper initially attempts at deciphering the traditional medicinal practices of the Bhutia and Lepcha (henceforth BL) peoples and then elucidating the present dynamics of the state, which has itself tried to accommodate religion and tradition for popular governance. In the process the validity of biomedicine at times becomes questionable and the efficacy of the traditional health care practices get reinforced.

Bhutias or the Denzongs and the Lepchas or the Rongs, as they prefer to call themselves, are the two indigenous tribal communities of Sikkim who once formed the ruling dynasty or the Chogyal. It remained a kingdom for long and a protectorate of India till its merger in 1975. "Sikkim is a small Himalayan state perched between Tibet to the north, Nepal to the west,

Bhutan to the east and Darjeeling district of India to the south-west. Covering 7,096 square kilometres, the state is 113 kilometres long and some 64 kilometres wide. Sikkim contains within its borders a variety of non-tropical and geographic environments from the low snow-free outer hills to the high peaks with permanent snow glaciers. Hills ranging from 300 metres above the sea level to 7,000 metres adorn the state. The varying altitude results in a climate that varies from sub-tropical to alpine. Sikkim has a rugged topography and flat pieces of land are rare to meet" (Bhasin, 2007). Administratively, the state has been divided into four districts – North, South, East and West. North district is the largest of the four.

Sikkim has witnessed hordes of migration of various caste and tribal population from Nepal and Tibet in the last hundred years. Due to it the Nepalis population stands to be almost 75 per cent population of the state and the BL people together do not figure more than 22 per cent. The migration factor has led to acute contests over control of natural resources and centres of power politics. The ethnic tussles have left their imprint on the traditional medicinal practices as hinted earlier. Quite like other tribes of north-east India, the BL medicinal or health care practices are pluralistic in nature. Both the allopathic and traditional faith-based aetiology are popular among them. In fact, though the modern medical facilities have become available, the BL people resort to the practices of the past. Their practices are quite like that of the Nishings of Arunachal Pradesh. The Nishings believe a disease which cannot be cured ordinarily through application of medicinal herbs is caused by evil spirits. There are a large number of benevolent and malevolent spirits. The malevolent spirits are always at odds with human beings and on the slightest pretext they cause harm to human beings. The harm may come either as disease, accident which, some times may prove fatal, and in any other unforeseen ways.

Before looking into details of the BL aetiology or health seeking behaviour let us get acquainted to the communities in brief at first.

The Lepchas

The Lepchas refer to Sikkim as their *nyemayellang* (Garden of Eden), while the Bhutias term it their *sbas yul Bras mo ljong* (Hidden valley of rice and fruits). Lepchas term themselves as Rong (A Lepcha word meaning ravine – folk or the dwellers of the valley) as they define themselves by their association with sacred mountain Kangchendzonga that is regarded as the source of their knowledge, culture, religion, wealth and resources and the place of their origin. They are the autochthones in their self-perception (Arora, 2006).

The Lepchas are distributed almost all over Sikkim. But the main area of their concentration is the Dzongu preserve in North Sikkim. In olden days, the Lepchas used to mainly survive on forest economy – hunting – gathering. They also used to practice shifting hill cultivation or swidden cultivation. But in the last fifty years or more, they have taken to settled terrace cultivation and cardamom farming. They engage Nepalis labourers on the farms. Some of the Lepchas have now joined the government services or are into cottage industries.

The Lepchas are divided into a number of clans. The clans claim to have mythical connections with particular mountain peaks which they propitiate as their guardian deity. Mount Kangchendzonga is regarded as a principal deity. The other revered mountains are Simvo and Sinolochu. The Lepchas follow patrilineal rule of descent. Although household is the smallest unit, there is multi-aid groups called lobo. They are based on reciprocity, consisting of neighbours and/or kinsmen, mostly on residential and customary lines to co-villagers in need.

The Bhutias

The Bhutias or the Denzongs are well spread around the state. But, like the Lepchas they too are more concentrated in the North district. The main areas of habitation are along the valleys of Lachenchu and Lachungchu rivers. In the higher reaches the Bhutias are mainly engaged in transhumance pastoralism, raising yaks, sheep, goats, horses and mules. In the lower reaches they practice terrace cultivation and cardamom farming. Horticultural practices too have gained popularity of late. Some of the Bhutias are engaged in trade as well. In the recent times, a good number of Bhutias are engaged in government offices.

The Bhutias are found mostly inhabiting clustered settlements. Their residential houses are made of wood with tin roofs. The cottages are of moderate size with ample space. Most of them have courtyards surrounding the house.

Among the Bhutias household is the smallest unit of production and consumption. However, in case of need, existing group structures – *chuchi*, larger than household and smaller than the *busti* are available. *Chuchi* are the mutual aid groups based on reciprocity, consisting of neighbours and/or kinsmen, mostly on residential and customary lines. Though these are informal groups, violation of its rules may lead it to actions at the formal level. In other words, both the BL groups are highly community centred and this gets reflected in all spheres of their lives, including health.

Health, Disease and Cure

The BL people suffer from many kinds of diseases and diarrhoea, dysentery and pneumonia are the most common among them. Tuberculosis and skin diseases are too quite frequent among them. The state has four hospitals in the different districts. There is a referral hospital in Gangtok, the state capital. There are also a good number of Primary Health Centres (PHCs) and Sub-Centres run by the government across the state. Though the private allopathic practitioners are far and few, the popularity of western allopathic medicine is now quite significant. However, in spite of availability of allopathic medicine, the traditional medical treatment or aetiology is almost as popular as before.

The concept of illness and disease is usually culture-based. While mental disorder may be considered to be a disease in one society, it may not be treated so in another. Bhasin (Internet) writes, "In the western world people usually do not make a distinction between illness and disease. Disease is an objectively measurable category suggesting the condition of the body. By definition, perceptions of illness are highly culture related while disease is usually not. To a great extent, research in medical anthropology, makes use of pragmatic orientation, but a powerful alternative also prevails, focussing on negotiation of meaning as key to understanding social life".

A study of Kabi village, about twenty kilometres north of Gangtok, by the author, revealed that the BL people are extremely religious in their bearings, affecting the entire lifestyle, including the arena of health, disease and cure. There is not a single BL household which has no 'Chesam' or altar with Buddhist markings and sometimes added with Hindu gods and goddesses. Multitudes of white and colourful prayer flags tied to bamboo posts hung from strings are strewn all over the village.

For the BL people any kind of illness is caused by supernatural powers. Bhasin (Internet) notes that illness may be caused by spirits of envy, hatred and quarrelling. The spirits of enmity and jealousy *Karo-mung* cause illness through evil thoughts. If a person is annoyed with a neighbour because his animals have strayed into his fields or he has done some harm or envies his possessions, the *mung* is released automatically. Illness is caused by evil spirits – Sabdok *Loo mung*, Dade *mung* sent by enemy. By divination the source is tried to be found out but no revenge of any sort is taken. Likewise annoyance or mischiefs of different *mungs* cause various ailments. Lepchas believe that quarrelling is the result of actions of three evil spirits: *su-mung* (enmity of speech), *ge-mung* (enmity of thought), and *thor-mung* (enmity of action). Besides the evil trinity of *sogo-thor*, *tamsi mung* causes quarrels and wars. Jaundice is caused by the *Londoon mung*. *Mang mung* produces many unpleasant symptoms apparently having no reason are the result of ancestral quarrels. A quarrel annoys deities – *Gebu Tabrong Pano*, who afflicts the offenders with all sorts of aches and pains; commencing with toothache as a punishment. Similarly, the antagonism of *rum* too punishes people by afflicting them with severe bodyache and prickly feeling.

Lepchas consider the people born in different years are distressed by specific *mung*. For example, Lepchas born in *Oon nam* (sheep year) are troubled by *chemen mung, loo desen mung, muzong rumloo and subdong loo*. The person under the spell of these *mungs* is always hungry and if catches sight of people having food, each time attacks for more food. Lepchas believe that if a child is born with a defect, his father must have committed an immoral act during his pregnancy. The death of such a child occurs in the year corresponding to the month of pregnancy when the act was carried out and is considered to be consequence of the endeavour.

The Bhutias also believe in ghosts and evil spirits quite like the Lepchas. The evil spirits among them are popularly called *shinde*. The mischief of *shindes* can cause stomach ache, miscarriage and other common diseases. Witchcraft and sorcery too is very common among Bhutias. People are always very suspicious of others and normally do not eat in the houses of unknown people. They are afraid of being afflicted by *kapat* or black magic.

The belief in evil eye too is very common among the Bhutias. Evil eye can be passed on to other through hypnosis, if scientifically observed. Causes vary from staring at someone for a long time, showing admiration or envy, gossiping on a person's look, which can have an effect whether negative or positive. Compliments are usually believed to be the cause of the evil eye. Common symptoms of the evil eye are strong headache, nausea, fatigue, or simply a bad mood. Only specialists are able to remove the spells of evil eyes. They try to cure the evil eye by amulets and charms or holy water, which they procure from religious practitioners.

Herbal cure among the Lepchas of Dzongu is widely prevalent. But hardly does one come across a herbal specialist. The elders are usually the repositors of knowledge of such elixir. The knowledge is usually guarded to ensure prudent use of herbs and shrubs and it also ensures retention of prestige to the experts. Names of a few of the herbal medicines and their uses are as follows:

Mei-hroom-rik:	Juice of the plant is used for curing sores in the mouth and tongue of infants.
Took-rik-koong:	Bark and root is used for ulcer, bleeding, piles and dysentery.
Sa-nao-koong:	Bark is used for diarrhoea.
Re-be-rip:	Rhizome and leaf paste is used for eye ailments and cataract.
Phozim Aeyok:	Whole plant is used for pneumonia and throat pain.

Pradhan and Badola (2008) state that a small state like Sikkim is rich in biota of which, there are at least 550 medicinal plants. They record in a study that in Dzongu, a tribal preserve of Sikkim, the Lepchas make use of 118 species of plants and herbs belonging to 71 families and 108 genera (8 species and 5 genera). As per use pattern, maximum 30.5 per cent species are to cure stomach related disorders/ailments,. Followed by 19.49 per cent for curing cuts, wounds, inflammation, sprains and joint pains. Administration of medicine orally is recorded in 75 per cent cases. Root and rhizome harvest targeted 30 species. The study revealed that 59.3 per cent plant species are used to cure more than one ailment. External applications as well as internal consumption are involved in the treatment of diseases. Analysis of species level data revealed that oral (75%), external application (44.4%), nasal (5.5%), eye (2.7%) and the ear (0.93%) are major administration routes of ethno-medicinal use. It was observed that most of the preparation includes single plant species and in rare case the combination of two or more species. It was also observed that different parts of a single species are used to cure different diseases.

The study finds the used administrations are not standardized in general, but depend on the age and physical appearance of the patient, illness and diagnosis of the disease. Children are given small doses of medicine than considered in case of adult patients, which further depend on the type of illness and treatment realized appropriate by the local medicine man. The type of disease and the level of its severity further decide the course of the frequency of the treatments. Each medicinal plant is used either raw or in dried form as medicine. Especially, the underground parts are used in the dried form, which is either cut into small pieces or powdered and stored.

There are a few plants and herbs which are commonly used for different kinds of cure. *Swertia Chirayita* is one of them, the extraction of which is used for treating fever, cold, cough, diarrhoea and stomach-ache. The rhizome of *Bergenia ciliate*, a threatened medicinal herb is used to cure fractured bone, fresh cuts and wounds. *Aconitum ferox* is a poisonous plant which is traditionally used for fever, skin diseases, cough and gout. *Oroxylum indicum* is yet another vulnerable taxa of Sikkim, which is used as a common appetizer and treatment for dysentery and throat pain. *Diocrea alata*, a common form of wild edible plant is occasionally used for curing fever, rash, itches, constipation and piles. Similarly, *Ageratum cornyzoides* is used by the Lepcha tribe for curing diarrhoea, dysentery, intestinal colic and flatulence in addition to cuts and wounds. The Lepchas have also learnt to use *Costus speciosus* for curing urinary tract infections and venereal diseases as well. The leaf of *Lantana camera* is used for curing diarrhoea and cough and soup prepared from it is served to pregnant women, which helps them in easy delivery of child. It also helps in healing bone fractures.

The biomedical treatment in recent years has gained tremendous popularity among the BL people. The Tibetan medical practitioners or the Amchee too have began gaining popularity. But 'folk' medicine provided by persons neither professionalized or bureaucratized hold a significant position. Shamanistic faith-healing along with indigenous medicines is perhaps the most important type of treatment adopted by the BL people. Thus they have mainly three sources of treatment in their framework: Treatment from herbs, Tibetan pharmacopea and magico-religious healing.

The Healers

The belief in supernatural powers and evil spirits is very strong among the BL people. Most of the diseases and illness are attributed to them. It is believed that the need for *shamans – bongthings, paus* and *jhankris* – is indispensible for the cure. They most often recommend charms and amulets. *Tse-sung* are recommended for prolonging life and warding off dangers.

Ri-sung are worn in times of epidemics.

Kunthup-sung are used to ward off general evil.

Za-sung is a charm for epilepsy patients and is worn to prevent attacks.

Gyal-sung is a charm for warding off evil influence of a special class of demons which are both inimical and useful to human beings, in proportion to the degree in which they are either propitiated or disregarded. These demons, which are believed to be the spirits of perverted Lamas, cause night mares, diseases of brain and the nervous system. For cases of childbirth and various diseases of nervous system, charms are written on thin strip of paper with Chinese ink. These are rolled into a pill, coated with butter and is administered to the patient. Such amulets are tied to the hair on the forehead of the pregnant mothers suffering from difficult labour. Strings of snail-shells are worn around the necks and wrists of children for their protection. Various plants and herbs are blessed and consecrated at auspicious time of wandering Lamas.

The BL people have lot of exorcists who are commonly called *bongthing* or *mun*. Many of the *muns* are women as well. The shamans acquire their traits usually through possessions. The *muns* must be present during occasions of birth, marriage and death. They also function together with Lamas during the annual well-being ceremonies like *Cherim* ceremony.

The *bongthing* or the *mun* usually attends an individual person. The disease is believed not due to soul loss but due to possession by some evil spirits. The *shamans* chant mantras and get into possession and spell out the solutions. The presence of family members and friends during the ceremony intensifies the whole experience. A patient gets courage through public acceptance of his battle and from knowing that so many people are on his side. Cooperation of the patient during exorcism is implied; and sometimes it is dramatically expressed. Followed by exorcism, animal sacrifice is often performed as per the directives of the possessed soul. Fowl and cattle are often sacrificed along with pig.

While most of the BL people think there are various kinds of spirits reside in trees, forests and hills, many think people fall sick due to spirit possession. The *bongthings* and other exorcists are invited to control the spirits and cure the patients. Quite often the women are believed to get possessed by spirits and make many kinds of pronouncements when in spell. They become vessels of the spirits. Such women tend to gain particular prominence in a male dominant world. Ritual healers use effigies of the victims and spirits and perform puja to get rid of the supernatural forces. The *shaman* gets into a trance voluntarily and communicates with the spirits to woo them away.

The Lamas are also often invited to treat the sick. The Lamas indulge in long prayers and instead of animal sacrifice they recommend raising prayer flags and offering figures made out of dough – popularly known as *torma*. Sometimes devil dancing or *kongso-klon* is performed by the Lamas to drive away the devils.

Community involvement in curing the sick is a marked trait among the BL people. This gets particularly manifest during the therapy of a sick person born in antagonistic year. Both the Lama and the *bongthing* operate together involving prayers and sacrifices. Most notably, colourful thread crosses tied to bamboo frames are placed at cross-road close to the house of the patient. The local people believe that the crosses operate as antennas inviting the benevolent spirits to drive away the evil ones. Thread-crosses are contraptions for catching demons (who causes sickness and harm the people) like flies in spider web. It is therefore necessary to renew the contraption and then to destroy the old thread-crosses when they have served the purpose and have become saturated with powers of evil.

According to the purpose they serve or the relation they have to certain supernaturals, the thread-crosses bear various names; often those of the one referred in the old Bon religion. This is interesting considering the fact that the thread-crosses are raised as per the divination of the Buddhist Lamas. When constructing the thread-crosses, strict rules concerning their colour, the way of arranging the knitting the coloured strings, etc., are maintained. While the work is progressing, prayers and incantations are chanted and the officiating priest blows breadth from time to time upon the structure.

More than directly providing the healing touch, thread-crosses have social functions as well. The colourful frames placed at the road junction in the locality of the patient makes people aware about somebody being sick around and silence has to be maintained. The thread-cross on the roof-top of the patient's house attracts the villager to the sick and they offer some gifts and money. This alleviates the moral of the sick person and the family members. Thus, the practice of thread-cross which the laity assailed as a kind of superstition, has a psycho-somatic implication.

Apart from the sticks, coloured threads and tufts of wood used for construction of thread-crosses, several other objects are required in the ceremonies to cure the sick. For the 'closing door of the Sky Demon' skulls of dogs are fastened to the thread-crosses. On the other hand, for closing door to the 'Earth Demon' ceremony, a ram's skull is tied to the Cross. The structural bianaries of mind are manifest particularly in the tradition where the horns of a goat are hung from the roof in front of the entry door and the hoofs are placed under the ground right below. Similarly, at many houses of the sick, namgo or talismans are put up. While the skull of a dog facing upwards (towards the heaven) is stuck against the wall above the main entrance on the first floor, a skull of a pig facing downwards (facing the hell) is stuck against the wall on the entrance door on ground floor. These indicate that many of the cures are also based on certain calculations and not based on random acts of the shamans. The Lamas, in fact, involve many other planetary calculations which create psychosomatic ambience for the cure.

Among the Bhutias of North Sikkim, the shamans are better known as *pau*. A *pau* is an exorcist. At times he works along with the Lamas and other monks. He also occasionally administers herbal medicines. He does practice *mumbo jumbo* but avoids any form of animal sacrifice. A *pau* holds a very important position in the Lachung town. His presence is indispensible during marriage, child-birth or settlement puja. He is also a member of the *Dzumsa,* a local statutory body for self-governance set up by the government. The *pau* thus plays an important role in the decision making process – development and maintenance of the social order as well.

Despite opening up of PHCs and massive propaganda, traditional beliefs about diseases and health prevail almost all over Sikkim, by and large. *Bongthings/Paus/Lamas* cure through the sight of physical body by means of an elaborate diagnostic system and pharmacopeia. It is believed by the tribals that traditional medical system is competent for restoring health of the body (herbalist) or the mind (*Bongthing/Pau*). Among the tribals, failure of the cure did not call for the efficacy of the system, but on the dissonance of ritual behaviour. The total commitment of the believers in the traditional system (which is sometimes doubted by failure) permits and so does the belief of the patient in the healer, regardless of the result. Pradhan and Badola (2008) too write, "Surprisingly, for some particular ailments like bone fracture and dislocation, most people still prefer herbal use rather than allopathic treatment, as they prefer to avoid undergoing painful therapies of the latter. Many natives still prefer and trust upon using traditional health care system as the excellent and much effective means to cure their ailments over allopathic drugs". These days, tribals do not fully rely upon ritual healers and often opt for herbal remedy as well. Compared to allopathic medicines, herbal remedies are cheaper and easily available in the vicinity. These herbal remedies are free from side effects which are seen with allopathic medicines.

In areas where biomedicine is available, there too tribals resort to traditional ritual cure. Biomedicine is usually criticized for failing to respond to wider emotional and spiritual needs of the patients. It is like a commodity delivered by health professionals and their assistants. Community members are not involved in the planning, implementation and evaluation. The dependence and confidence on ritual healers is the result of faith and trust among patients. Through them the tribals relate their needs to the supernatural powers and ask for assistance and clemency.

The pluralistic medical situation of doctors and deities in tribal areas provide flexibility and fulfils different needs of the community. The folk systems are often manifested by eclecticism of both the clients and practitioners, who adopt from array of co-existing medical traditions.

Dynamics of Tribal Medicine in Sikkim

The future of traditional medicinal practices is in doubt in Sikkim. Like any other state, it is under the throes of international forces and policies institutions like the World Health Organization (WHO). Although the WHO is staffed by technically qualified scientists and medical doctors, most of its policies are donor driven. In the present times there is a significant shift of WHO emphasizing on quality of life to vertical programmes. Powerful interest groups like the US and drug syndicates compelled the WHO to promote global programmes on AIDs, research on tropical diseases and human reproduction system (Walt, 2006). Falling in line, the Government of Sikkim too has paid considerable interest into AIDS research and extension programme. These programmes are being implemented even in the interior regions through the PHCs and Sub-Centres. Family planning activities too have gained ascendance through the efforts of the government agencies and the NGOs. General allopathic treatment too is being encouraged through the PHCs and establishment of new hospitals. A huge private hospital and medical college – Sikkim Manipal Medical College and Hospital (which has been presently takenover by the state) was started few years back near Gangtok.

It needs to be pointed out that even WHO is not a monolithic body and even it has duel policies. Due to the thrust of the developing nations, even WHO has been compelled to accept the efficacy of traditional medicines. It recommends holistic health care system as well – that of viewing man. In totality within a wide ecological spectrum, and emphasizing the view that if health or disease is disequilibrium of man in his total ecological system and not by causative agents and pathogenic evolution. The treatment strategies used in traditional systems of health include the use of herbal medicine, mind/body approaches including massage, acupuncture and exercise programmes. These are low-cost, locally available treatments which according to WHO are used as sources of primary health care among 80 per cent of the world's population. At present more than 20 centres around the world collaborate in the WHO Traditional Medicine Programme.

It is no wonder that the Government of Sikkim (under the global influence) too has been to some extent flexible in its health care policies. It is reported that the Health Department acknowledged the important socio-economic role played by the local medicine men and it instructed the medical officers in the PHCs to take them into confidence for them to be functional within their jurisdictions. The officers were instructed even to accommodate the shamans into their AIDS programme. The department also organized training programmes for the shamans in camps so as to orient them towards allopathic treatment and realize the nuances of AIDS treatment. Even otherwise the PHC doctors have been found advising the patients to consult the shamans simultaneously along with their own treatment. The Sikkim Health Department has of late been open to the idea of multiple therapies and it has also provided amenities for homoeopathic treatment in some of the PHCs. Besides, at the TNM Hospital, the largest government hospital located in Gangtok, an Amchee Tibetan doctor has been appointed to impart Tibetan medicinal practices.

When dealing with the future of the BL traditional medical system certain factors arise, similar to what Habib and Raina (2005) view, "The history of the encounter between modern allopathic medicine and so-called traditional medicine is one such field of cultural debate". Apart from culturological considerations, power and politics also have very important bearing on the medical practices. Of late, in many of the Third World countries, traditional medicinal practices are being revived even at times with the connivance of the state. Habib and Raina (ibid.) state in this regard, "In any case, political struggles for decolonization or cultural transformation have evoked traditional knowledge, values, and norms in order to establish parity with the hegemon. This counter-hegemonic ideology in each case evoked the tradition in a language that was more or less shaped by the idea of the modern. The tradition that was evoked was epistemically reconceived in the light of the modern. The theoretical vocabulary of this evocation is modern. This idea itself is a reflection of the conceptual engagement of the traditional with modern allopathic medicine. In historical; discourse this side of the engagement is invisible to the participants in a combat; just as the modernizers are unaware of how the 'traditional' steps into their own discourse, transforming it in ways not yet evident to us".

Ethnicity and Medicine

Intensive field studies in Sikkim have revealed that ethnicity has played a significant role in continuance of traditional medicinal and health care practices. The role of ethnic factors in the case of medicinal practices is usually not a very accepted phenomenon. But Rathwell (1984) has proved the relevance of it in the case of Great Britain, "In Britain ethnic minorities not only have marked different health care needs, but also different ways of making these needs manifest .... What is clear is that cultural differences predetermine, and to a large extent, predetermine the type of care of service the people seek. Asians for instance, tend to use traditional practitioners or hakims". He further writes, "Many minority group members mistrust doctors and hospitals. Many are unfamiliar with the system and distrust the bureaucracy that characterizes British society. Many lack the appropriate documents and thus find it difficult to obtain health care, and often do not understand why it is needed in order to receive care ... the hospital often ceases to be regarded as a place for the treatment of illness and instead is identified as a part of the forces of oppression". Lipton and Marbach (1981) too accept ethnicity to be a variable that effect health consciousness and treatment.

In the context of health and medicine among the tribes of India, Kumar (1993) too stresses on the importance of ethnicity. He writes, "It is generally believed that differences between the health status of the tribals and non-tribals, is a consequence of ethnicity. The health of the tribals is explained in relation to their tribalness, a cultural product of age-old historical process and inherited biological traits".

In Sikkim, there is an ambivalence with regard to the future of tribal medicinal practices. The laity and the intelligentsia in general believe that due to penetration of western education and medicinal practices through the proliferation of PHCs and Sub-Centres, the traditional age old system is on the wane. Pradhan and Badola (2008) write, "In recent years dependency on allopathic medicine has increased considerably over traditional health care systems. Loosening interest among young generation, and difficulties in procurement of plants and processing them and disappearance in the skills in locating the plants are the factors leading to gradual decline of traditional health care system. For living in the close proximity to the district headquarters and exposure to new livelihood options as well the availability of the PHCs and Sub-Centres in each village in recent years has further diverted youngsters from ethno-medicinal practices".

A very interesting contradictory observation has, however, been made by the author through a research on the medicinal practices among the BL people in Sikkim. It became evident that ethnicity has played a major role in the revival of traditional medicinal practices. In Sikkim there has been a simmering ethnic discontent for a long time between the autochthonous people and the migrants. This started there long before the state was merged (forcefully) with India and has continued even after. The seed of this conflagration is rooted to the large-scale immigration of Nepalese population to the state right from the beginning of nineteenth century to this day, and the subsequent competition over available limited resources. The BL people did not cultivate on their cardamom fields and engaged the Nepalese as labourers. From becoming Serfs, many of the migrants gained masterly possession of the lands they were tilling. The Nepalese migrants also drew the wrath of BL people since they sided with India in gaining political control over the state. The grip of the Nepalese has gained such a control over the state that except for the initial term all the other assembly terms have been under the control of a Nepalese Chief Minister. The ethnic divide is usually manifested in occasional petty scuffles, but at times has also flared up as communal pogroms (As in 1973). The occasional demand of the Nepalese population for attaining Scheduled Tribe status on the top of resource competition has of late created an intensely volatile situation and this has resulted in ethnic resurgence among all the native groups of the state. Even the state itself has succumbed to the ethnic assertions and has declared many minor religious festivals as public holidays. The state also has a seat in the Legislative Assembly reserved for the Buddhist Sangha.

Ethnic revivalism in Sikkim is marked by the emergence of several ethnic organizations like Survival Sikkimese. Apart from Survival Sikkimese, which enjoys support from both the Bhutias and Lepchas in the city of Gangtok, a few ethnic organizations owning allegiance exclusively to Bhutia and Lepcha too have surfaced in the last few years. The Tarzum in South Sikkim and Mutanchi Lom Al Shezum in North Sikkim are two such organizations which have been formed by the Lepchas exclusively for propagating their cause. These organizations have made deep inroads not only in the townships but also in remote villages. For instance, all the villagers of every village of Dzongu preserve are mandatorily made members of Mutanchi Lom Al Shezum. Every village has a separate branch of the Shezum with separate management committees at the branch level. The main objective of these groups is to unite the Lepchas and safeguard their identity by reviving their traditional cultural festivals like *Namsoong* or by making and distributing audio and video cassettes recording of their folk songs, myths and legends.

Ethnic revivalism in Dzongu is best manifest during Namsoong festival, which is being celebrated in a grand scale since the last few years. Namsoong is the festival to commemorate the new year among the Lepchas. It is celebrated in almost every Lepcha village. At Dzongu too, it used to be celebrated separately in each and every village. But presently all the villages are celebrating the occasion together at Namprikdam ground in Lower Dzongu. A week long fair is held along with sports competitions and cultural performances. Of late, Lepchas from Kalimpong and Darjeeling are found swooping down to the venue. The Governor of Sikkim and other dignitaries of the state too witness the event. Importantly, the opening ceremony of the festival is commenced by invoking the local gods and goddesses by a *Bongthing* – a Lepcha *shaman* and not by a Buddhist Lama.

Pang Lhabsol is another ritual that marks the ethnic bondage between the Bhutias and the Lepchas. It is celebrated at the Chogyal's (king's) palace to commemorate the blood treaty which was signed in AD 1275 between Thekok Tek, a Lepcha wizard and Khye Bumsa, a Bhutia chieftain at Kabi village sacred grove about 17 kms from Gangtok. The treaty necessitated the Bhutias to accept and respect the religious and cultural practices of the Lepchas and vice versa. This arrangement called *Chyu Rum Faat* in Lepcha language is believed to have been carried out by keeping Mount Kangchendzonga as the witness (Fonning, 1987). Consequently during the *Pang Lhabsol* Mount Kangcnedzonga and other mountain peaks are invoked. In the last few years this celebration is being organized at the state level in a big way at Kabi village. The celebration is solemnized by *bongthings*.

Indications to the phase of ethnic revivalism among the BL people can be gauged even from the fact that the number of Buddhist monasteries are rapidly increasing in the state. Apart from funding from the western sources, the state government too has been compelled to sponsor them. A new craving is witnessed even among the western educated tribes to send at least one of the sons to join the Lamasery in the monasteries. Surprisingly, the pre-Buddhist Bon religion is also regaining its lost splendour. In several villages the *paus* are now being invited to solemnize the weddings along with the Buddhist Lamas. Not surprisingly, at Sothing village in South Sikkim, a new Bon monastery has come up a few years back. The monks are encouraged there to propagate Bon medicine in the surrounding villages.

In Sikkim the revivalism of ethno-medicine appears to coincide with the ethnic resurgence. The revival of faith in traditional medicine may not be a deliberate ploy. In villages like Phoodong and Phensang in North Sikkim where practice of sacrificing cattle and pigs was given up so as to cure ailments, resurgence of the same is noticed in the present days. The community solidarity of the BL people appears to get reinforced and greater social support to the sick gets ensured. People are still continuing to consult the shamans to cure the sick through prayers and exorcism. They consult them even to determine the timings of operation in the hospitals. The practice of raising prayer flags, constructing prayer wheels and *chautaras* – resting places as part of vows to cure the seriously sick is ubiquitous in the state. The Tibetan medicine is too gaining fast popularity. In Gangtok itself three Tibetan doctors are operating. The Sothing monastery is too engaged in popularizing Bon medicines through its monks.

Interestingly, the Government of Sikkim Health Department statistics reveals that the number of patients treated in the government hospitals and health centres are gradually dwindling in the last few decades. While in 1983, 30,291 indoor and 4,02,401 outdoor patients were treated, in 1995 the figure receded to 3,257 indoor and 3,24,830 outdoor patients. While there has been only a marginal increase in the indoor patients, there has been a very significant fall in the number of outdoor patients. Importantly, there has been a population growth of 90,000 persons or about 28 per cent growth during 1981 to 1991. This has happened despite the fact that the number of PHCs and Sub-Centres have significantly increased within this period. While in 1983 there were 16 PHCs and 62 Sub-Centres, it grew to 24 PHCs and 144 Sub-Centres in 1995. The number of private allopathic or homoeopathic doctors in the state, however, is insignificant. Obviously traditional medicinal practices handled by the *shamans* have not lost their elan. This also can be construed as a dimension of ethnic consolidation. After all, *shamans* are considered to be the best repositors of the cultural traditions by the BL who use them best in the art of healing (Roy Burman, 2003).

Conclusion

It is apparent from the above study that the traditional health care practices are as pervasive as the western allopathic system. There is a pluralistic situation in the state. The Bhutia Lepchas do not follow exclusively one system of medication. In fact, being an extremely community-based society, the practices try to involve as many people as possible to ensure moral support to the sick and the family members. In between with the spread of western education and government policy to introduce western medicine through the hospitals and PHCs resulted in some loss of faith in the traditional medicines. The large-scale deforestation and rapid population growth too made it a bit difficult to find medicinal herbs and shrubs. But with the present ethnic revivalism there is a resurgence of ethno-medicines and faith in shamanistic healing.

Statistical figures from the health department too reveal that there is a gradual fall in the number of patients visiting the government hospitals and PHCs despite the increase in numbers of such centres. On the other hand sacrifice of animals during illness involving the community at large is on the rise. While Tibetan medicine is gaining popularity among the BL people Ayurveda is too gaining prominence among the ethnic Nepalese people. The Subbas or the Limbus who claim themselves to be indigenous have been asserting their rights by reviving many of their cultural traits, which included medicinal practices, have ultimately succeeded in gaining the Scheduled Tribe status.

The traditional medicinal practices among the BL people gained a fillip from the state itself. The government provided directives to its medical officers to incorporate the services of the shamans since they hold important positions in the society and that they should not be antagonized. Even the international institutions at times indicated its preferences in favour of the indigenous health care systems. Even the AIDS programme in Sikkim followed the inclusive policies of the WHO. Thus, in the times of globalization, tribal health care systems does not operate in isolation and even the western sources have been compelled to acknowledge the efficacy of some of the systems of tribal medicines prevalent in Sikkim. In a way, the scenario in Sikkim reveals an ongoing tussle between different forces – global and the local, both trying to outdo the other. It reflects upon a war between the moral order and the technical order in which the medicinal system or the health seeking behaviour is just an emblem.

References

Arora, V. (2006): *The Forest of Symbols Embodied in the Tholung Sacred Landscape of North Sikkim, India*, Conservation and Society.

Bhasin, V. (2007): "Medical Anthropology: Healing Practices in Contemporary Sikkim", *The Anthropologist*, No. 30, pp. 59–94.

Fonning, A.R. (1987): *Lepcha: My Vanishing Tribe*, New Delhi: Sterling Publishers.

Habib, I. and D. Raina (2005): "Reinventing Traditional Medicine: Method, Institutional Change and Manufacture of Drugs and Medication in Late Colonial India", in J.S. Alter (ed.), *Asian Medicine and Globalization*, Philadelphia: University of Pennsylvania Press.

Kumar, N. (1993): "National Health Policy: Some Issues", in A. Bose et al. (eds.), *Tribal Development and Development in Northeast India*, New Delhi: D.K. Publishers.

Lipton, T.A. and J.J. Marbach (1981): "Ethnicity and the Pain Experience", *Soc. Sci. Med.*, 19(12).

Pradhan, B. and H.K. Badola (2008): "Ethnomedicinal Plant Use by Lepcha Tribe of Dzongu Valley, Bordering Khanchendzonga Biosphere Reserve in North Sikkim, India", *Journal of Ethnobiology and Ethnomedicine*, 4: 22.

Rathwell, T. (1984): "General Practice, Ethnicity and Health", *Soc. Sci. Med.*, 19(2).

Roy Burman, J.J. (2003): *Tribal Medicine*, New Delhi: Mittal Publications.

Walt, G. (2006): *Health Policy: An Introduction to Process and Power*, London and New Jersey: Zed Books.

7

Body Mass Index Cut-offs to Determine the Nutritional Status (Thinness) of Gond Children of Mandla District, Madhya Pradesh

SUNEEL QAMRA, D.C. JAIN AND A. KAVISHWAR

Health of the people is the most important indicator of development of a nation, and nutrition is a vital determinant of health. Nutrition plays a significant role in physical, mental and emotional development of the child since conception. Poor and inadequate nutrition leads to malnutrition, morbidity and mortality among children (Vaid and Vaid, 2005). Child's growth is universal, inexpensive and simple measure to assess adequate nutrition, health and development of children and adults compared to other available assessment tools. During the growing age period, children have special nutritional needs because of their extensive growth and development (WHO, 1995; Blössner et al., 2006). Undernutrition among children is an important health problem in India. India has the highest incidence of childhood malnutrition in the world (Bamji, 2003) and among states, Madhya Pradesh has the highest. Earlier, childhood undernutrition (stunting, underweight and wasting) is generally assessed using Gomez and Waterloo classification in India following similar but different internationally and regionally recommended standards (WHO, 1995). These classifications had their own limitations. The body mass index (BMI) is now globally accepted and provides a simple measure of a person's 'fatness' or 'thinness', allowing health professionals to discuss overweight and underweight problems more objectively with their patients. Very recently, international cut-offs of child overweight and obesity for the age range of 2–18 (Cole et al., 2000) and for underweight or thinness (Cole et al., 2007) has been developed. In the latter study, undernutrition has been termed as thinness (as in adults) defined as low BMI for age. It has been graded as III, II and I (severe, moderate and mild, respectively).

Ever since, there is an increasing interest to evaluate nutritional status of children through calculating BMI [weight (kg) / height (m^2)]. Recently, scanty studies (Biswas et al., 2009; Das and Bose, 2011) have been delved to classify prevalence of different grades of thinness using the recently recommended age and sex specific cut-off values of BMI (Cole et al., 2007). The present study is an attempt to determine the nutritional status (thinness level) of Gond children of Mandla district of Madhya Pradesh following Cole's standards for grading rates of thinness. It is an important because there exist no published literature in Madhya Pradesh that has utilized these cut-off points to evaluate the rates of thinness (undernutrition) among children. Thus, the results of the present study will be useful for national and international comparisons of rates of thinness among tribal children.

Subjects and Methods

As per census 2001, the highest tribal population (22.8%) dwells in Madhya Pradesh. Tribal dominated Mandla district situated in the east central part of Madhya Pradesh was earmarked for the present study as high preponderance of Gond dwells in this district. This district has a total population of 12,91,263 scattered in four tehsils. Fifty two villages from three tehsils (Mandla, Nainpur and Bichhia) barring Niwas were selected for the study using clustering method in such a way that samples become representable for the entire area and identified villages are approachable in all seasons (Figure 1). The Niwas tehsil was excluded due to its nearness to urban area with lower tribal population.

Figure 1
Showing Study Area of Mandla District of Madhya Pradesh

The consent of the parents and community leaders was sought after explaining the purpose of the study. In total, 4,491 tribal households were selected for the study who had given their willing consent. 5,447 apprently healthy tribal children (2,829 boys and 2,618 girls) from birth to 12 years of age were able to screen from these households whose age/date of birth could be ascertained after preparing own calendar based on their local events, festivals and incidents. Sick children and children whose age could not be ascertained were excluded from the study.

Weight and height of the selected children were measured wearing minimum clothes and bare footed adopting cross sectional design using standard techniques and instruments (Weiner and Lourie, 1969). All measurements were recorded by a trained and qualified team of anthropologists.

Double keyed data entry was done on Microsoft Access 2003. Inconsistency and logical checks were carried out with the help of query design on Microsoft Access. Data validation and cleaning was done routinely during data entry for computation of body mass index. Nutritional status was evaluated using the age and sex.

Specific cut-off points of BMI as described by Cole et al. (2007) was used. Thinness was defined as low BMI for age and was graded as III, II, I (severe, moderate and mild, respectively) defined to pass through BMI values of 16.0, 17.0, and 18.5 kg/m2, respectively, at age 18 years (Cole et al., 2007). Student's *t*-tests were used to see the significance of differences in means between the sexes at each age group as well as between sexes on an overall basis.

Results

Anthropometric Characteristics

The mean weight, height and BMI of the subjects are presented in Tables 1 and 2. There was no significant sex difference in height in all age groups while weight of the boys was significantly higher at age groups 12–18 months and 108–120 months in comparison to girls (Tables 1 and 2). Thus, the boys were neither heavier nor taller than their corresponding girls. Similar to height and weight, mean BMI values were significantly higher ($p < 0.05$) only between 132 to 144 old among boys.

Mean BMI varied from 13.3 to 14.5 kg/m^2 between ages irrespective of sex following no consistent pattern. In comparison to Cole et al. (2007) standards, the Gond children averagely fell below Grade II level of thinness, thereby meaning that these children were moderately undernourished (Table 2).

Table 1

Age and Sexwise Mean Weight and Height of Gond Children

Age (in months)	*Weight*		*Height*	
	Girls	*Boys*	*Girls*	*Boys*
	Mean±SD	*Mean±SD*	*Mean±SD*	*Mean±SD*
<= 6	5.4±1.6	6.9±1.3	61.3±9.8	60.6±5.2
> 6–12	6.4±1.3	7.9±1.9	66.6±6.3	68.6±5.6
>12–18	7.4±1.4	8.3±1.42*	71.7±9.0	73.6±8.6
>18–24	7.9±1.6	8.8±1.6	75.9±6.8	77.1±6.9
>24–30	8.8±1.9	9.9±1.7	79.5±8.5	80.6±.2
>30–36	9.6±2.1	10.9±2.1	83.4±8.5	83.5±7.2
>36–48	10.9±2.4	12.5±2.2	89.7±9.5	89.7±9.6
>48–60	12.4±2.7	13.9±2.9	95.9±11.2	97.2±8.6
>60–72	14.0±2.8	15.7±2.6	104.1±10.1	102.5±10.3
>72–84	15.4±3.0	17.8±3.4	110.2±8.8	110.0±8.5
>84–96	17.4±3.3	19.2±3.2	115.9±8.7	116.1±9.1
>96–108	19.2±2.9	21.0±3.6	121.7±8.0	120.4±7.8
>108–120	20.7±3.3**	23.0±3.9	125.1±8.5	125.6±10.2
>120–132	22.0±4.1	25.0±3.9	128.0±11.1	128.8±9.4
> 132	24.1±5.1	24.1±5.1	133.3±10.7	132.9±12.8

*: P<0.05 and **: p< 0.01.

Table 2

Age and Sexwise Mean Values of BMI of Gond Children

Age (in months)	*BMI Male*			*BMI Female*			*t value*	*p value*
	N	*Mean*	*SD*	*N*	*Mean*	*SD*		
6	150	13.3	1.34	131	13.08	1.49	1.29	p>0.05
12	122	14.53	2.56	134	14.3	2.12	0.78	p>0.05
18	130	13.42	2.12	135	13.46	1.96	0.16	p>0.05
24	131	13.58	1.69	123	13.41	1.51	0.85	p>0.05
30	106	14.08	2.36	126	14.4	2.58	0.99	p>0.05
36	157	13.5	2.05	174	13.57	1.7	0.34	p>0.05
48	335	13.93	2.45	304	13.77	2.47	0.82	p>0.05

Cont'd...

...Cont'd

60	306	13.41	2.1	317	13.54	2.27	0.74	p>0.05
72	298	13.08	1.58	249	13.04	1.73	0.28	p>0.05
84	217	13.17	1.74	214	13.09	1.87	0.46	p>0.05
96	215	13.3	2.07	179	13.2	1.57	0.54	p>0.05
108	160	13.53	1.85	140	13.41	1.45	0.63	p>0.05
120	153	13.17	1.77	135	13.12	1.69	0.25	p>0.05
132	169	13.45	1.67	123	13.35	1.76	0.49	p>0.05
144	185	13.84	2.6	139	13.32	1.81	2.12	p<0.05

*: p<0.05 and **: p< 0.01.

Nutritional Status

Table 3 presents the prevalence of thinness by age and sex among Gond children. Overall prevalence of thinness was 79 per cent and 75.6 per cent among boys and girls respectively after combining all age groups from age two onwards. The rates of Grade III and Grade II thinness were higher among boys (Grade III = 36.4%, Grade II = 20.7%) compared with boys (Grade III = 34.4%, Grade II = 20.1%).

Table 3

Nutritional Level (Thinness) According to BMI (%) of Gond Children Using Cole's BMI Standard

Age	*Boys*					*Girls*				
	G-I	*G-II*	*G-III*	*Overall*	*Normal*	*G-I*	*G-II*	*G-III*	*Overall*	*Normal*
2	21	17.1	40	78.1	21.9	17.7	18.5	33.1	69.3	30.7
2.5	16.9	18.8	48.0	83.7	16.3	25	17.4	39.5	81.9	18.1
3	22	24.5	36.5	83	17	23.8	16.6	37.1	77.5	22.5
3.5	24.6	17.7	29.7	72	28	20.6	22.7	29	72.3	27.7
4	17.2	19.9	43.7	80.8	19.2	17.4	23	39.1	79.5	20.5
4.5	21.6	21.1	36.2	78.9	21.1	17.2	15.9	29.8	62.9	37.1
5	20.3	25.9	34.3	80.5	19.5	22.3	19	34.1	75.4	24.6
5.5	20.6	19.4	42.6	82.6	17.4	23.7	20.3	33.1	77.1	22.9
6	21.1	17.3	35.6	74.0	26	22.6	18.3	31.3	72.2	27.8
6.5	26.1	20.7	35.1	81.9	18.1	16.6	21.9	39.6	78.1	21.9
7	24.5	17	25.5	67	33	24.7	21.5	20.4	66.6	33.4
7.5	15.9	15.9	43	74.8	25.2	20.7	26.4	29.9	77	23
8	30	11.2	25	66.2	33.8	35.7	23.7	20.3	79.7	20.3

Cont'd...

...Cont'd

8.5	29.5	20.5	28.2	78.2	21.8	34.9	12.8	29.1	76.8	23.2
9	17.5	19.3	47.4	84.2	15.8	22.6	24.5	35.8	82.9	17.1
9.5	23.9	26.1	30.7	80.7	19.3	24.1	13.9	35.4	73.4	26.6
10	23.2	26.1	36.2	85.5	14.5	13.6	25.3	45.8	84.7	15.3
10.5	25.8	33	21.6	80.4	19.6	24.7	31.1	31.1	86.9	13.1
11	22.1	24.7	45.5	92.3	7.7	12.9	11.3	67.7	91.9	8.1
11.5	22.4	19.4	34.7	76.5	23.5	25.6	31.1	33.8	90.5	9.5
12	0	14.3	71.4	85.7	14.3	50	0	0	50	50
Total	21.9	20.7	36.4	79	21	22	20.1	34.4	76.5	23.5

Table 3 clearly reveals that thinness level of children of either sex keep changing depending upon the availability of the nutrition. The proportion of undernourished children (thinness Grade III, II and I) of the present study of both sexes in comparison to internationals standards of thinness cut-offs provided by Cole et al. (2007) was exorbitantly high as depicted from Figure 2.

Figure 2

Comparison of Present Study Children with Cole's BMI Grades of Thinness

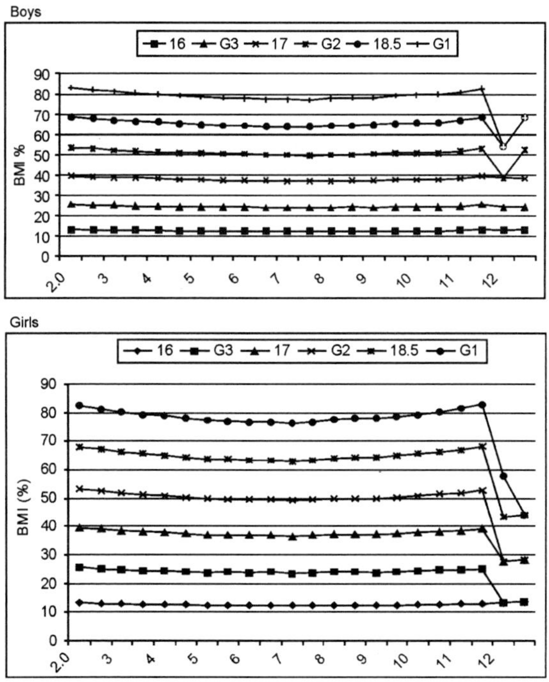

Discussion

The undernutrition continues to be a problem of considerable magnitude in India and is one of the reasons behind the high child mortality rate. Madhya Pradesh has the highest incidence of undernutrition among the Indian states and India has the highest incidence of childhood malnutrition in the world (Bamji, 2003). Further, the highest tribal population of the country dwells in Madhya Pradesh. The low nutritional status of tribal population in general and that of children in particular is a matter of a serious concern (Yadav and Singh, 1999). It is also highly detrimental for health of those children who survive to adulthood. India has adopted a multi-dimensional strategy to combat these problems and to improve the nutritional status of the population (Government of India, 2002–03). Needless to say, there is an emergent need to have tribalwise accurate information of undernutrition to assist policy planners. The present study is an endeavour to understand the prevalence of thinness of Gond children using BMI values and comparing the same with other available studies. BMI is known to track undernutrition significantly from childhood to adolescence, and then to adulthood as reported by Deshmukh et al. (2006). However, the less attention has been paid to the importance of assessing body mass index to monitor undernutrition.

Cole et al. (2007) developed international standards for BMI thinness cut-off points of children from age 2–18 years. They had also stated that undernutrition is better assessed as thinness (low body mass index for age) than as wasting (low weight for height). Prior to this report, there were no suitable thinness cut-off points for this age group. These cut-offs provide a classification of thinness for public health purposes and helpful for direct comparison of trends in child and adolescent thinness worldwide. The findings of the present study clearly revealed that the nutritional status of Gond children were poor with high rates of thinness in boys (79%) and in girls (76.5%). It is worth mentioning that there exists no significant sex difference in different rate of thinness (level of undernutrition). Further it is evident from Table 3 that high percentage of present children are suffering from Grade III, II and I level of thinness in comparison to international standards provided by Cole et al. (2007).

Figure 2 presents overall comparison of the prevalence (%) of undernutrition using thinness (BMI). Previous studies such as Bauri children (66.2%) (Das and Bose, 2009), urban slum children (57.4%) (Goel et al., 2007), ICDS children (63%) (Bhalani and Kotecha, 2002), urban children (60%) (Bhat et al., 1997), Bhopal children (58%) (Ray et al., 1990), rural Bengalee children 50.7 per cent, (Biswas et al., 2009), Odisha children

48 per cent (Mishra and Mishra, 2007), and slum children 51 per cent (Sen, 1994) have reported lower prevalence of thinness than the present study (77.7%). Most of these studies were delved on pre-school children. Thin children are more likely to grow into thin adults with a low BMI that would have an impact on their work productivity as well as lead to greater rates of morbidity and mortality.

The present study concludes that Gond children are severely undernourished in comparison to other studies. The findings of this study had important implication for policy makers and planners giving alarming message for immediate appropriate public health nutritional intervention programme.

References

Bamji, M.S. (2003): "Early nutrition and health: Indian perspective", *Journal of Current Science*, 85(8): 1–6.

Bhalani, K.D. and P.V. Kotecha (2002): "Nutrition status and gender difference in the children of less than 5 years of age attending ICDS Anganwadis in Vadodra city", *Indian Journal of Community Medicine*, 27: 124–129.

Bhat, I.A., S. Amin and G.N. Shah (1997): "Impact of socio-medical factors on pre-school malnutrition: An appraisal in an urban setting", *Indian Journal of Maternal and Child Health*, 8(1): 5–8.

Biswas, S., K. Bose, S. Bisai and R. Chakraborty (2009): "Prevalence of thinness among rural Bengalee pre-school children in Chapra, Nadia district, West Bengal, India", *Mal J Nutr*, 15(2): 155–164.

Blössner M., M. de Onis and R. Uauy (2006): "Estimating stunting from underweight survey data", in K. Bose (ed.), *Ecology, Culture, Nutrition, Health and Disease, J Hum Ecol*, 14: 145–152.

Census of India (2001): Govt. of India: Ministry of Home Affairs, Registrar General and Census of Commissioner, India.

Cole, T.J., M.C. Bellizzi, K.M. Flegel and W.H. Dietz (2000): "Establishing a standard definition for child overweight and obesity: International survey", *Journal of British Medical*, 320: 1240–1243.

Cole, T.J., K.M. Flegel, D. Nicholis and A.A. Jection (2007): "Body mass index cut-offs to define thinness in children and adolescents: International survey", *Journal of British Medical*, 335(7612): 194–197.

Das, S. and K. Bose (2009): "Anthropometric characteristics and nutritional status of Bauri preschool children of Nituria block, Purulia, West Bengal", *Internet Journal of Biological Anthropology*, 3(2).

——. (2011): "Prevalence of thinness among Santal pre-school children using new body mass index cut-off points", *Journal of Anthropology*, 2011: 1–4. (Article ID 602782)

Deshmukh-Taskar, P., T.A. Nicklas, M. Morales, S.J. Yang, I. Zakeri and G.S. Berenson (2006): "Tracking of overweight status from childhood to young adulthood: The Bogalusa heart study", *Eur. Journal Clin. Nutr*, 60: 48–57.

Goel, M.K., R. Mishra, D.R. Gaur and A. Das (2007): "Nutrition surveillance in 1–6 years old children in urban slum of a city in Northern India", *Internet Journal of Epidemology*, 5(1).

Government of India (2003): Economic Survey (Annual Report 2002–03), New Delhi: Government of India.

Mishra, B. and S. Mishra (2007): "Nutritional anthropometry and pre-school child feeding practice in working mothers of central Orissa", *Studies on Home and Community Science*, 1(2): 139–144.

Ray, S.K., P. Roy, S. Deysarkari, A. Lahiri and B.B. Mukhopadhaya (1990): "A cross sectional study of undernutrition in 0–5 years age group in an urban community", *Indian Journal of Maternal and Child Health*, 1(2): 61–62.

Sen, P.K. (1994): "Nutritional status of under five children in an urban slum community of Calcutta", *Indian Journal of Public Health*, 38(3): 113–114.

Vaid, S. and N. Vaid (2005): "Nutritional status of ICDS and non-ICDS children", *Journal of Hum Ecol*, 18(3): 207–212.

Weiner, J.S. and J.A. Lourie (1969): *A Guide to Field Methods*, IBP Handbook No. 9, England, Oxford: Blackwell Scientific Publication.

World Health Organization (1995): Physical Status: The Use and Interpretation of Anthropometry, Technical Report Series No. 854, Geneva: World Health Organization.

Yadav, R.J. and P. Singh (1999): "Nutrition status and dietary intake in tribal children in Bihar", *Journal of Indian Pediatrics*, 36: 37–42.

8

Determinants of Nutritional Status among the Dhodias in Coastal Region of Gujarat

SWAPAN KUMAR KOLAY

Malnutrition is a devastating problem, particularly among the poor and unprivileged. Children are most vulnerable to malnutrition due to low dietary intakes, inequitable distribution of food within the household, improper food storage and preparation, dietary taboos, infectious diseases, and care. Prevalence of malnutrition has remained a problem of considerable magnitude in most developing countries (Devi and Geervani, 1994). Malnutrition causes both emotional and physical suffering (Smith and Haddad, 2000) and is responsible for more than one-half of all children's deaths worldwide (Pelletier et al., 1995). Adults who survive malnutrition as children are less physically and intellectually productive and suffer from higher levels of chronic illness and disability (Smith and Haddad, 2000).

Among the Dhodias, prevalence of malnutrition among rural preschool children of coastal belt are remarkable. Empirical investigations have identified the problems of poverty and food insecurity which have prevailed among the low income population as well as high costs of living and dearth of animal protein among the causes of malnutrition.

The objective of this study is to measure the nutritional status of pre-school children, determine the factors that influence nutritional status and estimate the degree of nutritional status. It is expected that the findings from the study would serve as a guide to policy makers, extension staff, food nutritionists and households seeking to achieve some meaningful improvement in Dhodia children's nutritional status in Gujarat.

Method

Data Collection

The population of Gujarat in 2001 Census has been 50,671,017. Of this 7,481,160 persons are the Scheduled Tribes (STs) constituting 14.8 per cent of the total population of the state. In the coastal belt of Southern Gujarat, Surat and Valsad are two districts with largest concentration of tribal groups. Among the tribals, Dhodias constitute the largest percentage (about 37%) of all tribal groups in Valsad (3.59 lakh, Census of India, 2001) and Bhil and Chandhuri together constitute 40.5 per cent of all the tribal population in Surat with each having a strength of 2.06 lakh and 2.16 lakh respectively. Dhodias were, therefore a logical choice as it was the largest coastal tribe of district Valsad. The research work on Dhodias of Valsad has brought important information about nutrition and their bio-cultural determinants. The quantum of qualitative and quantitative anthropometric and other data is presented in Table 1.

Table 1

Quantum of Qualitative, Quantitative, Anthropometric and Other Data Collected During Fieldwork

District/State/ Population (Sample Size)	*Qualitative (Sample Size)*	*Quantitative (No. of subjects)*	*Anthropometric (No. of subjects)*	*Haemoglobin content estimation (No. of subjects)*
Valsad, Gujarat (Dhodia)	FGD= 14 Case studies= 25	Household Schedule= 450	382 Subjects	382 Subjects

Study Area

Valsad district is bounded on north by Navsari district of Gujarat, on the east by the Maharastra state, on the south by Dadra & Nagar Haveli and Maharastra state and on the west by the Arabian Sea. It is situated between 20°07' and 21°05' north latitude and between 72°43' and 73°00' east longitude (Figure 1). The total area of the district is 5,244 sq kms which comprise of 2.68 per cent of the total area of the state of Gujarat. Information on 450 households have been collected from nine villages from three of the five talukas, namely, Valsad, Pardi and Umergaon. The list of these villages along with taluka's name is given in Figure 1..

Figure 1

Location of Study Area

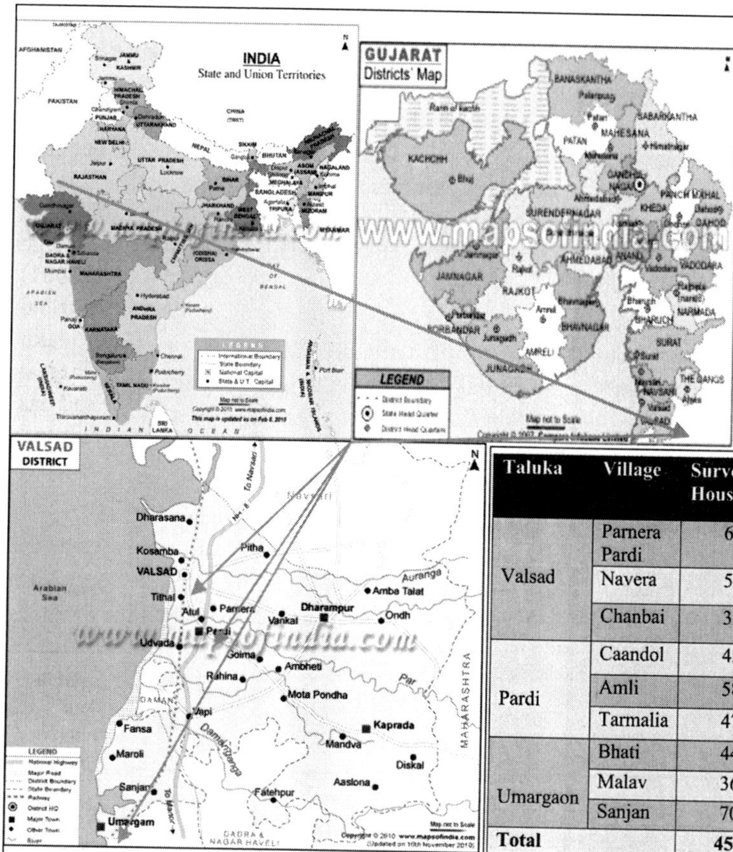

Taluka	Village	Surveyed Household
Valsad	Parnera Pardi	65
	Navera	50
	Chanbai	35
Pardi	Caandol	45
	Amli	58
	Tarmalia	47
Umargaon	Bhati	44
	Malav	36
	Sanjan	70
Total		**450**

There are two important parameters which are followed for determination of nutritional status of preschool going children: (1) haemoglobin estimation and (2) assessment of nutritional status through anthropometric measurements.

Collection of Blood Sample

1 ml intravenous blood was collected through disposable syringes in EDTA bulb. 1 ml blood was utilized for haemoglobin determination. A total of 382 blood samples comprising 131 males and 251 females were collected for the analysis for haemoglobin determination.

Haemoglobin Determination

Nutritional anaemia is a disease syndrome caused by malnutrition in its widest sense. It has been defined by WHO as a condition in which the haemoglobin content of blood is lower than normal as a result of a deficiency of one or more essential nutrients, regardless of the cause of such deficiency. Anaemia is established if the haemoglobin is below the cut-off points recommended by WHO. By far the most frequent cause of nutritional anaemia is iron deficiency and less frequently folate or Vitamin B_{12}. Details of procedure can be seen in *Laboratory Manual for Health Professionals in Tribal/Rural Areas* (Verma et al., 1994).

Results

The results of the analysis are presented in Table 2. It can be seen that mean Hb content for males was 14.25 g/dl±2.8 g/dl; and for females 12.27 g/dl ± 2.18 g/dl. Thus Hb values of both Dhodia men and women are towards the lower range of the normal values. It can be inferred that the degree of malnutrition in Dhodia is of moderate degree which is substantiate by the fact that a significant proportion of children also reveal to mild to moderate degree of malnutrition. The findings can be viewed in the context of their socio-cultural practices relating to environmental sanitation, personal hygiene, food habits and their attitudes towards modern medicines.

Table 2

Level of Haemoglobin Estimation

Sex	*Number*	*Mean value of haemoglobin (g/100 ml. blood)*	*S.D.*	*Max. Value*	*Min. Value*
Male	131	14.25	2.8	21.61	8.29
Female	251	12.27	2.18	18.75	6.85

Box 1

Major Observations

- Mean Hb values for men (14.25 gm/100 ml. blood) and women (12.27 gm./100 ml. blood) are towards lower range of normal values.
- Nutritional anaemia as reflected from haemoglobin determination, both in men and women Dhodias, is of moderate nature.

Assessment of Nutritional Status through Anthropometric Measurements

For assessing the nutritional status of the children less than or equal to six years old belonging to Dhodia tribal population group Valsad district in Gujarat, a set of anthropometric measurements was undertaken on them. Anthropometric data were collected from the Aanganwadi centres of different villages, the households and primary schools. The data were based on the cross-sectional sample of 332 children ages less than one through six years. Out of these 332 subjects, 174 were males and 158 females. Salient findings of the present study are discussed below. In all, 12 body measurements were taken, viz., crown heel length (up to two years)/standing height, body weight, skinfolds (skinfold at biceps, triceps, sub-scapular, supra iliac and calf sites), waist circumference, hip circumference, head circumference, chest circumference and mid-upper arm circumference.

The results of each of the 12 measurements mentioned above for both boys and girls are presented in Table 3. The statistical values provided for each variable include mean, standard deviation and standard error of mean and the range. It is clearly evident from the tables that irrespective of sex, there is even growth in each of the body measurements at successive ages. The *t*-values calculated for estimating the significance of the bisexual differences at different ages among Dhodia are presented in Table 3. It can be seen from the table that the bisexual differences, in general, are statistically non significance for most of the measurement below three years. The differences become significant only after three years of age for various measurements. However, standing height, waist circumference, hip circumference and the mid-upper arm circumference are the measurements, which do not show bisexual differences by and large. It can thus be inferred that Dhodia boys and girls under six years of age, in general, reveal similar pattern of growth for various body measurements in the present study.

Besides numerous other contributory factors, cultural practices among Dhodias are also responsible for these similarities. A girl child is never looked down upon in the society. There is no oppression and incidence of domestic violence is negligible. As far as diet is concerned, both sons and daughters get equal preference. Dhodia women enjoy respectable status in the society.

Data on Indian population is available for six measurements on boys and girls of various ages. ICMR Technical Report Series No. 18 (1994) which gives only four measurements, viz., body weight, standing height, crown heel length, chest circumference and head circumference are comparable to the present study. Similarly, Ghosh (1992) provides data on additional measurements, i.e., mid-upper arm circumference for the children belonging to better socio-economic class.

Table 3

The Statistical Values for Standing Height/Crown Heel Length among the Dhodias of Gujarat

Age Group (Year)	*Sample Size*		*Mean (Cm.)*		*S.D.*		*S.E.M. (cm)*		*Range*			
									Min.		*Max.*	
	M	*F*	*M*	*F*	*M*	*F*	*M*	*F*	*M*	*F*	*M*	*F*
0–1	23	23	63.57	62.82	5.35	3.84	1.11	0.80	52	58.2	68.3	70.0
1–2	24	22	74.76	74.28	4.87	4.78	1.00	1.02	61.2	65.8	80.4	84.5
2–3	30	18	86.26	84.69	4.59	4.57	0.84	1.08	77.1	77.0	94.4	92.3
3–4	37	28	92.68	93.10	6.43	5.37	1.05	1.01	69.1	82.2	102.3	105.0
4–5	24	24	98.30	98.54	5.36	4.94	1.09	1.02	86.8	89.3	108.3	106.1
5–6	36	43	105.72	105.76	6.20	5.24	1.03	0.80	92.6	93.2	118.2	115.1

Protein calorie malnutrition (PCM) has been identified as a major health and nutritional problem in India. It appears among children in the early childhood, generally below six years. It is an important cause of morbidity and mortality in children and leads to impairment of physical and mental growth of the individuals who survive. The incidence of PCM in India in preschool age children is one to 2 per cent. A great majority of cases of around 80 per cent are in the category of mild to moderate form, which frequently go unnoticed. To identify children requiring nutritional and health intervention, a number of classifications have been proposed. Gomez classification which is weight for age percentage is based on weight retardation. Water laws classification defines two groups for PCM. Malnutrition with retarded growth, which is height for age percentage indicating stunting and malnutrition with low weight, which is weight for height indicating wasting (Sadhukan and others, 2010).

Another indication of PCM is mid-upper arm circumference, which is a reliable estimate of body's muscle mass. Between age one and five years, mid-upper arm circumference hardly varies. Any arm circumference exceeding 13.5 cm is sign of a satisfactory nutritional status, between 12.5 and 13.5 cm indicates mild to moderate malnutrition and below 12.5 severe malnutrition.

Table 4

Nutritional Status of Dhodia Children According to Weight for Height and Height for Age

Nutritional Status	*% of Weight/Height*			*% of Height for Age**		
	Boys (n = 174)	*Girls (n = 158)*	*Total (n = 332)*	*Boys (n = 174)*	*Girls (n = 158)*	*Total (n = 332)*
Normal	37.20	35.92	36.60	39.63	42.25	40.85
Mild	43.29	36.62	40.20	43.29	44.37	43.79
Moderate	15.85	23.24	19.28	15.24	13.38	14.38
Severe	3.66	4.23	3.92	1.83	0.00	0.98

*Normal >90	<95
Mild 80–90	87.5–95
Moderate 70–80	80–87.5
Severe < 80	<80

Table 5

Assessment of Degree of Malnutrition of Dhodia Children to Weight for Age

Nutritional Status	*% of Weight/Age**		
	Boys (n = 174)	*Girls (n = 158)*	*Total (n = 332)*
Normal	11.59	16.20	13.73
Mild	46.34	42.25	44.44
Moderate	37.20	35.21	36.27
Severe	4.88	6.34	5.56

*Normal 90–110; Mild 75–89; Moderate 60–74; Severe <60

Tables 4 and 5 show frequency of undernutrition according to various classifications. It can be seen from the tables that about 59 per cent boys and 60 per cent girls suffer from mild to moderate forms of malnutrition according to weight for height whereas 58 per cent of boys and of girls suffer from mild to moderate forms of undernutrition with respect to height for age. Similarly, 77 per cent of girls 84 per cent of boys suffer from mild to moderate forms of malnutrition with respect to weight for age. In the present study boys are found to be more vulnerable as compared to girls in weight for age.

Moreover, mean mid-upper arm circumference among boys and girls are invariable above 13.5 cms in age groups two and above indicating their satisfactory nutritional status.

The entire ratios and mean upper arm circumference in the present study do not indicate any extraordinary situation regarding malnutrition. These children are apparently small but not unhealthy. One must also consider that this group of tribal children belongs to coastal population of Gujarat. Further few severe cases of clinical signs of malnutrition like marasmus and protein calorie malnutrition have been recorded in the annual report of civil hospital, Valsad district, Gujarat. The prevalence of the high frequency of mild to moderate forms of malnutrition can be attributed to infections like diarrhea, respiratory infections besides poor maternal health during and at the time of delivery, unavailability and underutilization of health services among many. Cultural practices relating to environmental sanitation, personal hygiene, food habits and their attitudes towards modern medical care go a long way in elevating their suffering.

Box 2
Major Observations

- Bisexual differences for 12 body measurements were not statistically significant for most of the measurements, revealing significant for most of the measurements, revealing similar pattern of growth among boys and girls.
- A comparison of Dhodia boys and girls with the comparable data on Indian rural boys and girls and girls and boys from better socio-economic class did not reveal any great differences with them.
- At least 58 per cent of boys and girls suffer from mild to moderate malnutrition according to weight for height and height for age.
- Mean mid-upper arm circumference among Dhodia boys and girls in the age group 2 and above (>13.5 cm.) does not indicate not any unusual nutritional status.

Factors Affecting Nutrition according to Place of Residence

Three talukas of Valsad district were studied under present investigation namely Valsad, Pardi and Umergaon. Among these three talukas, Valsad taluka is the centre place of the district and is the administrative centre. The

Zilla Panchayat Bhavan houses all the important administrative offices. The distance of different villages under study from taluka headquarters is as follow: The average distance of different villages from taluka headquarters in Valsad is 9 kms, while in Umergaon it is 15 kms and in Pardi it is 13 kms. Villages of Valsad taluka are nearer to the taluka headquarters while in Pardi and Umergaon talukas villages are situated far off and in remote area. A comparative study showed that rural children are more likely to suffer from chronic energy deficiency than children in urban areas. These higher rates of rural malnutrition were also reported by local district hospital, Valsad district, Gujarat (Morbidity Report 2003–04, Valsad Civil Hospital, Gujarat).

Household Economic Status

The pattern of annual household income obtained from different households in the present study is presented in Table 6. It can be clearly seen that 59 per cent of the total population of Dhodias are relatively poor. Middle income group constitutes 40 per cent of total population and slightly less than 1.5 per cent of Dhodia population can be considered as prosperous. As in the case of women, the economic status of a household is also one of the most important determinants of child nutritional status (UNICEF, 1990). Comparative studies on child nutrition for more than 15 countries (Sommerfelt et al., 1994) and Dhodia studies shows that the higher the level of economic status of the household, the lower the level of child stunting.

Table 6

Annual Household Income

Category	*Percentage of Household (n = 450)*
< ₹ 25,000 (Poor)	58.85
₹ 25,000– 60,000 (Lower-middle)	28.77
₹ 60,000–1,50,000 (Moderate)	10.97
> ₹ 1,50,000 (Prosperous)	1.41

Education of Mother

Literacy rate is evident from Table 7. Female literacy was found to be 73.6 per cent. Nearly 18 per cent of the men and women were illiterate. Literacy rate among Dhodias is much higher than its corresponding figure of 26 per cent in Indian tribal groups, 61.29 per cent for Gujarat and 58.38 per cent for Indian national population. Education is one of the most important resources that enable women to provide appropriate care for their children, which is an important determinant of children's growth and development

(Engle and Menon, 1996). Study shows a decreased incidence of malnutrition among young children with an increase in the level of mothers' education. The significance and direct relationship of the child's mother's education concurs with the assertion that maternal schooling is strongly associated with good child care and good health (Maxwell et al., 2000). More education for women is associated with higher levels of household food availability, higher quality diets, better care practices and behaviours and better nutritional outcomes. This finding makes a good case for the use of educational empowerment and capacity building of women as a means of promoting food and nutritional status of children in particular and household members in general.

Table 7

Literacy Rate Among Dhodias

Literacy	*Percentage (n = 2012; < 6yrs excluded)*
Illiterate	17.45
Literate	82.55
Total	100.00
Literates	
Primary	29.43
Middle	27.92
High School	26.83
Higher Secondary	9.12
Graduate and Other	6.70
Total	100

Employment Status of Mothers

Table 8 presents the pattern of occupation among Dhodias. It can be seen that there is a great degree of variability in the occupational pattern. Besides being primarily agriculturists, they have taken up to private and

Table 8

Types of Occupation Among Dhodias

Type	*Percentage (n = 450)*
Labour	24.23
Private Job	25.51
Agriculture	26.67
Government Job	13.30
Business	10.29

government jobs and also have started their own business. Although women's employment enhances the household's accessibility to income, it may also have negative effects on the nutritional status of children, as it reduces a mother's time for childcare. Some studies have revealed that mothers of the most malnourished children work outside their home (Popkin, 1980; Abbi et al., 1991). Another study argued that there is no association between maternal employment and children's nutritional status (Leslie, 1988).

Source of Water and Availability of Toilet Facility

In the present investigation it was found that 83 per cent of the household (Table 9) use water from the boring as primary source of drinking water. In 78 per cent of cases, the source was located within the village and in 21 per cent of cases within the house. Thus, quite a few Dhodia households have their own boring in the house.

Table 9

Sources of Drinking Water

Source	*Percentage of Family Users (n = 450)*
River	1
Boring	82.9
Tap (owned)	2.8
Well	14.2
Total	100

Table 10

Disposal of Wastewater in Dhodias

Disposal Category	*Percentage of Houses (n = 450)*
Closed drainage	0.3
Open drainage	0.8
No drainage	98.9
Total	100

Unfortunately, 85.6 per cent of the (n = 450) houses do not have their own toilets and they defecate outside. But 14.4 per cent of the houses have their own flash toilets. In the present study among the Dhodias, it can be seen (Table 10) that 99 per cent of the houses have no drainage which is a perpetual source of poor environmental hygiene. Unfavourable health environment caused by inadequate water and sanitation can increase the probability of infectious diseases and indirectly cause certain types of malnutrition (UNICEF, 1990; Engle, 1992). This study showed that unprotected water source and non-availability of latrine were associated with low child stature.

Child Morbidity

Diarrhea and other infectious diseases manifested in the form of fever affect both dietary intake and utilization, which may have a negative effect on improved child nutritional status. Crude death rate (CDR) has been estimated to be 8.7 for Indian national population and 7.9 for the population of Gujarat. CDR for Dhodias has been estimated to be 7.8, which is less than the figure of Gujarat and Indian national population. Infant mortality rate (IMR) is a very sensitive indicator of mortality indicating a pre-natal and post-natal care of mother and infants. IMR has been estimated to be 70/1,000 live births for Indian national population and 63/1,000 live birth for Gujarat. IMR for Dhodias was estimated to be 73/1,000 live births, which is comparable to both Indian national population and Gujarat. A comparative study on children's nutritional status (Sommerfelt et al., 1994) indicates that stunting was highest among children with recent diarrhea.

Childcare Practices in Dhodias

Table 11 presents childcare practices among Dhodias. It can be seen from the table that 85 per cent of the infants get their first feed as mother's milk

Table 11

Childcare Practices Among Dhodias

Childcare Practices	*Percentage*
I. First feed given to infant (n = 130)	
(a) Mother's milk with colostrums	84.9
(b) Mother's milk without colostrums	12.0
(c) Jaggery water	1.9
(d) Any other	1.2
II. Age at first supplementary diet (n = 114)	
(a) 6 months	48.0
(b) 6–12 months	30.2
(c) After one year	21.8
III. Duration of breastfeed (n = 308)	
(a) 1 year	6.7
(b) 2 year	74.5
(c) 3 year	16.5
(d) More than 3 years	2.1

with colostrums. Further, 86 per cent of infant also receives their feed within two hours of their birth. As far as initiation of supplementary diet is concerned, it is between 6 and 12 months of age. Similarly, 74 per cent of Dhodias new borns are breastfed up to two years. Only 7 per cent of Dhodia new born leave their mother's milk by the end of first year of life. In the present context two years of breastfeeding is a long duration and can be reasoned out from the fact that most of the Dhodia women are involved in household activities and in those income generation activities, which do not require them to leave their kids at home.

Age of Child

Children's nutritional status is also more sensitive to factors such as feeding/weaning practices, care, and exposure to infection at specific ages. A cumulative indicator of growth retardation (height-for-age) in children is positively associated with age (Anderson, 1995 as cited in Aschalew, 2000). Dhodia children have also shown an increase in malnutrition with increase in age of the child.

Immunization Status

Table 12 presents status of child immunization among Dhodias. It is clear from the table that Dhodias are highly motivated for immunization. In this regard efforts of the government have been appreciable. More than 95 per cent of the children have been vaccinated for DPT, polio and BCG. Performance in administration of vaccination for measles and Vitamin A prophylaxis needs further strengthening of efforts in this direction. Incidentally government institutions is the primary source of vaccination in more than 95 per cent of cases. By and large immunization coverage is very high in Dhodias of Valsad district.

Table 12

Status of Child Immunisation among Dhodias

Type of Vaccination	*Percentage of Responses*	
	Yes	*No*
DPT (n = 130)	95.0	5.0
Polio (n = 128)	96.1	3.9
BCG (n = 130)	96.1	3.9
Measles (n = 128)	69.9	30.1
Vitamin A (n = 127)	70.1	29.9

Birth Order

It has been found that Dhodia parents give less attention to older children when they give birth to a new child who needs much attention and care. One study showed that stunting is rare in birth order 2–3 (Sommerfelt et al., 1994), and higher birth order (5+) is positively associated with child malnutrition (Jeyaseelan, 1997).

Birth Interval of the Child

Closely spaced pregnancies are often associated with the mother having little time to regain lost fat and nutrient stores (ACC/SCN, 1990). Higher birth spacing is also likely to improve child nutrition, since the mother gets enough time for proper childcare and feeding. Studies in developing countries showed that children born after a short birth interval (less than 24 months) have higher levels of stunting.

Interrelationship between Maternal and Child Nutrition

Birth weight, child growth, and adolescent growth determine nutritional status before and during pregnancy (maternal nutrition). Maternal nutrition also influences fetal growth and birth weight (ACC/SCN, 1992). The presence of an intergenerational link between maternal and child nutrition means a small mother will have small babies who in turn grow to become small mothers. Some findings on the relationship between maternal and child nutrition (Loaiza, 1997; Teller et al., 2000; Genebo et al., 1999) showed that a high proportion of low-birth-weight and stunted children were observed among malnourished mothers.

Conclusion and Policy Implications

It was found that household economic status, education of parents, pre-natal care, visits of the mother (for access to health services), child's age, birth order and preceding birth interval are important determinants of child stunting.

This study arrives at the following conclusions to improve women and children nutritional status. Most of the socio-economic variables affect the nutritional status of children. It was also found that there exists a strong association between maternal and child nutritional status and maternal nutritional status and birth weight. This indicates that actions towards improving women and child nutrition should always be integrated for effective utilization of scarce resources and to reduce the risk (mother-child) of undernutrition.

This study revealed that children of very poor or low economic status households have the highest rates of malnutrition. This may be due to food insecurity in these households that negatively impacts the nutritional status of children in particular and the other household members in general. Therefore, measures should include government action to support the very poor, and to bring about rapid economic growth at the national level. It is important to develop community-based interventions giving priority to very poor households as a short-term solution. Urgent implementation of poverty reduction strategies and programmes designed by the government could also serve as a long-term solution to the problem.

It should be noted that over 27 per cent of women reported having no education. It is therefore necessary to promote universal education of girls and women. The results showed that education of parents is one of the important determinants of children's nutritional status. Children of educated parents are at a lower risk of malnutrition, if the risks observed for other variables are eliminated. This indicates that parents who receive even a minimal basic education (even in the poor households) are generally more aware than those who are not educated of the need to utilize available resources for the improvement of the nutritional status of their children. It is therefore imperative that young girls and boys be enrolled in compulsory primary school education and opportunities should also be given to adult women and men to take part in non-formal education. Health and nutrition education should also be an integral part of the education process.

Close spacing of births, i.e., having a preceding birth interval of less than 24 months, showed a significant nutritional deficit in the younger children, particularly in the rural areas of Valsad district of Gujarat. This may be associated with risk factors such as mothers' inadequate capacity for caring for her children. The mother herself may be biologically depleted from too frequent births, and this could also negatively affect the nutritional status of the newborn baby. Therefore, access to services for child spacing could benefit the youngest child and the mother. Prolonging the intervals between births, through increasing demand for family planning and/or fulfilling unmet need for family planning, could be important elements of strategies to improve child nutrition.

This study has also indicated that exclusive breastfeeding up to 6 months of age is not widely practised nor is the timely introduction of weaning foods at about 6 months. Therefore, education with this regard is also important intervention.

Therefore, further research on socio-cultural practices, intra-household food distribution, women's workload, seasonal food insecurity, and other related factors is suggested.

Acknowledgement

I am greatly indebted to Dr G. Kshatriya and Prof. A.K. Kapoor, Department of Anthropology, University of Delhi, Delhi for providing necessary help in connection with the presentation of this paper.

References

Abbi, R., P. Christian, S. Gujral and T. Gopaldas (1991): "The impact of maternal work on the nutrition and health status of children", *Food and Nutrition Bulletin*, 13(1): 20–24.

Administration Committee on Coordination, Sub-Committee on Nutrition (ACC/SCN) (1990): Women and Nutrition, Symposium Report, Nutrition Policy Discussion Paper No. 6.

Administration Committee on Coordination, Sub-Committee on Nutrition (ACC/SCN) (1992): Second Report on the World Nutrition Situation, Vols. 1 and 2, Global and Regional Results, New York.

Census of India (2001): Ministry of Home Affairs, New Delhi.

Devi, P.Y. and P. Geervani (1994): "Determinants of nutritional status of rural preschool children in Andhra Pradesh, India", *Food Nutr. Bull.*, 15: 335–342. www.unu.edu/unupress/food/8F154e/8F154 E0c.htm.

Engle, P.L. (1992): "Care and child nutrition", Theme paper for the International Conference on Nutrition (ICN), paper prepared for nutrition section, UNICEF, New York.

Engle, P.L. and P. Menon (1996): *Urbanization and Care Giving: Evidence from South and Eastern Africa*, San Louis, California: Department of Psychology and Human Development, California Polytechnic, State University, pp. 4–24.

Genebo, T., W. Girma, J. Hadir and T. Demmissie (1999): "The association of children's nutritional status to maternal education in Ziggbaboto, Guragie Zone, South Ethiopia", *Ethiopian Journal of Health Development*, 13(1): 55–61.

Ghosh, S. (1992): *The Feeding and Care of Infants and Young Children*, New Delhi: VHAI.

ICMR (1984): ICMR Technical Report Series No. 78, New Delhi: ICMR.

ICMR (1994): ICMR Technical Report Series No. 18, New Delhi: ICMR.

Jeyaseelan, L. (1997): "Risk factors for malnutrition in south India children", *Journal of Biosocial Science*, 1: 93–100.

Kshatriya, G.K. (2000): "Ecology and health with special reference to Indian tribes", in M.K. Bhasin and V. Bhasin (eds.), *Man-Environment Relationship*, Delhi: Kamla-Raj Enterprises, pp. 229–245.

Leslie, J. (1988): 'Women's work and child nutrition in the Third World", *World Development*, 16(1).

Loaiza, Edilberto (1997): *Maternal Nutritional Status*, DHS Comparative Studies No. 24, Calverton, Maryland, USA: Macro International Inc.

Maxwell, D., C. Levin, M. Armar-Klemesu, M. Ruel, S. Morris and C. Ahiadeke (2000): Urban Livelihoods and Food and Nutrition Security in Greater Accra, Ghana, Research Report 112, Washington, DC: International Food Policy Research Institute (IFPRI).

Pelletier, D.L., E.A. Frongillo, D.D. Schroeder and J.P. Habicht (1995): "The effects of malnutrition on child mortality in developing countries", *Bull. W. Health Org.*, 73: 443–448.

Popkin, B.M. (1980): "Time allocation of the mother and child nutrition", *Ecology of Food and Nutrition*, 9: 1–14.

Sadhukhan, S.K., Chatterjee, Shrivastava, Sardar, G.K. Joarda, Lahiri (2010): "Validity of arm circumference to detect protein energy malnutrition among 8–11 months old infants in a rural medical college of West Bengal", *Journal of Indian Medical Association*, Kolkata, Sept., 108(9): 559–562.

Smith, L.C. and L. Haddad (2000): Explaining Child Malnutrition in Developing Countries: A Cross Country Analysis, Research Report 111, Washington, DC: International Food Policy Research Institute (IFPRI).

Sommerfelt, A. Elizabeth and S. Kathryn (1994): *Children's Nutritional Status*, DHS Comparative Studies No. 12, Calverton, Maryland, USA: Macro International Inc.

Teller, H. and G. Yimar (2000): "Levels and determinants of malnutrition in adolescent and adult women in southern Ethiopia", *Ethiopian Journal of Health Development*, 14(1): 57–66.

UNICEF (1990): Strategies of Improving Nutrition of Children and Women in Developing Countries, New York.

Verma, I.C., M. Kaur and G.P. Das (1994): *Laboratory Manual for Health Professionals in Tribal/Rural Areas*, Genetic Unit, New Delhi: AIIMS.

9

State of Tribal Health in Odisha

With Special Reference to Maternal and Child Health

PRADEEPTA RANJAN PATTANAYAK

Health is an important indicator of the overall development of any society, as the importance of good health can never be underestimated in a progressive society. But it is a paradox that sometimes a sizeable section of the society does not have its rightful place in the health profile of the society, i.e., having a large number of malnourished people, having precarious premature mortality situation, not having proper access to health facilities owing to a host of reasons, and as a natural consequence, suffers from ill-health. A number of cross-country studies and micro studies have energized the potential linkage between the health profile and the GDP growth of states (Malenbaum, 1970; Wheeler, 1980). It has also been established that the contribution of a fit and healthy person to the economy is much higher as compared to those who suffer from ill-health (Martorell and Arroyave, 1984; Deolalikar and Behrman, 2002). The discussion on the relationship between nutritional status or health and labour productivity has found place in many other studies (Leibenstein, 1957; Mazumdar, 1959; Stiglitz, 1976; Bliss and Stern, 1978). Abysmal health condition and premature death reduces the life expectancy of the people and therefore also reduces their investment incentive on education and other areas. As it has a significant bearing on the future of economic growth, the vicious circle of poor health and slow economic growth rate moves on. The role of state intervention is important to the extent when development becomes equitable and its dividends accrue to all sections of the society. But, on the contrary, our experiences since the last sixty-five years of independence suggest a highly imbalanced picture, so far as the position of different sections in the health profile of the country is concerned.

The position of tribal health is even more alarming, as these groups inhabit in the remote forest and hilly areas far from civilization, they are largely unaffected by the developmental processes going on in the rest of the non-tribal areas of the country. The causes of poor tribal health are numerous and they present, to use Ogburn and Nimkoff's terminology, *spiralling feedback causation* among themselves. Malnutrition and mortality have a positive co-relation among themselves. However, it would be a knee-jerk generalization, if other variables affecting the above health indicators are not taken into consideration. They are poverty or poor economic conditions, illiteracy and/or low literacy, unavailable/inadequate/inaccessible health care services resulting in high morbidity, socio-cultural barriers preventing utilization of available health care services, etc.

Poverty or poor economic conditions lead to food insecurity especially during the lean period of summer and monsoon months. As a result of which the tribals have to take recourse to some other alternative to food grains. Here in this distress situation, unhealthy coping mechanisms come in to play to compensate the absence of food grains. At times it plays havoc with their health and life. Many lives were lost in the oft-repeated Kalahandi, Balangiri, Koraput (KBK) of Odisha in the early eighties, by consuming porridge made out of mango kernel powder out of hunger and in the absence of food grains. Poor economic conditions also reduce the chances of availing the better health care facilities. *Low literacy* or lack of proper education leads to lack of awareness of the better sanitation and hygiene practices. Poor sanitation and unhygienic practices aggravate infections and infestations leading to high incidence of morbidity and the consequent mortality (Bulliya and Kar, 2009). *Inadequate health infrastructure* is also a stumbling block in the efforts to improve the tribal health situation. Lack of access to health care facilities owing to a host of socio-economic reasons (i.e., poverty, road connectivity, transport facility, etc.) also contribute to the poor tribal health situation. *Social practices* of black magic, witchcraft and divinations prevalent in tribal communities are the recourse taken for diseases and prevent them from making use of the available health care services (Rout, 1966). The tribal culture has its own *norms of modesty* with regard to male-female interaction, which is also a barrier in achieving better health status for the tribals (Mohapatra, 1986, 1993). For instance, the treatment of the pre-natal stage of women has been opposed in many tribal communities as it deviates from the norms of female modesty. The doctor who examines a pregnant woman requires a certain degree of intimacy with her, which as per the accepted norms only the husband should have. *Pride and dignity* or *ethnocentrism* is also a factor which keeps away the tribal from the mainstream and as such posing a serious challenge to their assimilation with the great tradition.

Odisha: The Tribal Profile

Being the homeland of as many as 62 tribal communities, the state of Odisha continues to enjoy a unique position in the ethnographic map of India. It has got the largest variety of tribal communities vis-à-vis other states. From among the total of 62 tribal communities 13 are particularly Vulnerable Tribal Groups (PTGs). The state ranks third in the country in terms of its tribal population, i.e., 8.15 million, accounting of about 10.8 per cent of the tribal population of India. Tribals in Odisha constitute 22.13 per cent of the state's population. The literacy rate among the tribals of Odisha is not that encouraging even after sixty-five years of independence especially when a parallel is drawn with the other social groups in terms of their literacy rates. According to the Census Report of 2001, while the literacy rates among the men of general castes and Scheduled Castes (SCs) are little over 70 per cent, the men of Scheduled Tribes (STs) are lagging far behind with a literacy rate of just little over 50 percentage points. Similarly, when it comes to female literacy, the women belonging to the castes of general category and STs are having a literacy rate of more than 40 percentage points, whereas the women belonging to the STs are having a literacy rate of just little over 23 percentage points. For a precise understanding of the comparative literacy situation in Odisha, we can refer to the table given hereunder:

Table 1

General, SC and ST Literacy Rate in Odisha

Year	*General*		*SC*		*ST*	
	Male	*Female*	*Male*	*Female*	*Male*	*Female*
2001	73.3.5	50.51	70.47	40.33	51.48	23.37

Source: Census of India, 2001.

The concept of tribal health is either over-tuned or under-tuned depending on the researcher, the tribal community and the time period of the study. In Odisha, often the concept of tribal health is less felt and over said. The reasons are many – a study carried out in the most backward Kalahandi, Balangiri, Koraput (KBK) districts of Odisha reveals an indifferent attitude with less pragmatic understanding of the empirical practices of the tribals, and health care services made available to them has led to the present situation. Majority of the tribal groups in Odisha live in the remote forest and hilly areas far from civilization, as such they are largely unaffected by the developmental processes going on in the rest of the state. Therefore, these groups remain backward, particularly in health, education and other socio-economic aspects. Despite constituting a sizeable chunk of the state's population, their health status is in dire straits. Sixty-five years of independence does not carry any significance for them. They suffer from the terrible syndrome of relative deprivation as compared to other social groups and communities of the state so far as their health status is concerned. It is a matter of serious concern and poses a stiff challenge before the state, the civil society, and the policy makers. Of late, this problem of the tribals of Odisha has been recognized in the country and needs to be urgently remedied. However, very few empirical studies dealing with these problems were taken up in the past. This paper is a modest attempt to extend little help in analysing the tribal heath situation in Odisha (with special reference to maternal and child health) in comparison with other social groups, and its supposed remedy.

This paper makes use of the data from the secondary source – NHFS-2 and 3, Census Reports, Human Development Reports, 2004 and 2005 (published by Government of Odisha). It revolves around the comparative analysis of the health status of tribal women and children along with the other social groups, as every sane society places importance on protection and nourishment of its future generation and its nurturer – the children, their mothers, using all its might and mane.

For the purpose of analysis a pertinent parallel was drawn between tribal mother and children and the mother and children of other social groups to bring out the possible relative deprivation of the tribal groups. Health inputs like immunization, institutional delivery, ANC visits, etc., are used to arrive at a clearer picture as to where do the tribals stand vis-à-vis other social groups in the state. Considering the role of education for the promotion of knowledge and awareness of different diseases, their causes and consequences, education was used as an independent variable.

Comparative Analysis of the Health Situation of the Tribals

The Situation of Premature Mortality

IMR, UFMR and child mortality[1] in Odisha, in spite of their declining trend, continue to be at very high level, given the national standards. The table given hereunder makes a comparative analysis to this effect.

Table 2

Tribal Health Situation vis-à-vis Other Social Groups: Premature Mortality

Source	*Category*	*IMR*	*Child Mortality (1–4)*	*UFMR*
NFHS-3	SC	73.7	19.5	91.8
	ST	**78.7**	**62.5**	**136.3**
	OBC	66.0	18.8	83.5
	Others	53.1	11.7	64.2
	Total	64.7	27.6	96.6
NFHS-2	SC	83.9	42.4	122.7
	ST	**98.7**	**44.0**	**138.4**
	OBC	95.6	20.1	113.8
	Others	79.1	15.0	92.9
	Total	81.0	25.5	104.4

A sharp fall was recorded by SC, OBC, and among other castes in all types of mortality rates (as seen in Table 2). But among the STs, there is fall in IMR, but marginal fall in UFMR. What is more disturbing is that child mortality has experienced an increase during the period among the STs. It has increased by 18.5 percentage points. This implies that there must be some serious problem among the children. This may be in their food and nutrition deficiency or due to various infections which requires further study on their diet and nutrition.

Poor Tribal Health: Reasons

Considerably low weight at birth, non-availability of professional attendance at birth and lack of post-natal care are generally accounted as the reasons for high child death rate. Among the tribal women, proportion of deliveries at the health institutions is low; in Odisha it is 17.3 percentage points, compared to a fairly high of 91.6 percentage points in Goa and 1.5 percentage points in Uttar Pradesh – thus the professional attendance at birth is low (25.5% in NFHS-3). The following analysis tables helps us analyse the health situation of the tribal women and children as against the other castes of Odisha.

As per the data (taken from NHFS-3) presented in the above Tables 3, the health situation of the tribals in Odisha is not just a wake up call, but its a kind of alarm bell for all the stakeholders. It is found that Iron deficiency anaemia is highest among tribal women, i.e., 73.8 per cent, while the figures for the other three groups are fairly encouraging. Likewise, the professional ante-natal check up was lowest among tribals. In case of institutional delivery, the tribals also lag far behind the other social groups of the state. Iron deficiency, failure to get antenatal check-up may be accounted for reasons for low weight at birth and other related problems. In case of child immunization the tribals do not also stand on a better footing than the other social groups, which might have a direct bearing on infant and child death rates as well as poor nutritional status among the tribals.

Table 3

Child Immunization and ANC Visit

Category	*Child Immunization*		*ANC visit (3 or more) Percentage Points*	*Hospital Delivery*	*Delivery assisted by Health Personal*	*Anaemia*		*IFA Consumption (Mothers)*
	Complete	*Zero*				*Children*	*Mother*	
SC	59.5	03.7	58.6	30.2	39.1	63.5	64.2	64.7
ST	**30.4**	**22.3**	**46.0**	**11.7**	**17.3**	**80.1**	**73.8**	**58.3**
OBC	59.4	03.1	66.3	40.6	53.6	58.7	58.6	72.8
Others	58.0	15.9	74.4	60.4	66.9	58.2	53.4	72.1

Health Facilities: Still Far from Being Accessible

Another important factor which plays a pivotal role in improving the health status is the access to health facilities. Here, the information is collected from District Statistical Handbook of 1991 Census. Table 4 below shows that people in the tribal infested districts of the state have poor access to health facilities as against the industrially developed coastal districts of the state:

Table 4

Percentage of Villages in Different Districts: Tribal Infested and Coastal, without the Medical Facilities and the Transport Connectivity (within 5 km Distance)

Districts	*Medical Institutions*	*Transport Connectivity*
Cuttack	28	37
Puri	37	31
Balasore	36	35
Bolangir	50	41
Phulbani	59	59
Kalahandi	63	54
Sundergarh	54	41

From the table given above it is very clear that at least half of the villages in the tribal infested districts (indicated in bold letters) did not have medical facility within 5 km distance. But, in stark contrast to this, the coastal districts clearly have an improved situation so far as the availability of medical facility is concerned. Similarly poor transport connectivity in the tribal infested districts has obviously aggravated the health situation of the tribals.

Table 5

Availability of Medical Facilities (Districtwise) with ST Percentage and Doctors (per sq km)

District	*ST (%)*	*Doctors/Sq Km*
Cuttack	3.57	0.15
Khurda	5.19	0.08
Puri	0.30	0.05
Koraput	49.73	0.02
Malkangiri	60.32	0.01
Kandhamal (Phulbani)	51.98	0.02
Mayurbhanj	56.64	0.03
Nowrangpur	55.45	0.02
Raygada	56.31	0.02
Kalahandi	28.68	0.02

Sources of the computed data: Orissa HDR, 2004, Census Abstract, 2001, and OVHA, 1995.

The data given in the above table proves beyond doubt that the tribal dominated districts (given in bold letters) having 50 per cent or more tribal population have access to lesser number of doctors per sq km as compared to the districts of the coastal area having majority of non-tribal population, which have got comparatively higher number of doctors per sq km.

Economic Status and Health

Economic position of the people plays a very important role in achieving better health status. This is more so when the provision for public health care fails to achieve its desired objective. Private spending on health rises when the quality of public health care deteriorates. It is an established fact that owing to the absence of doctors in the government hospitals, people seek the help (paid services) of private physicians and also travel to distance places to avail the same even incurring high expenditure and as a consequence fall in the debt trap. This phenomenon is more acute in the interior and tribal dominated districts. Table 6 clearly reveals almost an inverse relationship between economic condition and the different categories of mortality rates (Data Source: NFHS-2 and NFHS-3).

Table 6

Wealth Index (Economic Position) and Premature Mortality in Odisha

Source	*Wealth Index*	*IMR*	*Child Mortality*	*UFMR*
NFHS-3	Lowest	79.8	42.3	118.7
	Second	73.2	27.4	98.6
	Middle	51.7	14.0	64.9
	Fourth	51.4	15.1	65.7
	Highest	28.2	0.0	28.3
NFHS-2	Lowest	101.1	40.9	137.9
	Middle	83.5	14.4	96.7
	Highest	32.8	1.4	34.1

It becomes crystal clear from the above table that those occupying highest position in the wealth index have got very less mortality rates compared to those placed in the lowest income group. Needless to say that the higher income group must have got better access to all types of resources including health, nutrition, and education. Majority of tribals do not belong to these classes.

Conclusion

After considering the state of tribal health in Odisha (especially maternal and child health) as discussed in the paper, it can be fairly concluded that the situation is alarming. The health condition of tribal children and women indicate a very bleak picture compared to that of the children of the other social groups. While SCs, OBCs and other castes have experienced sharp fall in all types of mortality rates, among STs, the situation is very discouraging. In health inputs like institutional deliveries, immunization, consumption of IFA tablets by expectant mothers, the tribals lag far behind the other non-tribal social groups. Comparatively, health care facilities are still far from accessible to them owing to a host of reasons. Poor health status of the tribals has got a positive and significant association with their economic condition. It was found that those occupying higher position in the wealth index have got better access to good health care facilities and as such present an impressive picture so far as their overall health status is concerned. Since tribals in Odisha live under the shades of abject poverty and sub-human living conditions, having a better heath profile is a far off dream for them. The chasm between health status of tribals and non-tribals as found out in the analysis of this paper, needs to be urgently bridged to live up to the dreams of our constitutional progenitors, who wanted to give India a sovereign socialist democratic republic, which secures to its citizens – justice – social, economic and political. Imbalanced growth of different sections of the society portends a dangerous signal for the future of our democracy (Pattanayak, 2004). Hence the problem in question – the alarming health status of the tribals needs to be addressed with a multi-pronged strategy with the involvement of all the stakeholders.

Based on the above analysis, the state needs to play a pro-active and responsive role, especially for the weaker sections in the backward areas of the state. Health related programmes in the tribal communities usually fail owing to lack of community participation and understanding of such programmes. Hence, there is no demand of the services offered but are imposed upon the community without a taker. As such, the health workers must have a pragmatic understanding of the practices followed in the community to ensure better community participation. Community behavioural change effort is needed to positively impact the indifferent attitude of the population for whom the programme is aimed at. Efforts should be spared to raise the physical access which will promote economic access and improve their health conditions. Promotion of female literacy (functional literacy for women) needs to be undertaken to reduce the IMR and UFMR. Attempts need to be made to see to it that there is an increase in the percentage of mothers making ANC visit. The government should raise the funds allocated to achieve the better health status of the people.

Note

1. *IMR*: The number of deaths to children under 1 year of age per 1,000 live births.
   Child Mortality: The number of deaths to children of 1 to 4 years of age per 1,000 live births.
   UFMR: The number of deaths to children under five years of age per 1,000 live births.
   Ethnocentrism: Used as a technical term for the view of things in which one's own group is the centre of everything and all others are scaled and rated with reference to it.
   Ethnography: The descriptive account of the way of life of a particular society.
   PTGs: Most backward and Particularly Vulnerable Tribal Groups facing extinction in the state.

References

Ali, Almas (1987): "Food Habits, Nutrition and Health Status of a Primitive Tribe of Orissa", Proceedings of Nutrition Society of India, New Delhi.

Ali, Almas and Sikha Nayak (1995): *Status of Health in Orissa*, Bhubaneswar: Information and Documentation Cell, Government of Orissa.

Bhattacharya, M. (1999): "Tribal Health: Food and Nutrition", in H.C. Upadhyay (ed.), *Status of Scheduled Tribes in India*, New Delhi: Anmol Publications.

Bliss, C. and N. Stern (1978): "Productivity, Wages and Nutrition, Part-II: Some Observations", *J. Development Econ.*, 5 (December).

Bose, N.K. (1971): *Tribal Life in India*, New Delhi: National Book Trust.

Bulliya, G. and S.K. Kar (2009): "Diet and Nutrition Issues of STs and Primitive Tribal Communities of India", *Critical Issues in Tribal Development*, Bhubaneswar: SCSTRTI.

Census Reports (1991 and 2001): Registrar General and Census Commissioner, New Delhi.

Deolalikar, Anil B. and Jere R. Behrman (2002): "Health and Nutrition", in Hollis Chenery and T.N. Srinivasan (eds.), *Handbook of Economics*, Vol. I, Amsterdam: North-Holland Press.

Leibenstein, Harvey, (1957): *Economic Backwardness and Economic Growth*, New York: Wiley.

Malenbaum, W. (1970): "Health and Productivity in Poor Areas", in Herbert Klarman (ed.), *Empirical Studies in Health Economics*, Baltimore: The Johns Hopkins University Press.

Martorell, R. and G. Arroyave, (1984): Malnutrition, Work Output and Energy Needs, (Manuscript), California: Stanford University Press.

Mazumdar, D. (1959): "The Marginal Productivity Theory of Wages and Disguised Unemployment", *Rev. Econ. Studies*, 26 (June).

Mohanty, S.C. (2009): "Tribal Development in Orissa: Some Areas of Concern", *Critical Issues in Tribal Development*, Bhubaneswar: SCSTRTI.

Mohapatra, L.K. (2008): "Tribal Health Situation: A Prospective Analysis in Orissa", paper presented in National Seminar on 'Critical Issues in Tribal Development', Bhubaneswar.

Mohapatra, Sitakant, (1986): *Modernization and Ritual: Identity and Change in Santal Society*, Calcutta: Oxford University Press.

——. (1993): *The Tangled Web: Tribal Life and Culture of Orissa*, Bhubaneswar: Orissa Sahitya Academy.

NFHS-2 (2000): National Family Health Survey-II (1988–99) India, Mumbai: International Institute of Population Sciences.

NFHS-3 (2007): National Family Health Survey-III (2005–06), India, Mumbai: International Institute of Population Sciences.

Orissa Human Development Report (2004): Bhubaneswar: Government of Odisha.

Orissa State Development Report (2001): Bhubaneswar: Government of Odisha.

Panda, M. (2002): "Poverty in Orissa: A Disaggregated Analysis", paper presented in NCDS Workshop on 'Poverty Monitoring', Bhubaneswar.

Pasayat, Chitrasen, (1998): *Tribe, Caste and Folk Culture*, Jaipur: Rawat Publications.

Pattanayak, P.R. (2004): "Democracy and Development: Conceptual Cousins or Counter Concepts?", *Indian Bar Review*, Vol. XXXI (1 and 2), Bar Council of India Trust.

Rath, G.C. (2006): *Tribal Development in India*, New Delhi: Sage Publications.

Rout, S.P. (1966): "Witchcraft among the Santhals of Mayurbhanj", in *Adibasi*, Vol. VIII, No. 4, THRTI.

Stiglitz, J.E. (1976): "The Efficiency Wage Hypothesis, Surplus Labour and the Distribution of Income in Less Developed Countries", *Oxford Economic Papers 28* (July).

Strauss, J. (1986): "Does Better Nutrition Raise Farm Productivity?", *The Journal of Political Economy*, Vol. 94, Issue 2 (April).

Wheeler, D. (1980): "Basic Needs Fulfillment and Economic Growth: A Simultaneous Model", *Journal of Development Economics*.

10

Saharia Primitive Tribal Group in Madhya Pradesh

Critical Evaluation of Welfare Measures Related to Health

YATINDRA SINGH SISODIA AND TAPAS DALAPATI

Tribal community originates from one of the oldest ethnological sections of population, lived in isolated areas as a distinct group both culturally and usually backward – socially, educationally and economically. Different tribal groups are living in various degrees of economic backwardness. They live generally in inhospitable terrain where productivity of soil is low and their hamlets are found in the interior forest areas along with the hill streams. There are no communication facilities between the various isolated groups, as well as between the tribal and the world at large. Their lands are dry and there are no irrigation facilities. The typical topography of undulating and hilly areas have made tribal area agriculturally less profitable. Because of distinct way of living, pattern of behaviour, customs and traditions, the programmes for their advancement ought to be in consonance with the social realities of their life. With this reason, various governmental programmes/schemes both from the centre and state are being chalked out and implemented for the upliftment of their lot, so that they may join the mainstream of national life.

India, after independence, became a welfare state wedded to the idea of democratic socialism and aimed at providing a minimum desirable standard of living to every citizen without any sort of discrimination. In order to meet this avowed objective, the whole developmental process is directed not only towards the advancement of resources, but also towards their equal distribution, so that every citizen of the country could get the fruits of development and his due share in the national wealth. This process involves protection of state, in order to bring them closer to the normal living standards of their fellow citizens by overcoming their helplessness caused by their social and economic backwardness. Keeping this goal in view, various legislative and welfare measures for the upliftment of these sections have been envisaged in the Indian Constitution, in the form of various concessions and special benefits and protection to them to raise their position in the social ladder alongwith their economic development.

The tribal development approach attempted to remove disparities between tribal and other developed areas and also to improve the quality of their life. The twin approach aims at forcing area development with problem solving with greater emphasis on (i) increase in productivity and income, (ii) development of human resources, (iii) elimination of exploitation, and (iv) infrastructure development.

The identification of the Scheduled Tribes (STs) is done on the basis of the following ideal characteristics: (i) primitive traits; (ii) distinctive culture; (iii) geographical isolation; (iv) shyness of contact with the community at large; and (v) backwardness. However, it is observed that not all these communities are at the same level of development. In fact, there are certain communities, which are at a much lower level of development even as compared to the other ST communities. It is also observed that in the matter of devolution of funds for the development of STs, the major share is taken by those communities that are more assertive and in a better position in demanding such benefits. As a consequence, the marginalized STs are left out in the process of development. In order to ensure the development of these communities, certain groups were identified for the first time in 1975–76 and thereafter in 1993, which are regarded as the poorest of poor amongst the STs and are called primitive tribal groups (PTGs). The criteria fixed for identification of such PTGs are: (i) pre-agricultural level of technology; (ii) very low level of literacy; and (iii) declining or stagnant population.

With the advent of the Fifth Five-Year Plan, a fresh diagnosis was made and it was decided to adopt a new strategy for the development of the tribal communities living totally a secluded life. These communities faced different type of problem due to their ecological settings, and were at a different level of agricultural development. Efforts were made to identify such primitive tribal communities on the basis of recommendations of the Working Group on Tribal Development and guidelines issued by the

Ministry of Home Affairs, GoI (1984) deciding three criteria to identify primitive tribal community, viz. (i) stagnant or diminishing population; (ii) pre-agricultural level of technology; and (iii) extremely low level of literacy. In this context, having small size of the community, pre-agricultural stage of economy, high extent of isolation, low level of literacy, etc., 75 tribal communities among all tribal groups of India have been scheduled as primitive tribes. In Madhya Pradesh, three tribal groups have been declared as primitive tribes on the basis of these criteria during the Fifth Five-Year Plan: (a) Baigas of Mandla, Dindori, Shahdol, Umariya and Balaghat districts of Madhya Pradesh; (b) Saharia of Gwalior and Chambal division of Madhya Pradesh; and (c) Bharias (of Patalkot) of Chhindwara district of Madhya Pradesh. The economy of these primitive tribes is based on agriculture and forest. The subsidiary occupation of the tribe is casual wage-earning and collection of leaves and other minor forest produce.

In Madhya Pradesh, Saharia is the largest primitive tribe demographically and its total population is 3.23 lakh. The term 'Saharia' means the companion of a tiger. According to legend, they have been blessed by the Lord Shiva and have access to the jungle like a *sher*, meaning tiger or lion. They live in the states of Rajasthan and Madhya Pradesh. The sporadical concentration of Saharia is not only limited by political boundary in Madhya Pradesh, but their dispersals are also located in Rajasthan, Andhra Pradesh, Odisha, Bihar and rarely in West Bengal. Etymological point of view expresses that the word 'Saharia' is the combination of two independent words like 'Sa' (companion) and 'Haria' (tiger) which means companion of tiger. All the settlement patterns of the tribe are found on the middle top of the hill.

In every dispersed Saharia village, hamlet or 'falia' is regarded as the first ecological unit. Most of the Saharia tribals depend on ecology, which plays an important role in forming their economic structure. The post-economic history implies that they traditionally practised shifting cultivation, hunting, gathering, pastoralism, etc., and sometimes adopted nomadic life also. Nevertheless, in the present time, most of the Saharias have become daily wage earners instead of their traditional way of occupation. Most of them are landless and poverty-stricken. Bread is considered their staple food. Nevertheless, sometimes, due to unavailability of wheat, they consume roots, tubers, leaves, etc., which are collected from the nearby forest. They are very much addicted to drinking local wine. They usually face shortage of water. Even their useable water from well and sometimes from tube-well is neither clean nor purified. Most of the Saharias are dominated by nuclear families. They are strictly clan exogamous and tribal endogamous. They generally practice negotiation and monogamy form of marriage at very early age. Influencing with their low socio-cultural pattern, most of the Saharias prefer to have a male child. Modern family planning contraceptive methods are rarely adopted among them. Literacy rate among Saharias is 23.2 per cent (which is very low), it accounts for 28.2 per cent and 17.7 per cent for male and female Saharias respectively.

The whole developmental process is directed not only towards the advancement of resources, but also towards their equal distribution, so that every citizen of the country can get the fruits of development and his due share in the national wealth. This process involves protection of state, in order to bring them closer to the normal living standard of their fellow citizens by overcoming their helplessness caused by their social and economic backwardness. Keeping this goal in view, various legislative and welfare measures for the upliftment of these sections have been envisaged in the Indian Constitution, in the form of various concessions and special benefits and protection to them to raise their position in the social ladder as well as their economic development. Because of distinct way of living, pattern of behaviour, customs and traditions, the programmes for their advancement ought to be in consonance with the social realities of their lifestyle. With this reason, various governmental programmes/schemes both from the centre and state are being chalked out and implemented for the upliftment of their lot, so that they may join the mainstream of national life.

Although there was progress as per Human Development Indices in the conditions of the STs, yet the benefits were not percolating to the PTGs, that lived in not only far flung regions but in remote and inaccessible areas and in small numbers. Therefore, in 1998–99, a Special Central Sector Scheme was introduced with the objective to cover those items/activities which, though very crucial for the survival, protection and development of PTGs, are not specifically catered to by any existing schemes, state or central or by guidelines governing the utilization of funds under Special Central Assistance to Tribal Sub-Plan and Article 275(1) of the Constitution. Such items/activities cannot be exhaustively identified at the central level as they may differ from state to state and even within a state, and from project to project. However, funds under the scheme could be used for helping the beneficiaries of the project to cope with extremely adverse pressures, which threaten their survival and protect them from various forms of exploitation thereby bringing them to a stage when they can demand and receive specific assets and services.

Health is a prerequisite for human development and is essentially concerned with the well-being of common man. The UNDP Human Development Index (HDI) comprises three components, i.e., health, education and income generating capacity. Health is a function, not only of medical care, but also of the overall integrated development of society – cultural, economic, educational, social and political. The health status of a society is intimately related to its value system, philosophical and cultural traditions, and social, economic and political organization. Each of these aspects has a deep influence on health, which in turn influences all these aspects. Hence, it is not possible to raise the health status and quality of life of people unless such efforts are integrated with the wider effort to bring about overall transformation of a society. Health development can be integrated with the larger programme of overall development in such a manner that the two become mutually self-supporting. Good health and good society go together. This is possible only when supportive services such as nutrition and improvements in the environment and in education reach a higher level (Basu, 2000).Though, good health is a foundation stone for holistic development of a society, unfortunately most of the tribes and especially primitive tribal groups in India are confronting several health problems, which are engendering their marginalization through a vicious cycle of poverty, malnutrition and ill-health. Therefore, several initiatives are undertaken by different state governments for ensuring health care facilities for conservation-cum-development of different primitive tribal communities within their state.

Studies on Saharia health depicts that the prevalence of malnutrition was more among Saharia females as compared to male. On comparing the socio-cultural norms and traditions among Saharias, it is found that the males are given preferential treatment for food and other necessities over females. The Saharia males are found to be under critical situation and females under serious situation as per prevalence of chronic energy deficiency classified as public health problem by WHO. It is clear that Saharias are severely malnourished, which is severely affecting their wage earning, thereby perpetuating a vicious cycle of poverty, malnutrition and ill-health (Kapoor et al., 2006). Analysing the dietary intake, Rao and his colleagues found higher prevalence of undernutrition both among children as well as adults in Saharia community. The prevalence of underweight and stunting among pre-school children and chronic energy deficiency among adults of Saharia tribe was significantly higher compared to their rural counterparts or those studied in drought affected areas indicates that the tribe was nutritionally highly vulnerable. Practices such as delayed initiation of breastfeeding, discarding of colostrum and faulty feeding habits seem to have significantly contributed to higher prevalence of growth retardation among infants and children of younger age group (Rao et al., 2006). In their study, Biswas and Kapoor (2003) reiterated that most of the

Saharias are landless and they are to be engaged in primary sector as wage earners. Due to paucity of water resources, they usually drink uncleaned and impured water. As interior inhabitation, they lag behind in the field of education and have achieved very little literacy rate. In respecting to their traditional society approved rules and norms, they are to come on marital alliance at very early age. The awareness of family planning contraceptive methods is almost nil. Therefore, early age at marriage and, family planning non-acceptance are the two important reasons which impose them to conduct frequent child births. In such circumstances, the early aged mothers are generally prostrated containing very low health status. Immunization and medical check-up for antenatal, natal and post-natal stages are mostly neglected among them. Even a major group of people are to be affected by various seasonal as well as nutritional diseases. So, poor socio-economic status, malnutrition, impured drinking water, high extent of illiteracy, early age at marriage and frequent child births, non-acceptance of family planning methods, unawareness on immunization, paucity of modern medical facility, worst environment, etc., are the attributed reasons of sharing various diseases which influence frequent deaths. Chakma and others also reiterated chronic malnutrition among pre-school Saharia children. Due to poor dietary habits, Vitamin A deficiency in the form of night blindness, bitot spot, xerosis acute respiratory infection and worm infestation were identified as the major morbid conditions among Saharia (Chakma et al., 1996).

Keeping in view the vulnerable health status of the Saharias, *Shaktiman** scheme and fortification of flour with micronutrients have been introduced by Government of Madhya Pradesh in the Saharia dominated areas. The objectives of this scheme are to arrest malnutrition among the children, improvement of awareness about personal hygiene, safe drinking water, sanitation and cleanliness among the Saharia families. Against this background an evaluation of the performance of welfare schemes specifically in operation in the area of health for the conservation-cum-development of Saharias of Madhya Pradesh has been done. It is well recognized by policy planners as well as by researchers that health is

---

*Shaktiman project is a nutrition development programme implemented in the tribal areas of Madhya Pradesh, where child malnutrition is crucial for their health. The basic objectives of this programme are to check and prevent acute malnutrition among children through Aanganwadi and to educate tribals about healthy food habits and hygiene. Under this programme supplementary nutritional foods and vitamins are distributed among children through Aanganwadi by enhancing frequency of food distribution to thrice a day. The project also encompasses prevention anaemia among pregnant tribal women, to prevent child and maternal mortality.

the most substantive and critical input for the development of child in particular and society in general and when we are talking in terms of primitive tribal groups, it becomes a matter of paramount importance. Special efforts have been made for the betterment of health for PTGs through various schemes. The evaluation study is carried out among Saharias of Madhya Pradesh to assess the role and performance of these schemes for the betterment of tribal community.

II
Fieldwork: Methodology and Context

The objectives of the evaluation study were as follows: to study the operationalization of the health schemes; to assess the impact and effectiveness of the delivery package of services; to know the level of participation of tribal people in the implementation of health schemes; to assess the status of infrastructural/physical facilities provided to tribals; to evaluate the role performance of officials in control, supervision, monitoring and inspection of the schemes; and to find out the practical problems of implementation of the schemes and to suggest viable measures for the betterment of the conservation-cum-development of Saharia primitive tribe in Madhya Pradesh.

The major concern of the evaluation project has been to study the implementation of health schemes for Saharias in Madhya Pradesh. The locale of the study is Gwalior region of Madhya Pradesh. For a proper special coverage, the selection of villages has been done based on operationalization of various health schemes operational in the villages specifically meant for the Saharias. Beneficiaries of the schemes were the unit of observation for this evaluation study. The size of the surveyed beneficiaries was 75. For primary data, interview schedule was administered among the beneficiaries. The interview schedule was broadly divided into two parts. First part dealt with questions related to socio-economic background of tribal beneficiaries. Second part was devoted to scheme specific questions. This part emphasizes on understanding of the schemes, perception about schemes and impact of the schemes. In each selected village, a directional group discussion was organized. The group discussion included the questions related to the specific problems of health among Saharia tribal community and how the governmental schemes have benefited the Saharias to come out of this poor situation. It was also important to make use of observational method to extract information and get insight into the issues involved. A diary was also maintained to record the observations throughout the fieldwork.

III
Findings

Social Background

The profile of the respondents is detailed here. Majority of the respondents are illiterate. The structure of family in Saharias is of mixed nature, more than half of the respondents have nuclear family structure; however, a considerable number has a joint family structure. The family size is invariably high in majority cases and that is the real worry for the attainment of health. Majority of the respondents do labour work either in agriculture or in non-agriculture sector. Majority of the respondents hold *kachcha* houses which are constructed with the use of local materials. More than half of the respondents have the *Antyodaya* card which is given to the extremely poor. One-third respondents have BPL card. This is indeed surprising that a small number of respondents do not have any card. The main source of drinking water is handpump whereas a few other sources like well, river, nallah, pond, tube well are also used by a small percentage of respondents. More than half of the respondents have no land whereas the land available for remaining respondents is also very less and therefore the livelihood base for the Saharias is mostly labour work. The asset holding with the Saharias is very poor, a very small number of respondents hold few basic amenities. Majority of the respondents still live below the poverty line. Considerable majority is still not aware of government's welfare measures available for their development. Usually girls are engaged in various household chores when they are not going to school. It is indeed a very mixed kind of opinion in terms of change in their status. Half of the respondents find no change, whereas a small number feel improvement. Nevertheless, a considerable number of them feel decline in their status. In majority opinion the improvement is discernible in terms of benefit of government schemes reaching to the people. The attitude of the local functionary is negligent and work not available round the year. The long list of different governmental efforts brings that many of the schemes operational in the field are known to the respondents; however, the numbers vary significantly from one scheme to another and their implementation is confined to a few places as compared to the people who know about them.

Schemes Implementation

The exposure and opinion about health related schemes are analysed here. There are two schemes related to health, viz., Shaktiman project for malnourished children and fortification of flour with micro-nutrients.

However, only one scheme of Shaktiman project for malnourished children was found operational in Karahal block of Sheopur district. For the evaluation of this scheme, out of Aanganwadi centres having this scheme, 15 such Anganwadi centres were listed out for survey and from each selected Aanganwadi, five households were chosen for survey. Thus, from 15 Aanganwadi centres, the size of sample was 75. In Saharia-dominated Sheopur district, the project is being implemented by the Women and Child Development Department.

During the survey, a discussion was held with Aanganwadi workers. After discussion it was observed that the Shaktiman project in the region was operational for five months in the year 2008 and out of which the money disbursed to them was only for two months and for the remaining three months the workers borrowed the required items for the implementation of the scheme for which the payment was still pending.

Almost three-fourth Aanganwadi centres opened at regular time however looking into the very important role assigned to Aanganwadi centres the remaining number is still very high. Out of the surveyed 15 Aanganwadi centres, six Aanganwadi workers used to commute distance of 8 to 10 kms. As a result there was uncertainty of opening of such centres and also these centres were more or less dependent on *Sahayika*. Out of 19 respondents who feel that there is irregularity in the opening of Aanganwadi centres, the reasons of irregular opening are different and also vary significantly in terms of opening in a week. Since the project like Shaktiman requires a set up to run its activities and in majority cases the Aanganwadi centres have their own building, however still considerable number depend upon rented accommodation. When the reason of irregularity was asked, they made the point that the irregularity was due to migration for work. Since the family is out for work, children alone cannot remain at home for availing the benefit of such scheme.

An overwhelming majority of the respondents feel that distribution of nutritional food to children is the main activity at Aanganwadi centre which is significant as the scheme under evaluation also falls under the same activity. When this specific question was asked from respondents regarding the frequency of distribution, almost two-third respondents were of the opinion that three months prior for around three to four months, there was distribution of food twice or thrice in a day but for the last three months the supply is only once in a day. Respondents feel that the Aanganwadi worker did not adhere to food chart whereas Aanganwadi workers were of the view that the distribution of nutritional food was based on availability of food items.

It is indeed a matter of concern that the quality of food is bad in the opinion of majority of respondents. The respondents were of the view that mostly the quality of readymade food items was very bad and even the food items cooked at the centre level did not adhere to certain minimum standard required for cooking of eatables. In majority of the cases the respondents have experienced inadequate supply of food items. Majority of respondents consider *Sabji-Roti/Sabji-Pudi* as expected food. Besides this, the demand for the *Dal-Roti, Dal-Chawal* and *Dudh/Kheer* is also very high. It is observed at the village level that many nutritional items listed in the Shaktiman project's diet chart is neither available at village level nor this is expected by the Saharia tribal group. Hence, it can be a better way to address the nutritional food item supply as per the expectations of the respondents instead of making a long exhaustive list of food items.

There is a provision in the Shaktiman project to distribute iron containing tablets to each child along with nutritional food. All the respondents categorically denied that no such tablets are distributed. It is indeed very disappointing to note that such an important provision of the project is not seriously implemented in the opinion of majority respondents. Even when the question of frequency of organization (where organized) of health camps was asked the response was that the camps were held once or twice only.

Shaktiman project is mainly operationalized to provide nutritional food to malnourished children. Besides this, there are certain other responsibilities which are bestowed on Aanganwadi centres keeping in view development of women and children. The health related issues/matters like vaccination are very popular among the respondents. It is indeed a bit disappointing to observe that majority of the respondents do not find the scheme any way effective.

The respondents have come out with a variety of suggestions to improve the scheme. Mostly, the respondents have suggested that the implementation of the scheme is in totality and is in right manner; continuity of the scheme; provision of full meal; and enhancement in the quantity of diet.

The Government of Madhya Pradesh initiated a new scheme for fortification of flour in the year 2007–08 for the PTGs. The scheme will provide micronutrients to the students of PTGs by which the problem of malnourishment will be eradicated. Under this scheme, there was no progress in all the three districts. During survey, District Coordinators of Sheopur and Shivpuri were contacted and they informed that due to unavailability of clear instructions, the scheme could not be implemented.

IV
Conclusion

Saharia is a primitive tribe that has its own cultural norms. Their integration with mainstream society and their development in health totally depends upon how they visualize importance of health in their worldview. Widespread malnutrition and morbidity among Saharias is a result of an alienation from the mainstream society and its health care system. This alienation is result of two-way process: (i) cultural isolation in relation to health, and (ii) inaccessible modern health care system. Saharia's dependence on primary activities like hunting and gathering, and their traditional food intake process with forest-based livelihood have threatened and their traditional sources of nutrition and medicine from traditional sources have been dwindling through widespread deforestation. In addition to this, adverse livelihood opportunities they are lacking minimum standard of well-being in relation to health. As their cultural life is different, it is the task of central government to understate their culture and initiate development programmes to bring them at par with the mainstream society.

Health is a major issue of concern for Saharias. Though, like other PTGs in Madhya Pradesh, their population has not dwindled in the last decade, their quality of human resource and life expectancy rate is very poor as compared to the mainstream society. The major diseases suffered by the Saharias are malaria, diarrhoea and cholera which are caused by poor sanitation habits and poor food intake. The sense of sanitation among Saharias is very poor. They live in traditional huts built by leaves and straws without proper sanitation facilities. The huts also leak very often during rainy season and Saharia live under a very inhuman condition. The first and foremost task should be to educate the Saharias to use safe drinking water, maintain proper sanitation and safe food habits. It is found that most of the Saharias children are malnourished and suffer from various diseases. The Aanganwadi centres and health workers seldom care about health of these PTG and blame their cultural practices for the same. To improve the health of children as well as mother's health care facilities should be exclusively targeted for Saharias and not to be clubbed with any general programme meant for the mainstream communities. Among Saharias there are traditional healers and *dais* who help the rural women during childbirth. These traditional healers and *dais* should be given training about modern health and sanitation practices so that they can educate the Saharias about health care practices and sanitation. The entire programme for Saharias is an extension of main development programme for the mainstream society. The programme for development of tribals like the Saharias should be culture-specific and exclusively target-oriented keeping in view their cultural practices and ways of living. Though government functionaries are ill-equipped to address such culture specific programme, capable NGOs should be entrusted to help build the capacities of Saharias to strengthen their healthcare practices.

Despite all such efforts, it is very clear from the evaluation that there is an urgent need to create awareness, sensitization and capacity among the Saharias for understanding the requirements of development and governmental efforts put in place. The health-related schemes need to be reformulated on the basis of needs assessment of the people. There is a culture of silence in the Saharia society and therefore the need of the hour is to make the society aware and responsive so that they can become active participators in the whole process.

References

Basu, Salil (2000): "Dimension of Tribal Health in India", *Health and Population: Perspectives and Issues*, Vol. 23, No. 2, pp. 61–70.

Biswas, Ranjan Kumar and A.K. Kapoor (2003): "A Study on Mortality among Saharia: A Primitive Tribe of Madhya Pradesh", *Anthropologist*, Vol. 5, No. 4, pp. 283–290.

Chakma, T., P. Vinay Rao, S. Pall, L.S. Kaushal, Manjulla Datta and R.S. Tiwary (1996): "Survey of Pulmonary Tuberculosis in a Primitive Tribe of Madhya Pradesh", *Indian Journal of Tuberculosis*, Vol. 43, pp. 85–89.

Kapoor, Satwanti, Renu Tyagi, Kiran Saluja, Anumeha Chaturvedi and A.K. Kapoor (2009): "Nutritional Profile and Socio-Economic Status of Saharia: A Primitive Tribe of India", *The Open Anthropology Journal*, Vol. 2, pp. 58–63.

Rao, K. Mallikharjuna, R. Hari Kumar, K. Venkaiah and G.N.V. Brahmam (2006): "Nutritional Status of Saharia: A Primitive Tribe of Rajasthan", *Journal of Human Ecology*, Vol. 19, No. 2, pp. 117–123.

Report on Working Group on Tribal Development during the Seventh Plan (1984), Planning Commission, New Delhi: Government of India.

Sisodia, Yatindra S., Ashish Bhatt and Tapas Dalapati (2010): Evaluation of Scheme related to Education and Health for the Conservation cum Development of Saharia Primitive Tribal Group: A Study in Gwalior Region of Madhya Pradesh, Report submitted to the Office of the Commissioner, Tribal Development, GoMP, Bhopal: Madhya Pradesh Institute of Social Science Research, Mimeo.

11

Towards Inclusive Health Management

Case Study of a Tribal Village of Madhya Pradesh

S.N. CHAUDHARY

In order to comprehend health and disease in the historical perspective, especially among tribes, scholars have heavily mainly relied on subjective interpretation across the world. Clements (1932) documented five fundamental reasons of disease as perceived by primitive people. These are: sorcery, breach of taboo, object intrusion, spirit intrusion and soul loss. Most of these reasons are related to spirit or what may be called 'ghost'. Hence, primitive people in particular, living across the globe, have faith in ghost and its ugly face. Under the subjective interpretation experience-based narratives and opinions of people have been elaborated. Their views about both health and diseases differ from culture to culture and from one social group to another. In India also subjective interpretations of health and disease have dominated in both rural and tribal societies. There are large number of studies on individual tribes across the country which disclose their fatalistic interpretation of both health and disease in the historical perspective. Kurian and Tribhuwan (1990), for example, studied perception of Thakur tribe of Raigad district of Maharashtra about disease. He found that causes of diseases as attributed by the tribe are highly supernatural in nature, i.e., visitation of gods and goddesses, warth of gods and goddesses, evil eye, possession by evil spirits, witchcraft and sorcery, breach of taboo and failure to perform divine duty or rites (p. 253). According to Chaudhari (1993), among Hos of Bihar (now Jharkhand), there is the Deuri or religious headman and Deonwa or the spirit doctor. The Deuri worship the deities and when epidemics or diseases are there, he offers a sacrifice at the sacred place. He is entrusted with the benevolent deities. The Deonwa, often through magical performances, controls the malevolent spirits. According to Mathur (1982) also, among Diyan tribe of Kerala, the "goddess Mariyamma cause epidemic like smallpox, chickenpox, measles, etc. Turmeric powder, a bundle of Neem leaves, coconut plantain and five Panams are generally given as the main offerings of Mariamma for curing the above-mentioned diseases" (p. 297). Among the Gonds of Baster, diseases are perceived as the legacy of god. Chaudhary (1998) observed that number of diseases are attributed to the wrath of some deity or spirit or are believed to be due to the violation of some norms, i.e., committing adultery or incest. For these diseases they seek the help of Valpa who diagnoses the cause and prescribes the remedies. They indeed make some distinctions between physical injuries, the cause for which is very obvious and which are not generally attributed to the wrath of the god or spirit and others which are attributable to the gods (p. 50).

It is true that subjective approach is largely based on perception but it has helped in the emergence of healing mechanisms of all varieties, i.e., magic, religion and science. Of course, the functioning of former two dominates in the rural and tribal societies, which is claimed to be relatively simple and isolated, but this does not mean that the latter is completely invisible there. In all the societies even at a given point of time not only more than one variety of treatment are found but also one can see practice of different sub-varieties of treatment which may be categorized within one variety. But as societies moves from tradition to modernity or from relatively homogeneous to relatively heterogeneous situation importance of science gradually increases. Number of modern health management institutions are made popular. And with this, scope and implications of objective interpretation of health also increases. Development of this variety have also taken place in the tribal world. Here, one can see radical departure from *jhar-phuk* practice to the massive use of herbs and medicinal plants in number of diseases. According to Joseph (1989), in Madhya Pradesh and Odisha, the tribal use 156 applications of mammals and their products, 32 of birds, 30 of reptiles, 10 of fish, etc. The use of blood and meat of pigeons is widespread in Odisha for the treatment of paralysis. Derivatives of bear, bat, tiger, wild boar, cow's urine, goat's liver, hen's eggs, honey, snake fat, flesh of earthworms, bones of elephants, etc., are used for various diseases. Lal (1987) attempted to know the role of herbs and medicinal plants to cure bone fracture among the tribes of Mandla, Sidhi, Raipur, Baster, Dhar, Bilaspur and Balaghat of Madhya Pradesh. To him, there are 21 important medicinal plants belonging to 21 genera and 16 families which are used for the treatment of bone fracture in case of both human being as well as domestic animals. These plants are well known to the local medicine men that are known by different names among different tribal groups throughout the state. These findings reveals that tribes have not jumped directly from the use of magico-religious prescription to the use of modern medicine. Rather they have been simultaneously using herbs and medicinal plants for treatment. But gradually with change in their mindset coupled with decreasing easy availability of local herbs and so-called popularization of primary health centre, community health centre and other institutional intervention, their dependence on traditional practices are decreasing and reliance on modern institutions are increasing.

As per objective interpretation of health, whether a person is healthy or not, it is determined by the modern health practitioner. And bases of such determination is also scientific, i.e., test of different organs and components of body purely on scientific basis. According to Lewis (1954), if the various organs work well enough not to draw attention to themselves and their owner is free from pain or discomfort, he usually supposes that he is in good health. This criterion is then a subjective one. But if he avails himself of the mass X-ray service and in consequence learns that his lungs shops strong evidence of tuberculosis disease, he ceases to consider that he is in good health: the criterion now he adapts is an extraneous one, viz. the assertion of a physician who relies on objective or pathological data.

Whether the concept of health is analysed subjectively or objectively, in a broader sense, health refers to a state of complete physical, mental and social well-being. And this well-being needs to be reflected at two levels, firstly, at the society level where one can call a person healthy if he/she is able enough to perform social roles assigned to them, i.e., if able to participate in the reproduction of society. Secondly from the standpoint of the individual where he/she is normally able to maximize growth and happiness. WHO defined the concept of health as "a state of complete physical, mental and social well-being and not merely the absence of disease and infirmity".

With the coming of the state in the tribal areas during pre-and post-independence, number of changes are taking place in both material and non-material culture of tribal masses. Change in health management is one among them. How tribes at large perceive health and disease today? What are the common diseases among them? Do the traditional and indigenous methods and the modern and exogenous interventions go hand in hand or there is conflict between the two? How they perceive and react to the new intervention which is by and large institutional? What is the state of functioning of traditional health management practices? Is there relevance and possibility of integration between the traditional and the modern treatment methods? How functioning of state induced modern health management mechanisms may be made inclusive and tribal-friendly in a sustainable manner? In order to address these issues this paper was written.

The paper is divided into three parts. Opening part deals with Gond tribe and their perception about different aspects of health and disease. It also deals with common diseases in the area and tribal response to these diseases. Part second examines role and status of both traditional and modern coping mechanisms to understand health status as well as techniques adopted to deal with health and disease related issues. Towards the end, some steps have been suggested to manage health and disease among tribes in an inclusive and sustainable manner.

Methodology

The study was conducted in Pathai village of Sahpur development block of Betul district. The logic behind selecting Sahpur block was numerical preponderance of tribal population (64%). In Pathai village more than 99 per cent population is tribal. The entire area of Sahpur is dominated by Gond population and only in some villages Korku tribe resides. Pathai is located at a distance of about 4 kms from Sahpur development block office and Betul-Itarsi National Highway. There are 200 households in Pathai and all of them participated in the study.

Pathai village is numerically dominated by illiterates, poor and non-workers. About 25 per cent households do not have land and villagers depend on wage work, farm work or both for their livelihood. The village is near to a forest. Historically tribes have been dependent on this forest for their social and economic requirements. Even today significant number of tribal women collect firewood from this forest in order to meet their day-to-day requirement. But, in the broader sense, the forest is now no more an important source of livelihood for the inhabitants of Pathai. Of 38 basic facilities required only 11 are available in Pathai. These are panchayat office, Primary Health Centre (PHC), metal road, electricity, Aanganwadi centres, primary and middle school, kirana shops, PDS shop, flour mill, handpump, tubewell and *jhar-phuk* facility.

Interview schedule, interview guide and case study were the three specific techniques used to collect data. Those who participated in the study were head of the household (usually male), Aanganwadi worker working at PHC, traditional medicine men (Bhagats), private practioners working at Sahpur and functionaries working at Community Health Centre (CHC),

Sahpur. Information was also collected from secondary sources, especially from records provided by PHC, CHC and mobile health facility working under Deen Dayal Antyodaya Upchar Yojana. Fieldwork was carried out during 2007–09.

I
Perceptions about Health and Disease

Villagers' Perception

Perceptions of both villagers, doctors and other health workers working in Pathai and Sahpur were mapped to get a comprehensive and comparative picture of different aspects of health and disease. So far as tribes are concerned, they have their own perception about health and a healthy person. To them a healthy person is one who eats properly, looks pleasant, has thin body, roam here and there easily, looks neat and clean, is active in day-to-day life, performs hard physical work, avoids alcohol and carries glow face. Happy life, consumption of vegetarian food and straight posture of body are also indices of good health.

Interpretations about roots of diseases in Pathai are also based on objective consideration. Fatalistic or metaphysical interpretation is today largely absent from the scene. Patel (1991) studied traditional health management practices among Baiga primitive tribe of Madhya Pradesh. He documented a number of religious beliefs, supernatural power, unhygienic food habit, faith in the concept of sin and virtue, birth and re-birth, violation of taboos etc., which were held responsible by Baigas for various diseases. He also found a number of traditional methods like worship, magic, herbs and medicinal plants etc., being used by them for treatment. There was no role of modern medicine in the treatment of about 44 diseases among them.

Among tribes of Pathai village, however, the situation is totally different. They have by and large objective interpretation of both health and disease. For instance, most of the diseases – both simple and complex – are perceived as due to lack of cleanliness. Here, cleanliness refers to cleanliness of one's body, clothes, houses, use of pure and safe drinking water, cooking utensils and so on. Many villagers said that people become ill because their food habit and meal time are not properly managed. Increasing use of chemical fertilizer in agriculture also contributes to illness. Carelessness, consumption of impure drinking water, consumption of rotten food, use of meat and regular consumption of Mahua liquor, which is very common in Pathai, and lack of proper and timely medical check-up on frequent basis also contributes to illness. Role of black magic or religion was hardly rated by any respondent as a key of disease and illness. Hence, all the villagers expressed objective views about indices and roots of both health and disease. Khera (1990) also observed the same thing while conducting study on Baiga tribe of Madhya Pradesh. According to him, "The Baiga are fully acquainted with the mosquitoes, the deadly cerebral malaria that infests the region as well as other poisonous insects and have developed special protective measures for it as well as for snake bite, bear bite, dog bite, etc. It is their knowledge about medicinal plants and herbs that has made them famous. Indeed a Baiga is sought after as the healer of the area".

Doctors' Perception

Some of the common diseases found in Sahpur area in general and Pathai village in particular, as narrated by two MBBS doctors who are practising at Sahpur, are fever, vomiting and loose motion, malaria, joint-ache, cough and cold, bodyache, swelling in leg, swelling in lever, TB, chickenpox, throat infection, pile, skin disease, STD, jaundice, abortion, anaemia, habit of eating soil, snake bite, delivery, fracture, teeth pain, wound, cut, itching and so on. Such diseases occur primarily because of malnourishment, lack of vitamins in food, poverty, wastage of time with Bhagats, lack of awareness about health, lack of sufficient treatment facility at Sahpur hospital, lack of de-worming scheme, etc. They observed that tribes not only make delay in approaching doctor/proper health service provider, but also there is total lack of follow-up on the part of patients. In an earlier study; Chaudhary and Singh (2006) observed a similar narrative made by the local medicine man which inhibits patient to approach modern health institution at the earliest. The healer narrated: "If somebody is bitten by scorpion crushed Kapur is applied on the bitten part to remove poison. If it fails, which is usually not, then *jhar-phuk* technique is used. If bitten by snake like Kobra, Kaili, Padmani and Patalhari, both *jhar-phuk* technique and very small tablet made out of poisonous Kalihari Kund is taken with water. If it fails then only patient is brought to hospital at Tamia".

The villagers also hesitate to revisit doctors even when they are asked to do so. As a consequence, the treatment remains incomplete which in many cases results in reappearance of some of the diseases especially malaria in a more complicated form, after few weeks or months. It was reported that in many cases most of the patients suffering from common ailments do not complete the total course of treatment as prescribed by doctors. Needless to mention that cataract, itch, ulcer and malaria are the very common diseases in the entire district since long.[1]

On the basis of these two sets of interpretations, especially of disease, it may be said that both experts and villagers have more or less similar perception about types of diseases as well as factors and conditions which originates and contributes to these diseases. Tribal perception about health and disease in an objective manner clearly refers to the fact that now gone are the days of magico-religious explanation of disease and illness. This development has taken place because of numerous exogenous factors, especially due to the state-initiated health management institutions at the village and at the district level.

II
Coping Mechanisms: Then and Now

Since the explanation of disease is now objective in nature, therefore, although both traditional and modern healing mechanisms are followed, but wind is blowing in favour of modern health practices. This is clear from the description in this section.

Traditional Treatment

To deal with most of the diseases historically tribes of Pathai have availed traditional medicines which include medicines made out of herbs and medicinal plants and practised and provided by local medicine men (Bhagats). Lakra (1997) conducted a study on Khairwar tribe of Surguja district of Madhya Pradesh. According to her, 99 per cent families have deep faith in traditional folk healing and generally follow traditional method of delivery. This is partially due to their poor economic conditions and the major cause being the tribes residing far away from PHCs in the interior areas. These parameters determine the medical facilities which the tribal people can avail and thus directly affecting their health status. Due to the far away location women are unable to get PHC services during the delivery time and the untrained *dais* attend them. Again absence of modern health management institutions has also encouraged tribals to depend on traditional medicine, besides their dependence on *jhar-phuk* technique. According to Kurup over 600 wild medicinal plants are often used for various diseases by tribal communities. Plant species like *Canarium evphyllum* (Andamans), *Paeonia obovata* (Western Ghats) and *Euphorbia acualis* of Madhya Pradesh, are found to be very effective against rheumatoid arthritis and inflammation. Similarly, *Adina cordifolia* and *Andrographis paniculata* collected from the forests of Madhya Pradesh are found to have remarkable hepato-protective and immunostimulant activities.

But today because of many reasons wind is blowing in favour of modern medicine. The following table clearly depicts the dynamics of treatment among them over the time:

Table 1

Treatment: Then and Now (multiple response)

Disease Name	*Then (20–25 years ago)*					*Today*				
	Traditional[2]	*Modern*[3]	*Both*[4]	*Nothing*	*No response*	*Traditional*	*Modern*	*Both*	*Nothing*	*No response*
Snake bite	194	5					194	6	0	0
Fracture	158	2			47		0	157	38	
Stomach problem	167	10			22		90	92	19	
Headache/bodyache	160	10			36		31	149	20	
Children illness	249	16			32		10	190		
Delivery	182	14		96			41	179		9
Teeth formation	158			49			23	151		26
Teeth pain	317	9		40			19	176		
Dehydration/vomiting	149	17		28				179	5	14
Feat	156	15		30			26	169		6
Fatigue	149	11		46			81	98		31
Fever	144	45		25			15	187		
Sleeplessness	97	6		101			32	94		76
Wound	163	21		17			12	188		6
Cut	176	11		13			5	181	10	7
Itching	164	19		21			20	180		7

On the basis of above data, it can be interpreted that barring snake bite villagers' dependence for treatment of all types of diseases have drastically increased on doctors, hospitals and modern medicine. In the same proportion their dependence on traditional and village-based health management practices have significantly decreased. This refers to expansion of modern health management system among them. But these modern practices are historically exterior to them. It has made them dependent-prone. The traditional practices which were indigenous, cost effective and available at any time at their doorstep are now thing of the past. Such traditional practices might have been semi-scientific but it has long history. Persons who carried on such practices had social acceptance and cultural legitimacy. But, the new health management system, which is said to be more scientific, is costly, not available at the doorstep and it contributes to psychological and cultural conflict in the life of many patients who try to adopt it and make delay in approaching modern health practices due to various economic and non-economic reasons.

In the past villagers used to depend on practices like Ojha and traditional medicine men. These traditional practitioners have significantly decreased over the time. And, with this, alternatives of treatment have also reduced. For instance, to get rid of fever they had eight alternative techniques in the past but today they follow only five such techniques. About 25 years ago, juice of *jari-buti*, other herbal medicine, help of Bhagat, patti of cold water on forehead, physical rest, consumption of mahua liquor, consumption of kutki and sama daliya, help of doctor/hospital, etc., was taken. Significant number of respondents were not using any such method now with the assumption that ailment will disappear automatically one day. But today maximum number of them (187) take recourse to doctor/hospital. They do not leave disease unattended. Those who used to take rest, use mahua liquor, take the help of Bhagat and body massage of coconut oil etc., their number have drastically decreased today. Also, to control dehydration and vomiting, they used to depend on eight techniques but today only three techniques are practised. Hence, with the passage of time, not only degree and amount of villagers' dependence on modern health management practices have increased but also number of alternatives of treatment have also significantly decreased.

The number of patients who could not avail any type of treatment during sickness in the past have decreased significantly. For instance, in the case of sleeplessness, 101 persons did not sought any treatment about 20–25 years ago but today number of non-treatment seekers for this disease has decreased upto 76. Similarly, in the case of dehydration and vomiting, 28 respondents could not avail any treatment about 20–25 years ago but the number of patients suffering from such diseases has also decreased today upto 14. This trend shows increasing amount of awareness among tribes regarding health and disease as well as their inclination in favour of modern health management practices being run especially by PHC and CHC at the local level. Treatment methods adopted in some of the diseases today support this conclusion.

Five Diseases and Its Treatment Today: Case Study

Pre-natal Death

During 2007 harvesting of soyabean crop was in progress. A pregnant Gond woman of 24 years of age was also engaged in harvesting. All of a sudden she experienced labour pain. She immediately rushed to Sahpur Community Health Centre (CHC), which is at a distance of about 4 kms from the said farm land for safe delivery. In course of treatment the doctor found it a critical case and the case was immediately referred to government hospital Betul. Betul is about 30 kms away from Sahpur. For want of money the patient could not go to Betul hospital on the same day. Next day, after managing money, she went to Betul District Hospital. In course of treatment at Betul, it was found that the expected infant was dead. Therefore, it was aborted. Needless to mention that in this case the patient was not dependent at all on Bhagat. But she was too late to approach the proper hospital. Her total dependence was on trained doctor but due to delay in treatment mainly due to lack of awareness she had bitter experience. Had she availed proper medical facility in time especially at Sahpur CHC, life of expected infant might have been saved.

Skin Disease

Asam Uikey is a 5 years' old boy. During 2007, he had so many wounds and itching on different parts of the body. He was suffering from pain and bodyache. Initially parents approached village Bhagat and *jhar-phuk* technique was followed but there was no relief. After few days the local medicine men asked him to take bath with water mixed with juice of neem leaf. This technique was followed for several days but this technique also could not extend any relief to the patient. Subsequently, the patient approached Sahpur CHC. At CHC proper treatment was provided. But this effort also could not succeed. Even today on occasions like full moon night and full dark night, there is itching on such wounds and by itching, these wounds become alive. The family do not have faith in Bhagat at all. Although till date he has spent about ₹ 500 on treatment but this has not harmed them economically. The family is suffering from mental tension due to this disease.

Pneumonia

Shubhan is a 4 years' old boy. About one and half years ago upper part of his backbone was not functioning well. Parents are wage-earner. Initially parents approached Bhagat Shankar Lal Dhurve. Dhurve adopted *jhar-phuk* technique and massaged the affected part of the body with the help of egg liquid. But such efforts could not succeeded. Subsequently, the patient visited to Shahpur CHC. Blood test was made. But they felt that the treatment was not proper and therefore, they approached private doctor at Bhawra. Here proper treatment was made for continuous 10 days. Parents had to spent about ₹ 1,500 which they had earned from wage work. Now, the patient is free from this disease.

Tuberculosis (TB)

Genda Lal Dhurve, a 70 years' old, was suffering from TB since last 15 years. Initially, he sought treatment from government hospital and he felt relief. He thought that he is free from TB and, therefore, he discontinued treatment. But, in the real sense, he was not free from TB. After few months, TB reappeared. Instead of approaching doctor he consulted Bhagat for treatment. Bhagat treated him in his own way locally known as Dana Uthana in which grains of rice or wheat is taken from the patient family and by uttering mantras it is thrown. It is thrown with the assumption that with this the disease will also go away. But, at the same time, on infrequent basis, he also continued treatment in government hospital. Since the treatment was infrequent and he continued taking inferior quality food for want of money and, therefore, even after spending about ₹ 10,000 he could not survive and ultimately died in 2007.

Accident

Ravindra Dhurve was 45 years' old, when he met road accident in 1998. He is in government job. He also owns cultivatable land. His monthly salary is around ₹ 5,000. He has two wives. From the first wife, he has one daughter and currently she is living with daughter at her maternal place after separation. Ravindra is living with his second wife and two small kids. His father was serving in the Forest Department. He died during job period. ₹ 2 lakh was paid to Ravindra's mother as a compensation. Ravindra was provided job in forest department on compassionate ground. He purchased one new motorcycle out of the compensation amount. He was habituated to consume mahua liquor every now and then. One day he was going to Ghoradongri town by motor cycle. He was in a drunken mood. On the way he met a serious road accident. Motor cycle was totally damaged and he had multiple fracture. He was in hospital for constantly three months. He went number of surgical operations. In the course of treatment he had to spent about ₹ 75,000 from the amount of ₹ 2 lakh which he had received as a compensation. During the course of treatment although salary was paid to him but his wife was forced to work as wage-earner. She was also forced to collect and market fuelwood to maintain family and continue study of children. Today, he is doing job but every now and then he suffers from pain.

Traditional Medicine Men in Pathai

As stated above, today, tribes of Pathai have more and more dependence on modern means of treatment. But this does not mean that their dependence on traditional treatment methods have totally disappeared. Even today, for various types of treatment they partly, totally or initially depend on traditional medicines. There are seven traditional medicine men (Bhagats) in Pathai. The traditional is local, historical and the practitioners are either from the village itself or from the neighbouring villages. These Bhagats are: Manak Parte, Bihari Batke, Sukh Lal Bhagat, Shankar Lal Dhurve, Rambharose Dhurve, Chatarpal and Swami Dada. They all are illiterate, although they have knowledge of basic mathematics. They learnt the treatment technique from family members. There are seven mohallas in Pathai and incidentally these Bhagat belong to six mohallas. This means in all the mohallas there is one Bhagat. All of them are men. They are available to villagers every time as and when their service is required. Treatment is by and large free and it is partly based on the local herbs and medicinal plants and partly on mantras. The following two cases of Bhagat deal with types of treatment extended by these traditional medicine men in different diseases over the time:

Shankar Lal Dhurve

Shankar Lal Dhuve is Gond. He is 55 years old. He belongs to relatively well-to-do family. Family economy is primarily based on farming. He is following both *jhar-phuk* technique and herbs and medicinal plants for treatment. He is engaged in this work since last 10 years. He could not receive any formal training for this work. Rather he learnt it in day-to-day life from villagers. Primarily he treats eight types of diseases with the following techniques:

Diseases	*Treatment*
tonsil	Paste of Bhasm khand is applied on the affected part of the body several times.
Phunsi	Paste of Bhasm khand is applied on the affected part several times.
Cut	Paste of neem tree kin is applied on the affected part several times.
Jaundice	Mixed juice of Amerbel and Jangli Haldi is both consumed and applied on the body. Mustard oil is also applied on the body. *Jhar-phunk* technique is also followed.
Fever	Juice made out of Kadu jeera is consumed continuously for 2–3 days.
Headache/Bodyache	Massage with kerosene oil is made.
Dehydration/Vomiting	Mixed juice of Pudina and lemon is consumed several times.

Shankar Lal said that most of the patients are affected by fever, tonsil and jaundice. They all are from Pathai itself. No fee is charged for treatment. However, once they get cure they offer coconut and agarbatti etc., to the Bhagat. Bhagat is follower of God Vishnu and he observed that by using both local herbs and mantras related to Vishnu, he provides treatment to villagers.

Bihari Batke

Bihari Batke is a 85 years' old Gond of Pathai. He hails from Gyaki Dhana. He uses both *jhar-phuk* and *jari-buti* since the age of 15 years for treatment. His father was also engaged in this profession. But his father died when Bihari was a child. Today, Bihari treats about 20 diseases. These diseases and treatment methods are as under:

Disease	*Treatment*
Stomach Problem	Paste made out of Silkajhar and Jaramtadi is applied on stomach as well as halwa/tablet made out of it is taken by patient continuously for 3 days and the patient gets cured.
Sukhi Bimari	Paste made out of Barahmas is applied on body as well as smoke created by burning raw Barahmas is inhaled for three days to get relief.
Cough and Cold	Tea made with the mixture of Phasi Jhar is consumed to get relief.
Asthama	Paste made out of Phasi Jhar is eaten as well as applied on body several times to get relief.
Jaundice	Mixture made out of Anidhara (Hathikan) and Amras are mixed together and it is both consumed and pasted on different parts of the body. Also *jhar-phuk* technique is used with the help of mustard oil and Dub grass.
Cancer	A tablet made out of leaf of Chatargoti and flower is consumed. Three tablets are taken each day for continuous 90 days with some food related restrictions.
TB	The above medicine used in the case of cancer is also used to cure TB.
STD/Piles	Root of Ramratan mixed with water is taken for 15–30 days.
Pneumonia	A tablet made out of Harra/root of Pulsa and root of Hatikan is taken two times each day for continuous 10 days.
Fit	A raw mixture made out of Pudina, Tulsi, Long and peppermint is consumed 2–3 times each day for few days to cure the disease.
Headache/Bodyache	A tablet made out of the mixture of Silka tree and part of Thingsaw is taken for few days.
Period Disorder	A tablet made out of the mixture of Ghatharu tree and Skin of Khendua Chal is consumed continuously for 8–10 days.

Cont'd...

...Cont'd

Itching	A liquid made out of Ghatharu tree mixed with coconut oil is fried for few minutes and it is used on affected part for several days to get cure from this disease.
Teeth-related problem of children	A dust made out of the mixture of root of Khara, a mango seed and skin of Kaira is mixed with milk and children are asked to drink it on several times.
Fracture	A paste made out of Hadjor and Rajkarna fruit is used on the affected part for several days. Besides strengthening bone it also reduces swelling.
Snake/Scorpion Bite	For scorpion bite liquid made out of leaf of Barahamas Khakara is applied on the affected part. Similarly in the case of snake bite the patient is asked to eat leaf of Bharu Cherota.
Fatigue	Dust made out of seed of Mudhari mixed with water is taken to get rid of fatigueness.
Wound/cut	A paste made out of the dust of root of Rajkarula and Hadjor is applied on the affected part.
Teethache	Paste made out of Theen Patiea Bela is applied on the affected part.

Modern Coping Mechanisms

As the interpretation of health and disease have become objective, coping mechanisms followed by tribes of Pathai have also become by and large objective. In comparison to the past, in spite of the presence of traditional health healers, villagers' dependence on modern health management institutions like Primary Health Centre (PHC), Aanganwadi centre and Community Health Centre (CHC) operating at the village and block level has tremendously increased during last few years.

Health-related coping mechanisms may be explained at two levels, i.e., preventive or precautionary measures and actual treatment. While the former creates an environment at the family and at the village level to take number of precautions to escape air and water-borne diseases, because these are the two major sources of diseases in the village, the latter provides treatment facility of different types. Both these steps are, however, interlinked. Under these two measures following specific efforts are in progress in Pathai. Both these measures, are institutional in nature. It shows increasing importance of state in health management in tribal villages.

Preventive Measures

At the family level many of the villagers take regular bath, use soap while bathing, they follow modern teeth cleaning instruments, take food in time, consume so-called clean water, wash hands after toilet and most of the them also do physical labour.

At the village level some efforts are made by Aanganwadi workers to make villagers aware about importance of environmental cleanliness and names and reasons of air and water-borne disease, villagers are also advised to take precaution in their day-to-day life in order to escape diseases.

In the recent past number of efforts have been initiated at the village level in order to improve health status of villagers. Important among these are:

Total Sanitation Campaign

Total Sanitation Campaign (TSC) also known as Nirmal Gram Yojna is an intervention for environmental upgradation. This project is directed to provide toilet facility in all the households where this facility is not available, in all the schools and in Aanganwadi centre. It is also directed to encourage cleanliness in the village and teach lesson to keep cooking place and space clean in and around house and the place where drinking water is kept.

So far as Pathai village is concerned, here during 2007–08 in more than 50 per cent households toilet facility was provided. It was promised that this facility will be extended to other households in the due course. It was assumed that villagers will use this technique and help each other in the environmental upgradation, which will subsequently keep them healthy.[5]

Safe Drinking Water

There are 11 handpumps in Pathai. However, during 2006–09, 28 wells were constructed under Mahatma Gandhi National Rural Employment Guarantee Scheme (MGNREGS) of which 18 are properly working today. These wells satisfy domestic requirement of water in a successful manner. In the past villagers at large used to face drinking water problem. Today, not only this problem is over but also this scheme has ensured supply of safe drinking water.

Public Distribution System (PDS)

In order to address the problem of food insecurity and malnutrition there is a special provision for the poor. Blue and yellow ration cards have been issued to obtain food grain at the cheaper rate from the local PDS shop. For instance, while APL (above poverty line) card holders receive wheat at the rate of ₹ 7 per kg, BPL (below poverty line) and most poor (Antyodaya Anna Yojana) card holders (yellow card) receives at the rate of only ₹ 3 and ₹ 2 per kg respectively. Other food grains are also provided to them at the cheaper rate.

Table 2

Food Grains Provided by PDS at Pathai

Category of Family	*Item*	*Quantity (in Kg/Litre)*	*Price (per Kg/Litre)*
APL (White Card)	Wheat	10 Kg.	7
	Kerosene Oil	4 Lt.	10
BPL (Blue Card)	Wheat	20 Kg.	3
	Rice	4 Kg.	6.50
	Sugar	2 Kg.	13.50
	Kerosene Oil	5 Lt.	10
Antyodaya Anna Yojana (AAY) (Yellow Card)	Wheat	31 Kg.	2
	Rice	4 Kg	3
	Sugar	2 Kg.	13.50
	Kerosene Oil	5 Lt.	10

Social Forestry

During 2007–08 efforts were made by panchayat to undertake plantation work in Pathai and Nishana village. In Pathai 27.5 acres of government land were undertaken for this purpose. Similarly, in Nishana village 32 acres of land came under social forestry project. Altogether ₹ 1.30 lakh was spent during 2007 and ₹ 1.50 lakh in 2008 for plantation purpose. By doing this panchayat created 7,875 man-days employment under MGNREGS. Towards the end of 2007 it was found that about 40 per cent of the seedlings had dried. To fill up the gap new seedlings were planted in 2008. Since this is a social forestry project, therefore, in the due course, besides environmental upgradation this project is also supposed to meet needs of fuel, fodder and non-timber forest produce to villagers.

Treatment

Number of institutional and non-institutional agencies/bodies are working both at the village and block levels to provide modern health facilities to villagers. Most of these arrangements have been made by the government. Important among these are:

Primary Health Centre (PHC)

PHC is working in Pathai since the middle of 2008. It covers four villages namely Nishana, Pathai, Bhagthandhana and Palaspani. It has one trained health worker (ANM). Besides serving at the centre the worker also moves in each of the villages for awareness generation as well as for extending treatment facility to the needy. Some of the important assignments performed by the PHC are: distribution of medicine free of cost, complicated cases are referred to Sahpur Community Health Centre, assist villagers to understand procedure to take medicine as prescribed by CHC, awareness generation relating to preventive measures, etc. Some of the diseases commonly treated at PHC are fever, cough, dehydration, stomach pain, knee pain, vomiting, eye ailment, cough and cold, headache, breast pain, teeth pain, pneumonia, wound, ear ailment, itching and so on. In the case of failure or partial issues the case is referred to the CHC.

During the year (October 2008 to September 2009) PHC treated altogether 1,013 patients belonging to Pathai village. Most of the patients were between the age group of 6 to 35 years. July and August were the peak months during which maximum number of patients received treatment.[6]

Table 3

Age and Monthwise Number of Patients Who Availed Treatment at the PHC

Months	*Age*						*Total*
	0–1	*2–5*	*6–14*	*15–35*	*36–60*	*60+*	
October 08	7	8	24	40	19	01	99
November 08	11	16	16	15	20	5	83
December 08	05	13	22	21	07	10	78
January 09	—	13	10	16	14	06	59
February 09	03	19	28	12	17	03	82
March 09	06	33	16	16	16	04	91
April 09	01	09	07	05	04	03	29
May 09	02	11	05	15	06	—	39
June 09	03	12	09	22	06	06	58
July 09	01	16	29	26	17	10	99
August 09	04	38	74	68	33	13	230
September 09	06	15	18	13	10	04	66
Total	49	203	258	269	169	65	1,013

Source: Register, PHC, Pathai village.

In spite of the fact that on an average 84 patients were treated in each month during 2008 and 2009, PHC and the ANM (auxiliary nurse midwife) is facing some of the fundamental challenges in its day-to-day functioning. These challenges are of two types, viz., challenges at the place of work and challenges relating to procedural mechanisms. While the former includes resistance by husbands or other male family members in the case of permanent sterilization of women, confusion among women that sterilization will contribute to number of ailments in the due course such as weakness, illness and fatness, problem of interaction between ANM worker who knows Marathi language and villagers who do not know this language and so on. The latter category includes shortage of essential medicines which PHC receives from CHC, lack of essential treatment facility and lack of instruments like delivery related package, pathological test facility and lack of helping hand. Today the coverage area is big and PHC worker has also to attend weekly meeting on Saturday at CHC, as a result of which she is not available at PHC on that particular day.

Aanganwadi Centre

Aanganwadi centre is working in Pathai since 1996. There is one Aanganwadi worker and one helper posted at the Centre. Aanganwadi worker is responsible to motivate villagers to follow institutional delivery, family planning devices, immunization and other modern health management methods. In order to strengthen health status of infant and children, iron folic acid (IFC) is frequently distributed among them. From 2007 to 2009, 61 children were provided this tablet.

Because of increasing health awareness among villagers as well as spread of state-led health management facilities number of children suffering from malnutrition is lower in comparison to the normal children. For instance, of 143 children up to five years in Pathai during 2009, 96 (67.13%) were normal, 35 (24.47%) were malnourished and remaining 12 (8.39%) were severely malnourished.[7] However, the problem of malnourishment is more serious among girls in comparison to boys.

Immunization programme carried out by the Anaganwadi Kendra is popular in the village. All the alive children of the specific age group are provided this facility. During 2007, 2008 and 2009, 31, 36 and 30 children were covered under immunization scheme respectively. Because of immunization project number of infant deaths have significantly decreased. During 2007, 2008 and 2009 there was death of 3, 4 and 2 infants, respectively. But, in spite of this facility, the rate of infant death is higher in comparison to death among other age groups. For instance, between 2006 to 2009 total 30 death occurred in Pathai of which maximum death (16) was of infant, i.e., 10 male infants and 6 female infants. Also, in all the age groups rate of death is higher among men (19) than women (11). There was no case of any maternal mortality during this period.

Community Health Centre (CHC)

Community Health Centre located at Sahpur is headed by Block Medical Officer (BMO). Besides running a 30 bedded hospital the centre is also managing Janani Suraksha Yojna (JSY) and Deen Dayal Mobile Hospital (DDMH). At Sahpur CHC hospital most of the time beds are engaged. For registration, APL patients have to pay ₹ 2 but for BPL patient registration is free. There are three doctors working at this centre. Some of the common diseases for the treatment of which patients at large visit CHC are: fever, cough, cold and headache. Facilities for delivery as well as family planning operation are also provided at this hospital.

During 2008, 32,665 patients visited Sahpur CHC for treatment. Pathai, which has a population of about 1,400, 896 patients visited this hospital. If we see monthwise variation, it is evident that during the months of July, August and September maximum number of patients visited to this hospital for treatment.

During these three months number of patients from the CHC catchment area was also highest. This shows that during these three months number of patients increases not only in Pathai but also in the entire catchment area.

Table 4

Number of Total Patients Registered at Sahpur CHC During January–December 2008

Month	*Sahpur*	*Pathai*
January	2292	52
February	2014	38
March	1948	51
April	1606	67
May	1886	65
June	2350	71
July	3508	153
August	4424	165
September	4569	116
October	4659	56
November	2559	40
December	850	22
	32665	896

Source: Data obtained from OPD Register of CHC, Sahpur block in December 2008.

Janani Suraksha Yojana (JSY)

This scheme was introduced to provide an opportunity of safe and institutional delivery to women from below the poverty line. Under this scheme economic assistance is provided to expected mother at the time of delivery. Earlier ₹ 700 was paid to the concerned woman but today the amount has been increased to ₹ 1400. From 2005 to 2007, 74 women from Pathai village have received the support of ₹ 68,100 under this scheme.

Success of JSY may be realized from the fact that between 2006–09 altogether 142 births took place in Pathai of which 96 took place at hospital and remaining 46 at home. While in the case of former service of nurse was received, in the case of latter *dai* (both trained and untrained) played crucial role. This data clearly reflects increasing trend in favour of institutional delivery.

Deen Dayal Mobile Hospital

Deen Dayal Mobile Hospital (DDMH) is directed to work in the development blocks which are numerically dominated by SC and ST population. Most of them are poor with having poor access to modern health facility. This facility is extended to them free of cost. In Madhya Pradesh this scheme was introduced on May 26, 2006 in a phased manner. Today, this facility is in operation in 86 tribal development blocks, with having 92 mobile units. If we see the statistics, it is obvious that from its inception (May 26, 2006) to February, 2009, 43,75,414 patients have received treatment. During 2008–09 alone at the state level a sum of ₹ 11.78 crore have been spent on this head. A large number of NGOs have been involved in this task.

Some of the health management activities done by DDMH are as under:

1. Medical advice to patients, first aid and free distribution of medicine,
2. Health check-up before and after delivery and free distribution of medicine,
3. Collection of blood and spittoon sample relating to malaria and TB disease,
4. Identification of serious patients in villages and referring the cases to CHC and other hospitals, immunization, and
5. Awareness programmes relating to various family planning devices, welfare schemes and education.

Mode of Functioning in Sahpur

So far as Sahpur Development Block (SDB) is concerned here a Delhi-based NGO named Jagran Solution (an unit of Jagran Prakashan Private Limited) is running this project since October 2007. There is an MoU between this NGO and Health Department of Government of Madhya Pradesh for three years which may be extended for another two years after review.

Under this scheme a properly equipped vehicle moves in the villages, attends all weekly markets and other common places. It has to follow a route chart prepared and provided by the Block Medical Officer (BMO). The vehicle moves between 10 am to 6 pm to provide treatment, free medicine and free advice. The mobile hospital examines 100 patients each day and 300 pregnant women in each month. This target is pre-fixed. Besides the facility of GPS, table for diagnosis, BP test instrument, instrument relating to treatment of pregnant women, IUD kit, contraceptive pills and other material, oxygen mask, blood counter, first aid kit, the vehicle is also loaded with instruments relating to popularization of population education such as TV, DVD, white board, chart, loudspeaker and so on. The mobile van receives medicine from CHC free of cost and it also distributes the same without any charge.

Besides these facilities in each mobile hospital there is a facility of pathological lab, one oxygen cylinder and stature, one MBBS doctor, one pharmacist, one trained ANM, one supervisor and one driver. The mobile hospital moves for 6 days in a week and on an average 26 days in a month. In the beginning of the month route chart prepared by BMOs in consultation with field staff, is provided to the mobile hospital in-charge. In most of the cases this chart is followed.

Sector Medical Officer (SMO), BMO, DMO, CMHO, Janpad Panchayat are the important institutions which have been entrusted to examine the functioning of mobile hospital.

In short, roughly about 1950 patients are examined and treated each month in the villages of Sahpur. Making comments on the achievement, dresser of this mobile hospital, said: "In spite of lack of ECG machine and spittoon slide in the mobile hospital, this project has reduced the cases of disease among poor dalits and tribal in a significant manner. People at large know about mobile hospital and they eagerly wait for it. Its intervention has provided them health facility at their doorstep."

Private Doctors at Sahpur

There are six chemist shops and private practitioners at Sahpur. The chemist shops provide advice to the patients on demand and accordingly they also prescribe medicine for various ailments even on credit. In different kirana shops also medicines for minor ailments are prescribed and sold. Similarly, there are six allopathic doctors and two homeopathic private practitioners at Sahpur. Villagers of Pathai also frequently visit to them for treatment.

III
Agenda for Action

Above observation clearly denotes that today tribes at large, especially those who are exposed to outside world, are no more dependent on their traditional healing practices in the case of most of the diseases. Only for snake bite, which is rare, they are still dependent on traditional system. Villagers dependence on state initiated health management mechanisms like PHC and CHC have significantly increased. Efforts and initiatives taken by CHC is very popular among them. More or less similar is the situation with PHC. The ever-increasing number of patients registered for treatment at both the centres is a testimony to this observation. Also, number of schemes managed by CHC is very popular in tribal villages. Villagers do not hesitate to consult these formal institutions in need.

But this is one side of the coin. The other side needs introspection and overhauling of the total health management mechanism especially in the light of the scattered and poorly connected geographical space where tribals are located and their limited psychological and economic carrying capacity. In spite of the presence of traditional medicine men in many tribal villages, tribals prefer to go to institutional arrangements. But the question is to what extent these institutions, especially PHC is well-equipped? Neither the ANM is properly trained to diagnose the disease nor the centre has sufficient medicine and other essential facility to address all patients in a proper manner. Catchment area of ANM is vast. Most of the time ANM is in the field and during this time at the PHC the visitors are unattended. Besides providing treatment the ANM worker has also to do number of official assignments. In case the ANM is an outsider and also from different cultural background and mindset, they do not associate themselves closely with villagers.

So far as CHC and its different activities are concerned, of course it has become popular over the time, but neither these interventions are well-equipped nor easily available to poor tribal in need. Even in the critical situation safe delivery is not possible at the CHC hospital. Patients are referred to Betul-based government district hospital. Mobile hospital is neither well-equipped nor very frequent in all the villages. There is no proper and frequent monitoring of its functioning. Medicines prescribed by chemist shop is one of the testimonies to this state of affair.

It is true that tribal dependence on modern health management institutions have increased over the time but still there is traditional healers.[8] For the treatment of some of the diseases villagers still go to them. But in spite of that there is no effort to modernize these traditional healers. Traditional knowledge possessed by these healers will disappear with their death because traditionally neither they share this knowledge with new generation nor the new generation is interested to learn this knowledge. But relevance of such knowledge specially from the point of view of poor tribal cannot be completely ignored.

In the light of these findings it can be said that modern health management initiatives have become very popular in tribal villages. Gradually it has made them dependant-prone. It has directly or indirectly created environment and mindset against the traditional healing methods. Under the given situation, if there is reluctance and apathy on the part of state and its initiatives pertaining to effective functioning of health management schemes, nobody is there to take care of health-related needs and requirements of poor tribal. This calls for formulation of action agenda in such a manner that it can ensure inclusive health management for tribal masses.[9]

Some of the steps needed to be undertaken in this direction may be as under:

1. Since tribal economy, by and large revolves around their basic need and if their health status deteriorates even for few days their basic need of food etc., will be negatively affected, therefore, their health condition has to be improved and retained. For this purpose there is need to ensure proper and fruitful functioning of all the preventive measures initiated at the community level, such as supply of safe and sufficient drinking water, proper functioning of schemes like public distribution system, immunization programme, total sanitation campaign, social forestry scheme and so on. These interventions, if properly managed, will directly or indirectly create enabling factors and conditions which will not only improve health status but also it may improve other aspects of their life in a proper perspective.

   However, functioning of all these ongoing initiatives can only be ensured provided beneficiaries at large are made aware about these schemes on constant basis. And for awareness generation, besides PHC and CHC initiatives, services of other institutions such as primary schools, Gram Panchayats, SHGs, NGOs, etc., may be taken.
2. It is true that over the time tribals' dependence on traditional healing methods have deteriorated and it is further likely to deteriorate but on this basis alone its contribution in the past cannot be undermined. Nobody can undermine cultural legitimacy and ecological foundation

of this practice. Hence, instead of discarding it, there is a need to document this knowledge in different local languages and dialects to make properties of each of the available herbs and medicinal plants popular among the masses for its wider use. There is a need to capacitate the traditional healers by linking them with modern health institutions. If properly linked and managed, they can be an integrating force between tribal masses and the modern health practices. We have to remember that modern medicine and treatment is a new entrant in the tribal world. There is also a need to organize and capacitate *jhola-chhap* doctors who are found in large number in villages. They are easily available, culturally accepted and many of them extend services even on credit. They have face to face relationship with poor clients. Hence, this institution needs to be capacitated and modernized in the light of current scenario.

3. There is a need to activise and strengthen PHC and CHC. Such institutions exists at their doorstep. Tribals' dependence on these institutions has increased over time. This trust has to be popularized and strengthened. PHC is neither properly equipped nor the ANM is able and capable enough to create needful environment. ANM number needs to be increased at all the PHCs. Also, an organized, structured and well-equipped training and orientation package needs to be formulated and implemented for them.

These are few suggestions from within. If implemented carefully, it can definitely bring some meaningful improvement in the health status of tribal masses.

Notes

1. People do not take very kindly to the operation of extraction of the lens; though evidence of successful operations is forthcoming in a large number of villages. They quite cheerfully undergo the dislocation performed by the native Sathyas, though these practitioners destroy about 80 per cent of the eyes operated on by them (Gazetteer of India, 1907, reprint 1999: 228).
2. Traditional Treatment: Black magic, herbal treatment, massage treatment by Bhumka, soil plaster, massage with garlic/soil, massage with boiled mahua, consumption of mahua liquor, consumption of raw bel leaf, consumption of mahi, consumption of root of banana plant, lemon water with sugar, kerosene oil massage, consumption of fried mahua, use of copper wire, consumption of jamun gutli, consumption of peepal leaf juice with milk, inhaling of lakh smoke, jharphunk, use of chandan, hot papaya juice, hot water massage,

turmeric powder massage, use of leaf of akau tree, steam of junglee brinjal, hot juice of guava leaf, lemon juice, massage with cow ghee/inhaling of cow ghee, consumption of kutki and sama dalia, sing song, pestering of neem leaf dust, juice of amla plant, bath in front of statue of god, paste of soil mixed with cow dung, bath with neem soap.

3. Modern Treatment: Trained and untrained doctor in the market, PHC and CHC and direct treatment by medical store.
4. Both: Initially traditional treatment but subsequently modern treatment as per the requirement or both are adopted side by side.
5. But the picture is altogether different in 2009. We observed that most of the toilets are not in a working condition. Length and breadth of toilet room is small and villagers hesitate to use it because of its narrow size. In certain cases it is used only by children. There are other inhibiting factors. The village is surrounded by forest and there is no paucity of open space. Therefore, by habit villagers prefer to defecate in the open space and the so-called awareness programme initiated by PHC and Gram Panchayat is totally failed to change mindset in the proper perspective. Also, villagers prefer open space because it requires less amount of water in comparison to their home-based recently constructed toilets. In some of the households, however, people use their toilet in the rainy season. It is needless to mention that in large number of houses mahua liquor is prepared for their own consumption as well as for market. We observed that some of the toilets, which is totally unused, villagers either use it as a store room or they prepare mahua liquor. We have observed that villagers at large neither know the negative implications of huge consumption of mahua liquor on their health nor they know the positive impact of use of family-based toilet on their health and environment.
6. In spite of the fact that on an average 84 patients were treated in each month during 2008 and 2009 however, PHC and the ANM is facing some of the fundamental problems in its day-to-day functioning. These problems are of two types, viz., challenges at the place of work and challenges relating to procedural mechanism. While the former includes resistance by husbands or other male family members in the case of permanent sterilization of women, there is also confusion among women that sterilization will contribute to weakness, illness and fatness, communication problem between ANM workers who knows Marathi and villagers who do not know this language and so on the latter includes shortage of essential medicines which she receives from CHC, lack of essential treatment facility and lack of instruments like delivery related package, pathological test facility and lack of helping hand because the coverage area is big and she has also to attend weekly meeting on each Saturday at CHC, as a result of which she is not available at PHC.
7. Indicators of malnourishment is both gender and age specific as per the indicators and guideline prepared by the WHO. For instance, female infant of

less than 6.5 kg and male infant of less than 7 kg are called severely malnourished. Similarly female infant between 7 kg to 8.75 kg and male infant between 7.75 kg and 9.5 kg are termed as normal infant respectively.

8. Such healers are also active in other parts of the world. According to Munguti (1997) despite the introduction of western medicine many Kenyan communities, including Tugen, follow traditional medicine because it is cheap, easily available, commands faith, while western medicine is very costly. It is beyond the reach of many.
9. By sustainable development we mean development which is productive especially in output and benefit sense of the term, stable even after formal withdrawal of the project by the state and other implementing agencies and equitable which can honestly and continuously take care of needs and concerns of even those who are at the end of the queue.

References

Chaudhuri, B. (1993): "Health, Culture and Environment: The Tribal Situation in India", in M. Miri (ed.), *Continuity and Change in Tribal Society*, Shimla: Indian Institute of Advanced Study.

Chaudhary, D. (1998): "Conserving Genetic Heterogeneity in North-East India", in M.K. Ruha and A.K. Ghose (eds.), *North-East India's: The Human Interface*, New Delhi: Gyan Publishing House.

Chaudhary, S.N. and R.P. Singh (2006): *Tribes of Pachmarhi Biosphere Reserve and Their Indigenous Knowledge*, Bhopal: Indira Gandhi Rashtriya Manav Sangrahalaya.

Clements, F.E. (1932): "Primitive Concept of Disease", *American Archeology and Ethnology*, 32(2), pp. 185–252.

Joseph, A.N.T. (1989): "Ethnozoology of Reptiles in Relation to Health Care among Tribals in Madhya Pradesh", *Social Action*, Vol. 39, No. 4, Oct-Dec, pp. 405–422.

Khera, P.D. (1990): "The Baiga and the Sal Forest", *The Eastern Anthropologist*, Vol. 43, No. 3, pp. 241–258.

Kurian, J.C. and R.D. Tribhuwan (1990): "Traditional Medical Practitioners of the Sahyadri", *The Eastern Anthropologist*, Vol. 43, No. 3, pp. 251–258.

Kurup, A.M. (2000): "Indigenous Knowledge and Intellectual Property Rights of Tribals: A Case Study", *Yojana*, April, pp. 5–9.

Lakra, Indumati (1997): "Health Status of Women of Khairwar Tribe of Surguja District", *Bulletin of the Tribal Research and Development Institute*, Bhopal, Vol. XXV, No. 2.

Lal, Brij (1987): "Traditional Remedies for Bone Fracture among the Trials of M.P. India", *Bulletin of the Tribal Research and Development Institute*, Vol. XV, Nos. 1–2.

Lewis, A. (1954): "Health as a Social Concept", *British Journal of Sociology*, Vol. IV, pp. 109–124.

Mathur, P.R.G. (1982): "Anthropology of Tribal Medicine: Disease and Curing Techniques among the Tribals of North Wynand (Kerala)", *Man in India*, Vol. 62, No. 3.

Munguti, K. (1997): "Indigenous Knowledge in the Management of Malaria and Visceral Leishmaniasis among the Tugen of Kenya", *Indigenous Knowledge and Development Monitor*, Vol. 5, No. 1.

Patel, G.P. (1991): "A Study of Traditional Healing Practices among Baiga Tribe of Madhya Pradesh", *Bulletin of the Tribal Research and Development Institute*, Bhopal, Vol. XIX, Nos. 1–2.

12

Tribal Health and Nutrition

Socio-ecological Issues and Ways Ahead in Contemporary Participatory Process of Natural Resource Management

D. DEBNATH

Webster's dictionary defines health as a noun which refers to the general condition of the body or mind. Health is associated with the state of functionality of the body of an organism, especially the human body. There is no general agreement about any definition of health since health itself cannot be measured. The concepts of health are thus an a priori condition; and to maintain this some formalities, which are interlaced with the cultural life of the given people, are necessary. Likewise, illness and disease, disability and death and so on are viewed by the learned group and various remedial measures are adopted by them to meet the situational exigencies. We now regard health and its proper upkeep as an integral part of development. Traditionally, health has been defined as "the presence or absence of disease". But, with the establishment of the World Health Organization (WHO), the definition of health has received a more holistic approach which reflects health in relationship with a variety of factors such as the individual's physical, social, psychological, and emotional condition; environmental and cultural factors, as well as the creativity and productivity of a person.

The World Health Organization's Constitution defined health in its broader sense in 1946 as "a status of complete physical, mental and social well-being and not merely the absence of disease or infirmity" (WHO, 1946). Illness is contradiction to health. Health and illness are continuous processes and are interlinked with each other in inverse proportions, molding the behavioural pattern of the community. The health is a universal natural and social phenomenon, but the concept is culture-specific. There are certain factors which make people healthy, these factors are called the determinants of health, and include:

1. the social and economic environment,
2. the physical environment, and
3. the person's individual characteristics and behaviours.

The World Health Organization listed the following as determinants of health:

1. *Gender:* Males and females vary in terms of acquiring diseases. For example, prostate cancer can only be acquired by men while ovarian cancer can only be acquired by women.
2. *Personal behaviour and coping skills:* Persons differ in terms of behaviour and coping mechanisms. These differences affect the state of health. For example, the ability to manage stress, eating habits, sleeping habits, etc.
3. *Culture:* Beliefs, customs, and traditions could also affect health. For example, the existence of fake healers and quack doctors in certain countries.
4. *Health services:* The accessibility of services provided for the community. For example, Third World countries could not avail advanced medical interventions for certain diseases due to lack of technology and facilities.
5. *Social support:* Health support from family, friends, relatives.
6. *Education:* Low education equal poor health. For example, unhygienic practices due to lack of knowledge and information.
7. *Working environment:* People who are health-risk in the workplace. For example, factory workers are more prone to acquire lung cancer.
8. *Social Status:* With higher income rates, people can easily avail quality medicines and health supplements.
9. *Genetics:* Hereditary factors play a vital role in health. For example, a young woman with a grandma who has cervical cancer is more prone to acquire cervical cancer as well.
10. *Physical environment:* Clean and fresh air, safe water, clean communities plays an important role in maintaining health. For example, a community with dirty waters are more prone to diseases such as amoebiasis, dengue fever, leptospirosis, etc.

Members of the United Nations met in 2000 and set themselves eight goals as "Millennium Development Goals (MDGs)" to be achieved by 2015.

Of these goals, reducing child mortality, improving maternal health, and combatting HIV/AIDS, malaria and other diseases related to the health segment were included. The first goal 'of eradicating extreme poverty and hunger' also contains a nutritional element which is health related. In the developing world, death rates in children under-5 are dropping, but not fast enough. Eleven million children are still dying every year from preventable or treatable causes. More than half a million women die each year during pregnancy or childbirth. AIDS has become the fourth largest killer worldwide, and in parts of Asia, HIV is spreading at an alarming rate. The blight of malaria and tuberculosis continues.

Clearly, the challenges for India are multifaceted. In rural areas, reducing child mortality and improving maternal health are major challenges. HIV is spreading fast in urban and slum areas. Health care in India has been neglected because of insufficient spending by the government. The central government has vowed to increase spending on health to 6 per cent of Gross Domestic Product (GDP) by 2010 (as revealed recently by Union Health Minister that India would be able to meet the UN Millennium Development Goals, of which health is an important segment), and has unveiled a National Rural Health Mission. If this dream comes true, villages would have 24-hour health care services provided by an army of paramedics.

Tribal Health

The tribal perceptions to nature, worldview, cosmogony vary among themselves and thus put them sometimes in identifiable isolation. Their health is the perceptions and conceptions in their own cultural system based on external stimuli emanating from astrological influences, witch-craft and evil spirits in the etiology of disease, with less awareness of the modern health care and health services for health-seeking behaviour The health status of any community is influenced by the interplay of health consciousness of the people, socio-cultural, demographic, economic, educational and political factors. The common beliefs, traditional customs, myths, practices related to health and disease in turn influence the health-seeking behaviour of autochthonous people (Balgir, 2004). Health is an essential component of the well-being of mankind and is a prerequisite for human development. If general health of an average non-tribal Indian is inferior to the Western and even many Asian counterparts, the health of an average Indian tribal is found to be much poorer compared to the non-tribal counterpart.

Tribal communities in general and primitive tribal groups in particular are highly disease prone. Also they do not have required access to basic health facilities. They are most exploited, neglected, and highly vulnerable to diseases with high degree of malnutrition, morbidity and mortality (ibid.). Their misery is compounded by poverty, illiteracy, ignorance of causes of diseases, hostile environment, poor sanitation, lack of safe drinking water and blind beliefs, etc. The chief causes of high maternal mortality rate are found to be poor nutritional status, low haemoglobin (anaemia), unhygienic and primitive practices for parturition. Average calorie as well as protein consumption is found below the recommended level for the pregnant as well as lactating women. Some of the preventable diseases such as tuberculosis, malaria, gastroenteritis, filariasis, measles, tetanus, whooping cough, skin diseases (scabies), etc., are also high among the tribals. Some of the diseases of genetic origin reported to be occurring in the Indian tribal population are sickle cell anaemia, alpha- and beta-thalassemia, glucose-6–phosphate dehydrogenase (G-6-PD) deficiency, etc. (ibid.). Night blindness, sexually transmitted diseases are well-known public health problems of tribals in India.

Madhya Pradesh is the largest state of the country. The state has a total population of 603.48 lakh as per 2001 census and ranks sixth in the country, with a total tribal population of 120.69 lakh. There is about 23 per cent of the total tribal population of the country. There are 46 Scheduled Tribes (STs) spread over in 45 districts of undivided Madhya Pradesh (henceforth Madhya Pradesh means undivided Madhya Pradesh). Out of these 46 tribes, seven tribes are most backward tribes and are identified as primitive tribes (Tiwari, 1985) based on certain parameters of the Government of India. These are their pre-agricultural level of technology, low level of literacy and stagnant or diminishing population. The three primitive tribes of divided Madhya Pradesh are Baigas, Bharias and Saharia.

The health status of tribal population is very poor and worst of primitive tribes because of the isolation, remoteness and being largely unaffected by the developmental process going on in India (ICMR, 1998). Some of the factors which are responsible for this state of affairs are:

1. *Alcoholism*: An increased number of chronic active blood-borne diseases like Hepatitis B, cirrhosis of liver cases and virus infection are likely to be high in the tribal population because of the common social practice of tattooing and together with alcoholism.
2. *Problem of drinking water and water-borne diseases*: Water-borne diseases like helminthiasis, amoebiasis, giardiasis and diseases are rampant in the tribal population.
3. *Malaria and vector-borne diseases*: A number of tribal areas still continued to harbour malaria, primarily because of their inaccessibility and lack of community participation.

4. *Genetic disorders*: Sickle cell anaemia, glucose-6-phosphate dehydrogenises deficiency are common in the tribal populations
5. Traditionally permissive in sexual matters.
6. *Malnutrition*: Not only is protein-calorie malnutrition common, deficiency of micronutrients like iron is also very common.
7. Snake bites, suicides and accidents.
8. Inadequate access to services and inadequate indoor residual spraying.
9. The role of the NGOs is found to be minimal and insignificant in the sample villages covered in Madhya Pradesh.
10. Non-availability of government health workers and inadequate number of laboratory technicians in PHCs.

In India National Rural Health Mission has been launched in April 2005 to

(i) augment and ensure appropriate public health focus, people's orientation and ownership of public health programmes;
(ii) encourage community-based approaches to disease control;
(iii) promote public-private partnership in service provision;
(iv) involve local bodies and Panchayati Raj Institutions (PRIs); and
(v) promote gender equity.

These initiatives are intended to improve access to primary health care, thereby impacting the prevention and control of communicable diseases including vector-borne diseases, reduction of infant mortality rate and maternal mortality ratio by 50 per cent by the year 2012 and promotion of healthy lifestyles.

The paper aims to analyse the etiology of disease, procedure of treatment, major problems and issues with some suggestions to upgrade the health status and health-seeking behaviour of the primitive tribal groups (PTGs) of Madhya Pradesh.

Methodology

The data gathered for the study was collected through primary and secondary sources. The primary data collection was carried out through (a) individual interviews, and (b) informal discussions. The interview schedule was designed to collect detailed information regarding etiology of diseases, health facilities, and health-seeking behaviour and also discussing the issues that were raised during the individual interviews. The data were collected from six villages each from three primitive tribal groups:

(a) Bharia of Patalkot in Chindwara district
(b) Baiga of Dindori district
(c) Saharia of Sheopur district

Table 1

Socio-economic Profile of Villages of Three PTGs: Baiga, Saharia and Bharia

Socio-demographic Data	*Baiga of Dindori*	*Saharia of Sheopur*	*Bharia of Chhindwara*
Total sampled villages	6	6	6
Name of the villages	Talwar Tola, Kapoti, Kharideeh, Bangladadar of Karanjia block and Kandavani and Sarai of Bajag block in Dindori district	Upri Khoree, Nichli Khoree, Parond, Chak Bilari, Sonipura of Karhal block and Sironi of Vijaypur block in Sheopur district	Chimptipur, Gal Dubba, Rather, Kariyam, Gurhi Chetri, Ghat Linga of Tamia block in Chindwara district
Total HH in sampled villages	360	344	218
Total ST population in sampled villages	1711 (100%)	1506 (100%)	1469 (100%)
Total ST males in sampled villages	923	804	748
Total ST females in sampled villages	788	702	721
Sex ratio in sampled villages	854	873	964

Health and Nutritional Status of PTGs in Madhya Pradesh

Health and nutritional status of the population largely depends on the consumption of food in relation to their needs; which in turn is influenced by the availability of food and purchasing power and the nutritional values of the food intake. The health status depends upon the frequencies of diseases, natural or viral under different socio-economic conditions. For instance, in recent times fluorosis has emerged as a new public health hazard among the tribals of Madhya Pradesh. In Mandla district dental mottling and genuvalgum was seen in children and young adults of less 20 years of age. Fifty per cent drinking water sources of Mandla and Dindori districts had high fluoride contamination.

The health status of three PTGs is discussed below using secondary sources:

(a) *Baigas:* Baigas are one of the oldest autochthones of Madhya Pradesh, living in the five districts of Madhya Pradesh, i.e., Mandla, Dindori,

Shadol, Anupur and Umaria. But the biggest concentration is found in the Baigachak area of Dindori tehsil (now Dindori district). The area is surrounded by thick forest patches, rivulets and hillocks. Baigas economy mainly depends on agricultural pursuits and collection of non-timber forest produce. The other employment opportunities are unskilled labour and work in forest. They also love to work in the baris (land attached to the house) and grow maize, mustard, vegetables, roots and bulbs. Maize, Kodo, Kutki and Ramtila are the main crops grown by the Baigas. Maize and millets form the major foodstuffs consumed by the Baigas. These are consumed in the form of 'Pej', often supplemented by vegetables. Health and nutrition survey carried out by the centre in 1988–89, revealed that mean cereal intake was 425 + 11.6 gm/cu/day. Pulses consumption was much less 17.6 + 2.8 gm/cu/day as compared to RDA (40 gm.). Oil and fat consumption was negligible (2.2 + 0.7 ml/cu/day). The mean energy intake was 1615 + 57.2 kcal/day with protein intake of 50.2 + 1.9 gm/day (RMRCT 1988–89, 1996–98; Chakma et al., 2006). The severely malnourished Baiga preschool children were 7.3 per cent though percentage of normal preschool children was highest (33.3%) as compared to other primitive tribes. The consumption of calcium, thiamin, riboflavin and niacin were also lower than RDA. Goitre was also common in the areas of Baigas (Chakma et al., 2006).

(b) Bharias are one of the smaller primitive tribal groups of Madhya Pradesh found in the Patalkot area of Chhindwara district. The area is a unique deep depression in the Satpura plateau. There are about 12 villages spread over 79 sq km area with a total population of about 1600. The approachability is extremely difficult as the ridges are almost vertical. The economy of Bharias depends on 'Baris' attached to their hutments. They grow maize, jowar, Kodo and Kutki and non-timber forest products like mahua, amla, harra, etc. Preparation of deo-baharis (brooms) and selling them in the local market is also an important source of cash income. Though the valley is said to be very rich of medicinal plants, they are yet to be exploited as a source of income by the tribe. Maize consists the staple diet along with coarse millets like jowar, Kodo and Kutki, which are consumed in the form of 'Pej'. Green vegetables are scanty. Vegetables like gourds and vejra are grown in their baris. Apart from it 'Kaccharia' is consumed during winter season, which is then preserved by drying and later consumed during summer/rainy season (RMRCT, 1992). Acute respiratory infection (78.0%) and malaria (24.5%) were the major morbid conditions observed apart from sickle cell disease, which is 22.3 per cent (Chakma et al., 2006).

(c) *Saharia:* Saharias are mainly located in the Chambal division, i.e., Gwalior, Morena, Guna and Shivpuri bordering Rajasthan. Though as per record they are spread over in 21 districts of Madhya Pradesh, their main concentration is in Shivpuri district. Their economy lies mainly on minor forest produce. Because of unemployment the young people migrate to nearby district or town in search of employment specially during summer. Though their staple diet is jowar, bajra and maize in the form of Chapati, their detail diet survey is yet to be carried out. Nutritionally only 16.3 per cent of the preschool children were normal, 40.7 per cent were mildly malnourished, 34.5 per cent moderately and 8.5 per cent were severely malnourished (Table 3). Vitamin A deficiency in the form of night blindness, bitot spot and xerosis was 53.3 per cent. Acute respiratory infection (38%) and worm infestation (9.4%) were the major morbid conditions observed (Table 4). There were complete absence of sickle cell disease among this tribe, but b-thalessaemia was found to be 5.2 per cent. Cervical lymphadenopathy was observed in 20.4 per cent of the available individuals, which prompted us to take up an in-depth survey on tuberculosis in Karhal block of Morena district, where more than 50 per cent population were tribals. The prevalence of sputum positive pulmonary tuberculosis was 12.7/1000 (ibid.).

The following table shows the percentage of the people of three PTGs suffering from various diseases:

Table 2

Intensities of Diseases Among Three PTGs

Type of Disease	*Baiga*	*Saharia*	*Bharia*
Sickle Cell	22%	Nil	19.7%
Thalessaemia		8.7%	
Malnourishment preschool children	7%	9%	9%
Goitre			Over 10% among 15 year age
Hookworm infestation	13%		7%

Source: RMRCT Annual Reports 1988–89, 1996–98; Chakma et al., 2006.

Observations in the Three PTG Villages

In the studied villages main causes of diseases are as under:

1. *Natural:* Malevolent action of some planets and belief in doctrine of karma or bad deeds of the past, failure of performing rituals; environmental effects, wrong combination of foods, contact with some living organisms.

2. *Supernatural:* Evil spirits intrusion, evil eye effects, wrath of gods and goddesses.
3. *Human agencies:* Sorcerer and witches in finding out the causes of diseases like injury, paralysis, eczema, vomiting, rickets etc.

Procedure of Treatment

1. Folk Medicine:
   (a) *Religious*: Preventive procedures – includes use of charms, amulets, animal sacrifices, propitiation of disease causing gods and goddesses
   (b) *Magical:* Curative procedures – domestic methods, magical spells, shamanistic treatment
2. Modern Medical System:
   (a) Allopathy
   (b) Homeopathy

Table 3

Health Facilities for Three PTG Villages

Name of PTGs	*Availability of Primary Health Centre (PHC) Facilities*	*Availability of Sub-Health Centre (PHC) Facilities*	*Immunization*	*Doctor Visit from PHC*	*Drinking Water*
Baiga	100% villages	100% villages	100% villages	100% villages once in a week	100% villages available
Bharia	83.33% villages	100% villages	100% villages	100% Nurse visit rarely	100% villages available
Saharia	100% villages	100% villages	100% villages	100% villages once in a week	100% villages. Acute shortage

Baiga Villages

1. Severely malnourished preschool children are found, because milk is not available.
2. Drinking water availability is there but content have the high fluoride.
3. The consumption of calcium, thamin, riboflamin, iron and niacin and other micro-nutrients are lower among Baigas.
4. Sickle cell anaemia is the major morbid condition and goitre is common.
5. Malaria cases are highly reported.
6. The use of medicinal plants is found to the larger extent.

7. They depend on primary clinic as the access to PHC and SHC is difficult.
8. Cases of anaemia and RCH among the women are found.

Saharia

1. Severely malnourished preschool children are found among the Saharia.
2. The environment in the habitation is highly unhygienic and inhuman condition of living, e.g., because of toilet constructed at wrong place in front of their houses leading to overflow of dirty water, foul smell.
3. Inbreeding ground for houseflies and mosquitoes leading to illness.
4. Due to shortage of water they do not bathe so no concept of hand washing before food.
5. Animals die due to thirst.
6. As per government, the Saharia Aanganwadi children are given three times meal a day. No such distribution was found over there.
7. Mid-day Meal (MDM) distribution is also irregular.
8. Saharia habitat is geographically drought-prone area, hence drinking water is one of the major problems.
9. In Saharia land night blindness, bitot spot and xerosis are prevalent due to Vitamin A deficiency.

Bharia

1. The Bharia children are in the better condition regarding health and nutritional status in comparison to Baiga and Saharia children.
2. The boys and girls in Ashram school are getting proper mid-day meals.
3. There is lack of infrastructure, e.g., drinking water and hospital facilities
4. The people get improper food and habitation.
5. There is no tap water supply. The women and children carry water on their head for miles.
6. Due to topography the medical emergency cannot be provided.
7. They have to consume much energy due to undulation in the habitation of them for the fulfilment of daily requirement.
8. The crop varieties are limited as they cultivate only maize and consequently get less nutrients.
9. Due to inaccessible habitation, the state government health scheme like Janani Suraksha Yojana is implemented only in few villages …

The following table shows the health condition under universal determinants of health status:

Table 4

Determinants of Health Status among Three PTGs

Determinants	*Baiga*	*Saharia*	*Bharia*
Gender	Nutritional and health status are same among males and females.	Marked differences occurred in nutritional and health status among males and females.	Differences occurred in nutritional and health status among males and females.
Personal Behaviour	Sense of hygiene not so good, especially in the sense of sanitation.	Sense of hygiene not existing at all in all health-seeking behaviour.	Sense of hygiene is moderate, but not so good, especially in the sense of sanitation.
Culture	Causes behind the diseases are supernatural effects. High dependence on medicine men or quack doctors.	Causes behind the diseases are supernatural effects. High dependence on quack doctors.	Causes behind the diseases are supernatural effects. High dependence on medicine men or quack doctors.
Health Services	Government health services are there, but not so effective. Drinking water available.	Govt. health services are there, but not so effective. Acute shortage of drinking water.	Government health services are there, but not so effective. Drinking water available.
Social Support	During illness or sickness family, friend's or relation's support is available.	During illness or sickness family, friend's or relation's support not found to that extent.	During illness or sickness family, friend's or relation's support not found at all.
Education	Unawareness of health and hygiene.	Unawareness of health and hygiene.	Unawareness of health and hygiene.
Working Environment	People who are health-risk in the workplace.	People who are health-risk in the workplace.	People who are health-risk in the workplace.
Social Status	Due to poor income the people are incapable of spending money.	Due to poor income the people are incapable of spending money.	Due to poor income the people are incapable of spending money.
Genetics	Hereditary factors are there.	Hereditary factors are there.	Hereditary factors are there.
Physical Environment	Living in natural conditions with safe drinking water and lack of sanitation facilities.	Living in unhygienic situations with acute shortage of safe drinking water and lack of sanitation facilities.	Living in poor infrastructure with safe drinking water and lack of sanitation facilities.

Some Suggestions

In the course the investigation following suggestions have been made:

1. Health education is to be provided from the school level education to make freed from the traditional bindings.
2. Health care and health services to be provided in the tribal area for the treatment of the highly frequent diseases.
3. Community participation in the implementation programme is to be increased.
4. The tribal association with the medicinal plants are to be better utilized to generate green jobs.

Community Forest Management and Medicinal Plants

Community forest management covering the joint forest management (JFM) and community forestry has significant role in involving the people in protection, management and development of the forests. In course of time the participatory process of management demonstrated potential to make important contributions to poverty alleviation and conservation objectives. Thus, sustainable harvesting, cultivation, conservation of rare and endangered herbal species have been being taken in various JFM/FDA projects, in achieving multiple social, economic and conservation benefits. Tribals have been involved in managing the medicinal plants in collection, cultivation and utility for long time. So, in the project like SGSY programmes under Ministry of Rural Development, the Madhya Pradesh Forest Department cultivated 10 medicinal plants involving self-help groups. Madhya Pradesh Forest Department conducted several training programme for awareness generation, capacity building in processing and trading among the tribal women. Workshops of medicine man were held for inventorization of rare and endangered species in different territorial forest divisions. Being aware that several efforts and innovative strategies are under implementation in India, currently, there is a platform National Medicinal Plants Board, Department of Ayush, Ministry of Health and Family Welfare, Government of India, which provides an opportunity to all tribal and rural people to share and disseminate such efforts and help in developing 'mature' systems of medicinal plant management with potential to become part of the multi-crore businesses growing rapidly. They have taken initiative in promotional and commercial schemes for conservation and cultivation of medicinal plants. Thus community forest management has lot of scopes in conservation and cultivation of the medicinal and aromatic plants (MAPs) for support to the solution to the health issues of the tribals and also livelihood generations among them for poverty alleviation or reduction in the institutional process.

Conclusion

Health status and health-seeking behaviour are the important parameters and criteria in the development process. The dimensions of tribal health are philosophical, social, economic and developmental. As the tribals have their own system of healing their diseases in the traditional practices, mostly they depend on that. Now various schemes of the government have been implemented in the tribal villages for developing their health status. But the tribal peoples have not benefited to that extent due to unawareness, inaccessibility to their habitation, negligence of the administration, inefficiencies of the implementer. The approach and methods are to be participatory, as it is in normal practices in the community forest management, where the production and utility of the medicinal plants can help in institution building, livelihood generation and developing health status and health-seeking behaviour.

References

Balgir, R.S. (1998–99): Physical Growth, Health and Nutritional Status of Ashram School Children, Annual Report, Bhubaneswar: Regional Medical Research Centre, p. 37.

Chakma, Tapas, P. Vinay Rao, P.K. Meshram and S.B. Singh (2006): "Health and Nutrition Profile of Tribals of Madhya Pradesh and Chhattisgarh", Proceedings of National Symposium on Tribal Health, Jabalpur: RMRCT.

Indian Council of Medical Research (1998): *Health of Tribal Population in India: Results of Some ICMR Studies*, New Delhi: Indian Council of Medical Research.

RMRCT (Regional Medical Research Centre for Tribals) (1988–89): Annual Report, Jabalpur.

RMRCT (Regional Medical Research Centre for Tribals) (1996–98): Annual Report, Jabalpur.

RMRCT (Regional Medical Research Centre for Tribals) (1992–93): Annual Report, Jabalpur.

Tiwari, D.N. (1985): *Primitive Tribes of Madhya Pradesh*, New Delhi: Government of India, Ministry of Home Affairs, Tribal Development Division.

Wikipedia (n.d.): Social Determinants of Health. www.en.wikipedia.org/Social_determinants_of_health visited on 14th June, 2011

13

Health Status of the Baigas of Madhya Pradesh and Chhattisgarh

Y.G. JOSHI

The Scheduled Castes and the Scheduled Tribes, constituting about one-fourth of the Indian population, represent that section of the society which had been socially and economically deprived for centuries and still lags behind in all the standard parameters of development. Number of studies conducted in India clearly indicate that widespread poverty, illiteracy, malnutrition, absence of safe drinking water, poor sanitary and living conditions, poor maternal and child health services and ineffective coverage of national health and nutritional services have contributed to dismal health conditions prevalent in the tribal population of the country.

The present paper is focused on the Baiga primitive tribal group residing in the eastern Satpura region of central India. Baiga is relatively a small group, constituting nearly 2 per cent of the total Scheduled Tribes (STs) population of Madhya Pradesh and Chhattisgarh. The present paper is based on a part of the larger study conducted under the directives of the Ministry of Home Affairs, Government of India, to bring about the changes which this primitive tribal group has undergone, especially in response to government programmes, as compared to other population residing in the same area.

The scope of the primary survey, as far as the health status is concerned, is restricted to availability of health care facilities, maternal and child health, incidence of illness and death and adoption of family planning measures among the Baiga tribal group, as compared to other population living in the same area.

Methodology

The paper is solely based on the empirical data collected during fieldwork in the Baiga belt of central India. The coverage of the empirical study includes all those districts from Madhya Pradesh and Chhattisgarh where at least 5 per cent of the Baiga population resides. Thus, the districts included in the study are Shahdol, Sidhi, Umaria, Mandla, Dindori and Balaghat from Madhya Pradesh and Surguja, Korba, Bilaspur and Rajnandgaon from the state of Chhattisgarh. A total of 40 sample villages were included in the survey. The selection of 40 sample villages was made by the use of random table from the list of villages where at least 50 persons belonging to Baiga community resided.

Three types of schedules were used in the field survey, namely, village schedule, household schedule and the ethnographic schedule. Household schedules were canvassed in 25 households belonging to Baiga community and 15 households belonging to general population in each sample village. The selection of the households was done randomly, using the pre-prepared sampling frame of house list of each sample village. During survey some respondents had to be dropped out due to non availability. Finally the survey includes 983 household from Baiga community and 600 from other population.

Availability of Health Care Facilities

During the household survey it was ascertained from the respondents whether in their opinion the medical services were easily available to them and where did they take the patients for treatment for normal and serious ailments. The responses received have been set out in Table 1. The table brings out that only 27 per cent of the Baigas and 36 per cent of people from other communities perceived that the medical services were easily available, while the opinion of a majority of population was that medical services were not easily available. This clearly brings out a poor state of medical facilities in the entire region. Surprisingly, the tribal medicine man, called as *Gunia*, still holds an important position amongst the Baigas and nearly 58 per cent of the Baiga population was found to depend on him for treatment for normal ailments. The Primary Health Centre (PHC) and private doctors were found to be second and third order choice among Baigas where respectively 28 and 8 per cent of the patients were taken for normal ailments. The choice pattern for the type of health care facility of other population with respect to normal ailments was found to be significantly different than Baiga. Amongst non-Baiga, the gunia was the choice for only 24 per cent of the people, while the PHC and the private doctors were preferred by 38 and 23 per cent of the respondents respectively.

Table 1

Per cent Distribution of the Households According to Type of Health Care Facility Available

	Category	*Baiga ST*		*Other than Baiga ST*	
		In general	*In case of major ailments*	*In general*	*In case of major ailments*
A	Easy accessibility				
	Yes	26.6	—	36.3	—
	No	73.4	—	63.7	—
B	Access to type of health care facility				
i	Government Hospital	2.9	48.8	4.4	54.8
ii	PHC	27.7	22.2	38.3	24.9
iii	Sub-centre	2.5	6.6	3.4	4.5
iv	Family planning clinic	—	—	—	—
v	Mobile clinic	v	—	—	—
vi	Government paramedical	—	—	—	—
vii	Private hospital or clinic	—	0.2	1.3	0.5
viii	Pharmacy/drug store	—	—	—	—
ix	Private doctor	7.8	11.7	22.9	11.9
x	Village quack *(Gunia)*	58.2	8.6	24.1	2.3
xi	Field worker	0.8	2.8	4.0	0.3
xii	Other	0.1	0.1	1.6	0.6

As far as the treatment of major sicknesses is concerned, the preference in Baiga and other population was found to be more or less the same. Nearly half of the respondents preferred to take the serious patients to government hospitals and one-fourth to PHC where government hospitals were not accessible. The private doctors were found to be the third choice where nearly 12 per cent of the serious patients were being taken by both the Baiga and others.

The responses of the respondents regarding their faith in the medical system are presented in Table 2. The table brings out the perceptional difference between the Baigas and non-Baigas. While Baiga's first choice was still the traditional tribal medicine and occult prescription of 'jhad-phukh', in the case of 83 per cent of the respondents in other population, only 40 per cent of the respondents preferred them, while nearly 37 and 20 per cent of them preferred the ayurvedic and allopathic system respectively.

Table 2

Per cent Distribution of the Households According to Preference for System of Medicine

Category	*Baiga ST*			*Other Population*		
	First Pref.	*Second Pref.*	*Third Pref.*	*First Pref.*	*Second Pref.*	*Third Pref.*
Allopathic	17.0	23.9	60.0	55.7	20.1	33.3
Ayurvedic	0.1	15.2	15.4	4.3	37.0	9.1
Homeopathic	—	—	2.2	0.5	0.2	15.2
Unani	—	—	0.1	—	—	—
Siddha	—	—	—	—	0.4	0.2
Naturopathy	—	0.4	1.6	—	1.1	2.0
Yoga	—	—	—	—	—	—
Tibetan	—	—	—	—	—	—
Tribal medicine	1.4	50.3	12.5	1.2	28.9	13.2
Occult prescription	81.5	9.9	4.7	38.3	12.3	18.6
Any other	—	0.3	3.5	—	—	8.4

Maternal Health Care

In order to ascertain the availability and extent of utilization of maternal health care services some questions on antenatal care pertaining to number of visits of health workers made by expected mothers for pre-natal check-up, tetanus-oxide vaccination, nature of assistance acquired at the time of delivery, etc., were asked to male members. This information was collected for 708 Baiga and 436 couples pertaining to other population who had at least one issue. This information is presented in Table 3.

Table 3 reveals that only 21 per cent of the Baiga respondents reported about the visit of the health workers to inspect their pregnant wives for pre-natal check-up, this percentage was a bit higher at 29 with respect to other population. Nearly three-fourth of the Baiga respondents reported that the visit of the health worker was once or twice, while one to two visits were reported by nearly 50 per cent of household in the case of other category.

In spite of the claim of the government to have provided special facilities under Baiga Development Authorities, 92 per cent of the Baiga respondents reported that their wives did not visit the hospital for pre-natal check-up. In the general population also 79 per cent wives of the respondents did not go for pre-natal check-up. This situation testifies to the lack of awareness of the people about the need to have a pre-natal check-up at the time of pregnancy in general, and the Baigas in particular. Only 19 per cent of the Baiga males reported to have the knowledge that ATS was given to their wives during pregnancy, this percentage was higher at 37 in the case of other population.

Table 3

Percentage of the Youngest Married Couples in the Households having at least One Live Birth According to Type of Medical Care Received During the Pregnancy and at the Time of Delivery

	Category	*Baiga (Percentage)*	*Others (Percentage)*
I	Visit of health worker		
	Yes	21.0	29.4
	No	79.0	70.6
	No. of visit		
1	One visit	29.5	18.0
2	Two visits	45.0	38.3
3	Three visits	18.1	28.9
4	Four or more visits	7.4	14.8
II	Visit for pre-natal check up		
	Yes	7.6	21.0
	No	92.4	79.0
III	Titanus toxoid injection		
	Given	19.0	36.9
	Not given	81.0	63.1
IV	Assistance during delivery		
1	Doctor (allopathic)	1.0	4.8
2	Doctor (ayurvedic)	—	—
3	Nurse/midwife	1.3	6.2
4	ANM/LHV	0.6	4.8
5	Trained *dai*	2.6	1.8
6	Traditional *dai*	42.6	43.5
7	Relative/friend	51.5	38.9
8	Other	0.1	—
9	None	0.3	—

As far as the assistance during delivery is concerned, nearly 94 per cent of the Baigas were found to depend on either traditional *dai* or their relatives and the help acquired from the doctor or midwife was as low as 2 per cent. In the general population also the dependence on the traditional *dai* or relatives for delivery was found to be nearly 82 per cent, while the doctors, midwifes or ANM performed deliveries in 15 per cent of the cases.

Thus, in spite of modern health infrastructure created for Baigas, there has not been any perceptible change in their traditional practices.

Child Health Care

In order to have an insight into the prevalent practices of child rearing and the adoption of the immunization schedule for the healthy growth of the children some questions were introduced in the schedule. The responses received from the young couples have been listed out in Tables 4 and 5.

Table 4

Per cent Distribution of Youngest Eligible Couples having at least One Child According to Particulars of Breastfeeding and Initiation of Solid and Semi-solid Food

	Item	*Baiga (Percentage)*	*Others (Percentage)*
I	Breastfeeding		
	Yes	97.6	97.0
	No	2.4	3.0
II	Sex of child		
	Male	47.9	47.2
	Female	52.1	52.8
III	Duration of breastfeeding		
	<1 month	0.4	0.2
	1–3 months	1.6	1.2
	4–6 months	2.5	2.4
	7–9 months	1.8	2.1
	10–12 months	32.6	27.1
	> 12 months	61.1	67.0
IV	Use of lotion/paste for weaning		
	Yes	1.4	5.5
	No	98.6	94.5
V	Reasons for not breastfeeding		
1	Mother ill/weak	11.2	25.0
2	Child ill/weak	44.4	50.0
3	Child died	44.4	25.0
4	Nipple/breast problem	—	—
5	Insufficient working	—	—
6	Mother working	—	—
7	Child refused	—	v
8	Other	—	—
IV	Initiation of solid/semi-solid food		
	Within 4 months	0.6	0.2
	4–12 months	94.1	95.5
	After 12 months	5.3	4.3

Table 4 lists out the particulars about the breastfeeding and the initiation of solid food in infants. The table brings out that in Baigas, as well as the general population, nearly all of the children were found to be breastfed for a period of 10 to 12 months or above. There was no gender bias reported on this count. The insignificant number of children which could not be breastfed were those who were either too weak or had died. The initiation of solid food was also found to be during 4 to 12 months in both the Baiga and other population. It was observed during fieldwork that prolonged period of breastfeeding, without giving proper nourishment in solid form, was resulting in undernutrition of the infants.

Table 5

Per cent Distribution of Youngest Eligible Couple According to Vaccination Given to their Last Child and Prevalence of Diseases Among Them

	Category	*Baiga (Percentage)*	*Others (Percentage)*
A	Vaccination given to last child		
I	BCG		
	Yes	34.0	53.8
	No	56.2	37.8
	Not known	9.8	8.4
II	DPT		
	Yes	31.8	52.7
	No	57.7	38.2
	Not known	10.5	9.1
III	Polio drops		
	Yes	69.3	79.3
	No	24.6	15.2
	Not known	6.1	5.5
IV	Injection against measles		
	Yes	35.4	55.8
	No	53.7	34.1
	Not known	10.9	10.1
B	Prevalence of disease (no. of cases)		
1	Whooping cough	8	6
2	Measles	—	—
3	Polio	—	—
4	Diphtheria	1	—
5	Chickenpox	2	—
6	Rickets	1	2

The adoption of immunization schedule as suggested under the National Health Programme was not found to have gained ground, as expected with regard to the population of the area in general and the Baigas in particular. Table 5 reveals the fact that adoption of the immunization programme was significantly higher in the general population, as compared to Baigas. Against 34, 32, 69 and 35 per cent of Baiga youngest child who had been vaccinated against BCG, DPT, polio and measles respectively the percentage in general population was higher at 54, 53, 79 and 56 respectively. Whooping cough was found to be most prevalent in the infants of both in the Baiga and other population from amongst the diseases which are preventable by vaccination.

Incidence of Illness

Information collected on different types of diseases reported in the surveyed household, the age of persons reporting sick, duration of illness, and the type of medical facility availed for treatment is presented in Tables 6 and 7.

Out of all the family members of the surveyed household 6.2 per cent of the Baiga and 7.9 per cent members from other communities were reported to have been sick during the period of 12 months preceding the time of survey. No significant difference was noted between male and female in the incidence of illness. Agewise, the age group of 15–49 years was the modal group in both the Baiga and other household, accounting for around 40 per cent of the total persons reported sick. The incidence of illness in the age group of 1 to 4 years was found to be twice in Baiga, as compared to general population.

No significant difference between the Baiga and other population was noted with regard to duration of illness. The maximum number of persons reported sick remained ill for a period of 7 to 14 days. Nearly one-fourth of the Baigas who reported sick, remained ill for more than 90 days; this percentage in general population was 21.

A probe of Table 6 brings out the fact that the entire area was malaria infested and more than three-fourth of the patients were directly or indirectly affected by malaria. The persons reporting fever were also mostly those whose malaria was not properly cured and they became chronic patients and the carrier of the parasite. The enquiry revealed that a majority of patients who reported severe headache with loss of consciousness were the cases of cerebral malaria. Besides malaria and related disorder, diarrhoea was a common disease in the area resulting from infected water. Chickenpox and skin diseases were found to be more prevalent among Baigas as compared to general population. The skin diseases in Baigas may be ascribed to their poor personal hygienic habits. The asthma was found to be more prevalent in the coal-mining areas.

Table 6

Distribution of Persons Reported Ill by Age and Sex, Type and Duration of Illness

	Item	*Biaga ST*			*Other than Baiga ST*		
		Total	*Males*	*Females*	*Total*	*Males*	*Females*
	All persons (No) (%)	273 (6.2)	130 (5.9)	143 (6.5)	243 (7.9)	122 (7.7)	121 (8.1)
I	Age of persons reporting sick (%)						
	<1 year	0.3	0.4	0.2	2.8	3.0	2.4
	1–4	8.4	10.4	9.1	4.6	6.3	3.7
	5–14	15.2	16.3	10.9	14.7	14.0	14.2
	15–49	42.6	36.7	46.3	41.4	38.7	43.0
	50–59	18.7	20.0	17.8	16.7	16.0	16.2
	>=60	14.8	16.2	15.7	19.8	22.0	20.5
II	Duration of Illness (%)						
	<7 days	8.4	7.7	9.1	12.8	11.5	14.0
	7–14 days	31.1	25.4	36.4	22.2	22.1	22.3
	15–29 days	15.4	16.2	14.7	23.5	22.9	24.0
	30–59 days	14.7	17.7	11.9	14.0	18.0	9.9
	60–90 days	5.5	5.4	5.6	6.6	5.8	7.4
	>=90 days	24.9	27.6	22.3	20.9	19.7	22.4
III	Type of illness (%)						
1	Malaria	31.9	32.3	31.5	38.3	35.2	41.3
2	Fever	25.3	21.5	28.7	21.8	22.1	21.5
3	Severe headache	20.5	21.5	19.6	17.7	17.2	18.2
4	Chickenpox	5.1	6.2	4.2	—	—	—
5	Diarrhoea	6.2	6.2	6.3	4.9	3.2	2.5
6	Skin disease	2.9	2.3	3.5	—	—	—
7	Tuberculosis	1.5	3.1	—	1.6	2.5	0.8
8	Pneumonia	0.7	0.8	0.7	2.9	4.1	1.6
9	Measles	0.7	0.8	0.7	2.1	0.8	3.3
10	Asthma	2.6	3.8	1.4	4.1	7.4	5.0
11	Other*	2.6	1.5	3.4	6.6	7.5	5.8

*All other diseases in which cases reported were less than 5.

As far as the type of medical facility availed was concerned, 21 per cent of the Baigas and 11 per cent from the other communities did not avail any medical facility. Table 7 reveals that among Baigas merely 64 per cent of the patients got their treatment from the infrastructure created by the government, like hospital, PHC or sub-centres, mobile clinics, or field workers, while 28 per cent were treated by the private doctors. This percentage was found to be respectively 57 and 37 for other population, meaning thereby that other than Baiga population was depending more on private health facilities, as compared to Baigas.

Table 7

Distribution of Persons Reported Ill According to Medical Treatment Availed/Not Availed and Its Source

	Item	Baiga Scheduled Tribe			Other than the Baiga Scheduled Tribe		
		Total	Males	Females	Total	Males	Females
	Persons taking medical treatment (%)	79.5	82.1	77.3	83.8	90.8	86.6
	Source of medical treatment (%)						
I	Government/Municipal Hospital	13.5	13.6	13.4	23.1	25.2	20.9
II	PHC	16.6	17.3	16.0	15.3	14.3	16.4
III	Sub-centre	12.7	14.5	10.9	9.6	7.6	11.8
IV	Mobile clinic	13.2	10.9	15.2	3.9	3.4	4.5
V	Government paramedical	—	—	—	—	—	—
VI	Private hospital or clinic	0.4	—	0.8	0.9	0.8	0.9
VII	Pharmacy/drug store	0.8	1.8	—	—	—	—
VIII	Private doctor	27.9	28.2	27.7	35.8	38.7	32.7
IX	Field worker	7.9	7.3	8.4	5.2	5.0	5.5
X	Other	7.0	6.4	7.6	6.2	5.0	7.3
	Persons not taking medical treatment (%)	20.5	17.9	22.7	11.2	9.2	13.4
	Reasons for not availing medical facility (%)						
I	Not deemed necessary	10.2	12.5	8.6	—	—	—
II	Not customary	23.7	33.3	17.1	24.1	8.3	35.3
III	High financial cost	15.3	16.7	14.3	34.5	41.7	29.4
IV	Inconvenient due to long distance	6.8	8.3	5.7	6.9	8.3	5.9
V	Lack of knowledge of services	—	—	—	—	—	—
VI	Poor quality service	1.7	-	2.9	—	—	—
VII	No time to go	1.7	—	2.9	—	—	—
VIII	Not permitted to go	—	—	—	—	—	—
IX	Other reasons	40.6	29.2	48.5	34.5	41.7	29.4

Out of the persons who did not avail any medical facility 41 per cent of the Baiga representing the category of other reasons were those who depended either on gunia or tribal medicine man or took local herbs. The percentage of such persons in other than Baiga was 35. The second important reason for not availing medical facilities in Baigas was that it was not customary, or was not felt to be necessary. Prohibitive cost was termed as the second important reason in other population. Nearly 7 per cent of those persons who did not avail any medical facility in both the Baiga and other communities were those who could not go to hospital due to long distance.

Incidence of Death

A total of 21 deaths in Baiga household and 13 in other category were reported in a period of 12 months preceding the date of survey. The age and sexwise break up, together with the cause of death and type of medical attendance provided is set out in Table 8.

Table 8

Distribution of Deaths According to Age of the Deceased, Cause of Death and Type of Medical Attention Received Before Death

	Item	*Baiga ST*			*Other than Baiga ST*		
		Total	*Males*	*Females*	*Total*	*Males*	*Females*
I	Number of deaths	21	12	9	13	7	6
II	Age of deceased (%)						
	Less than 1 year	14.3	16.7	11.1	15.4	28.6	—
	1–4	9.5	8.3	11.1	7.7	—	16.7
	5–9	14.3	16.7	11.1	—	—	—
	10–19	4.8	8.3	—	—	—	—
	20–49	9.5	—	22.2	53.8	42.9	66.7
	50–59	9.5	8.3	11.1	—	—	—
	60 and above	38.1	41.7	33.4	23.1	28.5	16.6
III	Cause of death (%)						
1	Accident and injury	—	—	—	7.7	14.3	—
2	Childbirth	—	—	—	23.0	—	50.0
3	Fever/TB/jaundice	52.4	50.0	55.6	38.5	42.9	33.3
4	Digestive disorder	14.3	25.0	—	15.4	28.5	—
5	Respiratory disorder	9.5	—	22.2	—	—	—
6	Senility	23.8	25.0	22.2	7.7	—	16.7
7	Other	—	—	—	7.7	14.3	—
IV	Medical attention (%)						
	Provided	76.2	90.9	60.0	84.6	85.7	83.3
	Not provided	23.8	9.1	40.0	15.4	14.3	16.7
V	Medical attention provided by (%)						
1	Doctor	57.1	75.0	33.3	76.9	85.7	66.7
2	Ayurvedic doctor	—	—	—	—	—	—
3	Nurse/midwife	—	—	—	—	—	—
4	ANM/LHV	—	—	—	—	—	—
5	Trained *dai*	—	—	—	—	—	—
6	Traditional *dai*	—	—	—	—	—	—
7	Relative/friend	4.8	—	11.1	—	—	—
8	Other	38.1	25.0	55.6	23.1	14.3	33.3

In Baigas maximum deaths were reported in the age group of above 60, while in the general population the highest number of deaths occurred in the age group of 20 to 49. Nearly half of the deaths in Baigas occurred due to malaria, TB and jaundice. This percentage in other group was 39. Nearly 24 per cent deaths in Baigas were due to old age and 14 per cent died due to digestive disorders. In the other population deaths during child birth and due to digestive disorders were respectively the second and third order cause. Among Baigas medical attendance could be provided to nearly three-fourth of those who died and 38 per cent of those were treated by gunia or the tribal medicine man. Among other communities nearly 85 per cent of the persons who died were provided medical treatment and 77 per cent among them were attended by the doctor.

Fertility

There are numerous variables on which data may have been collected for analysing levels and trends of fertility in the demographic surveys. However, keeping in view the scope of the present study and operational constrains, information on a few variables like age at marriage, number of children ever born, children who died and those who were not staying with the household was collected. The information was collected by the interviewers from the head of surveyed household and pertained to ever married women aged 15–49 years. It may be mentioned, on the onset, that the information about children who were born, those who died and about the adoption of family planning methods, etc., is quite sensitive one and many of the respondents were hesitant to give proper information with the fear that they may have to undergo family planning operation. In some cases male members were not found to have proper memory of births, deaths, age of marriage, etc. The data would have been more dependable if the deeper probe could have been made by female interviewers with the female members of the family. However, this could not be done due to time and money constraints.

Marital Status

Considering first the distribution of ever married women aged 15 to 49 years into currently married, widowed and divorced category it may be observed from Table 9 that out of respectively 853 and 601 ever married Baiga and other women of this age group, nearly 96 per cent were in the currently married category and there was no difference with respect to marital status between Baiga and other communities. However, in the age group of 40 to 49, the percentage of widowed women in Baigas was 12.9, being nearly twice than the other population.

Table 9

Per cent Distribution of Ever Married Women Aged 15–40 by Marital Status

Age Group	*Baiga Marital Status*			*Others Marital Status*		
	Currently Married	*Widowed*	*Divorced/ Separated*	*Currently Married*	*Widowed*	*Divorced/ Separated*
15–19	99.1	0.9	—	98.0	—	2.0
20–29	98.4	0.3	1.3	98.4	—	1.6
30–39	97.6	0.7	1.7	96.5	2.5	1.0
40–49	85.7	12.9	1.4	91.5	6.6	1.9
Total	96.0	2.7	1.3	96.5	1.5	2.0

Age at Marriage

As regards distribution of ever married women with respect to the age at marriage was concerned, Table 10 clearly reveals that age of marriage in Baigas was significantly lower, as compared to other population. In Baigas nearly 76 per cent of the ever married women were married at the age below 15 years, while this percentage in other population was lower at 67 per cent.

Table 10

Per cent Distribution of Ever Married Women Aged 15–49 by Age at Marriage

Age Group	*Age at Marriage*					
	<15	*16*	*17*	*18*	*19*	*>19*
Baiga Scheduled Tribe						
15–19	81.0	10.9	50.7	1.8	0.6	—
20–24	70.5	11.8	4.9	4.9	3.0	4.9
25–29	71.3	10.8	5.6	5.6	2.6	4.1
30–34	77.8	14.2	2.3	1.7	0.6	3.4
35–39	74.1	12.1	4.3	2.6	—	6.9
40–44	86.0	4.4	3.2	3.2	—	3.2
45–49	74.5	14.5	3.6	—	—	7.4
Total	75.8	11.4	4.4	3.3	1.3	3.8
Other than the Baiga Scheduled Tribe						
15–19	87.4	4.4	5.9	2.3	—	—
20–24	55.6	15.6	5.9	14.8	2.2	5.9
25–29	54.7	11.1	6.8	15.4	0.9	11.1
30–34	63.0	11.8	4.2	7.6	1.7	11.7
35–39	62.7	14.5	3.6	4.8	4.8	9.6
40–44	76.7	11.7	3.3	6.7	—	1.6
45–49	72.3	4.3	2.1	14.9	—	6.4
Total	66.7	10.8	5.0	9.3	1.4	6.8

At the opposite end the girls being married at or after 18 years in Baigas were nearly 8 per cent, while this percentage for other population was nearly 18. The agewise break up of the ever married women depicts the general tendency of early marriage throughout the area in all the communities and there had not been any noticeable change in this tendency in recent generation, as compared to previous ones.

Number of Children Ever Born and Surviving

Number of children born to women in the reproductive age group reflects trends and differentials in fertility to the women of different cohorts. While parity distribution of women reveals shifts in the fertility pattern of women of reproductive age group, average number of children ever born and living reveal trends in fertility performance of these women. Data collected on these items from the surveyed household pertaining to children ever born and living, excluding the cases of abortions, has been presented in Tables 11 and 12.

Table 11

Distribution of the Ever Married Women (Aged 15–49) According to Age at Marriage and Number of Ever Born, Dead and Surviving Children

Age Group	*No. of Ever Married Women*	*No. of Children Ever Born per 100 Women (Both Sexes)*	*No. of Children Not Alive per 100 Women*	*No. of Children Surviving per 100 Women*
Baiga Scheduled Tribe				
15–19	109	54	10	43
20–24	116	172	20	152
25–29	189	328	51	277
30–34	171	400	64	336
35–39	121	445	68	377
40–44	89	463	72	391
45–49	58	423	63	360
Total	853	313	47	266
Other than the Baiga Scheduled Tribe				
15–19	51	56	9	47
20–24	118	152	20	132
25–29	125	296	36	260
30–34	115	405	39	366
35–39	86	462	61	401
40–44	58	495	67	428
45–49	48	458	42	416
Total	601	326	38	287

Table 12

Per cent Distribution of Women (Aged 15–49) Belonging to Baiga and Other Population According to Number of Children Ever Born and Staying Within or Outside the Households

Age Group	No. of Ever Married Women	Number of Children Ever Born (%)								No. of Children			
		0	1	2	3	4	5	6	7	Total Born Children No.	Staying in the Household (%)	Not Staying in the Household (%)	Those Who Died (%)
Baigas (Both Sexes)													
15–19	109	58.8	34.8	5.5	0.9	—	—	—	—	53	79.2	1.9	18.9
20–24	116	28.6	45.0	17.0	7.7	1.7	—	—	—	326	61.3	27.0	11.7
25–29	189	7.4	32.3	32.3	20.0	5.8	2.2	—	—	621	45.4	39.1	15.5
30–34	171	3.0	29.2	30.8	21.1	13.0	1.6	1.3	—	684	41.4	42.5	16.1
35–39	121	1.5	28.2	30.3	22.8	15.5	1.1	0.6	—	503	35.4	49.3	15.3
40–44	89	2.0	22.4	21.7	25.7	15.8	10.5	1.3	0.6	412	30.8	53.7	15.5
45–49	58	1.7	22.7	31.8	21.1	9.1	10.2	2.3	1.1	220	27.3	57.7	15.0
Total	853	12.2	32.8	30.9	11.9	8.0	3.4	0.7	0.1	2819	41.6	43.2	15.2
Other than Baigas (Both Sexes)													
15–19	51	48.8	41.4	9.8	—	—	—	—	—	25	80.0	4.0	16.0
20–24	118	24.1	51.8	19.4	4.1	0.6	—	—	—	179	66.5	20.7	12.8
25–29	125	9.5	36.0	36.0	15.0	3.0	0.5	—	—	335	53.4	34.4	12.2
30–34	115	4.5	30.6	34.4	15.3	8.3	5.1	0.9	0.9	466	41.8	48.5	9.7
35–39	86	4.0	27.1	23.2	23.2	11.3	7.3	1.3	2.6	379	36.7	50.1	13.2
40–44	58	3.9	17.3	28.8	20.2	15.4	9.6	2.9	1.9	287	29.3	57.1	13.6
45–49	48	3.6	21.2	32.5	18.8	10.0	8.8	3.8	1.3	206	30.6	60.2	9.2
Total	600	10.6	33.2	28.5	14.7	6.9	4.2	1.0	0.9	1877	42.6	45.6	11.8

The data presented in Table 11 on average number of children born and living reveals that the fertility pattern at all age groups in Baiga and other communities was more or less the same. The ever born child per 100 Baiga women on an average worked out to 313, as compared to 326 for general population. However, the number of children who died per 100 women was higher at 47 in Baigas, as compared to 38 in other communities.

The child birth at early age group of 15 to 19 years was more or less the same in all the communities of the area. The percentage distribution of ever married women by number of children born according to women's current age is presented in Table 12. The table shows that nearly one-tenth of the ever married women aged 15–19, both among Baiga and other categories, did not give birth to any child, while nearly 40 per cent among them gave birth to two or three children. The average number of children ever born worked out to nearly three in both the Baigas and other communities. There was also no difference with respect to the children remaining with the household, being around 40 per cent.

Knowledge and Practice of Family Planning Methods

The information pertaining to the knowledge and practice of family planning methods was collected from the male members of the youngest eligible couples in the surveyed villages. A total of 715 respondents from Baiga household and 432 from amongst other than Baiga were covered under this sample survey and this information is set out in Tables 13, 14 and 15.

Table 13 lists out the knowledge, practice and adoption of family planning methods currently in vogue. It was observed that nearly 90 per cent of the Baiga young couples and 94 per cent of the respondents from other community were aware of some or the other method of family planning. Male and female sterilization was known to nearly all of them. Awareness of condom or 'Nirodh' was found amongst 59 per cent of the Baiga respondents and 75 per cent amongst other communities. Knowledge about pills and Copper 'T' was found to be much higher at respectively 67 and 41 per cent in other communities, as compared to respectively 51 and 13 per cent in Baigas. The responses regarding injection, periodic absence or withdrawal were rejected because during field checks it was observed by the principal investigator that the majority of respondents were not clear about the basic scientific concept of the above methods and had replied to the questions just casually. Nearly one-tenth of the respondents of both the community responded to have used some herb to prevent conception, however, the response to this question were also not found to be specific. As far as the adoption of family planning methods was concerned nearly all of the respondents both from Baiga and other community, were found to use only one method and in 72 and 26 per cent of the cases in Baigas and 82 and 90 per cent in other communities it was respectively male and female sterilization. The adoption of male sterilization was relatively more pronounced in other communities, as compared to Baigas. Nearly 6 per cent of the respondents from other communities also had adopted Copper 'T' however, in Baigas the adoption of all other methods was more or less non-existent.

Table 13

Per cent Distribution of Youngest Eligible Couples having Knowledge of any Contraceptive Method and Its Practice by Them

	Method	*Baiga Scheduled Tribe*	*Other than Baiga Scheduled Tribe*
A	No. of couples	715	432
	Couples having knowledge of any method (%)	89.5	93.5
B	Knowledge of FP method (%)		
1	Pill	51.1	67.1
2	IUD/Copper 'T'	13.4	40.5
3	Condom or Nirodh	59.1	74.8
4	Female sterilization	100.0	100.0
5	Male sterilization	99.1	99.0
C	Practice of FP method (%)		
	Yes	22.4	36.1
	No	77.6	63.9
D	Use of herb/plant (%)		
	Yes	7.8	10.4
	No	92.2	89.6
	Any other	—	—
E	Adoption of FP method (%)	22.9	33.3
1	Immediately after marriage	0.6	—
2	After one child	9.8	11.1
3	After two children	26.2	29.9
4	After three children	31.7	23.6
5	After four children	14.6	17.4
6	After five children	9.8	8.3
7	After six or more children	7.3	9.7

Table 13 clarifies that none of the respondents, either from Baiga or other communities used any family planning method immediately after marriage. In Baigas the highest per cent of persons used some family planning method only after the third child, while in other communities it was after the second child.

Table 14 lists out the age distribution of the persons who knew or adopted any family planning method. The table brings out that it was the middle age people of the age group of 35 to 39 who were mostly aware and used family planning method in both the communities and it was mostly sterilization.

Table 14

Per cent Age Distribution of Youngest Eligible (Male) Couple Knowing and Using any Family Planning Method by Age

Age group	*Baiga Scheduled Tribe*		*Other than Baiga Scheduled Tribe*	
	Knowledge	*Practice*	*Knowledge*	*Practice*
< 20	0.8	—	0.3	—
20–24	10.8	1.3	9.8	0.7
25–29	24.3	9.4	19.9	12.2
30–34	20.3	21.5	23.3	26.5
35–39	23.8	34.2	24.1	32.0
40–44	11.5	20.1	14.6	19.8
45–49	8.5	13.5	8.0	8.8

Table 15

Per cent Distribution of Youngest Eligible (Male) Couple Knowing and Using any Family Planning Method by Duration of Marriage, Educational Level, Work and Marriage Status

Category	*Baiga ST*		*Other than Baiga ST*	
	Knowledge	*Practice*	*Knowledge*	*Practice*
Duration (years) of marriage <1	0.3	0.6	1.0	1.2
1–4	7.0	0.6	8.0	3.8
5–9	18.8	5.0	20.9	9.6
10–14	24.1	18.1	20.0	21.2
15–19	20.6	26.9	21.7	31.4
>=20	29.2	48.8	28.4	32.8
Education				
Illiterate	76.0	78.1	39.4	39.1
Below primary	11.2	9.7	18.0	16.0
Primary	6.8	7.1	13.4	14.7
Middle	3.6	2.6	12.7	9.6
Matric	1.1	—	4.8	7.1
Hr. Sec./Sr. Sec.	0.8	0.6	6.6	7.1
Graduate and above*	0.5	1.9	5.1	6.4
Any other**	—	—		
Worker				
Main	81.5	78.3	92.8	90.6
Marginal	8.9	10.9	3.2	4.4
Non-worker	9.6	10.8	4.0	5.0
Migration				
Inmigrant	1.2	1.3	2.6	2.0
Non-migrant	98.8	98.4	97.4	98.0

*Including all persons having technical and non-technical degree/diploma.

** Including unspecified.

Data of certain selected characteristics of the eligible males having knowledge or practising any family planning method pertaining to duration of marriage, education level and work status were also collected during the survey and is presented in Table 15. The table brings out that in both the communities the family planning methods were used only after 4 years after marriage. The majority of persons knowing or practising any family planning method in Baigas were illiterate, main workers, and non-migrants. In non-Baigas the majority were literate and had the work status similar to that of Baigas.

Salient Findings

1. Nearly three-fourth of the respondents, both among Baiga and general population, opined that the government medical facilities were not easily available.
2. More than half of the Baiga population was still found to depend on *Gunia* or the tribal medicine man for normal ailments. However, for major sickness, patients were being taken to nearby government hospital, PHCs or to private doctors.
3. The information about maternal health care collected from married couples revealed that in nearly three-fourth of the cases, in both Baigas and others, no health worker visited their wives for pre-natal check-up.
4. The lack of awareness regarding the need to have a pre-natal check-up at the time of pregnancy in people in general and in Baigs in particular, was clearly noticeable.
5. As far as the assistance during delivery was concerned, nearly 94 per cent of Baigas depended on their traditional *dai* or their relatives.
6. Nearly all of the infants in Baigas were found to be breastfed for a period of 10 to 12 months and above. It was observed that the prolonged period of breastfeeding, not properly supplemented by solid food, was resulting in the undernourishment of the infants.
7. The survey brought out the fact that the adoption of immunization schedule suggested under National Health Programme was poor in Baiga population. The adoption of vaccination against BCG, DPT, polio and measles was 34, 32, 69 and 35 per cent respectively. The situation of general population was found to be marginally better.
8. The entire area was found to be malaria infested and more than three-fourth of the patients in both the Baigas and other population were directly or indirectly affected by malaria. A sizable percentage of patients were of cerebral malaria.

9. Besides malaria, diarrhea was noted to be another common disease resulting from infected water.
10. Skin diseases, resulting from poor personal hygienic habits, were found to be more prevalent in Baigas, as compared to other population.
11. As far as the type of medical facility availed was concerned, one-fourth of Baigas did not avail any medical facility and among those who availed it, 64 per cent depended on the infrastructure created by the government and 28 per cent depended on private doctors. The dependence on private doctors was found to be more in general population.
12. In Baiga males maximum deaths within the duration of one year were reported in the age group of above 60 years and nearly half of them were from malaria, TB and jaundice. With respect to women the deaths during delivery were comparatively much higher in Baigas.
13. The age of marriage in Baigas was significantly lower as compared to general population. More than three-fourth of Baiga girls were married at an age below 15 years.
14. The fertility performance of the Baiga women with respect to number of children ever born was more or less similar to the general population. However, the reported death of children in Baigas was found to be nearly 24 per cent higher.
15. More than 90 per cent of the respondents, both among Baigas and other population, were found to be aware of some or the other method of family planning.
16. The male and female sterilization was known to nearly all the respondents, however, the knowledge of other methods, viz., pills, copper 'T' and condom was significantly higher in general population, as compared to Baigas.
17. As far as the adoption of family planning methods was concerned, in both the Baigas and other population, nearly all of them were found to have used only one method, and for two-third of them, it was sterilization at the age of 35 to 39.
18. The adoption of male sterilization in other communities, as compared to Baigas, was relatively more pronounced.
19. None of the respondents in both the communities used any family planning method immediately after marriage. In Baigas a majority of them used it after the third child, while in other communities it was after the second.

In conclusion, it may be said that in spite of significant investment made by the government under the special assistance programme for the development of this primitive tribal group, the ground realities are far from being satisfactory. The high death rate of female during child birth, high child mortality rate and a majority of deaths occurring due to preventable diseases, like malaria, diarrhea and jaundice, speaks itself of the sorry state of affairs with respect to the availability of health care facilities in the area.

Besides poor geographical accessibility, access, affordability and lower education and awareness levels, the corruption and non helping attitude of the functionaries, together with mismanagement and poor coordination between different components of health care delivery system are largely responsible for the poor state of health of this primitive tribal group, even after so many decades after independence.

14

Health and Nutritional Status of Santhal and Birhor Tribes of Hazaribagh, Jharkhand

An Analysis

CHATURBHUJ SAHU

The study of indigenous knowledge of health and disease is a new revolution set in the domain of anthropology. In its wake, this new knowledge interface has created a new awareness on the part of anthropologists to critically look at their conventional methodological armour. This knowledge, as an area of anthropological interest, deal with a variety of hybrid studies borne out of a battle of different perspectives, leading to a critique of our understanding of knowledge as such. A holistic perspective on human knowledge would help us to understand the implications of indigenous knowledge especially in the areas of health and disease.

The health of an individual is dependent on hereditary nutritional, environmental and other factors. Except hereditary factor all are within the control of the individual and the community. The people being one of the living organism depend upon the environment. Environment includes the conditions, circumstances and surroundings which affect the development and growth of an organism. It also includes biological, ecological, physical, social and economic factors. Nutritional, environmental and lifestyle factors much depend on the socio-economic status of an individual and family as well as community. Hence, the state of health and nutrition, disease and illness, etc., must be analysed in the light of socio-physical and ecological background.

Concept of Health

Health of the people is the natural wealth of a nation and therefore, health problem is a problem of national importance. It is a well-known fact that health is an aspect of cultural life. In fact all communities, especially tribals have their own concepts of health, as part of their culture. The tribal people have adjusted themselves with their surrounding by developing knowledge including health, disease and treatment. Thus, they have their own concept of good health. They explain that health is the most valuable thing on this earth. They clearly identify about the good health and bad health. A man who is free from disease possesses good health. In this healthy situation he looks energetic and feels fit in performing his daily work smoothly and comfortably. Healthy man is regarded as an asset for family, society and nation. Health in broad sense is quality of life rather than only the absence of disease. It is also regarded that health is the primary factor and foundation stone of human personality.

Tribals generally feel that good health is the outcome of pious and disciplined life while illness is regarded as the punishment given by gods or spirits. Hence, their health culture is centred around magico-religious practices besides other therapeutic practices, which are still in persistence among them. The health of a tribal community by and large is a function of the interaction between socio-cultural and socio-biological particles, the genetic attributes and the environmental conditions. The widely varying prevalent health practices, use of indigenous herbal drugs, taboos and superstitions are also responsible for determining the health behaviour and nutritional status of the tribal groups (Sahu, 1998).

The WHO has defined health as "a state of complete physical, mental and social well-being and not merely the absence of disease or infirmity" (citied in Lewis, 1976). The basic concept of health and disease, in this sense, needs an empirical investigation in various societies for acquiring specific details.

To maintain good health the people require certain food in certain quantities and proportion. Food is a basic need from pre-natal stage to extreme old age. It is the main source of body which yields heat and energy for building-up of new tissues and for repairing damaged tissues as well as for the regulation of metabolic process. In addition to satisfy physical and social needs, food also satisfies our emotional needs. Such emotional needs generally include sense of security, love and affection. That is why man's deep concern in food began before the dawn of civilization and continued to grow throughout the ages to the present time and has finally resulted in the growth of science of nutrition.

Nutrition includes everything involved from the moment food is taken to its use in various functions of the body. Nutrients are the components of food that are needed by the body in balanced amount in order to grow and lead a normal healthy life. Nutrients include water, proteins, fats, carbohydrates, minerals and vitamins (Shukla and Rastogi, 1999).

Keeping all these, an attempt has been made to elaborate the facts about the health and nutritional status of Santhal and Birhor tribes of Hazaribagh district, Jharkhand. Both tribes are expert in diagnosing about different kinds of health and diseases. They also know about the cause of disease and method of curing disease. The data have been collected from Churchu block for Santhal tribe and three Birhor Tandas, viz., Demotanr (Sadar block), Kandsar (Katkamsandi block) and Sijhu a (Ichak block) of Hazaribagh district.

Study Area: Hazaribagh District

Situated on the 24°59'30" latitudes and 85°22' longitudes respectively and rich in flora and fauna, Hazaribagh is a natural museum of rocks and topological in equalities. It is the headquarters of North Chotanagpur commissionary and the Hazaribagh district. It is a region of plateaus, residual hills and valleys. It is surrounded by seven hills and hillocks namely Sitagarha, Babhanbay, Silwar, Kanhary, Banadag, Musan and Belian. The climate of the area is very pleasant (Sahu, 2001).

Hazaribagh is also one of the tribal dominated districts of Jharkhand. It is the home of socially and culturally important tribes, viz., Santhal. Munda, Karmali, Bedia, Mahli and Birhor. The Oraon and Kherwar are also seen in a limited pocket.

Santhal and Birhor

Jharkhand is characterized by having 32 tribal communities in which Santhal is largest tribe while Birhor is nomadic and vanishing one. According to Vidyarthi and Rai (1977) Santhals belong to settled agriculturist and Birhors are food gatherer and hunter one. Both tribes are ancient, most aboriginals of India. It consist a rich culture with well-defined social system and life structure. Both are specialized in recognizing herbal medicine and they are known as herbal doctors in their locality. They are in great demand not only by the other tribal communities but also by many other non-tribals even (Sahu, 1995, 1996).

The Santhals are settled agriculturist and grow paddy, millet, maize, marua, Gondali, Urda, Alhar, Chana, Khesari, etc., but the economic condition is not favourable for providing meals for majority of the Santhal family. The cereals consumed by them is not found in uniformity throughout the year. About 70 per cent of their calorie intake is provided from cereals. Though they grow verities of pluses but the quantity is not good. Inadequate intake of pluses is a serious matter for them. Earlier studies indicate that the consumption of cereals and pulses is same for the Santhal of this area (Kumari, 1998, 2001).

The Birhor is hunter and gatherer tribe so the Birhors' activities remain confined in the forest. Forest is the backbone of their life. Right from birth to death their each and every activity is related to procure food. They have to do lot of strenuous work for their survival. Their economic condition is very pitiable. This condition is directly related to the health and nutritional status of the people. Due to this fact symptom of undernutrition and malnutrition are bound to appear not only among the children but also among the adults. It is useful to examine time to time the nutritional status of these poor tribal people.

Development of Health Scenario

Before adopting the National Health Policy, the health system in the country was urban-based, elite-based and curative oriented. The people of rural and tribal areas were sufferer of getting facility of health services.

British government took a serious step in 1943 and constituted the health survey and development committee under the chairmanship of Sir Joseph Bhore. The report was published in 1946. The Bhore Committee report had indicated four areas of health priority – overpopulation, widespread incidence of communicable diseases, malnutrition and poor health care infrastructure.

After independence special programmes for tribal development have been implemented to benefit the tribal people through the five-year plans. In the First Five-Year Plan (1951–56) the main emphasis was given on health and housing. Primary health centres were opened in rural areas. This was strengthened during the next plan periods.

In 1973, the government decided to introduce a health guide scheme. Accordingly, trained male and female health workers were appointed to assist the health services. Another decision was taken in 1977 to appoint a worker from within the community to render assistance in maternal care.

Health for All by 20th Century

In September 1978, the World Health Organization (WHO) and UNICEF sponsored International Conference on Primary Health Care recommended "Health For All by 2000 AD". Soon India's health services underwent a new zeal after signing of the Alma Ata Declaration. Early in 1980 a study group of the Indian Council of Social Science Research (ICSSR) and the Indian

Council of Medical Research (ICMR) was constituted which came up with a wide range of suggestions in 1981 (Prasad and Sahu, 2009).

National Health Policy, 1983

The National Health Policy (NHP) came into existence during December 1983. Since then a creditable progress has been registered in elevating the people's health status (Srivastava, 2001). The criteria of opening Primary Health Centres (PHCs) was viewed for tribal and rural areas. Previously PHCs were opened for the population of 30,000 but now it has relaxed to 3,000 only. Now, the country has more than 1,20,000 rural sub-centres, 19,000 PHCs and 35,000 Community Health Centres (CHCs), 1,100 allopathic dispensaries, 120 allopathic hospitals, over 1,000 ayurvedic dispensaries, about 40 Unani and Siddha dispensaries, 28 homoeopathic hospitals and 250 dispensaries.

The number of registered medical practitioners is increasing day-by-day. Significant achievements have been made in the production of drugs, vaccine and hospital equipment. The life expectancy at birth which was around 30 years in 1950s has become doubled in over 60 years.

In spite of this impressive expansion of health care facilities, the health status of the tribal population has not improved along the desired lines. They are still practising their traditional medicine to cure the diseases. In the recent years there is a growing interest among the medical scientists to accept and practice of indigenous knowledge of health and disease in the management of positive health and well-being. As a result WHO, UNICEF and developing countries like ours have recommended the inclusion of traditional medicines and its practitioners in primary health care. Since the beginning of civilization mankind has always been able to find rudimentary medicines in order to ameliorate pain and disease and lead a productive socio-economic life in the society. In fact, this instinct has led man to search for empirical techniques and methods of healing, which in due course of time has crystallized into traditional health care system. Thus the tribal communities have build-up reservoirs of health and medical knowledge over years for good health.

Health Status

A medicine man is called *Ojha* in Santhal and *Sokha* in Birhor. Ojha is male only while Sokha may be female. Each and every village/*tanda* (Birhor colony is known as *tanda*) has one medicine man or women. Phaguni Birhorni of Kandsar *tanda* is very famous as herbal doctor. She is practising medicine for the last 37 years. People from far and wide come to her for having the treatment of various diseases. She is trying to cultivate few of the medicinal herbs so that she may be in a position to prepare medicine within a moment.

Ojhas are believed to be having a direct control and communication with particular *bongas* (spirits) usually evil or malevolent ones. Though these bongas they claim to cure and help their people. Besides this, they are expert in the knowledge of herbs and prescribe them for the physical illness.

According to the herbal doctors of both tribes, the disease usually occur from three different sources:

(i) *Natural sources:* Change of season brings many diseases.

(ii) *Human agencies:* The human agency helps in spreading contiguous diseases, such as skin diseases, leprosy, tuberculosis, veneral disease, etc.

(iii) *Supernatural agencies:* All diseases are caused by the work of the supernatural beings.

The diseases, which occur, may be divided into two categories:

(i) Physical illness

(ii) Mental illness

Physical illness is cured by giving proper herbs while for curing the mental illness they apply mantras to drive away the evil bongas from the individual body supplemented by herbs. Among them most of the diseases are mental and caused by supernatural agencies.

In case of a person having high fever or any other ailments, the Ojha is immediately informed and the patient is usually taken to the Ojha. He tries to diagnose the ailment by applying oil on the two leaves of *Sal* (Sohrae Robusta) and then sprinkles *Sindur* (vermilion) along with it he chants mantras. Finally he looks and reads into the leaves. In this way he becomes able to know the source and type of disease and finally proceeds for treatment. If he proclaims that the person is possessed by an evil spirit, then the treatment is very different. In this case the patient is left alone with the Ojha, who by burning certain herbs creates smoke. He chants mantras, uses his hypnotic powers, and at time even beats the patient with his stick. By treating the patient thus, it is believed that the spirit runs away leaving the patient tired and exhausted. This treatment continues for a few hours, days or weeks and sometimes even for months. If a Ojha fails in his task the patient is shown to another renounced Ojha.

There is a strong belief that the ancestral spirits play an important role in the prosperity and protection of the family so they remain conscious about the malevolent spirits as serious harm in the sphere of their healthy life. They do not try to consult modern doctor for common disease, but in acute situation Santhal go to hospital to receive the allopathic medicines.

Table 1

Curing of Disease by Using Indigenous/Medicine/Both Way

Tribe	*Sex*	*Indigenous Treatment*		*Medicine*		*Both Way*		*Total*
		No.	*%*	*No.*	*%*	*No.*	*%*	
Santhal	Male	144	55.4	26	10.0	90	34.6	260
	Female	82	68.3	16	13.3	22	18.3	120
	Widow	80	77.0	06	5.8	18	17.4	104
Birhor	Male	40	93.0	—	—	03	7.0	43
	Female	25	92.6	—	—	02	7.3	27
	Widow	06	100.0	—	—	—	—	06

From the Table 1 above it has been observed that there is difference between Santhal and Birhor tribe regarding treatment of the disease. 55.4 per cent Santhal male undertake indigenous treatment for the disease while it is 93 per cent in case of Birhor tribe. Regarding Santhal women 68.3 per cent believe in indigenous treatment including Jharphunk while almost 92.6 per cent Birhor female undertake this treatment. A total of 100 per cent Birhor women has not taken advantage of other method of treatment. In all 77 per cent Santhal widows' diseases are cured by indigenous treatment whereas only 5.8 per cent referring belief on medical treatment. And, about 34.6 per cent Santhal males have believe in both treatment together.

It is clear that Santhals are becoming conscious for taking advantage of allopathic treatment. It also indicates that there is a lack of the way of proper treatment hence an attempt needs to be made to make the people more and more conscious about it.

Table 2

Patients Admitted in Hospital or Not During Last Three Years

Tribe	*Sex*	*Admitted*		*Not Admitted*		*Total*
		No.	*%*	*No.*	*%*	
Santhal	Male	40	34.48	76	65.52	116
	Female	14	36.48	24	63.52	38
	Widow	8	33.33	16	66.66	24
Birhor	Male	2	14.3	12	85.7	14
	Female	—	—	4	100.0	4
	Widow	—	—	2	100.0	2

It is found from Table 2 that during last three years there is difference among the Santhal and Birhor male, female and widow patients admitted in hospital or any other nursing home for curing the disease, because 33.33 to 36.48 per cent among the Santhal admitted whereas 14.3 per cent male Birhor admitted in Sadar Hospital with the pressure of government administration. It can be said that among the Santhal the tendency of getting treatment from medical doctor is increasing day-by-day. Previously, they were also in the option that if a modern doctor treats a patient, he/she will surely die.

Nutritional Status

Assessment of nutritional status is one of the most important health indicators of population group. It largely depends on the socio-economic profile of a group which in turn influences the capability of a group to produce and consume food of their choice. It has been found that majority of the tribal people of Jharkhand are economically very weak. Due to this situation they are not in a position to provide proper food for their family members throughout the year. Consumption of balance diet in results proper growth of body.

Human diet is not restricted to any special category of food. Man can and does eat a variety of food. This is all the more important in the tribal population. A diet containing all the required nutrients in proper quantities and proportion has, therefore, to be taken by an individual depending upon such factors as age, sex, working conditions etc., to meet the requirements of the body. A diet which satisfies these needs is known as balanced diet.

Table 3

Balanced Diet for Adults (Men and Women)

Food item	*Sedentary Work (gm)*		*Moderate Work (gm)*		*Heavy Work (gm)*	
	Men	*Women*	*Men*	*Women*	*Men*	*Women*
Cereals	460	410	520	440	670	575
Pulses	40	40	50	45	60	50
Leafy vegetables	40	100	40	100	40	100
Other vegetables	60	40	70	40	80	50
Roots and tuber	50	50	60	50	80	60
Milk	150	100	200	150	250	200
Oil and fat	40	20	45	20	65	40
Sugar and jaggery	30	20	35	20	55	40

Source: Recommended Dietary Intakes for Indians, 1984, ICMR.

The food requirements of Santhal and Birhor are met through agricultural subsistences and forest products. Their food is very simple and natural. Their daily diet consists of cereal, pulses, leafy vegetables (Sahu, 1994, 1996; Kumari, 2000, 2006). Cereals are good source for minerals and vitamins. Pulses are important source of protein. Pulses are rich in protein and also called poor men's meat. Urad and Kurthi are the common pulses used by them. But consumption of pulses is very low in comparison to rice, so the protein intake is very low. It has been observed that no special diet is given to the pregnant and lactating women. They have the clear knowledge that there is a need of extra diet for these women than the normal women but due to economic hardship they do not take this matter seriously. The worst condition has been seen among the Birhor of Hazaribagh district.

Table 4

Balanced Diets for Children (Boys and Girls)

Food item	*Children 1–3 years (gm)*	*4–6 Years (gm)*	*7–10 Years (gm)*	*7–10 Years Boys (gm)*	*10–12 Years Girls (gm)*
Cereals	175	270	350	420	380
Pulses	35	35	40	45	45
Leafy vegetables	40	50	50	50	50
Other vegetables	20	30	40	50	50
Roots and tuber	10	20	25	30	30
Milk	300	250	250	250	250
Oil and fat	15	25	30	40	35
Sugar and jaggery	30	40	40	45	45

Source: Recommended Dietary Intakes for Indians, 1984, ICMR.

Table 5

Additional Diet During Pregnancy and Lactation

Food Item	*During Pregnancy*	*During Lactation*
Cereals	35	60
Pulses	15	30
Milk	100	100
Fat	—	10
Sugar	10	10

Source: Recommended Dietary Intakes for Indians, 1984, ICMR.

Table 6

Recommended Daily Allowances of Nutrients by ICMR

Nutrients	*Recommended Daily Allowances*
Calories	2875
Protein (gm)	60
Calcium	400
Iron (mg)	28
Vitamin A (fag)	2400
Vitamin B1 (mg)	1.4
Vitamin B2 (mg)	1.6
Vitamin C (mg)	40
Niacin (mg)	18

Table 7

Average Nutrient Consumption of Santhal and Birhor Women in Normal and Special Condition

Tribe	*Food Content*	*Normal Case*		*Pregnancy Period*		*Lactation Period*	
		RDA	*Consumption*	*RDA*	*Consumption*	*RDA*	*Consumption*
Santhal	Calories	2875	2000	3300	2200	3400	2200
Birhor	Calories	2875	1700	3300	1800	3400	1800
Santhal	Protein (gm)	60	45	60	45	70	50
Birhor	Protein (gm)	60	35	60	40	70	45
Santhal	Calcium (mg)	400	475	900	650	900	650
Birhor	Calcium (mg)	400	550	900	650	900	650
Santhal	Iron (mg)	28	25	40	30	32	25
Birhor	Iron (mg)	28	20	40	20	32	20
Santhal	Vit. A (fg)	2400	2000	3000	2500	4600	2500
Birhor	Vit. A (fg)	2400	1600	3000	2000	4600	2000
Santhal	Vit. B1 (mg)	1.4	0.8	1.7	1.0	1.7	1.0
Birhor	Vit. B1 (mg)	1.4	0.5	1.7	0.5	1.7	0.5
Santhal	Vit. B2 (mg)	1.6	0.8	2.0	1.6	2.0	1.6
Birhor	Vit. B2 (mg)	1.6	0.8	2.0	1.0	2.0	1.0
Santhal	Vit. C (mg)	40	32	40	32	80	50
Birhor	Vit. C (mg)	40	20	40	20	80	50
Santhal	Niacin (mg)	18	12	22	18	23	18
Birhor	Niacin (mg)	18	8	22	12	23	12

The nutrients may be divided into five major groups – carbohydrates, protein, fat, vitamins and minerals. Carbohydrates and fats provide energy which is expressed in calories. Protein and minerals supply the materials for building up and keep the body tissues well.

Vitamins are the most active nutrients which regulate the body process. In this way human body in being maintained. If food ingested fails to sub-serve these functions adequately, the architecture of the living tissues becomes imperfect and transformation of energy in the body become disturbed and metabolic process disordered.

Table 7 shows that every content consumed by Santhal and Birhor is deficient. From nutritional point of view, it has been observed that the status of diet of the women of both tribes is very low. The worst condition has been found among the Birhor. They take mainly cereals in their diet. Cereals are the major source of nutrient but less consumption creates malnutrition among them. Consumption of pulse is very less. The consumption of vegetables is far better than pulses because they get green leafy vegetables from the jungles, from local market and from their own *Bari* in case of Santhal. The present study confirms the study of Gupta (1980) and Basu (1992).

Conclusion and Suggestions

The above-cited results indicate that both tribes of study area are living in adverse health situation. From nutritional point of view it has been observed that the status of diet of both tribes is very low which effect the proper growth specially of the children. In each meal they should take cereals in various forms but consumption of calories is not satisfactory. They are undernourished and susceptible to many communicable and vector-borne diseases.

There is strong belief among them that spirits play an important role in the prosperity and protection of the family. In controlling or driving away the disease they remain conscious about the malevolent spirits.

Health is a basic requirement, not only for the fulfilment of human aspirations, but also for the enjoyment of all mankind of better quality of life. It is also indispensable for a balanced development of the individual within the family and as a part of the community and the nation.

No doubt, from Seventh Five-Year Plan emphasis has been given towards delivering of health care and family welfare services to the rural community in general and tribal community in particular, but there is a need of popular understanding of the different health aspects of the Santhal and Birhor tribes. Increasing number of health care facilities is not going to solve the health problems so the attention should be given towards understanding their indigenous knowledge of health, felt needs and acceptance of the modern facilities.

Balanced diet is essential to sustain good health so each and every person should take food not just to make life possible but to lead a healthy and active life. Each and every person should know about the recommended diet.

Cultural factors regulate consumption aspect of nutrition. Thus the study of cultural factors in nutrition has to be taken into consideration compulsorily.

Looking into the various aspects of health and nutritional status, it seems that the situation can be improved by giving proper nutrition education.

There is strong need to create the awareness among them on various programmes so that they should be able to understand their right and duties and achieve better quality of life.

Since most of them are quite ignorant of the proper ways and means to maintain good health and nutrition, it has been extremely difficult to achieve good health for such people. In view of the need of these people some effective and efficient ways and means should be developed.

It is also suggested that the proposal to promote cooperation between biomedicine and indigenous medicine will be of great help and advantage to develop collaborative health care programmes.

The research should be mission oriented and directed towards improvement of the quality of life of Santhal and Birhor in particular and other tribes in general.

References

Basu, Salil (1992): "Nutritional Status, Physical Growth Trends and Health Problems among the Tribal Population of Baster District (M.P.)", in P.D. Tiwari and R.S. Tripathi (eds.), *Dimensions of Scheduled Tribes Development in India*, New Delhi: Uppal Publication House.

Gupta, S.P. (1980): "Nutrition and Health Problems of Primitive Tribal Group of Chotanagpur and Santhal Parganas (Bihar)", *Biology in National Development*, Ranchi.

Kumari, Parnita (1998): "Cultural and Environmental Aspects of Health in the Santhal Tribe", in Chaturbhuj Sahu (ed.), *Tribal Culture and Identity*, New Delhi: Sarup & Sons.

——. (2001): "Food Habits and Practices of Santhal Tribe", in Chaturbhuj Sahu (ed.), *Indian Tribal Life*, New Delhi: Sarup & Sons.

Prasad, N. and C. Sahu (2009): "Tribal Health Development", in Chaturbhuj Sahu (ed.), *Approaches of Tribal Development*, New Delhi: Adhyayna Publication and Distributors.

Sahu, Chaturbhuj (1989): "Nutrition and Health Problem of the Birhor: A Vanishing Tribe of Bihar", in A.N. Sharma (ed.), *Modern Trends in Anthropology*, New Delhi: Northern Book Centre.

—. (1995): *Birhor Tribe: Dimensions of Development*, New Delhi: Sarup & Sons.

—. (1996): *The Santhal Women: A Social Profile*, New Delhi: Sarup & Sons.

Sahu, Chaturbhuj (ed.) (1998): *Tribal Culture and Identity*, New Delhi: Sarup & Sons.

—. (2001): *Indian Tribal Life*, New Delhi: Sarup & Sons.

Shukla, B.R.K. and S. Rastogi (1999): *Physical Anthropology and Human Genetics*, Delhi: Palka Prakashan.

Vidyarthi, L.P. and B.K. Rai (1997): *Tribal Culture of India*, New Delhi: Concept Publication.

15

Status of Tribal Health and Nutrition

Evidence from Rural Odisha

ANJALI DASH

Tribals are often referred to as Adivasi, Vanyajati, Vanvasi, Pahari, Adimjati and Anusuchit Janjati, the latter being the constitutional name. The concept of tribe emerged in India with the coming of the British. Gradually, the concept of reservation emerged and through that emerged the idea of Scheduled Tribe in independent India. The Scheduled Tribes (STs) differ considerably from one another in race, language, culture and beliefs. Notwithstanding so much diversity, there are certain broad similarities between the mutually divergent tribal groups. Striking similarities are noticed in their modes of living, each tribe lives in a definite area, has common dialect, cultural homogeneity and unifying social organization. The tribal population of India has been found to speak 105 different languages and 225 subsidiary languages indicating a great deal of variety.

The Scheduled Tribe (ST) population in Odisha (22%) is larger than the national average of 8 per cent. The Scheduled Caste (SC) population is 16 per cent. Together they account for 38 per cent of the population. Historically, tribal communities were characterized by a lifestyle distinct from agrarian communities. They subsisted on different combinations of shifting cultivation, hunting and gathering of forest products; all activities linked with forest. Their cultures celebrated and fostered this close bond with nature while also emphasizing communal ownership and consumption, closely-knit kinship structures and minimal hierarchies. However, available disaggregated indicators point to a poorer health status among these deprived social groups.

Undernutrition stunting of growth and underweight are higher among SC, ST and other backward communities. Coverage of antenatal care is lower among deprived socio-economic groups. Geographic and other reasons have led to lower access and utilization of health care. Efforts have been made by the state on a priority basis to redress this lacuna. For indigenous people, a package of services will be made available and accessible. This would include nutrition services (education-cum-supplementation); communicable disease control especially malaria, tuberculosis, leprosy yaws; services for specific diseases such as sickle cell anaemia and special norms for health services including training and induction of health workers and professionals from this social group into the state health services. Persons of SC origin are spread throughout the Odisha in all districts, while STs are more concentrated in certain districts. Primary care, access to complete treatment, follow-up and referrals to secondary and tertiary care hospitals at very subsidized rates is very much necessary for STs. Side by side local health traditions need to be acknowledged and respected. In this context, sensitization training is necessary for health providers to reduce negative social attitudes. The tribal population is among the poorest, most vulnerable and exploited groups in the state. The tribal economy in the state is primarily subsistence oriented and based upon a combination of agriculture, forestry and wage labour (HDR, 2004).

This paper is divided into three sections. The first section deals with the situation of health at the national level with reference to the situation in Odisha state. The second parts examines health-related issues in the studied village. Towards the end some concluding observations have been made.

I
Status of Health

Health is a prerequisite for human development and is essentially concerned with the well-being of common man. The UNDP Human Development Index (HDI) comprises three components, i.e., health, education and income generating capacity. Health is a function, not only of medical care, but also of the overall integrated development of society – cultural, economic, educational, social and political. The health status of a society is intimately related to its value system, philosophical and cultural traditions, and social, economic and political organization. Each of these aspects has a deep influence on health, which in turn influences all these aspects. Hence, it is not possible to raise the health status and quality of life of people unless such efforts are integrated with the wider effort to bring about overall transformation of a society. Health development can be integrated with the larger programme of overall development in such a manner that the two become mutually self-supporting. Good health and good society go together. This is possible only when supportive services such as nutrition and improvements in the environment and in education reaches the masses. Studies have shown that the acceptance of a particular health care system among the tribal people mostly depends on its availability and accessibility (Guite and Acharya, 2006). Another study among the Meitis of Manipur reveals that though the people are educated enough, the concept of deities and their effect on human health are widely prevalent among them (Devi, 2003). The individual and the local community in primary health care works not as a social necessity; rather as a medical necessity (Bryant, 1988).

In the case of health care services, access is a basic requirement and an important aspect. One can distinguish between two kinds of access: physical and economic. Physical access can be either population coverage-based or area coverage-based. Economic access refers to direct cost of accessing the services. In Odisha, the population covered per public health facility is good and the coverage is better than in nine other major states. However, the area coverage is very poor. The problem of physical access is compounded by two other factors; poor roads as well as transport connectivity. The economic access refers to a situation in which a majority of population will have adequate treatment at affordable prices given their income. It is thus not surprising to find that poor physical and economic access affect the utilization of public health care facilities. Equitable access to health care requires that all citizens be able to secure an adequate level of care without excessive burdens. Discussions of a right to health care have frequently been premised on offering patients access to all beneficial care, to all care that others are receiving, or to all that they need – or want. By creating impossible demands on society's resources for health care, such formulations have risked negating the entire notion of a moral obligation to secure care for those who lack it.

However, it is influenced by various factors like the degree of awareness about illness, the educational level and the accessibility, availability and affordability of health care services, drinking water facility and other factors like caste, sex and religion, choice and preference pattern. Demand is determined not completely by price and income but by occurrence and extent of illness. Some time moral hazard types of situation occur in the demand side. In rural underdeveloped areas majority of the people are too poor to afford payment. Poor quality of health services might be another major factor for low level of utilization of health services. Odisha is well known for its backwardness not only in terms of per capita income but also in human development indicators as well. Especially in the health sector despite the intervention of government and NGOs, the infant mortality rate in the state remain at 69 per cent in 2008, which is much higher than national level (53 per 1,000). To reduce this IMR rate, mother and child health care National Rural Health Mission (NRHM) was implemented where ASHA play an important role. But there is no coordination between Accredited Social Health Activist (ASHA) and Aanganwadi Worker (AWW) in many villages.

Health Culture

The culture of community determines the health behaviour of the community in general and individual members in particular. The health behaviour of the individual is closely linked to the way he or she perceives various health problems; what they actually mean to him or her, on the one hand, and on the other his or her access to various relevant institutions. The holistic concept of health culture provides a valuable framework for analysing the work of anthropologists in health fields. However, a very few studies are available in this direction, especially among the tribal population. Among tribals modern medicine system is not in full fledge, the tribal people primarily take indigenous herbal medicine at the time of their need. Traditional healers are more accessible than medical doctors to care for the patients. The cost of consultation with a traditional healers and the price of herbal drugs are relatively low in comparison to the modern health care system.

Health Problems

The health problems need special attention in the context of tribal communities. The tribal population has distinctive health problems which are mainly governed by their habitat, difficult terrains and ecologically variable niches. The health and nutrition problems of diverse tribal groups have been found to be unique and present a formidable challenge for which appropriate solutions have to be found out by planning and evolving relevant research studies. Insanitary conditions, ignorance, lack of personal hygiene and health education are the main factors responsible for their ill-health. Some primitive tribal communities are facing extinction like the Onges, Jarwas and Shompens of Andaman and Nicobar Islands mainly due to lack of adequate health care facilities. Some of the problems as indicated by investigations include: (a) endemic diseases like malaria, introduced from outside or otherwise like tuberculosis, influenza, dysentery, high infant mortality and malnutrition, (b) venereal diseases, induced abortion, inbreeding, addiction to opium, custom of eating tubers of Disscera (may cause sterility as they contain substances used in oral contraception), and (c) disturbed sex ratio leading to shortage of women.

The health and nutrition problems of the vast tribal population of India are as varied as the tribal groups themselves who present a bewildering diversity and variety in their socio-economic, socio-cultural and ecological settings. Anaemia is a major problem for women in India and more so in the rural and tribal belt. This is particularly serious in view of the fact that both rural and tribal women have heavy workload and anaemia has profound effect on psychological and physical health. Anaemia lowers resistance to fatigue, affects working capacity under conditions of stress and increases susceptibility to other diseases. Maternal malnutrition is quite common among the tribal women especially those who have many pregnancies too closely spaced. Tribal diets are generally grossly deficient in calcium, Vitamin A, Vitamin C, riboflavin and animal protein.

The forest-based tribal economy in most parts of the world was women-centred. Women made provisions for the basic necessities like food, fuel, medicine, housing material, etc., from the forest produce. Food was obtained from shifting cultivation and from minor forest produces (MFP) like flowers and fruits collected from the forest. Extraction from herbs, roots and animals were used for medicine. All these efforts incurred an excessive workload on women. A study on the Kondhs revealed that women put in an average of 14 working hours per day as compared to 9 hours put in by men (Basu, 2000). Given this additional workload, even women in advanced stages of pregnancy were required to work in the agricultural fields or walk great distances to collect fuel and minor forest produce. The overstrain on tribal women however, was not adequately compensated due to the non-availability of minor forest produce and decrease in food grain production. To add to the malnutrition and additional workload, there was destruction of traditional herbs through deforestation and the lack of access of the tribal to modern medicine. All areas along with the increasing ecological imbalance resulted in diseases such as TB, stomach disorders and malaria etc.

Nutrition

Health status of a community depend upon his access to adequate food, nutrition, portages worth and good sanitation facilities. While action is called for through different departments, the specific role of the Health and

Family Welfare Department is very important. The following steps are necessary towards better nutrition: (i) nutrition education of mothers and families through health workers in collaboration with ICDS functionaries, (ii) improvement in nutritional content of supplementary feeding using low cost locally available food through self-help groups, (iii) improved training of health professionals regarding nutrition, (iv) nutrition and growth monitoring with trend analysis, (v) Vitamin A, iron and folic acid supplements for women and children, under supervision, (vi) early detection and treatment of childhood illnesses to prevent deterioration of nutritional status, and (vii) de-worming. All these effort are very crucial for nutritional development of a community. Good nutrition was a requirement throughout life and was vital to women in terms of their health and work. Nutritional anaemia was a major problem for women in India and more so in the rural and tribal belt. In developing countries, it was estimated that at least half of the non-pregnant and two-thirds of the pregnant women were anaemic (U.N., 1984).

The schemes like Aanganwadi (ICDS) and Mid-Day Meal (MDM) are in operation in Odisha. The Aanganwadi scheme is taking care of children below six years of age in the state. The basic objective of this scheme is to help children and pregnant women for their nutritional as well as mental growth.

Childbearing and Maternal Mortality

Neonatal mortality rate (NMR – infant deaths within four weeks of life per 1,000 live births) at 49 (SRS, 2007) accounts for 69 per cent of the IMR, while early NMR (infant deaths within one week of life per 1,000 live births) at 37 (ibid.) accounts for 76 per cent of the NMR. An evaluation of Janani Suraksha Yojana (JSY) in Odisha in December 2008 highlighted that only 27 per cent of the beneficiaries surveyed stayed for at least two days in the health facility after delivery. With the huge offtake in JSY in the state (3.09 lakh beneficiaries in 2008–09), this is clearly a missed opportunity to address early neonatal mortality (Economic Survey, 2009–10).

Childbearing imposes additional health needs and problems on women – physically, psychologically and socially. Maternal mortality was reported to be high among various tribal groups. The consumption of iron, calcium and vitamins during pregnancy is poor. As far as childcare is concerned, both rural and tribal illiterate mothers are observed to breastfeed their babies. Vaccination and immunization of infants and children have been inadequate among tribal groups. In addition, extremes of magico-religious beliefs and taboos tend to aggravate the problems.

In Odisha, according to a study, there is a high incidence of spontaneous abortions – an indicator of pregnancy wastage and a possible contributor to pre-natal and maternal mortality (Padhi and Mishra, 2000). One reason for the high incidence of spontaneous abortions and the high MMR is the poor nourishment of women and high prevalence of anaemia.

Crude birth practices were found to exist in some tribal groups among Kharias, Gonds, Sandals, Kutia, and Khondhs of Odisha. Institutional delivery is very little in tribal areas. A high incidence of malnutrition was observed in some primitive tribal groups in Phulbani, Koraput and Sundergarh district of Odisha (Basu, 2000).

Infant Mortality Rate (IMR)

IMR is significant in rural areas (see Table 1). The tribal population has much higher IMR as compared to the SC and other non-tribal population.

Table 1

IMR in Odisha

	Urban	*Rural*	*Total*
NFH-1	85	117	112
NFHS-2	81	81	81
NFHS-3	40	69	65

Source: NFHS-2 and 3.

Infant Mortality and Undernutrition in Odisha

Infant mortality is a traditional indicator of the overall access to health services of the maternal health. Studies suggest that as much as half of all infant mortality and morbidity is preventable by better access to or improved medical care (see Figure 1).

Figure 1

BR, DR, and IMR of Odisha and India

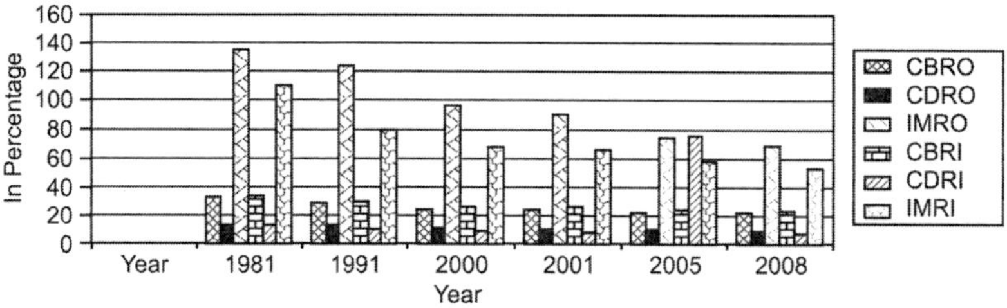

Note: CBRO-Crude Birth Rate of Orissa, CDRO-Crude Death Rate of Orissa, IMRO-Infant Mortality Rate of Orissa, CBRI-Crude Birth Rate of India, CDRI-Crude Death Rate of India, IMRI-Infant Mortality Rate of India

It is observed that IMR, CDR and CBR reduced in Odisha from 135 to 69, 13 to 9, 33.1 to 21.4 whereas in India from 110 to 53, 12.5 to 7.4, 33.9 to 22.8 during 1981 to 2008. Figure 1 shows the trend of IMR of both Odisha and India. During the period both Odisha and India witnessed a downward trend of IMR.

Table 2

Social Categorywise Nutritional Status

Background characteristics	*Neonatal, post-neonatal, infant, child and under-5 mortality in Odisha, 2005–6*		*Prevalence of anaemia in 6–59 months children (status by haemoglobin level)*	*Nutritional status of children in India, Odisha, 2005–6*		
	Infant mortality	*Under-5 mortality*	*Any anaemia (<11.0 g/dl)*	*Stunted (height for age)*	*Wasting mortality (weight for height)*	*Underweight mortality (weight for age)*
India	57	74.3	69.5	48.0	19.8	42.5
Odisha	64.7	90.6	65	45.0	19.5	40.7
Caste/tribe						
SC	73.7	91.8	63.5	49.7	19.7	44.4
ST	78.7	136.3	80.1	57.2	27.6	54.4
OBC	66.0	83.5	58.7	40.8	17.8	38.1
Others	53.1	64.2	58.2	33.6	12.8	26.4

Source: NFHS 2005–06.

In all cases like IMR, under-5, stunted, wasting and underweight mortality case ST are high (see Table 2). Overall, 11.7 per cent children under-5 had diarrhoea in the two weeks prior to the NFHS Survey. It is observed that use of ORS was poor in households where children suffered from diarrhoea. Only 9.4 per cent of households gave more liquids and 39 per cent gave less liquid to children with diarrhoea. Four out of every five households (80.2%) in Odisha do not have sanitation (NFHS-2); 21.5 per cent of households do not use improved sources of drinking water and only 18.3 per cent treat their water for drinking purposes.

Given the critical situation in health care system in Odisha the present study has high relevance as it would be covering a large issue of demand side, supply side and livelihood of the tribal people; which could immensely contribute to the overall health scenario of the state and hence of the economic growth of the country.

II
Health-related Issues in the Study Area

Tribal population is one of the weaker sections of the society and lies at the lowest rung of the process of development. The study is mainly based on primary information collected from a village Brahmanipali situated in the Sonepur district of Odisha. During the study responses were collected from patients and other members of households belonging to different households. The households are selected using a stratified random sampling procedure. Out of the 139 households of the Brahmanipali village, 98 households were selected from the study village. The population of the village is 662 according to 2001 census and 37 per cent, 26 per cent and 21 per cent population belongs to SCs, STs and OBC categories respectively.

The average size of the sample household is 4.7. Of the total population 337 (51%) are male and 325 (49%) are female. Out of these 98 households, 33 per cent are SC, 42 per cent are ST and the rest include OBC and general category. Worker-dependent ratio in the very poor category is more compare to other, i.e., 51. In rich category dependent ratio is 47 because in these groups there are servicemen and businessmen. Overall, the worker-dependent ratio is 45 among the sample households (see Table 3).

Table 3

Categorywise Socio-economic Condition

Category	*No of households*	*% of SC population*	*% of ST population*	*% of other population*	*Worker dependent ratio*
Rich	5	20	20	60	47
Middle	24	21	33	46	31
Poor	30	33	50	17	46
Very poor	39	41	44	15	51
Total	98	33	42	25	45

Source: Field Survey.

Socio-Economic Profile

The studied village is divided into three units. One unit is inhabited by SCs, other by STs and last one is dominated by OBCs and other caste people.

Drinking Water, Sanitation and Housing Facilities

Tube well is the main source of drinking water in the village. The village has two tube wells, one is located in the main settlement and other one is situated at primitive locality. The quality of this tube well is not good due to lack of proper maintenance. People have to consume the dirty water that comes from the tube well located in their locality. The surrounding of tube well is also very dirty as the used water get logged and absorbed into the nearby area of the tubewell. In Odisha the coverage of safe pipe drinking water was hardly 9 per cent as per 2001 Census. Further, hardly three households in the study village have toilet. In Odisha 14.89 per cent of households have access to toilet. Majority of households use metal pot, earthen pot and cement pot for storage drinking water. As about 82 per cent of households use firewood for cooking, they are susceptible to environmental diseases like TB. Dwelling structure of the house also influence the health condition of the family members. The housing condition of the study village is not satisfactory. In the study village there is no drainage facility.

Health Infrastructure in Rural Odisha and the Studied Village

According to the Indian public health norms, there should be one Sub-Centre (SC) for 5,000 people (3,000 in hilly areas), one Primary Health Centre (PHC) for 30,000 people (20,000 for hilly areas) and one Community Health Centre (CHC) for 1,20,000 people (80,000 for hilly areas).In rural areas of Odisha, there are only 6,688 sub-centres against the requirement of 7,283 and 1,279 PHCs as against the requirement of 1,171 and lastly 231 CHC as against the requirement of 292. Moreover, the number of health institutions in rural areas is more or less stagnant since late 1990s.There has not been any significant improvement in health care infrastructure.

Due to lack of adequate number of public health institution, existing institutions in rural areas are overburdened in terms of persons dependent on them. On an average population coverage per SC is 31,619 for one PHC, 1,59,328 population for one CHC and 21,599 population for one medical institution. There is deficiency in doctor population ratio, i.e., 1:75, one doctor for 7,513 population. As a result many medical institutions are without doctors and beds. Thus the shortage of doctors in rural areas is common in rural Odisha.

Other health infrastructure in the village includes one Aanganwadi worker (AWW), one Accredited Social Health Activist (ASHA) which comes under National Rural Health Mission (NRHM). Before ASHA, AWW was working as a health practitioner. She was providing some medicine. But when NRHM was launched in 2005, this mission provided an ASHA to all rural village especially for mother and child health care. Government established this mission in 2005 but its progress is very slow, hence many rural villages are unable to get this facility. One Mobile Health Unit (MHU) vehicle comes on last Friday of the month. There is also provision of immunization on the third Wednesday of the month which is called Mamata Divas. On that day, many health related check-up are done, such as BP check-up, weight check-up, child weight check-up, etc. (once in a month). On immunization day they provide polio DPT to 0–6 month children, megels to 9 month children, children of 1–2 years age given polio DPT buster, 5 years age children are provided DPT buster. Because due to lack of awareness and lack of information and illiteracy among the people they are excluded from these services. If we consider allover the village only 5 or 6 families have radio. Only one family reads newspaper.

Table 4

Socio-economic Condition of People in the Studied Area

Variable	*Type*	%
Caste	SC	33
	ST	42
	Other	25
Categories	Rich	5
	Middle	24
	Poor	31
	Very poor	40
House	Kucha	82
	Pucca	9
	Semi-pucca	9
Drain	Yes	0
	No	100
Toilet	Yes	4
	No	96
House-Clean	Daily	68
	Alternate day	29
	Weekly	3
Drinking Water Sources	Tube well	90
	Well	10
Store Water	Earthen pot	21
	Metal pot	57
	Cement pot	21
Drinking Water Safetyness	covered	65
	uncovered	35
Electricity	Yes	23
	No	77
Use mosquito net	Yes	28
	No	72
Cooking	Firewood	82
	Gas	5
	Others	13

Source: Field Survey.

Aanganwadi worker was the first health practitioner provided by the government at the village level. Before NRHM come to the village, AWW was the health care provider. AWW provided special care to mother and child. For each day NM gets 190 gram of rice and 30 gram of *dal* up to six month of her child was born. After that, the child gets 80 gram of rice and 30 gram of dal up to one year. By providing this AWW gives some suggestion about their health care check-up. AWW also provides some iron medicine for the better health care if available. She provides this nutritious food 25 days for a month. But question here is; is the food sufficient for the NM and ANM with her child? Certainly not. In that case how the NM and ANM get nutritious foods. Sometime AWW is also busy with her personal work.

After getting training AWW does not work properly. Many of the villagers have expressed their dissatisfaction on her work. Sometimes she gives more importance to her caste. At the delivery time she is not accessible. Due to her absence delivery occurs unsupervised. Many people avoid her due to caste background. She also provides medicine to the NM and ANM after delivery and before delivery. ANM come to the village once in a month. She comes on Mamata Divas, i.e., days of the mother. She provides check-up to the mother and child including all other members of the village. She attends to other health problems. She also observes and tries to cure that. Institutional delivery in rural Odisha is only 40.4 per cent. In urban area it is 74.4 per cent and total 44.3 per cent. Delivery at home is more in rural areas, i.e., 58.5 per cent (DLHS-3).In our study village this ratio is more in case of SC/ST households.

We have discussed the role of AWW, ASHA and ANM. But there is not any coordination among them. They have very jealous attitude towards each other. For one delivery case ASHA get 600 but for a month AWW gets 1,000. For that AWW feel jealous some time. ANM takes a neutral view because she never wants to interfere anything between AWW and ASHA. In this context the NRHM is a failure in the Brhamanipali village.

Morbidity Situation in the Study Village

The total number of patients suffering from different diseases in the study village during the survey year 2009 (January to December) based on the responses of the households, were 175 and there were 215 episodes of diseases. Out of these patients, 35 patients (20%) have fallen ill twice during the year and two patients had illness more than twice and one of them had illness four times during the year. Of the total number of patients, 89 were male and 86 were female which account for 51 per cent and 49 per cent respectively. Similarly, out of total patients, 31 patients (18%) belong to the age group of 0–5, 38 patients (22%) belong to the age group of 6–15, 93 patients (53%), belong to the age group of 16–60, and rest 13 patients (7%), belong to the old age group.

The nature of illness suffered by members has been classified broadly on the basis of WHO guidelines. The illness of these patients have been classified into four categories, namely: (i) communicable diseases (malaria, brain malaria, PFR, fever), (ii) water-borne diseases (diarrhoea dysentery, typhoid, jaundice, stomach pain), (iii) Non-communicable diseases (pneumonia, TB, appendicitis, sugar, heart problem), and (iv) others (accident and injury, operation). Majority of patients suffered from infectious, communicable and water-borne diseases in the study village. It has been found that the prevalence rate of communicable diseases is common in different classes of patients. Of the total patients malaria consisted 28 per cent (49), PFR 9 per cent (15) and fever in 13 per cent (23). The number of patients suffering from communicable diseases is relatively higher in comparison to other diseases. Five patients had communicable diseases at one time and water-borne disease in other time of the year. The proportion of water-borne disease is more among the children and adult age group in comparison with other groups; Communicable diseases are found more among adults.

Table 5

Diseases Pattern According to Age Group in Terms of Episode

Age	*Communicable diseases*	*Water-borne diseases*	*Non-communicable diseases*	*Other*	*Total*
0–5	14(11)	17(35)	3(19)	1(4)	35(16)
6–15	27(22)	10(20)	7(44)	5(19)	49(23)
16–60	72(59)	17(35)	6(38)	20(74)	115(53)
Above 60	10(8)	5(10)	0(0)	1(4)	16(7)
Total	123(57)	49(23)	16(7)	27(13)	215

Note: Figures in the bracket represent percentage.

Source: Field Survey.

Surprisingly, the reported morbidity prevalence rate among the ST is considerably higher than that among the other social groups, given their low level of socio-economic condition, illiteracy and hygiene situation is not unexpected. It is observed that prevalence of illness increases with age. While acute ailment is responsible for high morbidity prevalence among the children, chronic ailments has caused the rise in morbidity prevalence among the elderly and affected their nutritional status. The high prevalence rate of chronic illness among the aged population points to the need for special targeting of health care services for the elderly.

Poor access to proper drinking water, lack of proper storage of drinking water ponds to various types of diseases. The occurrences of communicable diseases have been due to menace of mosquito, which occurs more during the rainy season. Only 28 per cent of the households have used mosquito net and rest have never used the same.

The impact of health providers on well-being and financial outcomes depend upon both preventions taken and the curative care. Timely preventive care can ameliorate adverse health outcomes and there will be less financial burden in the future. Effective treatment for sick persons can reduce the time span of the illness and the income losses associated with morbidity and premature mortality. From economic perspective, health care utilization depends on the relative magnitude of costs and benefit involved from the view point of persons, for themselves and for other family members. The cost of seeking care basically includes financial expenses and income losses that may incurred. As a result, income losses can be high if considerable time is spent in commuting queues to obtain medical care (Duraisamy, 2000; Gartler and Gaag, 1990). Further, the cost for health care services, such as consultancy fee for doctors and hospital charges, are likely to influence the cost of health care utilization (Gartler and Gaag, 1990).

In case of SC and ST categories, they mostly prefer to go government hospital for treatment. Only in emergency cases they had preferred for private treatment. This type of situation arises when they have no alternative option. This evidence is consistent with findings of both rounds of National Sample Survey (NSS) in Odisha. According to it the high percentage of poor patients have preferred to such treatment from government hospital. The composition of patient in terms of age groups is discussed in Table 5. The patients have been divided into four groups. They are 0–5, 6–15, 16–60 and above 60. The first two groups are children, the third group is adult and the last group belongs to old age persons.

Gender Bias

One of the most striking features of the child mortality in rural India is the male female discrimination. This differential mortality is also reflected remarkably in regional differences in the sex ratio of the rural population. The male child is a potential source of economic support and gets the lion's share of parental attention and nourishment in comparison to girl child. Women's lives are shaped by customs that are centuries old. *May you be the mother of a hundred sons* is a common Hindu wedding blessing (Kishor, 1993; Dasgupta, 2005). There is a urgent need for undertaking a region-specific study of the status and role of tribal women which alone can throw light upon tribal health situation to make planning for their welfare more meaningful and effective. The status of tribal women has gone from bad to worse as a result of the impact of social change which has affected the social structure of tribal society.

Excess female mortality is widely recognized as rooted in economic and cultural factors, few attempts have been made to evaluate the simultaneous contribution of such factors to its persistence. The relatively greater female mortality in response to higher fertility is consistent with micro-level research that has found greater mortality among girls born into families that already have a daughter (Dasgupta, 1987; Muhuri and Preston, 1991; Rajeswari, 1996). The deaths of young girls in India exceed those of young boys by over 3,00,000 each year and every sixth infant death is specifically due to gender discrimination. A primary way that parents discriminate against their girl children is through neglect during illness by delay for treatment. IMR in Odisha during the year was 68 for male and 70 for female whereas 52 and 55 for India (2009). Gender disparity is less in case of educated people, who have schooling for more years in comparison to illiterate.

Based on indicators such as sex ratio, literacy rate, work participation, poor nutrition and health status of women in Odisha is considered to be low. The sex ratio of Odisha declined from 1,022 (1951) to 971 (1991) and 972 in (2001). The sex ratio for 0–6 years declined from 967 in 1991 to 950 in 2001 (estimated). However, the sex ratio of Odisha is comparable to some demographically developed southern states. It has an equitable gender balance in the SC population, and tops the list in sex ratio amongst the ST population. Compared to other parts of India, there is not a strong son-preference in many parts of the state. The status of tribal women is considered to be relatively better than that of women in coastal districts.

Cost of Treatment

Poverty is the general bane of tribal, which arises due to economic factors. Some of the factors responsible for poverty among them are low agricultural productivity, shifting cultivation, land alienation, indebtness, lack of irrigation facilities, low education, and unawareness of institutional credit facilities, market prices, traditional living condition, malnutrition, diseases, isolation and exploitation by traders.

The high cost of health care has serious implication for the livelihood of the households in general and for poor households in particular. Households responding to medical need and spending a large share of annual income on health care may affect their other essential expenditure. The expenditure incurred for treatment of diseases has been estimated by us from the primary information collected from the study village. Because of the hospitalization of a patient a household has to spend a large sum of money which is beyond his capacity. In such a case he has to borrow from different sources because he cannot postpone such urgent expenditure. In that situation the family has to forgo a substantial part of its income for repaying the debt and it may end up in indebted situation (Selvaraj and Karan, 2009; Singh, 2010).

The cost of health care has grown enormously with adverse effect on the health and economic status of disadvantaged groups. Hospitalized ST/SC people spend more than half of their total annual expenditure to buy health care, while 45 per cent borrow money/sell assets to cover expenses and 35 per cent fall below the poverty line. Out of pocket medical costs alone may push 2.2 per cent of the population below the poverty line in one year. The number of disadvantaged poor, who did not seek treatment because of financial reasons increased from 15 per cent to 24 per cent in rural areas and doubled from 10 per cent to 21 per cent in urban slums in the decade 1986–96.

Apart from geographic, social and economic adversity, low awareness of ill-health affecting health-seeking behaviour of ST/SC and other disadvantaged groups remain an important barrier to better health outcomes in the state as a whole. A majority of their ailments are preventable and easily curable with timely medical attention and with a little money, yet unsatisfactory public health programmes and public facilities, force them to spend their meagre earnings on private health care.

Table 6

Different Component of Health Expenditure Incurred by Indoor and Outdoor Patients and Source of Treatment

	TC	*DC*	*MC*	*Test*	*Other*	*Total*
Indoor						
Private	1574	6642	1432	184	4205	14037
Govt.	360	2450	1033	117	1556	5516
Sub Total	773	3854	1152	138	2443	8359
Outdoor						
Private	381	166	971	185	866	2569
Govt.	156	40	534	46	189	954
Sub Total	198	64	613	73	320	1261
Overall	344	1037	746	89	863	3074

Source: Field Survey. Notes: TC: Transport Cost, DC: Doctor Cost, MC: Medicine Cost.

The expenditure related to health care by individual patient includes doctors fee, medicine cost, diagnostic test, transport, and other cost. The other cost relate to the expenditure such as food, lodging charges, etc., incurred by relative of patient when they are accompanying the patients to the hospital or private clinic but excluded the transport cost. It relate to the expenditure incurred for carrying the patient and accompanying members to the health care centre from home and back.

In this study the overall health expenditure incurred per episode was ₹ 3,074. It was ₹ 1,261 and ₹ 8,359 for outdoor and indoor patients respectively. It is seen that the expenditure incurred by patients seeking treatment in the private sector both, as indoor and outdoor patients, was much higher in comparison with that expenditure incurred in the government health care sector (see Table 6).

For out patient treatments, in private sector, the average expenditure was one and a half times higher than it is incurred for that treatment at public sector hospital. Unfortunately, government health care facilities, which used to offer services free of cost earlier is not so today and patients have to buy drugs and diagnostic services from private sector providers. It has increased the cost of health care even in public health sector and has narrowed the cost difference between public and private health care sector (see Selvaraj and Karan, 2009).

Components of Health Expenditure

In the study overall household health expenditure constituted 15 per cent of total income for all households with wide variation across different size classes. Household income of ST are lower in compare to other social groups (see Table 7).

Debt Position

The most important source of livelihood of tribals today is settled agriculture. However, tribal land alienation is the most important cause of the pauperization of tribal people, rendering their economic situation, which is extremely vulnerable at the best of times, even more precarious. Studies have indicated that in Odisha 54–56 per cent tribal land has been lost to non-tribals over a period of 25–30 years through indebtedness, mortgages and forcible possession. What is more significant is that tribals have lost possession over the most productive land, leaving them to cultivate poor quality land that makes their economy more vulnerable to natural calamities.

Table 7

Percentage of Health Expenditure, Borrowing and Without Interest Rate Borrowing

Category	*House-hold Income (₹)*	*Avg. health exp. per HH (₹)*	*% of health expendi-ture out of total income*	*% of expendi-ture out of total income*	*% of health expenditure out of total expenditure*	*% of borrowing out of total health exp*	*% of health expendi-ture out of their own source*
SC	27284.38	2437.5	15	85	24	95	5
ST	22146.34	2535.36	20	87	17	95	5
Others	66068	11816	14	65	28	30	70

Source: Field Survey

Expenditure on medical care seems to have a negative impact on economic condition of the households. Borrowing or sale of assets is widely prevalent among the patients belongs to poor and very poor in the study village. During the study year 2009 out of 98 households, 35 patient household had borrowed to meet their health expenditure (see Table 7). The main source of borrowing was moneylender and the interest charges on such loans varied from 36 per cent to 120 per cent per annum. It is found that most of the poor households have borrowed money for meeting their health care expenditure on harsh terms and condition. Indebtness situation are found more in case of small and marginal farmers (Singh, 2010).

III
Conclusion

The Scheduled Tribes are at different stages of social, cultural and economic development. The cultural pattern varies from tribe to tribe and region to region. The economic life of the tribals is local which is also specific in nature. Tribals primarily depend upon local resources to make their living. The primitive tribes of Odisha and their health scenario presents a kaleidoscopic mosaic of various communicable and non-communicable disease profile keeping in pace with their socio-economic development. Among these there are communities who still depend primarily on hunting and food gathering as primary source of livelihood. The widespread poverty, illiteracy, malnutrition, absence of safe drinking water and sanitary conditions, poor maternal and child health services, ineffective coverage of national health and nutritional services, etc., have been found, as factors of dismal health condition prevailing amongst the primitive tribal communities of the state. The non-communicable diseases like diabetes and hypertension are conspicuously absent indicating that the primitive tribal communities are still far away from the modern civilization and developments. In spite of the tremendous advancement in the field of preventive and curative medicine, the health care delivery services in these primitive tribal people are still poor and need to be strengthened in order to achieve the goal of 'health for All' in the country.

The study concludes that 95 per cent SC/ST households borrowed for health care and in this way they became the victim of indebtedness. These poor households had to borrow at exorbitant rate of interest transferring collaterals to the lenders. They have been suffering from income and assets loss and falling into debt trap. Given such a situation in the rural Odisha there is urgent need for provision of primary health care (doctors as well as paramedical, medicare) and drinking water to reduce the morbidity rate and burden of diseases. From this study we found that not only in tribal area alone but also in heterogeneous village primitive tribals are suffering in case of health and nutritional status. The tribals encounter with mainstreams restructuring their patterns of kinship, economy, religious institutions. Poverty is the general bane of tribals, which arises due to economic factors. Some of these factors are responsible for low agricultural productivity, shifting cultivation, land alienation, indebtedness, lack of irrigation facilities, low education, and unawareness of institutional credit facilities, market prices, traditional living condition, malnutrition, diseases, isolation and exploitation by traders and moneylenders.

Policies promoting growth would also have the desirable effect of reducing poverty. Overall, there is a compelling reason for stepping up both public and private investment in health which would pay off in the long run. There is a strong association between per capita income and health status (LEB and IMR) of the population. Therefore, two way solutions should be chalked out for well-being of tribal health: (i) alleviation of poverty, and (ii) more accessible health care facilities in the tribal areas.

References

Basu, S. (2000): "Dimension of Tribal Health in India", *Health and Population: Perspectives and Issues*, 23(2): 61–70.

Bryant, J. (1988): "Health for All: The Dream and the Reality", *World Health Forum*, 9(3): 291–302.

Castro-Leal, Florencia, Julia Dayton, Lionel Demery and Kalpana Mehra (1999): "Public Social Spending in Africa: Do the Poor Benefits?" *The World Bank Research Observer*, 14(1): 49–72.

Dasgupta, M. (1987): "Selective Discrimination against Female Children in Rural Punjab", *Population and Development Review*, 13(1): 77–100.

——. (2005): Public Health in India: An Overview, Policy Research Working Paper Series 3787, The World Bank.

——. (2005): "Explaining Asia's 'Missing Women': A New Look at the Data", *Population and Development Review*, 31(3): 529–535.

Devi, L.S. (2003): "Ethnomedical Practices in Manipur: A Case of Evil Eye", *Anthropologist*, 5(1): 25–40.

DLHS-2 (2002–04) and 3 (2007–08): Orissa, Ministry of Health and Family Welfare, Government of India.

Duraisamy, P. (2000): "Health Status and Healthcare in Rural India", paper presented at International Seminar on 'Human Development', New Delhi, November 27–29.

Gartler, Paul and J. van der Gaag (1990): *The Willingness to Pay for Medical Care: Evidence from Two Developing Countries*, Johns Hopkins University Press, Washington, DC, The World Bank.

Guite, N. and S. Acharya (2006): "Indigenous Medicinal Substances and Health Care: A Study among Paite Tribe of Manipur, India", *Studies in Tribes and Tribals*, 4(2): 99–104.

Human Development Report (2004): Planning and Co-ordination, Department of Orissa, Bhubaneswar.

Kishor, Sunita (1993): "May God Give Sons to All: Gender and Child Mortality in India", *American Sociological Review*, 58(2): 247–265.

Muhuri, Pradip K. and Samuel H. Preston (1991): "Effects of Family Composition on Mortality Differentials by Sex among Children in Matlab, Bangladesh", *Population and Development Review*, 17(3): 415–434.

Padhi, Sakti and Srijit Mishra (2000): "Premature Mortality, Health Status and Public Health Care Facilities in Orissa: A Case Study in Accessibility and Utilisation", Nabakrushna Choudhury Centre for Development Studies, Bhubaneswar, Mimeo.

Rajeshwari (1996): "Gender Bias in Utilisation of Health Care Facilities in Rural Haryana", *Economic and Political Weekly*, 31(8): 489–494, February 24.

Singh, N.D. (2010): "Rural Healthcare and Indebtness in Punjab", *Economic and Political Weekly*, Vol. XIV, No. 4, January 22.

Selvaraj, Sakthivel and Anup Karan (2009): "Out-of-Pocket Health Expenditure and Impoverishment in India: What Causes Households to Incur Catastrophic Payments?", paper presented at the 7th World Congress on 'Health Economics' held at Beijing, 12–15 July.

16

Tribal Health

Problems and Prospects

VINITA SINGH AND JAY PALAK

World Health Organization (WHO, 1946) defines health as a complete state of physical, mental and social well-being and not merely the absence of disease or infirmity. Hence, it is perceived as a dynamic state of well-being characterized by a physical and mental potential, which satisfies the demands of life commensurate with age, culture and personal responsibility while others talks of health as a condition of well-being free of disease or infirmity and a basic and universal human right. Australian aboriginal people generally define health as not just the physical well-being of the individual but also refers to the social, emotional, spiritual and cultural well-being of the whole community. It is a whole of life view and includes the cyclical concept of life-death-life (NHMRC, 1996). The various factors affecting people's health are as follows:

Food: People regard food as the major factor influencing health. The sources of good health are fresh food items which include green leafy vegetables (self-grown) milk, etc. People distinguish between hot and cold food and there is belief that consumption of inadequate or dirty food causes health problems.

Physical work: High value is attached to physical work. Physical work tones up the body and is quintessential for healthy living for men and women. With the advent of machines, there is little scope for physical work. It is believed that one should strictly follow the traditional practices of going deep into the forest for defecation or for collecting 'datun' to clean teeth as this exposes the person to fresh air and also tones the body.

Mental state: People take due note of the mind-body interaction. Most of the new age diseases are because of rise in mental tensions which are the natural consequences of modernization. Besides that, weak economic conditions and matrimonial disharmony are other sources of mental tension.

Alcoholism: The tribal people are known for their indulgence in alcohol as alcohol is a part of tribal culture.

Code of conduct: There is a strong notion of good and evil. Evil or immoral acts result in punishment in the form of illness, accidents or mishappenings. It is believed that in order to remain healthy one must maintain good moral conduct.

Magic: Diseases can be the outcome of magic. Magical powers can inflict diseases. The 'Dayans' are living females who are born with evil, they think evil of somebody and the evil happens to that person. Magic is believed to be not only inflicting diseases but also curing them.

Cognised environment: Tribal people believe in unseen powers in their environment which influence the course of their lives. These powers are the deities of different order who can cause illness (Devta). These powers are also vested with the power of healing. Besides devtas, there are evil spirits or *churail* – ghost of women who die during parturition. The *chhaya* of these powers result in illness and accidents.

The belief system pertaining to etiology of diseases can be split up into Personalistic beliefs – in which supernatural beings are taken to be causative agents and Naturalistic beliefs in which natural causes like wrong food, weather, etc., are taken to be factors of illness (Gaur, 2001).

Health Problems of Tribals

The chief causes for the poor health status of tribal people are poverty and undernutrition in both macro and micronutrients, poor environmental sanitation, hygiene and lack of safe drinking water. Also, lack of access to health services, social barriers preventing access and utilization of health services and specific diseases such as malaria, TB, yaws, sickle cell anaemia and thalassemia (RCH II, 2006).

The tribal population have distinctive health problems which are mainly governed by their habitat, difficult terrains and ecologically variable niches. The health, nutrition and medico-genetic problems of diverse tribals groups have been found to be unique and present a formidable challenge for which appropriate solutions have to be found out by planning and evolving relevant research studies (Basu, 1999). Primitive tribal groups of India have special health problems and genetic abnormalities like sickle cell anaemia, G-6–PD red cell enzyme deficiency and sexually transmitted diseases. Insanitary conditions, ignorance, lack of personal hygiene and health education are the main factors responsible for ill-health among tribals. Some primitive tribal communities are facing extinction like the Onges, Jarwas and Shompens of Andaman and Nicobar Islands (Verma, 1978). Some of the problems are: (a) endemic diseases like malaria, introduced from outside or otherwise like tuberculosis, influenza, dysentery, high infant mortality and malnutrition, (b) venereal diseases, induced abortion, inbreeding, addiction to opium, custom of eating tubers of Dioscera (may cause sterility as they contain substances used in oral contraception), and (c) disturbed sex ratio leading to shortage of women. Urgent studies are therefore required on different primitive tribal groups of India (Basu, op. cit.).

The health and nutrition problems of the vast tribal population of India are as varied as the tribal groups themselves who present a bewildering diversity and variety in their socio-economic, socio-cultural and ecological settings. Nutritional anaemia is a major problem for women in India. This is especially so because tribal women have heavy workload and anaemia has profound effect on psychological and physical health. Anaemia lowers resistance to fatigue, effects working capacity under conditions of stress and increases susceptibility to other diseases. Maternal malnutrition is quite common among the tribal women especially those who have closely spaced pregnancies. Tribal diets are generally deficient in calcium, Vitamin A, Vitamin C, riboflavin and animal protein.

Childbearing and Maternal Mortality

Childbearing imposes additional health needs and problems on women – physically, psychologically and socially. Maternal mortality was reported to be high among various tribal groups but no exact data could be collected. The chief causes of maternal mortality were found to be unhygienic and primitive practices of parturition. Similar crude birth practices were found to exist in various tribal groups. Expectant mothers, to a large extent, are not inoculated against tetanus. From the inception of pregnancy to its termination, no specific nutritious diet is consumed by the women. On the other hand some pregnant tribal women (Dudh Kharias, Santhals) reduced their food intake because of the simple fear of recurrent vomiting and also to ensure that the baby may remain small and the delivery may be easier. The consumption of iron, calcium and vitamins during pregnancy is poor. The habit of taking alcohol during pregnancy has been found to be usual in tribal women. Almost all of them are observed to continue their regular activities including hard labour during advanced pregnancy. More than 90 per cent of the deliveries are conducted at home by elderly ladies of the households. No specific precautions are observed at the time of conducting deliveries which results in an increased susceptibility to various infections. Services of paramedical staff are secured only in cases of difficult labour.

As far as childcare is concerned tribal mothers are observed to breastfeed their babies. But, most of them adopt harmful practices like discarding of colostrum, giving prelacteal feeds, delayed initiation of breastfeeding and delayed introduction of complementary feeds. Vaccination and immunization of infants and children have been inadequate among tribal groups. In addition, extremes of magico-religious beliefs and taboos tend to aggravate the problems. The tribal population has much lower IMR as compared to the Scheduled Castes but moderately higher than the other population. The expectation of life is the average number of years remaining to be lived by those surviving to that age. Thus, this is far below the average life expectancy at birth of 58.6 years for the Indian population.

Genetic Disorders

Genetic disorders especially sickle cell disease and G-6–PD have been found to occur in high frequency among various tribal groups.

Sexually Transmitted Diseases (STDs)

They are most prevalent disease in the tribal areas. VDRL was found to be positive among polyandrous tribes (Jaunsaris of Chakarata, Dehradun). The number of females suffering from the disease was proportionately higher than the number of males.

Forest Ecology and Women's Health

The forest-based tribal economy in most parts of the world was women-centred. Women made provisions for the basic necessities like food, fuel, medicine, housing material, etc., from the forest produce. Food was obtained from shifting cultivation and from minor forest produces (MFP) like flowers and fruits collected from the forest. Extraction from herbs, roots and animals were used for medicine. All these efforts incurred an excessive workload on women.

Because of extensive cutting of trees by vested interests, the distances between villages and the forest areas have increased, forcing tribal women to walk longer distances in search of MFP and firewood. In this rapidly changing milieu, tribal women are confronted with an extraordinary workload. Given this additional workload, even women in the advanced stages of pregnancy are required to work in the agricultural fields or walk great distances to collect fuel and minor forest produce. The overstrain on tribal women however, is not compensated due to the non-availability of minor forest produce and decrease in food grain production.

Clearly tribal people especially women and children require special attention if their health status is to be improved. There is low utilization of health services in tribal areas because of sparsely distributed tribal population in difficult forest and hilly regions, poorly located sub-centres, PHCs and CHCs. Service providers do not remain in post, lack of suitable transport facilities for quick referral of emergency cases, lack of appropriate HRD policies to encourage/motivate the service providers to work in tribal areas, inadequate mobilization of NGOs, lack of integration with other health and sector programmes, Behavioural Change Communication (BCC) activities may be inappropriate, services are not client-friendly, there are cultural barriers to accession of health service, non involvement of local traditional faith healers and a weak monitoring and supervision system.

Strategies for Improvement of Tribal Health

The goal of RCH II in tribal areas is to improve RCH health outcomes for tribal people. The specific objectives are:

- Assess the unmet RCH needs in tribal communities
- Provide integrated, appropriate and quality RCH services
- Ensure equitable access to these services
- Stimulate demand for these services
- Improve service coverage and acceptability
- Promote community participation and inter-sectoral coordination
- Provide opportunity for employment of tribal people
- Promote and encourage tribal systems of medicine

Strategies to be Adopted for Improving Health Outcomes

Basic health and RCH services need to be integrated in the overall development of tribal areas. Tribal communities have many strengths such as strong community feeling, positive value towards health and strong faith in the traditional healing system. Close partnership can be developed with NGOs which are active in tribal areas. They should be involved in the planning, management and delivery of health care services. The approach to tackling tribal health problems has to be multipronged, area specific and need-based. This is important because tribal population is not homogenous.

In order to increase utilization of health services by the tribal population the suggested innovative approaches should include involving the community in the planning process as well as the management and implementation of the services and programmes, using community-based workers as social mobilizers, educators and providers of non-clinical services, involving locally elected bodies, involving NGOs, and promoting tribal systems of medicines and tribal healers wherever appropriate.

Promoting Community Participation

Working with Panchayati Raj Institutions (PRIs) will be important to bringing health on to the local political agenda. They need to be actively involved in the planning and management of health care delivery system. Community-based organization should be motivated to take active part in the management of local services. Community-based providers shall be trained to improve access and demand for services among the tribal population. Community-based volunteers can play an important role in extending reach services to tribal populations. In difficult terrain and sparsely populated areas it may be an advantage to have a team of men and women, preferably a married couple, working as community-based development (CBD) workers. This has been successfully implemented by SARTHI in 150 tribal villages of Gujarat and SEWA – Rural in Bharouch district of Gujarat. By having a male worker the reproductive health needs of men can be addressed.

BCC should be carefully developed with full community involvement. Community could either provide land for its construction of facilities or input in terms of time. A large network of Aanganwadi workers is available in the tribal areas under the ICDS scheme. They will be involved in creating awareness and demand for services for women and children.

NGO and Public-Private Partnerships

Mapping of NGOs will be useful in tribal areas, and credible NGOs especially with a proven track record of clinical service provision should be encouraged to take responsibility for managing RCH and other health services in sub-centres, PHCs and CHCs where the public health system is deficient. NGOs and the corporate sector should be encouraged to take up community-based development projects covering minimum of a population in the block and be assigned coordinating function for the mobile health services, referral transport, awareness creation and social mobilization.

ISMPs and tribal system of medicine practitioners may be provided orientation and training to provide counselling services for RCH services. They can potentially be depot holders and refer clients to public health facilities for IUDs, sterilization, immunization, antenatal care (ANC) and other services.

Communication Strategy

BGG needs to be carefully developed to prioritize local behaviour change objectives. In order to stimulate demand for RCH services, the BCC strategy must be appropriate for the tribal population to be served. A communication strategy needs to be based on the values, beliefs and practices of the tribal population with regional differences. Tribal dialects should be used in audio-visual presentations. Local tribal artists and cultural groups needs to be involved in designing and testing BCC materials.

Support to Infrastructure and Service Delivery

Facilities for Emergency Obstetric Care (EmOC) needs to be established at block level. PHCs and sub-centres shall be strengthened and the skills of public sector providers upgraded, not just in terms of technical training; special emphasis should be given to developing skills in counselling, the appreciative inquiry approach to quality improvement, supportive supervision and infection prevention.

Mobile clinics can be very useful in providing curative and preventive care through regular visits on fixed days to sub-centres. Teams may comprise doctors, auxillary nurse and midwives (ANMs) and health workers (HWs) (M), 'Aanganwadi workers (AWWs), Sahayika, PRI, NGO and traditional tribal medicine practitioners may provide local assistance. Facilities needs to be reequipped and strengthened according to the local RCH needs. Mini sub-centres may be established in limited hilly remote and difficult to approach areas, staffed by ANMs, with flexible population norms between 700 to 2,000.

Human Resource Development

Skilled assistance for birth will be promoted by piloting community midwife training. One approach might be to recruit local married women for training and assistance setting up their services. This need to be closely monitored to assess the quality of the services offered. More suitable and responsive human resource development policies for tribal areas needs to be explored (e.g., the possible relaxation of entry qualifications for ANM training for local tribal women, possibly involving a longer duration of training at the ANM training schools). This will be subject to the approval of Nursing Council of India. New ANM schools may be considered for tribal areas or special batches of ANM training exclusively for tribal girls at existing ANM schools may be considered.

Conclusion

In retrospect, it becomes clear that the behaviouristic and culture specific studies are not going too far in improving health status in tribal areas. An interdisciplinary approach to tribal health is necessary to improve their health status. It is necessary to have a better understanding of their living conditions and bring 'women' to the centrestage of development. Safe drinking water, roads, electricity, schools and functional and affordable health services need to be provided in the vicinity. Also, there is a need to ensure livelihoods and food security to the tribals, especially for women and children. Further, we need to ensure and protect their rights over the forest and other natural resources in their areas.

It is imperative to take cognizance of the tribal situation vis-à-vis their ecosystem. There is need to recognize and protect the traditional knowledge, customs and practices of indigenous people. Further, there is a need for ethno-botanical investigation and scientific inquiry to preserve their knowledge and protect their valuable source of knowledge from vanishing. Women should be fully involved in decision making and in the implementation of sustainable development activities. Priority should be given to gender-sensitive, participatory action oriented research and policy analysis. Measures should be taken to develop and include environmental, social and gender impact analysis as an essential step in the development and monitoring of programmes and policies. Thus, there is need for a holistic approach to environment, economy, energy, equity and development. Further we need to assess the levels of deprivation, nutritional status, food security, unemployment, housing, wages, access to land, forest, water resources, safe drinking water and electricity among various tribal groups.

There are several other issues which need attention. Detailed information are needed on maternal malnutrition, nutritional anaemia, nutritional status of pregnant women and the nature of their workload, food allocation and distribution within the family and its effect on the nutritional status of women, the complications of pregnancy and child birth, practices for parturition, maternal mortality, birth weight of children, infant and childhood mortality and their sex differentials, nature of maternal and child health care practices, attitude towards family planning, etc. A database on all the tribes has to be generated.

Tribal development strategies have to be more human centred, which means having an agenda that consists of provisioning of basic education, basic health care and capacity building within the framework of a stable and sustainable land use policy, where there is a basic inter-linkage of the individual activities. It also means better targeting so as to ensure an equitable development process. Thus the development paradigm will need to make health, centrestage in the overall development strategy.

Primary health care for tribal areas will have to be planned. The priority problems must be decided based on the disease pattern of the concerned tribal population. Problems like accidents, burns, sickle cell disease, Malaria, TB, leprosy, sexually transmitted diseases, endemic goitre may need special attention. Trained workers from outside may not be stable in tribal areas, so the tribals need to be selected and trained. Indigenous systems of health care and indigenous practitioners should be incorporated into health care planning. Greater role for voluntary organizations is required.

In order to generate data bank, compilation of all the microstudies published and unpublished in various states should be done. Further there is need to conduct a national survey and produce desegregated data on the health condition of various tribes. More studies need to be carried out to see the implications of development and tourism in the scheduled areas on the health of the tribes. Strict laws should be implemented to protect the rights of the tribal people. Policy related to use of forest land and health of tribes need to be in their favour (Reddy, 2008). Taking note of the above recommendations will certainly go a long way in improving the health status of tribals.

References

Basu, S. (1999): "Dimensions of Tribal Health in India, Health and Population: Perspectives and Issues", Lecture delivered at National Institute on 'Health and Family Welfare', New Delhi, Oct. 6.

Gaur, Mokshika (2001): "Health and Society in a Himachal Village", *Indian Anthropologist*, 31(2), Dec.

National Health and Medical Research Council (NHMRC) (1996): Promoting the Health of Indigenous Australians: A Review of Infrastructure Support for Aboriginal and Torres Straits Islanders Health Advancement, Final Report and Recommendations, Canberra: NHMRC.

RCH II Document 2 (2006): The Principles and Evidence Base for State RCH II Programme Implementation Plans (PIPs), Chapter 1: Improving Health Outcomes.

Reddy, Sunita (2008): "Health of Tribal Women and Children", *Indian Anthropologist*, 38(2).

Verma, I.C. (1978): "Medico Genetic Problems of Primitive Tribal Communities", in I.C. Verma and R.K. Puri (eds.), *Medical Genetics in India*, Vol. 2, Pondicherry: RK Auroma Enterprises.

WHO, Preamble to the Constitution of the WHO as adopted by the International Health Conference, New York, 19–22 June, 1946, and entered into force on 7th April 1948.

17

A Consumption and Nutritional Profile of the Birhor

A Vanishing Tribe of Jharkhand

RAM NARAYAN SAHU AND CHATURBHUJ SAHU

The ethnic people, confined to a particular geographic area, are called tribes. The tribes as we know are among those people who had been historically known as different from the Aryan people. They are believed to be the earliest settlers of the country. They are found throughout the country in different ecological and geoclimatic conditions in different concentration except Punjab and Haryana states and union territories of Delhi and Chandigarh. There are 427 (Roy Burman, 1971), 609 (Sharma, 1978), 635 (Singh, 1992) tribal communities which constitute the weaker section and form a significant proportion of population (8.28% in 2001). They are having some salient features which make them unique. Some of the tribes still cling to their abodes in forest and crude technology and simple way of life while at the same time there are others with higher levels of economy following gradual adaptation to the nature and ecology and practising pastoral economy, slash and burn cultivation or agriculture with plough and some others depending on simple industries having some sort of socio-economic symbiosis with their neighbouring communities (Bhowmick, 1990)

In Jharkhand 32 tribal groups are found in which we have included primitive tribal groups. By and large, inclusion of a population into primitive tribal group indicates its minority in demographic number as well as its primitive socio-economic activities.

The Birhor is one of the most backward primitive tribes of Jharkhand. They are nomadic, semi-nomadic, hunters, food gatherers and rope makers. They are on the verge of extinction even. This decline may not be due to low level of fertility but to a rather high level of mortality and existing bad health practices. Their total population is 4,377 as per 2001 census. Their population was 2,438; 3,461; 4,377 and 8,083 in 1961, 1971, 1981 and 1991 respectively.

The distribution of the Birhor is mainly confined to forested region of Hazaribagh district. They are probably one of the earliest settlers in the hills and forest of Jharkhand. Though they are wild but a very harmless race. Hunting and gathering is the main occupation and all the members of Birhor are found to be highly expert in hunting and gathering right from the childhood. They are also expert in rope making from indigenous fibres. The Birhors are found in hilly areas of Jharkhand, Odisha, Chhattisgarh, Madhya Pradesh and West Bengal, but their main domain is Jharkhand (Sahu, 1989, 1995, 1998).

Forest is the backbone of the life. It is very difficult to live without forest. Right from birth to death their each and every activity is related with the forest. From childhood they come and acquaintance with every plants, trees, animals, birds, etc. They have to do lot of strenuous work for their survival. They have to ride on the hills, move one forest to another in search of edible food and games. Due to this they become extremely introvert, shy and confined themselves only.

Hazaribagh District

Hazaribagh is one of the oldest district of Jharkhand. It forms the northern part of north Chotanagpur division, lies between 23° 25' and 24° 48' North latitude and between 84° 29' and 86° 38' East longitude. Hazaribagh town, situated at an elevation of about 2,000 feet, is the home of socially and culturally important tribes. The district has enjoyed a distinct identity since long from the historical, political and cultural points of view. Eco-cultural factors have added uniqueness to this area and have produced a way of life showed by all despite their living in different stages of economy (Sahu, 1995, 2001).

Material and Method

The Birhor like other tribal groups have been adjusted themselves in the surrounding ecology for getting food and doing other activities of life. All creature of the universe require certain food in certain quantities and proportions to ensure an acute life and successful reproduction. The data on food, food habits and food consumption pattern have been collected with the help of interview schedule, observation and interview techniques. The mean daily food intake has been analysed with respect to different food groups, viz., cereals, pulse, green leafy vegetables and other vegetables, fats and oils and sweeteners. The respondents have been asked to estimate the amount of different food consumed in possible unit. The mean nutrient has been computed using food tables as suggested by Indian Council of Medical Research (ICMR, 1984).

Results and Discussion

Today, the health and nutrition is probably an area which has attracted the attention not only of medical professional, but also of social doctors in general and anthropologists in particular. Health provides the ground for examining relationship between biological and social phenomenon. Medical anthropology in its present form represents an important application area in anthropology. It deals with the culturally constituted treatments for the categories of sickness as well as the categories of western scientific medicine, where the perspective is biologistic.

It has already been studied by the scholars related to this field about the functions of nutrition and nutritional problem. Mention may be made names of Puffer and Serrano (1975), Chojhacka and Adeghola (1984), Pandey et al. (2000). It has also been described that food is the only source of nutrition for regularizing the metabolic and socio-mental activities of life. Nutrient function in the body in three ways:

(i) It may provide the body with fuel, which when oxidized releases energy for its activities.
(ii) It may provide materials for the building and upkeep of body tissues.
(iii) It may provide the materials that are necessary to regulate body processes.

A single nutrient may take part in any one of these functions or two or even all three. The food taken by the people is not in a position to function adjectly than the architecture of the living tissues become imperfect and finally damages the several body system. Regarding the Birhor it has been described that they are the hunters and gatherers. So they have to compel themselves to depend on the forest produces and daily wages. The unavailability of food as well as poor economy are responsible for malnutrition among them. Their daily food and calorific intake has been shown in the Table 1 and nutritional value of food has been examined from the level of consumption content, requirement content and deficiency content.

Table 1

Consumption Pattern among the Birhor (in gm)

Individual		*Cereals*	*Pulses*	*Leafy veg*	*Other veg*	*Fat/oil*	*Sugar/ jaggery*
	Consumption	310	12	40	40	15	15
Men	RDA	575	30	50	50	40	45
	Deficiency	265	18	10	10	25	30
	Consumption	300	10	45	45	15	10
Women	RDA	575	30	50	50	35	45
	Deficiency	275	20	10	10	30	35

Cereals is main food consumption of the Birhor. For this they have to purchase these items from the village or nearby market but the consumption of this item is not found equal throughout the year. In average the male consumes 310 gm whereas it has been recommended 575 gm per day by ICMR (1984). This is equally true for female. In this case we find that Birhor is more deficient in comparison to other tribes, because more than 265gm cereals are lacking for them.

The average consumption of pulses is observed extremely inadequate among both the sexes. They often take any kind of pulse on any occasion. On and average it is 11 gm/day for male and female. Regarding leafy vegetables and other vegetables it has been found that they are in better condition than all the other consumed items. This is because of the fact that they are the man of forest, their entire life-cycle moves in the forest, and they have good knowledge about the useful and harmful product of the forest. In average they consume 80 gm for both the sexes. Deforestation has created this problem otherwise they were in a position to take more than the recommended daily allowances (RDA) as found by Sahu (1989, 1995).

The dietary intake of fats and oils are also observed inadequate among both the sexes but the worst situation has been seen among the female. The same situation is found for consumption of sugar/jaggery.

Though the Birhor are non-vegetarian as being the hunters but they do not take the meat of hunted animal. They sell them and purchase food item and alcoholic item.

Nutrients Intake

The nutrients have been categorized into five major groups – carbohydrates, protein, fat, vitamins and mineral. Carbohydrates and fats provide energy which is expressed in calories. Protein and minerals supply the materials for building-up the tissues and vitamin regulates the body process.

Table 2

Pattern of Nutrients Consumption

	Calorie	*Protein (gm)*	*Calcium (mg)*	*Iron (mg)*	*Vit.A (fg)*	*Vit.B_1 (mg)*	*Vit.B_2 (mg)*	*Vit.C. (mg)*	*Niacin (mg)*
Consumption	1700	45	550	20	1600	0.5	0.8	20	8
RDA	2875	60	400	40	2400	1.7	2.0	40	22
Deficiency	1175	15	150 (excess)	20	800	1.2	1.2	20	14

Table 2 shows the pattern of nutrient consumption among the Birhor of the study area. It is again studied from the consumption, RDA and deficiency basis. It shows that in all nutrient consumed by them is inadequate. So far as the calory in concerned they get only 1,700 kcal while 2,875 kcal is required for a normal and healthy people. 1,175 kcal becomes too much inefficient for any person which is found among the Birhor. Consumption of protein recommended is 60gm/day/person, but Birhor receive only 45gm, which is again deficient in this nutrient. They use forest product in every season, so they get high quantity of calcium which is found 550 mg/day/head. This is the only item which is being received in excess quantity.

Cereals are the major source of iron which provide only 20mg for each person. This is just half as per the recommended allowances. In case of vitamin or niacin the same situation has been observed.

In this way we find that every food content consumed by the Birhor is remarkably deficient except calcium. This deficient situation effect the resistance power of the bodies. Hence they are kept under the categories of malnutrition.

Before encroaching the forest by the outsider, the Birhor were happy in all aspects including consumption of food and nutrient but presently in the changed situation they have become poorest among the poorer. They are not in a position to give the proper food even for pregnant and lactating mother. In this critical situation they move in the forest for getting herbs and other edible roots and fruits.

The proverb "health is wealth" is also equally important for this minor and vanishing tribe for the leading of healthy and better quality of life. No doubt government. is trying to improve their quality of life through implementation of various welfare programmes, but all programmes have largely failed due to ignorance of the felt needs, cultural values and ecosystem of the people of study area. Thus the study of cultural factors and other factors have to be taken into consideration compulsorily along with giving proper nutritional education.

References

Bhowmick, P.K. (1990): *Applied Action Development Anthropology*, Calcutta: Institute of Social Research and Applied Anthropology.

Chojhacka, H. and O. Adeghola (1984): "The Determinants of infant and child morbidity/mortality in largos", Nigeria, *Social Science Medicine*, 19: 799–807.

Pandey, B.N., P.K.L. Das, A.K. Jha and A.K. Ojha (2000): "Socio-biology and nutritional status of Korwas: A primitive tribe of Bihar", *The Anthropologist*, 2(1): 21–26.

Puffer, R.R. and C.V. Serrano (1975): *Birth Weight, Maternal Age and Birth Order: Three Important Determinants of Infant Mortality*, Scientific Pub. No. 294, Washington, DC: Pan American Health Organisation.

Roy Burman, B.K. (1971): *A Preliminary Appraisal of the Scheduled Tribes of India*, New Delhi: Office of the Registrar General, India.

Sahu, Chaturbhuj (1989): "Nutrition and health problems of the Birhor: A vanishing tribe of Bihar", in A.N. Sharma (ed.), *Modern Trends in Anthropology*, New Delhi: Northern Book Centre.

——. (1995): "Food and health condition of the Birhor: A vanishing tribe of Bihar", *Indian Anthropologist*, 25(2): 13–24.

Sahu, Chaturbhuj (ed.) (2001): *Indian Tribal Life*, New Delhi: Sarup & Sons.

——. (2009): *Approaches of Tribal Development*, New Delhi: Adhyayan Pub. and Dist.

Sharma, B.D. (1978): *Scheduled Tribes and Scheduled Areas in India*, New Delhi: Prachi Prakashan.

Singh, A.K. (1992): *Tribal Development in India: Issues and Strategies*, New Delhi: Amar Prakashan.

18

Health and Nutrition of Tribal Women

Challenges and Possibilities

KALI NATH JHA

Sociologically, health, a counterpart to medical models of explanation which concentrate on organic disease mechanisms, sociological explanation redirects attention to social relationships as powerful determinants of changing health experience. Drawing on epidemiological knowledge and technique to reveal the distinctive social distribution of medically defined conditions in a population, attention is focused on variables like gender and class as possible direct influences in the 'etiological' process. A related concern in the development of new concepts of health and ill-health from non-medical perspectives.

In the analysis of individual experience, the onset of illness is conceptualized as a process characterized by a complex sequence of interactions between physiological, psychological and social factors. Social variables appear either as mediating mechanisms determining the individual's capacity to cope with negotiation of critical life events such as bereavement, divorce and unemployment which are seen as the underlying or prior causes of disease onset, or they are themselves accredited an independent causal role (Mann, 1983).

There have been a number of studies on the tribes, their culture and the impact of acculturation on the tribal society. There have also been studies on the status of women relating to their socio-cultural problems, their economic rights, their participation in management, their access to employment, food, health, etc. But these issues have not been properly focused in relation to tribal women. There are only a few studies on the status of tribal women in India (Mann, 1987; Singh, Vyas and Mann, 1988; Chauhan, 1990 and Chaudhary, 2011). Thus, the study of tribal women cannot be ignored.

Gender: Health and Nutrition

The subordinate status of women in the Indian society deeply influences their health status. Excessive emphasis on one biological aspect (childbearing) leads to early marriage, repeated pregnancies, abortions and reproductive problems are compounded.

The determinants of health and ill-health are well known, the socio-economic, cultural and political dimensions are often forgotten. The causes of disease are often looked for within the narrow biomedical model framework and solutions attempted to be found within this with a reductionist approach – which are 'technological fixes' for the 'worms and germs'. Women are seen as womb and tubes and their health problems seen related to this, i.e., contraceptives and reproductive health related. Their occupational health concerns and mental health concerns are systematically neglected. The gender dimension has often been absent, and the epidemiological approach missing. The social and gender roots of ill-health do not ever register.

These are painfully demonstrated in the planning and the implementation of three health programmes, the preparations of training and functioning of health personnel which are Family Planning, AIDS and tuberculosis (Kapur, 2001).

Mental Health – the most neglected area concerning tribal women – has been her mental health. Stress generated due to major life events such as break up of marriage, widowhood, illness in the family, financial hardship and substance abuse destroy an individual's ability to cope with and function effectively (Nair and Nair, 2002). Suppression of the extremities of an abusive relationship results in acute mental stress and trauma. In countries like India, economic dependency along with social and financial pressures trap women in abusive relationships, both physical and mental, forcing them to hide their anguish. Social workers and psychiatrists are approached by husbands to issue 'mentally unfit' certificates so that they can flash them in a court of law to demand divorce. Relatives do not want to keep mentally ill women in the family (ToI, 2002).

The high incidence of depression, anxiety, neurosis, psychomatic disorders, hysteria, increasing rate of suicide in women, especially in states like Kerala, clearly shows that in keeping of the projections of World Mental Health Report this is emerging as a major cause of morbidity. The impact of globalization, economic crisis in the lives of thousand of women who have lost their livelihoods or are being deserted, there is an increase in the number of women being forced into prostitution for survival, with many girls and women being tricked into it with false promises of jobs, marriage or promises of undying love by men who use them as commodities, desert them or sell them (Kapur, op. cit.).

As family programmes targeted women, with an increasing number of contraceptives made available for them including some with potentially serious side effects, with unethical clinical trials conducted on women treating them as guinea pigs, with greater push for female terminal methods of contraception, provides controlled long acting hormonal contraceptives and increasing use of abortion as a family planning method. What was never challenged was the role of men and their irresponsible sexual behaviours in matters related to reproductive health (ibid.).

Added to this, lack of adequate nutrition – partly due to poverty and partly due to lack of freedom – limited or no opportunity to rest and relax further aggravates women's reproductive health. As evident from 85 per cent of pregnant women being anaemic, 20 per cent stunted and many suffering from calcium deficiency presenting as Osteoporosis, thinning of bones, especially after menopause, severe back pain and fractures obviously reflects that the nutritional neglect is of a longer nature starting right from girlhood. Over one-fifth of the deaths that occur during pregnancy and child birth are anaemia related. That is why Chaudhary (2011) has rightly remarked that health and nutrition are two sides of the same coin. Without having intake of proper food and availability of pollution free environment no one can ensure proper health. But proper nutrition and safe environment are only necessary conditions and not the sufficient condition to ensure balanced health status in a sustainable manner. Even if we restrict to these issues, its relations with social structure, life chances, opportunities and value system needs to be examined. In a patriarchal society like India there are different social groups in general and women in particular who take food of having low nutritional value (Brief Outline: Seminar).

A diet that provides sufficient calories and micronutrients is essential for a pregnancy to be successfully carried to term. Proper nutrition and avoidance of unnecessary pregnancy related taboos can reduce serious complications during pregnancy and child birth. Infant mortality rate is an important index of the level of socio-economic development and quality of life. It is a sensitive indicator of the availability, utilization and effectiveness of the health care particularly pre-natal care. It is persistent undernourishment of women and girl child in particular, that is emerging as critical factor responsible for infant mortality. Poor maternal health results in low birth weight and premature babies. Infant and childhood diarrheal diseases, acute respiratory infections, and malnutrition contribute to high infant mortality rates.

The ill-effects of food and nutritional insecurity can be linked to the life cycle of an individual. When a child is weaned from mother's milk to other foods, very commonly the protein and energy requirements are not met. Due to inappropriate complementary or supplementary feeding practices, the energy gap widens. This is because for the proper growth after months of age, the requirement of the extra energy cannot be fulfilled by breast milk alone. This is displayed as protein energy malnutrition (PEM), which is very common form of malnutrition. The onset of malnutrition starts from the period between 7–8 months of age and if not mitigated then effects persists for the whole life. In the existing scenario where we see gender disparity existing in families, the male child may make up for these nutritional losses, but this cannot be always the case with a girl child.

Inverse Sex Ratio: Gender Violence Attitude towards Women's Health

There have, however, been areas of concern as reflected in worsening inverse sex ratio, increasing violence against women, the still unacceptably high maternal mortality, much more so in some states in India. The continued discrimination against women, the low status, unacceptably high illiteracy rate, ignorance about how to access services, low health awareness, denial of decision making, access to resources as well as to health services has negatively affected women's health.

The worsening of the inverse sex ratio is due to female foeticide, female infanticide deaths due to violence by burns, poisoning and death due to maternal mortality and communicable diseases. Increasing violence against women has emerged as the most disturbing phenomenon. The worsening inverse sex ratio is a matter of our collective shame as it reflects a widespread boy obsession, gender discrimination as well as increasing misuse of newer technologies (Kapur, op. cit.).

Trafficking of Tribal Women and HIV/AIDS

There is an increasing number of tribal women being forced to migrate or work within or outside the native place. And also being forced to work in sex-trade. For the SAARC region trafficking of girls has been identified as matter of key concern and also the increasing entry of minors in the trade often following rape. Demand for minors has increased with the AIDS awareness and also because of the old myth that sex with a virgin treats veneral disease.

Women are and will be the worst sufferers as innocent wives, as trafficked minors forced to provide sexual services to infected men, as mothers passing on HIV unknowingly to their babies, having been infected by their single sexual partner, their 'protector', their husband suffering doubly at the discovery that the child is infected and at its loss and that they were infected by their own husband. The physical, mental, economic price of illness is very high for any nation more so for a nation in debt, a nation with around 40 per cent of its people below poverty line, with 80 per cent of the health care being provided privately, with medical care having emerged as the second commonest cause of rural indebtedness, and AIDS drugs being outrageously priced, a nation with one billion people with ever increasing unemployment, loss of livelihoods, a nation where the media influences behaviour without creating health awareness, and the impact of globalization perpetuating individualism, conspicuous consumerism have led to erosion of human values, personal family, societal values as caring and compassion, interfere with unbridled profit making as mere economic growth defines 'efficiency' – totally disregarding social costs (Kapur, op. cit.).

Availability of Health Care

Generally, tribal women avail many types of health services. First of all, the majority of women try home remedies, failing which they approach either a man with indigenous knowledge of herbal medicine or an 'ojha' (with full of superstitions) or a homeopath or ayurvedic doctor or unani healer or at last the allopath. And while going through the phased process of treatment many times either she is failed to reach the last station or even if she reaches to the modern hospital/doctor the ailment becomes out of order. And for this state of affair multiple factors operating at macro and micro level are responsible.

Conclusion

There is a need to situate tribal women's health in the overall macro parameters. Gender divide in the access of health care and health cost is so sharp that women have to access informal providers and informal care. Gender audit in health should be done on the basis of identifying issues for reorientation at each stage of women's life cycle and focussing on the problems of each age group of women.

To address the problems concerning women's health, a holistic life span approach is needed (Gupta, 2001). Women's health is determined by the material reality generated by socio-economic, cultural forces as well as gender relations based on subordination of women. It is important to make men aware about women specific health needs. Improvement in women's health is a precondition for the development of her family. For an effective public education on the above-mentioned issues, charismatic personalities should teach the 'women and health' module. How to engender medical education? This question needs to be addressed. There is also, a need for gender sensitive books for the health practitioners (Patel, 2002).

Women and health movement in India has come of an age. Women's groups are examining health issues of women from political economy perspective. With the worsening economic crisis, especially due to massive deforestation nutritional needs of tribal women are not fulfilled. Structural adjustment programme has affected budgetary allocation for women's overall health needs.

The International Conference on Population and Development in Cairo in 1994 and IV World Conference on Women, 1995 emphasized the importance of reproductive rights and placed reproductive health both for men and women at centre stage of demographic objective instead of fertility reduction. The Cairo Conference reorganized women's right as individual rights. Gender equity and equality was accepted as goal for sustained and substantial development. Demographic indicators, internal migration and the provision of universal access to reproductive health services, including family planning services are some of the areas for achieving gender equity and equality (Nagla, 2003).

References

Chaudhary, S.N. (2011): National Seminar, Bhopal: Brief Outline.

Chauhan, Abha (1990): *Tribal Women and Social Change in India*, Etawah: A.C. Brothers.

Gupta, Nisha (2001): "Social and Gender Perspectives in Women's Health", *Health for the Millions*, Vol. 27, No. 3, May-June.

Kapur, Promilla (2001): *Empowering the Indian Women*, New Delhi: Publication Division.

Mann, M. (1983): *Encyclopedia of Sociology*, London: Macmillan Press.

Mann, K. (1987): *Tribal Women in a Changing Society*, Delhi: Mittal Publications.

Nagla, Madhu (2003): "Gender Equality: Perceptive Threat to Health", *Nucleus*, Vol. III, No. 1, January-June.

Nair, Jayashree Ramkrishna and Hema Nair (2002): "Engendering Health: A Brief History of Women's Involvement in Health Issues", *Samyukta: A Journal of Women's Studies, Women's Initiatives*, Vol. II, No. 1, January.

Patel, Vibhuti (2002): *Women's Challenges of the New Millennium*, New Delhi: Gyan Publishing House.

Singh, J.P., N.N. Vyas and R.S. Mann (1988): *Tribal Women and Development*, Jaipur: Rawat Publications.

ToI (*The Times of India*) (2002): 26th January.

19

Status of Tribal Health and Nutrition

A Case Study of Hajong and Lisu Tribes of the North-East Region

CHURA GIRI

The World Health Organization (WHO) at its inception in 1946, defined health as, "a state of complete physical, mental and social well-being and normally the absence of disease or infirmity". It is a fundamental human right and the attainment of the highest possible of health is a social goal. Health implies a sufficient reserve of physical strength, agility and endurance, as well as mental poise to meet the demands of everyday life. All communities wish to keep themselves healthy and adopt with the changing environment. The beliefs, traditions and customs handed down through many generations usually play a vital role in determining individual and community health care in the most of Indian societies. It is recognized by all governments that investment on health is an investment on man and in improving the quality of life as such is a part of the strategy of human resource development. The Constitution of India envisages the establishment of a new social order based on equality, freedom, justice and dignity of the individual, it aims at the elimination of poverty, ignorance and ill-health and directs the state to regard the raising of the level of nutrition and the standard of living of its people and the improvement of public health as among its primary duties, securing the health and strength of all citizens especially ensuring that women and children are given opportunities and facilities to develop in a healthy manner.

The sociological interest in the problems of health is a recent development. Medical sociology can be said as an area where sociological knowledge is used in understanding of the distribution of disease in society, human medical behaviours and cultural perspectives on disease, the role, attitudes and values of health providing institutions and the relationship of treatment and support facilities and any other health and disease related issues. The Rights to Health in general Article 25 of the Universal Declaration of Human Rights 1948 lays down that everyone has the right to a standard of living for the health and well-being of the family. Article 12 of the International Covenant on Economic, Social and Cultural Rights provides the right to enjoyment of the highest attainable standard of health. Undoubtedly women form an important social category. The basis of this category is not simply the biological entity but also the socio-cultural construct. In India within the given socio-cultural matrix women get low access to medical care. Women belonging to the low strata of the socio-economic hierarchy and to the rural areas have seen the critical manifestation of this aspect. Women's health is effected by a series of inter-related economic and socio-cultural factors, viz., level of earnings and educational background and the attitudes to marriage, age of marriage, value attached to fertility and sex of the child, the pattern of family organizations and the role demanded of women by social conventions (NPPW, 1988: 97). Individuals must learn about the basic health care practices at the time of any emergencies. Some of the general health services have been implemented by the government and some services are also available from local medical practitioners. Calnan (1987) on the basis of his study suggested that government, general practitioners and individuals all have a role to play in the maintenance of health. Health may be conceived as a product of many factors and the communities contribute to and share the responsibilities of its maintenance and grow consciousness towards health. Under the constitution health is a state subject. The areas of central government like eradication of major communicable and non-communicable disease, broad policy formulation, medical and para-medical education along with regulatory measures are important. Nutrition plays a critical role to the overall health status of women. Massive population size is a barrier to development and better quality of life. Fertility which is directly related to population growth is affected by number of factors such as cultural preferences of diverse roots and strength, family structures that distribute power over fertility decisions in various ways, customs and taboos related to sexual behaviour, child birth and childbearing, varying and rapidly changing economic condition and increasing government concerns. In rural areas, a strong family orientation is found. The family is the source of physical and emotional support and fulfils most social needs. Awareness and availability of family planning methods may not effectively control fertility unless people are properly motivated to reduce fertility (Jaiswal, 2008). This study is related to tribal health with special reference to Hajong tribe of Assam and the Lisu of the Arunachal Pradesh. Broad objectives of the paper is to analyse the health conditions of the women, their consciousness towards health and importance of health in their life.

The Survey Context

In Assam there are 23 communities recognized as Scheduled Tribe (ST), out of 23 communities nine communities are recognized as ST (plain) and the rest 14 are ST (hill). Hajong is recognized as ST (hill) only in Karbi Anglong and NC. Hills district of Assam. According to the 2001 Census 1,80,000 Hajong are distributed all over Assam. Basically, the Hajongs are Hindu and so amongst other tribes they are lagging behind in case of many schemes and provisions. The study is designed to examine the factors behind the health of women and its importance in the society. The selection of locale of the study and sample is based on the Hajong women, a Scheduled Tribe (hill) of Assam residing in Kothasema village of Jagun gaon panchayat of Margherita subdivision of upper Assam. Jagun is one of the farthest places of Assam situated at Tinsukia district. It is situated at the north bank of the Buridihing and the surveyed village named Kothasema gaon is situated on the southern bank of the same river. The village is approximately 8 km far away from the National Highway 153. Vital changes occurred in this village. This village constituted of Sema Nagas but after the division of Greater Assam, the Nagas went to Dimapur and Hajongs migrated to Kothasema in search of job and started to settle. This is a situation which took place from 1970–71 from Dhemaji as they were eroded by flood. Four villages constituted the No 4 Jagun village panchayat ward. The Kothasema has many neighbouring villages namely Chandrapur, Wagon-4, Adarsha gaon and Ramnagar.

Concept of Disease

The concept of disease similarly varies greatly depending upon the type of society, culture or individual. Usually it is defined as a deviation from the normal functioning, which may adversely affect the future health status. Since a diseased person is unable to perform his normal social responsibilities, his behaviour is viewed as deviant and hence dysfunctional by the society, which undertakes to cure him as early as possible to a person normal.

The notion of disease was never governed by the 'objective facts' rather it depended on the decision of the society. The disease and illness were believed to be caused not only by the individual's biophysical conditions but also by the supernatural beings. Violation of religious rules or norms, disobedience towards local deities and the resultant wrath of the gods and semi-gods and goddesses and the sins committed by the people in his present life and past lives. The internal disorders are believed to be the result of the tumours of human body, namely, wind (Vayu) blie (Pitta) and flagum (Kaf). Such notions about diseases have been the root causes of many Aryuvedics and Sidha medicine practitioners in treatment of diseases which tend to make the task of health care and consciousness towards health.

According to Hajongs (respondents) of the surveyed village of Kathasema the concept of 'well-being' stands for a state of being healthy, happy and prosperous. A healthy physique or beautiful features or muscular power may not be criteria for good health. In their opinion health, like happiness is an elusive concept, the ability or capacity to do manual work carrying out normal day's routine and having a clear eyesight and memory is the sign of being healthy. If on the other hand, a person is unable to carry out the normal routine and if subsequently the amount of food intake falls to almost a possible nil, then the person may be considered to be sick or ill or to be unhealthy. Petty ailments like fever or stomach trouble do not mean that the person concerned is unable to carry out the daily routine. But once the daily routine is disturbed, the family members of the person get alarmed and take precaution. These concepts are gradually changing and today a person without having serious diseases which may lead to death, is taken as a healthy person. The Hajongs of Kathasema tends to explain illness largely in terms of deviances from socio-moral norms that lead to an ebbing of the life force. According to them, a patient's moral nature or purity is also taken into consideration during an illness episode.

In Hajongs perception 'bemar' (disease) denotes a natural phenomenon and forms a part of the routine transactions between man and environment and presents disruption in the normal balance. The use of the term disease conveys different meaning in different contents. Like any story or drama in life there are three components of the drama of disease. In the context of former it consists of a hero, villain and the circumstances while in the latter the components are;

(a) The host or the man who enjoys health or suffers from disease.

(b) The agents, living such as bacteria and non-living such as temperature, pressure, etc., which act on the man.

(c) The environment such as air, water, food, housing and place of work etc., in which host and agent live and interact.

The end-result of interactions between man or host and the agents arising from the environment is health discomfort, disability, disease or death depending upon the factors or causes in all the three. Illness is either suggestive or descriptive term. It was, however, found that Hajong have equivalents words for disease like cholera, cancer, smallpox, and the like. The appearance of these many names and concepts in traditional system of nomenclature and disease of the Hajong are due to cultural values and tradition. According to literate and young generation youths there are three identifiable categories of disease, those which the doctor can cure and the folk-medicine man cannot (such as gallstone disease). Those which the folk-medicine man can cure but the doctor cannot (such as person attacked by evil spirits) and those which both can cure (such as tuberculosis). The Hajongs generally believe that some diseases are naturally caused and some by supernatural powers. They believe that it is most inauspicious thing if vulture perch on the roof of a house and when this happens the death of one of its inmates is thought to be imminent. The continuous crying of owl at night is also believed as inauspicious and it heralds disease for the family members of the locality where the owl is crying.

The Hajongs has a certain set of beliefs about factors causing diseases and their relation to other aspects of the society such as religion, morality, etc. Disease and its treatment are frequently supposed to be interlinked with these aspects. The types of diseases are caused by biological or natural factors, viz., infections, stress and decline in physical capabilities due to old age, accident or physical injury and infection of bodily injuries due to violent quarrels, infection results from invasion of the victim's body by tiny insects or germs. Infection generally occurs when a wound or cut is left open. So the Hajong always tie a bandage made out of a piece of clean cloth when they suffer from cut and other wounds. The diseases or ailments caused by supernatural agencies are fate or personified ill luck, impairment of health due to use of by a human being, attack by evil spirits and suffering due to bad dreams. Traditionally the Hajong's belief in many spirits is prevalent in the village. The older generation still believe in such phenomena and could not give up their beliefs on unseen supernatural beings and the spirits who influence the life of the Hajong are said to haunt peculiar places, some dwell in hill and forest, in huge trees and bamboo groves, the deserted house or some specified area in the village. The traditional belief in the activities of such evil spirits have led to the use of amulet and other metal ring made of five metals known as 'panch dhatu' – iron, lead, copper, silver and steel are there to counteract the attack by evil spirits.

The Hajongs of Kathasema have been practising several indigenous methods for the identifications of the causes of various diseases. Symptoms have been said to be basic criteria to diagnosis an illness type. In the Hajong perception dreams play a pivotal rote in interpretation of the imminent attack of diseases. If the person dreams riding a black horse or police personnel caught by the hand, a buffalo, etc., it may sure the person will fall in disease. It is general belief that the person should narrate the dream to the person senior to him or her not the person junior to him or her. If he or she does such narrations, the danger of the disease may be discarded.

Interrogation is another method to diagnose disease. The folk-medicine man and the folk-medicine woman and bone setter try to identify different types of diseases and illness by interrogating the patient and his close kith and kin. In any kind of illness, the pulse is examined and it is considered to be an identifying factor for diagnosis of disease and illness.

Dietary System and Health

The staple diet of Hajong is boiled rice. Generally they are non-vegetarian and take curries of fish, mutton, chicken and egg, etc. They are permitted to drink alcohol and eat pork. In addition to these essential proteins, minerals and carbohydrates essential for the growth of the human body can be acquired from the locally common edibles which have medicinal properties also. The Hajong women are expert in food preservation. They preserve food in a very traditional way not in modern method like freezing. Generally they preserve the following edibles which also carry the medicinal properties

1. *Sukati hak:* During *Ashwin* month when the cutting of Marapat (jute) is held the good leaves of *hukati hak* is dried in strong sunlight and packed nicely and eaten when the normal ailments like cold, stomachache occurs.
2. *Shewali hak:* During autumn they collect the coral jasmine flower and dry up them and with small fish they fry and eat the leaves of these flowers which have strong medicinal properties. For the diabetic patients it is very useful.
3. *Tea of wooden apple:* The unripe wooden apple after grinding and drying in the sun is kept for use. Instead of tea leaves the Hajong put a pinch of powder of wooden apple into hot water. It gives aromatic flavour. The Hajong use these type of tea in the ailment of constipation and ailments of stomach

Though it is a remote area, awareness towards health is found in womenfolk. They are aware about the diseases and the causes of diseases at least. They are found taking medical aid for the prevention of the fatal diseases. Due to poor communication they face problems to consult doctors in nearby town in Jagun and there is no such hospitals at Kathasema.

A Brief History of Yobin (Lisu)

People of India Vol. (III) (Singh, 1994) study counts some 5,653 distinct Indian communities. Out of 5,653 communities in India, 635 are tribals, out of 635 tribals, a little over 200 categories are found in the north-east. The very last among them must be the Lisu (Yobin) a Sino-Burmese tribe which entered the portals through the country's eastern most extremity in Vijaynagar region in Changlang district in Arunachal Pradesh from Southeast China just at or after Indian independence in 1947 (Verghese, 1996).

Now they are a small group of people lesser known to others, are found in Vijaynagar areas in Changlang district of Arunachal Pradesh. The matter is under consideration of Indian government. In temperament they are very docile, peace loving and gentle people. The population of the Lisu (Yobin) in Vijaynagar region is approximately 3,000 only. They prefer to address them as Lisu. The name Yobin is addressed by the Singpho community as the Lisu addressed the Singpho (a ST ethnic group mostly found is the valley of Assam and the hill region of Arunachal Pradesh) as "Afaphu'. It is crystal clear that the community under study is better known as the Lisu and they feel happiness to call themselves Lisu as this name is given to them from their forefathers. They are also called Yobin since time immemorial by other neighbouring community especially by the Singpho. Etymologically, of the word 'Lisu' the first part is Li which means four or wrapping and 'Su' means person. Generally they used to wear long belt wrapping around the waist and hence called Lisu. It is important to note that the belt wrapping around the waist is called *Jala* in their local dialect and made from Ganja leaves (Marijuana)weaving on handloom by the women. They are born and brought up in the midst of natural surrounding. Nature is the means of their survival.

The Yobin is an ethnic group who inhabit Myanmar/China, Thailand and one of the states of north-east region, i.e., Arunachal Pradesh. The Lisu of Arunachal Pradesh believes to originate from eastern Tibet. The Lisu form one of the 25 major ethnic groups officially recognized by the Government of Arunachal Pradesh. Lisu in Arunachal Pradesh are generally Christian, A section of missionarized Lisu migrated from China to Myanmar (erstwhile Burma). Later the community was ordered to leave Burma by the government and at that time this group of Lisu settled in Arunachal Pradesh. It is true that the isolation from the forces of change and natural geographical situations have circumscribed in very low stage of socio-economic formation.

Material and Method

The locale for the study is Lisu inhabited areas at Miao and Kharsang of Changlang district, Arunachal Pradesh. The Lisu community generally migrated from Gandhigram of Vijaynagar circle of Changlang district and settled in Miao and Kharsang. The households of these areas are 200. A sizeable sample of married Lisu women is selected for the study through various techniques of data collection like interview schedule, observation and in-depth interview related to reproductive health and their status in the society.

Conception and Pregnancy

The Lisu know the biological or physiological cause of conception. But they do not believe that sexual intercourse always follows conception. They ascribe the cause of conception to their god named Phula. Blessing of Phula is essential for becoming a mother. A physically fertile Lisu woman may not become a mother unless she is showered with the blessing of Phula. A sterile Lisu woman is considered unlucky because she is deprived of the blessing of Phula. Generally, no prebirth ritual is performed by the Lisu, but the movement of pregnant woman is restricted by the different taboos and works. These are as follows:

(i) During the period of pregnancy a Lisu woman should not visit the place where the evil spirits or ghosts are supposed to reside.

(ii) She should not visit the place where the traps are set up for hunting animals, birds and fishes.

(iii) She should not cross over the fishing net *(shague)* and arrow *(chey)* straight scythe *(atha)* etc.

(iv) It is a taboo to cross over the rope by which the pig, goat or cow is tied upon.

(v) She is debarred from taking the things which are bitter in taste *(khaosha)*

(vi) She should not carry heavy load.

(vii) She should not fall on the ground by any means.

(viii) The belief behind all these taboos is that they help in the successful delivery, otherwise as per their belief the woman will definitely get troubles like serious pain, abortion, deformed baby, delay in delivery, etc.

Birth

Generally delivery or the birth of a child takes place in the husband's house. For delivery a room is selected where the pregnant woman stays. Delivery is attended by the women only. In every Lisu village there are a few women who specialize as delivery nurses named *Jhojasu.* When the labour pains starts jhojasu is informed. Mother of the pregnant woman also attends and generally stays with her daughter. No male members including the husband are allowed to enter the delivery room. The Lisu mother never becomes polluted after the delivery. After three days of delivery she cleans herself, no purification ceremony is observed by the Lisu. So the question of employing washerman and barber does not arise at all in the case of the Lisu. Physically handicapped or deformed baby is attributed to the act of evil spirit *(nio).* Such baby is killed immediately after birth and buried in a suitable place but not in the burial ground and sometimes the baby is kept floating without killing in current water of a nearby river. Their presence is believed to bring calamities and misfortune to the Lisu.

Name Giving Ceremony

On any day after three days of birth of the baby a name giving ceremony is performed. Here the consanguineal relatives of baby's father are invited. Name of the baby is given by grandfather of mother. Grandfather or mother announces the name of the baby before the relatives. A hog is sacrificed on that day. Invitees or relatives are provided with a feast consisting of rice, pork, and beer. Then according to suitability, mother with the baby after two or three months of birth goes to her parent's house with some presentations and remain there for some days. There also a ceremony is observed where the relatives of the mother's side are invited.

No feeding ceremony is performed by the Lisu. When the baby begins to cut the teeth, mother put some solid food to the mouth of the baby after chewing them properly. No feed day or time is selected for the purpose, mother does it according to her suitability.

The Lisu do not believe in birth control and they do not use any contraceptive for the purpose. They consider birth control a kind of genocide and vehemently oppose it. It is one of their foremost sacred duties to increase their population or follow beings rather to procreate as many children as possible.

The Lisu do not believe in rebirth of their ancestors and there is no system of preparing the horoscope of the babies born to Lisu. Preference of male or female child varies from one family to another. A Lisu mother prefers female baby only to get an extra helping hand in her daily work and similarly a Lisu father prefers a male baby to get assistance in his work.

Child Care and Rearing

A great care is taken to protect a Lisu baby from the clutches of evil spirits. A Lisu baby is never left alone. One is always deputed to remain with the baby. It is believed by the Lisu that the spirit cannot do any harm to the baby in presence of human beings.

Old Age and Lisu Society

One of the most important aims of the Lisu is to produce as many children as possible. Intention behind the producing of a number of issues is that at least one of them will surely look after the Lisu parents at their old age. As a sequel to the norm of the Lisu society the parents at their old age prefer to live with their youngest son. Old men and women command respect from their society. Generally the Lisu men and women continue their normal household activities even after the age of fifty-five or sixty. After menopause when they are relieved of the burden of childbearing, Lisu women again turn their attention to the heavy work of the plantations, harvesting, collection of firewoods etc., at par with men. In old age some Lisu women becomes mid-wives and pursue their profession till death. As old age approaches women settle down to performing the skilled tasks in the households, to weaving, superintending the children, feeding the cocks and pigs. Similarly men settle down to preparing bow and arrow, fishing nets controlling and burning fire in the house, guarding the house and giving advice to the young men The Lisu men and women do not want to live up to the very old age when they are not in a position to participate in any work. The old Lisu men and women become very much delighted if they could see their actual burial place and the coffin before death.

Death

Belief to the cause of death is generally attributed to a natural phenomenon. But when a Lisu man or a women dies due to old age it is thought to be a natural death and the cause is imputed to the will of God *(Wusa)* a present to Jesus Christ. Now they believe that the allotted span of life in this world is over so Jesus Christ has taken him or her to himself. Death due to prolonged diseases, death by accident such as a fall from a tree, drowning, rolling boulders, by the attack of ferocious animals etc., are not uncommon. Death at pregnancy or at the time of delivery death of a child and epidemic death are ascribed to the evil actions of different spirits commonly known as *Ni.*

Stereotype Role and Women's Health

No doubt stereotype roles have impact on women's health. An individual woman's position in her family and in society was responsible for the formation of stereotyping roles which impact on women's health is immense. While examining the position of health of woman in Hajong society and Lisu society, we have observed some important cause which threats on woman's health such as the patrilineal family is responsible for the deteriorated condition of woman's health at the same time. Woman's mental and physical health is affected by such roles and expectations. Women work long and tedious hours often under difficult and unhygienic condition. Food discrimination is like the boon for women and girls. We know that discrimination emerges from the kitchen first by this we mean that men and boys eat first and are given the larger and more nutritious portions. Traditionally women eat after men in our society and when there is lifted food to be distributed they automatically get less. Improvement in the health status of the women has been one of the major thrust areas for the social development programmes of the country. This will be achieved through the awareness of the women towards health. The social scientists, policy planner and the media generated enormous data on women's issue. Hence, women's health as one of the issues have emerged to be crucial contemporary women's issues in India. In Assam the role of National Health Mission in this regard is much emphasized.

References

Calnan, M. (1987): *Health and Illness: The Lay Perspective*, London: Tavistock Publication Ltd.

Jaiswal, Neeraj (2008): "Fertility and Health of Rural Women," (ed.) Pandya Rameshwari, *Women Welfare and Empowerment in India*, New Delhi: New Century Publication.

National Perspective Plan for Women (1988–2000): Department of Women and Child Development, New Delhi: Government of India.

Singh, K.S. (1994): *People of India*, National Series Vol. III, Delhi: Oxford University Press.

Singh, K.S. and S. Manmohan (1983): *People of India*, Vol. IX.

Verghese, B.G. (1996): *India's Northeast Resurgent*, New Delhi: Konark.

20

Breastfeeding among Tribes in Western Madhya Pradesh

An Analysis

PARUL JOSHI

Mother's milk is the nature's gift to the baby. This is nutritionally a most balanced food for the infant. This is a very complicated mixture of fats, proteins, sugars, minerals and water that can provide all the food elements required by a baby for the infancy period. Breastmilk is nutritionally adequate and balanced, safe and hygienic and provides immunity against gastrointestinal and respiratory infections and allergies (Bhatt, 1993). Breastfeeding practices affect both mother and child. Breastfeeding is affected by the duration of exclusive breastfeeding, weaning or time of introduction of semi-solid and solid food and total duration of breast-feeding. It influences the child's nutritional status, which in turn has an effect on child survival. "If the babies are placed directly on to the breast after birth, it is possible that infant infection and consequent malnutrition could be reduced substantially" (Bairathi, 1991). The World Health Organization (WHO) recommends that a baby should be given breast milk immediately after birth and it should be given the same exclusively till the fourth and sixth months.

"In the first few days after delivery, the breast yields a clear yellowish secretion known as colostrum, should be given to the baby immediately after birth because it prevents a number of ailments and diseases in the new born. Early introduction of the breast also stimulates milk production and therefore, assumes importance" (Banerji, 1982). A lot of work has been done to promote the breastfeeding practice by the government. What is the real situation for the breastfeeding in the tribal area? This study was conducted with the following specific objectives:

1. To study the status of breastfeeding practice in the tribal area; and
2. To analyse various administrative, socio-economic, cultural and psychological factors affecting the breastfeeding practice.

To achieve these objectives, Dhar district of western Madhya Pradesh was selected for the study. The study was focused on tribes, so only those blocks of Dhar district were selected in the study where the tribal population was more than 70 per cent. According to Census of 2001, there were six blocks of Dhar district where tribal population was more than 70 per cent. These were Bagh, Umarban, Dhai, Gandhwani, Kukshi and Tirla.

In the above six blocks the total number of villages, as per census of 2001, were 615. Out of 615 villages, only medium sized villages with a population of 500 to 2,000 were included in the sampling frame. Thus, in the sample, 295 villages were included. The actual selection of 5 per cent villages, i.e., 15 villages was made randomly from the population range of 500 to 1,000 and 1,000 to 2,000 in proportion to number of villages in each category from six designated blocks.

From the selected 15 villages all those available women, who were pregnant and had children upto five years, were included in the study. The actual number of such women available in the village during the survey were 250, all of them were included in the survey. For quantitative data collection, interview schedules were used as a tool. The schedules were finalized after pretesting. To have a deeper qualitative insight of the problem, observation and directional group discussions were held.

Both the primary and secondary data has been collected for the analysis of the problem.

Secondary data was collected through various published material like published books, census report, five-year plans including state five-year plans, statistical abstracts, government publications, annual report of the Ministry of Health and Welfare, National Family Health Survey-India, National Family Health Survey-Madhya Pradesh, research reports, journals and periodicals, letter-magazines, and newspapers, etc.

With the help of interview schedules primary data were collected through personal interviews with the respondents, observations and group discussions were conducted in the villages and government hospital (SC/PHC/CHC/FRU). Interviews and discussions were also held with the functionaries of the health department and Women and Child Development department.

The information collected through the schedules was properly codified using the code book and entered on the master chart in the excel framework with the help of computer. Then, the data was tabulated and analysed. Following are the findings.

Profile of the Sample Population

Being a tribal-dominated region the sample reflects the dominance (84.8%) of Scheduled Tribes, in the surveyed households. Among the tribals the majority were Bhil followed by Bhilala and Patlya. Rest of the 15.2 per cent surveyed population belonged to Scheduled Castes.

Table 1

Analysis of Socio-Economic Profile of the Respondents

Characteristics (Personal and demographic)	*Categories*	*Frequency*	*Percentage*
Caste	Scheduled Tribes	212	84.8
	Scheduled Castes	38	15.2
Present Age	18–20	22	8.8
	21–25	80	32.0
	26–30	96	38.4
	31–35	40	16.0
	36–40	12	4.8
Type of Family	Nuclear	148	59.2
	Joint	94	37.6
	Broken	08	3.2
Number of Children	1 to 2	40	16.0
	2 to 5	113	45.2
	6 to 8	75	30.0
	8 to10	22	8.8
Education	Illiterate	213	85.2
	Literate	17	6.8
	Primary	12	4.8
	Middle	08	3.2
Age at the Time of Marriage	12 to 15 year	44	17.6
	15 to 18 year	109	43.6
	Above 18 year	97	38.8
Main Occupation	Agriculture+	104	41.6
	Labourer Only	91	36.4
	Labourer Agriculture	44	17.6
	Business	08	3.2
	Government Service	03	1.2
Annual Family Income (in ₹)	5,000	63	25.2
	5,001 to 10,000	111	44.4
	10,001 to 15,000	38	15.2
	15001 to 20,000	16	6.4
	20,001 to 25,000	12	4.8
	Above 25,000	10	4.0

The age structure of the respondents reflects the younger population. This is so because in the survey, only pregnant women were included. Out of these 38.4 per cent expectant mothers belonged to the age group of 26 to 30.

Bhils prefer to live in nuclear families, and therefore, in the surveyed household nearly 60 per cent families were found to be nuclear.

The table clearly reflects that small family is still a far removed concept among the rural areas in the tribal region. In the surveyed population the average size of family was seven and nearly half of the respondents were having 2–5 children and a perceptibly higher percentage of 30 was of those who were having 6–8 children. Nearly 9 per cent of the respondents were having even more than eight children.

In spite of the legislative provision regarding the age of marriage, nearly 61 per cent respondents were married below the age of 18 and 17.6 per cent of the pregnant mothers were 12 to 15 years old at the time of marriage.

Table 2

Breastfeeding Profile

Particulars	*Number of Respondents*	*Percentage of Respondents*
Time when breastfeeding was started or initiated		
Within two to four hours of birth	19	7.6
After four hours but same day	25	10.0
After one day	47	18.8
After three days	156	62.4
Not breastfed at all	3	1.2
Women who fed breastmilk with colostrum	94	38.0
Women who fed breastmilk without colostrum	153	62.0
Women who fed direct breastmilk with colostrum without feeding any other thing	23	9.2
Women who fed breastmilk with colostrum after feeding any other thing	71	28.4
Time for which the babies were fed exclusively on breastmilk		
Only fifteen days	31	12.5
One month	45	18.2
Two to three months	77	31.1
Three to four months	59	23.8
Four to six months	35	14.1

Despite intensive state efforts to propagate education among women, 85 per cent of the surveyed respondents were illiterate and only 3.2 per cent had an education above primary level.

As far as the occupational status was concerned the data reveals that only 17.6 per cent households were depending on agriculture alone while 78 per cent were either labourers or were working on others' fields as labourers, besides cultivating their own fields. The presence secondary and tertiary sector was found to be less than 5 per cent.

With an average of seven members in a family, annual income of an average household was less than ₹ 10,000. Thus, a majority of surveyed households were below poverty level.

With regard to socio-economic condition as per the overall picture, which has emerged in the surveyed household were mostly tribal, with more number of children, mostly illiterate, and belonging to predominantly labour category with low income. Details of breastfeeding practices in study area are given in Table 2.

Table 2 shows that only 8 per cent respondent's breastfed their babies within two to four hours of their birth and most of the respondents (62%) breastfed their babies after three days from birth. The practice was in vogue because of a custom in the community to breastfed the babies after one to three days from birth and a solution of jaggery and water, cow's and goat's milk with water was given to the babies for one to three days from birth. It may be concluded that culture plays a dominant role in the decision about time for starting breastfeeding. As per only one per cent respondents their babies were not breastfed at all, because mothers could not produce breastmilk so they did not put the babies to the breast. Only 38 per cent respondents were such as breastfed their babies with colostrum while 62 per cent respondents were such as had squeezed out breastmilk with colostrum and then fed the babies. The initial breastmilk contains colostrum which is necessary for the growth of the children. The baby could be easily protected from illness because the colostrum provided to the baby gives strong resistance power and immunity.

Out of the total respondents who had fed breastmilk with colostrum to their babies, only 9 per cent women had fed direct breastmilk with colostrum without feeding any other thing to the babies, which is right method. While about 28 per cent respondents had fed breastmilk with colostrum after feeding a solution of jaggery and water, cow's and goat's milk with water for one to three days from birth.

The table further shows total number of respondents who fed their babies exclusively breastmilk (without giving water or any other supplementary food during the time) for a certain period. Only 14 per cent mothers were such as fed their babies with only breastmilk for four to six months. The remaining respondents were fed (water and other supplements) before time. Though it should be given the same exclusively till the fourth to sixth month.

Table 3

Reasons for not Feeding Colostrum to the Babies

Responses Given by Respondents	*Percentage of Responses*
The breastmilk that comes initially has to be discarded five times in the name of god or goddess because failing on that account could result in illness of both the mother and the child.	35
Breastmilk that comes initially is not good for child's health.	35
Age-old custom, so elders stopped the women from feeding colostrum to their babies.	30

Table 3 shows the reasons for not feeding colostrum to the babies. Out of the total responses received to know the reasons for not feeding colostrum to the babies, 35 per cent responses were in favour of the fact that the breastmilk that comes initially had to be discarded five times in the name of god or goddess failing which both mother and child could fell ill. A total of 35 per cent responses were in favour of the fact that the initial breastmilk becomes dirty or improper for intake because it has remained in the mother's body for nine months. If the babies are fed, then the babies would fall prey to diarrhoea or other stomach disorders. According to 30 per cent responses, it was an age-old custom which had been practised in their community since a very long time, so elders in the family stopped the women from feeding colostrum to their babies. Solution of jaggery and water, cow's milk and goat's milk was given to the baby for the first three days in place of mother's milk, so colostrum was squeezed out and thrown.

Weaning

The term 'weaning' is used to denote the process by which an infant changes from breastmilk to a mixed diet. It is the shifting of the child from breastfeeding to other forms of nourishment. Breastfeeding is an ideal food for the infant, but it cannot be continued for a long period. The quantity of milk reduces when the times passes and hunger of infant increases with the growth, so weaning is necessary for infant. Weaning is a process in which an infant is gradually introduced to a variety of liquid, semi-solid and solid foods to effect a smooth shift to the adult or family food pattern. Table 4 shows the distribution of 250 mothers according to their responses on times for starting weaning.

Table 4

Time of Weaning of the Children

Age of Children	*Number of Respondents*	*Percentage of Respondents*
Between three and four months	27	10.8
Between four and six months	38	15.2
Between six and eight months	70	28.0
Between eight and twelve months	61	24.4
Between twelve and fifteen months	54	21.6

It is emphasized by nutritionists, pediatricians and others concerned with child health that satisfactory growth and development of the infant and the young child depends on adequate breastfeeding and timely introduction of supplementary food. It is stated that the need of supplementary food starts between fourth and sixth month. In the present investigation, though it is heartening to see prolonged breastfeeding. Since most mothers cannot produce sufficient milk after six months, addition of some other form of food in the baby's diet is extremely important. If solid foods are not introduced at the right time, the child may become malnourished. But Table 4 shows that about 11 per cent mothers had introduced supplementary food to their babies between the age of three and four months, only 15 per cent mothers had given supplementary food to their babies between the age of four and six months, which is the correct time to introduce the supplementary food for the children. While a large number of respondents, i.e., 74 per cent had introduced supplementary food to their children between the age of six and fifteen months. This indicates the mothers' complete ignorance about nutritional requirement of children and type of weaning food which can be given easily. This also indicates the need for proper nutrition and health education of the mothers.

Conclusions and Findings

It is very important for new born babies to be fed with breastmilk which is rich in colostrum but among the villagers, there is lack of awareness about it. During the study it was found that culture plays a dominant role in deciding time for starting breastmilk. Only 17 per cent respondents started breastfeeding on the day of birth and a large number of them started it after third day. Direct breastfeeding with colostrum was also not in practice. Only 38 per cent respondents breastfed their babies with colostrum. Out of them very few women had breastfed their new borns with colostrum without any other food, which is the right method while a large number of respondents had breastfed with colostrum after feeding other type of solution. Since there was a custom in their community to feed the new born babies with solutions of jaggery and water, or with cow or goat milk mixed with water for about two to three days from birth, only after which the baby was breastfed. During the study, prolonged breastfeeding was found. Since most mothers can not produce sufficient milk after six months, addition of some other form of food in the baby's diet is extremely important. Though only 15 per cent mothers had given supplementary food to their babies between age of four and six months, which is the correct time to introduce the supplementary food. While a large number of respondents had given supplementary food and their children before or after the proper time. This indicates the mother's complete ignorance about supplementary food and nutritional requirement of child.

References

Banerji, Debabar (1982): *Poverty Class and Health Culture in India*, New Delhi: Prachi Prakashan.

Bairathi, Shashi (1991): *Tribal Culture Economy and Health: Health Care Practices*, Jaipur: Rawat Publications.

Bhatt, I.A. (1993): "Who is Responsible for Artificial Feeding? An Evaluation", *Indian Journal of Mother and Child Health*, 4(2).

21

Status of Health in Relation to Cultural Practices

Reference to Tribe of Koraput District of Odisha

SOUBHAGYA RANJAN PADHI

Importance of good health has been well recognized over time. However, many times a section of the society does not have much access to health facility and suffer from ill-health. Despite remarkable global development in the field of diagnostics and curative and preventive health, there are many indigenous communities far away from modern medication facility, living in isolation in natural surroundings adhering to their traditional values, customs, beliefs and myths. About half of the world's indigenous people, comprising 635 tribal communities including 75 primitive tribal communities live in India. Odisha, the most picturesque state in eastern India, occupies a unique place in the tribal map of the country having largest number of tribal communities (62 tribes including 13 primitive tribes) with a population of 8.15 million constituting 22.3 per cent of state's population (2001 Census).

The status of tribal people is intimately linked to the issues of health and human rights. Gender consideration often leads to denial of various human rights – including the access to adequate nutrition and other health services. According to the modern human rights law, which guarantees equality in every sphere, many of the health disadvantages of tribals can be classified as injustice. But in many countries social research has tended to overlook the consequences of these health inequality and violation of human right of tribals and neglected to examine fully the different social, cultural and economic context within which tribals work and live. To delineate the sickness and health vulnerability experienced by tribals, one has to probe into the inner world of their experience. This would unearth their sense of identity, role acceptance, compliance, susceptibility and many other personal issues. It is crucial that the dominant human rights discourses should address the health issue of tribals in general and reproductive health and gender equality in particular. There is an urgent need to come out with benchmarks and indicators to examine the status of tribal people in the context of health disparity and human rights violation. Cross-sectional studies have estimated the positive co-relation between better health and nutrition and higher GDP (Chaudhuri, 1990; Basu, 1993; Wheeler, 1980). Various micro studies also explored the economic contribution of a healthy man to be higher compared to others. Poor health reduces the life expectancy of the people and therefore, also reduces their motivational level and future levels of economic growth. This way the vicious circle moves (ICMR Bulletin, 2003). Thus, there is a need to break this vicious circle by apt public provision of health on a sustainable basis. This is even more appropriate for the poor and marginalized tribal communities who suffer from pitiable health conditions and severe health disparities. In this paper an attempt is made to examine the health status of the tribal community of the Koraput district in Odisha.

In the study of health the most perplexing and ambiguous issue has been its definition. However, the most widely accepted definition is what is stated in the Constitution of World Health Organization (WHO), which defines health as a "state of complete physical, mental and social well-being and not merely the absence of disease or infirmity". In a broader perspective health refers to the promotion of social and related services and prevention of the barriers for the realization and maintenance of one's physical, mental and social well-being. The challenges of securing tribal's health focus attention not simply to physical and mental health services, but to the justice of the foundations upon which societies function.

The broader perspective of health prescribe for giving attention to the full range of human rights that go beyond the provision of medical, nursing and related health services and to contribute in different ways and at different levels to the achievement and maintenance of health (Cook, 2004). Therefore, the rights relevant to the promotion and protection of tribals' health include:

- The right of tribals to be free from all types of discriminations
- The right with regard to survival and safety
- The right to information and education

- The right regarding tribals' empowerment, including right to freedom of thought and the right to political participation
- The right to health care and the benefits of scientific progress

The familiar WHO concept that health is determined by reference to "physical, mental and social well-being and not merely the absence of diseases or infirmity" emphasizes the significance of social welfare of populations and not merely the medication of diseases. Medical science occupies a central position in health, but health is the outcome of a combination of factors – biological, genetic, environmental, political social and economic. The elements that condition a population's health go beyond physiological factors to include economic condition, literacy level, accessibility to different opportunities, exposure to the larger society, developmental processes, political and bureaucratic inventiveness. Against this backdrop the circumstances affecting health of tribes can be analysed through various statistical indicators and other socio-economic functioning of their community.

Methodology

The study was conducted using a combination of qualitative and quantitative methods. Participatory Rural Appraisal (PRA) technique was adopted to collect wide-ranging information from the tribals regarding their health status. Nevertheless this is an empirical study (a case study of Ranikana village of Semiliguda block) and various research techniques were employed to investigate tribals' perception of their health problems. In view of the present study the researcher has used the observation technique to collect the first-hand information from field. Observation has been used in this study as a method in the field to scrutinize the responsibility of various complex socio-religious institutions and the ethics of their cultural practice which play a major role in determining health status of these people. Besides the observation method, a structured interview schedule has also been used deliberately to achieve reliability and study the health issue more intensively. The interview schedule has collected the general information regarding their health conditions. Data has been collected on several belief system and practices by interviewing a purposive sample of pregnant women, as well as from *dais* and others who have suffered from certain diseases. The information collected in this manner is supplemented with data from other relevant secondary sources like official records of UNICEF, NFHC, NRHM, PHC and other published materials.

Situation Analysis

Tribal people have distinct health problems, mainly governed by multi-dimensional factors like their habitat, difficult terrain, ecologically variable niches, illiteracy, poverty, isolation, superstition and deforestation. Odisha is one of the ten states in the country covered under the National Nutrition Monitoring Bureau (NNMB). According to the report of NNMB (2000–2001), Odisha continues to have second highest level of undernutrition among the ten states. When compared with the aggregate figures for chronic energy deficiency (BMI < 18.5) among adults in these states, the level is higher in Odisha. The prevalence of chronic energy deficiency (CED) in adult men in the state is 38.6 per cent compared to aggregate of 37.4 per cent, whereas the CED prevalence in the adult women is 46 per cent against 39.3 per cent aggregate figure. As malnutrition is known to potentiate susceptibility to death due to infectious diseases, the high mortality rate amongst the tribes is attributed to this. The majority of tribes of Odisha had different grades of anaemia. Anaemia is more common in females than males. Statistical analysis revealed a positive correlation between hookworm infestation and anaemia possibly due to indiscriminate defecation, barefoot and lack of health awareness. Orissa Health Strategy (2003) has advocated for improving the health status of tribal population by reducing mortality and morbidity. It indicates that the tribal people suffer disproportionately from malaria, sexually transmitted diseases, tuberculosis, genetic disorders, deficiency, sickle cell, anaemia and nutritional deficiency diseases. These are some of the special health problems attributed to these communities. Various epidemiological studies and malariometric surveys carried out in tribal population reveal a high prevalence of malaria in the forest regions of Odisha, because malaria control in such settlements has always been unattainable due to technical and operational problems.

The situation analyses of health indices of the tribal population in Odisha are worse than the national level. The health status of tribal people is miserable and this is a neglected field for many years. There is a need to address this neglected area at the policy level. The health of tribal people is influenced by interplay of various factors including social, economic and cultural ones. The common beliefs, customs, practices related to health and treatment of disease in turn influence the health-seeking behaviour of the community. There is a consensus that the health status of the tribal population is very poor and most awful among the primitive tribes because of their isolation, remoteness, cultural practices, illiteracy and being largely unaffected by the developmental processes going on in the country. Time is ripe now to evaluate seriously the health scenario in tribal communities of Odisha. There are wide gaps in knowledge regarding the levels, determinants and consequences of tribal's health problems in Koraput district, which is one of the most underdeveloped regions of our country. In this context the present paper focuses on various cultural practices and its effect on the emerging health issues of tribal people in the Koraput district of Odisha. The present study has explored various circumstances guided by their socio-cultural values under which tribal people manage their health. Information has been collected on various levels, trends and determinants of morbidity to obtain a clearer understanding of the socio-cultural and religious context in which their health problems arise.

Major Findings of the Present Study

The present study has been conducted in the Ranikana revenue village of Semiliguda block, Koraput district. This village is dominated by tribal inhabitants. In the village there are 90 households and among them 70 households belong to tribal community. The demographic profile depicts that the total tribal population of this village is 276. Among them males are 136 and females are 140.

Health Condition

"Health care" is one of the greater human rights and it is observed that apart from other inequalities, tribals of the village are deprived of basic health facilities. Their accessibility to professional standards of health is limited due to several causes. The main causes of low health status of tribals of the study area have been discussed below:

- Poverty has played havoc on the health and nutrition condition of tribal people
- Lack of education always creates hurdles for health treatment of tribes.
- Language is said to be a barriers between tribal and non-tribal and sometimes prevents access to health services, which are dominated by non-tribal people with having different dialect/language.
- Lack of accessibility and communication often create hurdles for the enhancement of health status of these people.
- Apart from this the traditional socio-cultural belief and practice is also another bottleneck for improved health status of tribals.

Provision of proper health care facility is an important aspect of human resource development. Tribes have their traditional method of health system. The concept of health in these communities is associated with certain traditional belief system and rituals. For them health and sickness are reward or punishment for harmonious relationship with the maintained or not maintained deities, ancestors, neighbours and natural surroundings. They believe that sickness is caused by (i) a breach in relationship with a neighbour who, displeased or envious and employ witches or cast the evil eye. (ii) An act of someone who has displeased the village deity (*hundi)* or has broken moral and religious norms. (iii) A breach of relationship with ancestors for whom the requisite death rituals (*dasa)* have not been performed. (iv) Intrusion into the territorial jurisdiction of deities presiding over hills, forests, streams, rivers, etc., or the failure to propitiate them, as through sacrifices.(v) Improper celebration of seasonal or annual feasts, festivals, rituals, etc. (Nayak, Boal and Soreng, 1996).

Accidents, it is believed, are a punishment for relationships broken with the deities. They believe that not offering sacrifice to the god of wild animals will bring such kind of incidences. To escape from these accidents they seek the treatment only from a priest (*dissari)* or a magic man (*gunia).* It is believed that only dissari or gunia can please the angry deity and save the victim/patient from all sorts of troubles. If by chance the sick person is cured, due to the application of some herb by the dissari, the medicine man (dissari) gets all credit. Nobody recognizes the curative qualities of that herb used for a particular sickness.

Accessibility of health facilities are considered important in determining the health condition of the tribals. Earlier for the treatment of disease or solving any health problems usually tribals took only the help of local quacks. Treatment of diseases is primarily based on indigenous sources. For every minor disease they used to go to dissari or gurumai. For serious disease they only prefer modern medication facility. However, now some of them have started to avail modern health services to cure diseases. But it is evident that, till now tribal people prefer dissari for the treatment of their diseases.

Table 1

Preferences of Sample Households for the Treatment of Diseases (Single Response)

Preferences for Health Treatment	*No of Households*
Dissari	36(51.43%)
Health Worker	19 (27.14%)
Doctor	15(21.42%)
Other	00(0%)
Total	70(100%)

The present study reveals that a majority of tribal people, i.e., 51.44 per cent give first preference for indigenous health treatment. 27.14 per cent give first preference to health workers and only 21.42 per cent give first priority for modern medical facilities for their health treatment. It is observed that tribal people's giving priority to indigenous health practices is more due to the profound association of tribal society with its cultural and religious systems. The first preference for availing modern facility is comparatively less due to lack of communication facility, and predominantly owing to their illiteracy as well as poor economic conditions.

Besides physical accessibility, economic accessibility to health facilities is also important. It takes care of the private expenditure on health. In spite of the public provision of health care facilities people have to spend a lot on health. Private expenditure on health depends on the better economic conditions of the people. In the study area majority of the households (69%) are from below poverty line. They even cannot dare to bear for transport cost required for reaching government hospitals. For serious health problems they cannot spend for outside medicines. Moreover, what is more important is the share of income devoted for food and social functions is very high in tribal areas. Due to illiteracy and poverty they do not give much importance to their health aspect and spend less for their health treatment.

Earlier, the cases of institutional delivery were very low. But now it has been increasing gradually due to the consistent effort of ASHA and other health workers. In this regard the intervention of government initiated programme, UNICEF and involvement of civil society is significant. In the present study 59 per cent of total deliveries are institutional. The study revealed that unhygienic and primitive birth practices are mainly responsible for ill-health of pregnant women. It is observed that among tribals of this area, the delivery is still conducted by the mother herself or with the help of untrained birth attendant (Dhai) and they just consult with *Dishari* (traditional priest) or *Gurumai* (magic man) in case they get some complicacy. In complicated labour, obviously it leads to maternal as well as child mortality. The pattern of beliefs concerning diet during pregnancy is quite complex in this population. Nevertheless, the data on belief system reveals about the restrictions in terms of food quantity and food types. Tribal women of this area are deprived of the basic health facilities. Their accessibility to professional standards of health is severely limited. Women's choice in dealing with unwanted pregnancies is limited. Malnutrition during pregnancy is a common problem, which causes many health tragedies like anaemia, low weight, and other psychological catastrophe. Lack of awareness leads to risk of early pregnancy, complications in pregnancy, reproductive tract infections, contraceptive side effects, etc., among them. The antenatal care provided is not adequate. Due to their poverty and customary taboos the women are not taken to the hospital for antenatal care. It is a practice among tribal communities that pregnant women work throughout the day without rest. She has to resume her work within a day or two after delivery which clearly reflect the gender bias and exploitation of women in tribal society. The average age of tribal women at marriage is very low. The age at marriage among tribal girls is 13–15 years. Early marriage is a curse for tribal women. Ignorance, illiteracy, age-old practice and tradition, etc., forces the women to marry at a younger age. They do not know why the children should not be married in a younger age and what harm it can cause to the girl child when she become pregnant in a very young age.

A society is healthy when its sanitation situation is healthy. Good health is possible only when there exist, a balanced relationship between human thought and external sanitation situation. In this village due to illiteracy and lack of awareness, the sanitation situation is worse. Uncleanly habits have made the tribal people victims of several diseases. Apart from malaria, in sample village, the tribals generally suffer from skin diseases, diarrhea, cold and fever, eye-infection, stomach-ache, etc.

Table 2

Name of the Diseases Most Frequently Occurring in Family (Multiple Response)

Name of the Diseases	*Number of Households*
Malaria	64(91.42%)
Cold and Fever	61(87.14%)
Dysentery	58 (82.85%)
Skin diseases	66(94.28%)
Goiter	02(2.85%)
Others	48(68.57%)

In the study the diarrheal diseases including cholera are found to occur throughout the year attaining its peak during the rainy season (From July to October). In the present study, the members of 66 households (94.28%) have been suffered from skin diseases, 64 households (91.42%) from malaria and 58 households (82.85%) from dysentery, which depict that the sanitation awareness of these people is very less.

Sanitation and Hygienic conditions

Sanitation and Hygienic condition also refer to housing condition, cleanliness of the houses and cattle sheds, source of drinking water, personal cleanliness, washing of cloths, disposal of waste water and garbage, etc.

The sense of personal hygiene among the tribals is very poor. Majority of members in the studied families do not take bath on daily basis. Their nails are uncut, filled with dirt. Bathing and washing of clothes with soap is occasional. The sense of public hygiene is very poor. The scattered pattern of village habitation has deprived them of the idea of living in a community. Dung heaps are found all through the village lanes. During the rainy season the village lanes have ankle deep mud. The idea of keeping the public places clean such as the *Sadar*, village well and tube well, etc. seldom occurs in the studied village.

In spite of all developmental programmes of government, the tribal's living conditions has not improved and still most of them are living in miserable and unhygienic houses. The construction of kachha houses is more (68.57%) in this village. No doubt now it is observed that the tribal households whose financial conditions are comparatively better have even two or three living rooms. But still in majority of the houses (72.86%) there is one living room. Only 6 houses have separate kitchen facility which constitutes 8.57 per cent. Like earlier days the ventilation of their house is very poor. Only 13 houses have window facility which constitutes 18.57 per cent of the total houses. Out of 70 households, 36 (51.43%) have earth floor, which causes unhygienic conditions in rainy season. But the rest houses (48.57%) have concrete floors in their houses.

Table 3

Sanitation Facility in the Village

Various Facilities	*Total Sample HH*	*No*	*Yes*
Pukka type of houses	70(100%)	48(68.57%)	22(31.43)
Separate kitchen facility	70(100%)	64(91.43%)	06(8.57%)
Window facility	70(100%)	57(81.43%)	13(18.57%)
Concrete floors	70(100%)	36(51.43%)	34(48.57%)
Washing cloth on daily basis	70(100%)	62(88.58%)	08(11.42%)
Bathroom facility	70(100%)	70(100%)	00(0%)
Using toilet	70(100%)	69(98.57%)	1(1.42%)

Table 3 depicts that the members of only 8 households (11.42%) wash their clothes on daily basis whereas the rest 88.58 per cent do wash their cloth on daily basis. Even today majority of tribal houses (98.57%) do not have proper toilet facility. No particular change has come to their mind and attitude to construct toilet and bathroom facilities in their houses. Mostly they go to nallah or stream for toilet and bath in the sample village. They do not have apposite drainage system in their house and village; the road within the village is *kachha.* This reflects the poor sanitation system in the tribal village.

As regards drinking water, majority of families use tube well. But still some families are taking stream water for their drinking purpose. It is interesting to note that often some villagers take the tube well water for bathing purpose, but drink the stream water without boiling it. When asked about the reason of it, they reply that the bad smell of tube well water discourages them to use it for drinking purpose. Some respondents also inform that the tube wells often go out of order and it takes a longer period to repair. During that period they depend on stream or well to fetch water for drinking purposes. This lack of habit of taking safe drinking water also causes various serious diseases among them.

Literacy Level

Education is the most important social input for the development of any society. Literacy enhances the awareness level of people and augments the health status of any community. However, this is the most neglected aspect in tribal society. In Koraput district the tribal literary rate is only 18.7 per cent. It is 29.2 per cent for male but just 8.4 per cent (2001 census) for the tribal female, which indicates that female literacy is very poor in tribal society. The total literacy rate of the sample village is only 18.12 per cent. Female literacy rate is less than their male counterpart in sample village. This has adversely affected the health condition of the tribal people in general and reproductive health of their women folk in particular.

Table 4

Literacy Rate of Family Members of Sample Households

Name of village	*Total Literates*			*Total Illiterates*			**Total Eligible population*
	Male	*Female*	*Total*	*Male*	*Female*	*Total*	
Ranikana	16 (9.35%)	15 (8.77%)	31 (18.12%)	63 (36.85%)	77 (45.03%	140 (81.88%)	171 (100%)

*The total eligible population for the calculation of literates is total population – the population found in the age group of 0–6. Out of the total sample population of 276, 171 are eligible (above 6 years) for the calculation of literacy rate.

Source: Field study.

Due to poor sanitation, unhygienic conditions, low literacy, low socio-economic status, less access to medical facilities, lack of safe drinking water, habit of taking stream water for drinking purpose, unwillingness to take tube well water, vacancies of posts of medical staff and also their absenteeism coupled with their cultural belief and practices cause and promote severe health problems in the tribal areas of the Koraput.

Among a plethora of factors, impact of religion is observed as the most dominant one, responsible for the low health status of tribal. Tribal world view is full of different benevolent and malevolent supernatural forces such as *Jogini*, *Devis*, etc. Health is realized in great mysteries. Various diseases are attributed to supernatural or religious forces (*Dharma* diseases) and effects of ancestral deeds (*Karma* diseases) or evil spirits. This may be viewed as a built-in cause of their health problem. Witchcraft, sorcery and evil eye, have a greater impact on the health of tribals. The belief in witchcraft and magic are deeply rooted in the traditional customary ideas. Tribal system of medicines is largely magico-religious, under which the tribals subscribe to supernatural agencies through traditional healers (*Disaries*) and perform a wide variety of rituals and sacrifices in order to propitiate the angry spirits. This excessive dependence on supernatural form of treatment is primarily due to its easy accessibility and absent of other alternatives. Even though health facilities are available, they consult local healers. Tribals are strong believers of natural theory of diseases. They feel when man falls out of harmony with nature suffers from illness and becomes susceptible to diseases and accidents. Hence, various rituals are observed to restore harmony with nature. The prevention of diseases includes use of charms, amulets, animal sacrifices for the propitiation from diseases attributable to nature and evil spirits. The effects of the cultural practices and belief system on the health aspect in tribal society have been discussed below:

- The common beliefs, customs and practices connected with health and disease have been found to be intimately related to the treatment of disease.
- It is necessary to make a holistic view of all the cultural dimensions of the health of a community.
- The religion plays a significant role in determining the reproductive health status of tribal women.
- To solve their reproductive health problem they first go for magico-religious treatment.
- When magico-religious treatment fails, they go for modern treatment.
- Heavy dependence on magico-religious practices has severely challenged the service of ASHA and ANM.

Suggestions

Tribal people had specific problems, some of these were built-in problems of these tribal communities and some were imposed upon them, which jeopardized their overall development and progress inclusive of their health. Nevertheless some of the suggestions are given below to enhance the health status of tribal communities.

- Health legislation has a great role to play in promoting public health and could be used more vigorously to promote tribal's health.
- The wisdom and experience of traditional medicine man on the use of various herbs for cure of diseases are to be learnt by the service providers. The government should take maximum care for the development of herbal gardens. Due importance must be given for the documentation of traditional method of treatments.
- The traditional beliefs of tribal people that the cause of an ailment or a disease lies in the anger of the divine power or the ancestors need to be handled carefully.
- Community involvement, mutual interaction between the service provider and the beneficiaries, health consciousness of the tribals, etc., are some of the greatest challenges, which need to be effectively monitored and tackled.
- The Aanganwadi workers, the multipurpose health workers, voluntary organizations, primary school teachers, etc., can play vital role in the implementation of various health programmes. Proper motivation, practical training, handsome incentives to these workers can definitely bring better results.
- The experience of tribal people towards the development functionaries is not pleasant. It is frequently observed that tribals have been exploited, while receiving a benefit from the service providers. This perception has to be changed through the honesty, commitment and involvement of the officials.
- Healthy nutrition should be encouraged through local produce and local recipes. The tribal themselves through a better utilization of their locally available cheap but nutritious food should solve nutritional needs.
- Maintenance of personal hygiene in connection with health childbirth, abortion or menstruation should be properly communicated to tribals.
- Tribal women in their advanced stage of pregnancy should be advised to reduce their workload and take adequate rest.
- The habit of taking alcohol and drugs during pregnancy should be discouraged.
- Tribal health healers should be invited to participate in modern health projects introduced by government and different voluntary organizations.

Conclusions

The tribal people of Odisha and their health scenario presents a kaleidoscopic mosaic of various communicable and non-communicable disease profile keeping in pace with their socio-economic development. Among these there are communities who still depend primarily on Dishari or Gurumai for their health treatment. The widespread poverty, illiteracy, malnutrition, absence of safe drinking water and sanitary conditions, poor maternal and child health services, ineffective coverage of national health and nutritional services, etc., have been found as possible contributing factors of dismal health condition prevailing amongst the tribal communities of Odisha. Many of the infectious and parasitic diseases can be prevented with timely intervention and health awareness. Some of the intervention programmes can be included in the national programme also. The presence of reproductive health problem indicates that the tribal communities are still far away from the modern civilization and developments. In spite of the tremendous advancement in the field of preventive and curative medicine, the health care delivery services in these primitive tribal people are still poor and needs to be strengthened in order to achieve the goal of health for all in the country.

The health framework for tribal people should go beyond the narrow con-fines of physical health and to encompass all aspects of human well-being. It has to critically examine tribal people's relation with their socio-religious structure, livelihood, and life situation. There is a need to explore varied information in the areas, where there are information gaps. Against this backdrop synergy between traditional and modern medication facility must be carefully examined. Various studies should highlight on the ground reality experience of what works and what does not and why, in different socio-cultural contexts.

References

Basu, S.K. (ed.) (1993): *Tribal Health in India*, New Delhi: Manak Publishers.

Chaudhuri, Buddhadeb (ed.) (1990): "Social and environmental dimensions of tribal health", *Cultural and Environmental Dimensions of Health*, New Delhi: Inter-India Publications.

Cook, R.J. (1994): *Women Health and Human Rights*, Switzerland: World Health Organization.

Directorate of Economics and Statistics, Orissa (2001): District Statistical Hand Book of Koraput, Bhubaneswar.

Haque, M. (1990): "Height, weight, and nutrition among the six tribes of India", in B. Chaudhuri (ed.), *Cultural and Environmental Dimensions of Health*, New Delhi: Inter-India Publications.

ICMR Bulletin (2003): Health Status of Primitive Tribes of Orissa, Vol. 33, No. 10.

Nayak, R., B.M. Boal and N. Soreng (1996): *The Gadabas: A Handbook for Development*, New Delhi: Indian Social Institute.

Regional Medical Research Centre for Tribal Health (1992): *Tribal Health Bulletin*, Bhubaneswar.

Wheeler, D. (1980): Human Resources Development and Economic Growth in Developing Countries: A Simultaneous Model, Washington, DC: World Bank Staff Working Paper No. 407.

Index